UNTOLD STORIES

UNTOLD STORIES
on Women, Gender and Architecture in Denmark

Jannie Rosenberg Bendsen
Svava Riesto
Henriette Steiner

Strandberg Publishing

Contents

Preface
On Writing a New
History of Architecture 8

Introduction
Where Are the Women
in Danish Architectural History? 16

Chapter 1
Visions – A Revolution in the Kitchen 50

Chapter 2
Love – Three Houses Built for
Women's Work, Family and Love Lives 96

Chapter 3
Growth – Stories of a More
Caring Approach to Urban Planning 150

Chapter 4
Alternatives – A New Architecture for a New Society 202

Chapter 5
Collaboration – A Story About how Architecture Comes Into Being 248

Postscript
Feminist Architects Who Wanted to Change the World 296

Notes 306
Bibliography 321
Index 330
Acknowledgements 333
About the authors 334
Photo credits 335

Preface

On Writing a New History of Architecture

This book presents a new history about twentieth-century architecture in Denmark. We bring to light previously untold stories about women's contributions to architecture and introduce an understanding of the profession that illuminates, interprets and celebrates the many and varied collaborations across genders, disciplines and skills inherent to it. In this preface, we discuss the methods underpinning our work and the reason we chose to write the way we have. Existing books and articles on the history of architecture often describe twentieth-century architecture in Denmark by highlighting a very few men and their work on designing canonised buildings. This book adopts a different approach, exploring instead last century's architecture by focusing on some of the women who also contributed to shaping the buildings, cities and landscapes of the modern Danish welfare state, yet who rarely get mentioned in the many architectural histories about the period.

In order to change this bias in Danish architectural history, it is necessary not only to shed light on the work of forgotten women but also to develop new ways of studying, researching, interpreting and writing about twentieth-century architecture. Because architecture does not simply spring into being through the creative efforts of individuals; rather, it is a result of collaborations. Design is an important part of what makes architecture happen, but it never takes place in a vacuum; design is only one part of the often much more multifaceted work carried out by architects. Furthermore, it always takes place in an ongoing interaction with other forms of knowledge and skills as well as site-specific conditions. By taking the work of women as our point of departure, we have the opportunity to include a wider range of contributions – from architects and those in other professions – which have contributed to shaping physical environments, yet been overlooked or relegated to the margins of architectural literature. Rather than adding individual women to the canon of architectural history, thereby fuelling the patriarchal hero-worshipping narrative of the modern architect as a solitary genius, in this book we examine how architecture is created through collaborations. These are collaborations that cut across gender divides as well as draw on various knowledge forms and skill sets, some of which do not contribute to constructing built or physical structures at all. As we shall see, these collaborations are based on creative synergies, reciprocity and alliances, but they also offer tales of power struggles, conflicts and disappointments. Our choice to shed light on collaborations and overlooked contributions points to one of many new possible paths for the study of architecture in order to provide a more accurate understanding of how architecture is created. We hope that this book will do exactly that.

We write these words in times that call for collaboration. But deeper reflections on the various formats and challenges of collaboration in architecture are rarely articulated directly or considered within a broader political and historical context. In light of the many crises associated with climate, resources, ecological, political and social issues that we face as a society today, architecture falls short if we maintain an understanding which perceives it simply as beautiful forms made by 'great heroes' – regardless of their gender identity. On the contrary, we need a new and expanded understanding of architecture. This book's historical narrative is therefore written from our point of view, in our own time, with a goal of ensuring a more nuanced and accurate understanding of the past. In other words, we want to contribute fundamental knowledge that is necessary for us to develop fairer and more sustainable built environments and landscapes in the future.

The book focuses on a historical period characterised by major societal changes which made an imprint on the built environment in different ways: from the economic crisis of the 1930s and the architects' contribution to reform political agendas, including the handling of the housing shortage, followed by a vast building boom and the growth of urban areas in the post-war period up to the 1970s' energy crisis and general decline in construction. Working across these historical contexts, we focus on women whose professional work was undertaken within the architectural professions in Denmark. We are curious about what a reading focused on gender can contribute to the understanding of various design practices within construction, urban spaces, landscapes and urban planning which were developed in response to a succession of societal challenges associated with the rise of the modern Danish welfare state. Based on these parameters, we ask: Which women have contributed to shaping Denmark's cities, buildings and landscapes in the period from 1930 to 1980? How did they work, with whom did they work and how, and what significance did their gender have in terms of their professional endeavours? And, finally, what can all this tell us about how architecture comes into being?

Looking back from a present-day perspective, it is important to understand the significant transformation of society and the forces and values that underpin the gradual creation of the twentieth-century welfare state in Denmark. The huge development of cities and landscapes that took place from 1930 to 1980 has left a greater physical legacy than any other period in the history of architecture – not only in terms of the number of buildings and the volume of infrastructure projects, but also regarding the great social and cultural significance of the period's many schools, homes, roads, parks and public institutions.[1] Large parts of the Danish population have grown up interacting with these physical environments in their everyday comings and goings, and today even more people enter into daily contact with the architecture and infrastructure of the period. This means that personal and collective memories and experiences are embedded in the built environment, and buildings, landscapes and infrastructure from the very period under review in this book have contributed to shaping the institutions and modes of interaction we see in Denmark today. As individuals and as a society, we are connected to this physical context, which is under renegotiation at present as the ideological basis for the Danish welfare state is shifting and changing.

Within the architectural disciplines, extensive work is currently being undertaken to assess, repair, renovate and transform the buildings and infrastructures of the period so that they can be adapted to present-day needs and challenges.

There is growing recognition that we cannot continue to uncritically launch resource-intensive new construction projects within a profit-oriented, investor-determined time horizon while demolishing existing buildings. We need to create a more caring, equitable and socially sustainable approach to the physical development of the buildings, cities and landscapes we already have – as part of a necessary green transition – just as we need to carefully consider where, why and how we build anew.[2] In order to do this, we need a nuanced historical understanding of the practices and values that underpin twentieth-century architecture and urban and landscape development.

The basis for this book is a collective effort which has seen us explore vast and varied source material. Along the way, we have been surprised by the sheer number of women who have contributed to the architectural professions during the period, and by how different their positions, working methods, conditions and collaborations have been. We do not devote equal amounts of space and attention to all the women who appear in the book, but because in many cases this is the first time they are presented in an architectural historical context, we have elected to write brief biographies of all the women mentioned. These biographies can be read separately in the margins. Despite our best efforts, it has proven impossible to find photographs of three of these women, meaning that no images accompany their information. We hope that pictures will emerge of these women so that their images can be shown in future books on architectural history. Just as we ourselves have made specific choices to include or exclude certain people and places, we have been confirmed in our view that historical archives are not neutral reflections of the past but rather places that testify to more or less conscious selections and de-selection of documents and sources.[3] The ways in which materials have been selected to be kept for posterity in the existing architectural archives – reflecting choices conditioned by the research found within the field, by changing perceptions of history, by structural and economic conditions and by chance – has resulted in women's work often being assigned a marginal position. This is a vicious circle. Because if some contributors – in this case women – are not visible in the literature available because their work falls outside the usual canon, meaning that it is not recorded in either physical or digital archives, then the opportunity to understand and interpret their contribution to posterity disappears.

Fortunately, we have discovered that in many cases materials can still be found – often in unexpected places. However, this requires a different and differentiated approach. For example, we have searched for uncatalogued material that contains information about women's work, and we have looked through archive folders about some of the better-known men. This is to say that we have looked beyond the official architecture archives – for example, in the protocols of various places of educations, in professional magazines and newspapers, and in municipal and state archives – and we have also visited the buildings and landscapes that women have contributed to shaping. What is more, we have found important sources of information in television footage, radio broadcasts and the daily press, since an astonishingly large proportion of the women whose work we have examined were visible in media back in their own day, even if their work has been overlooked in later literature on the history of architecture.

We have also engaged whenever possible in an ongoing dialogue with the women themselves, or with their descendants, former employees, business partners or spouses. All these people have generously helped us gain access to material often unknown to the public, such as private photo albums, diaries, letters, drawings and records. They have also passed on knowledge orally: through conversations and interviews, they have shared stories and memories which have been of great importance to our research. We have thus been given the opportunity to help expand some of the official collections with new material, thereby contributing to a development already underway in several archives.[4]

In 1971, the American art historian Linda Nochlin described how historiography reproduces a patriarchal view of history which focuses on concepts of 'greatness' and 'genius', even when such perspectives are not directly articulated.[5] Nochlin believed that the reason why we do not know about 'great' woman artists has to do with basic structures in society and a specific outlook on history. This means that the question of women in the history of art or architecture cannot be considered a marginal niche issue for feminist studies. Rather, it offers a welcome opportunity to rethink the very way we speak and write about our shared history and the ways in which we now manage the buildings, landscapes and infrastructures of the past. In this book, we have focused on making room for many different contributions that are important for architecture to come into being. We have done this based on the hope that a more comprehensive – and therefore more accurate – understanding of the past can lead to more inclusive and collaborative practices in the future. We set out to investigate a group that has been marginalised in various ways in society and in the historical narratives of posterity, as doing so can in itself lead to new ways of understanding the familiar world and our common context. We believe that such a new understanding can help to outline alternative, hopeful notions about the cities and landscapes of the future.[6] One might describe our position as one of utopian feminism: fundamentally hopeful about the future, it carries with it the implicit notion that the world can be different and more equitable – for men as well as for women and other gender identities – and also more caring, inclusive and sustainable in the ways people interact with each other and the surrounding world.[7]

One objective of our research has been to gather knowledge about the many women who have contributed to the architectural professions in

Denmark in the period from 1930 to 1980, but of course creating a complete overview of women's contributions to the architectural professions in Denmark in a single book is not realistic.[8] What is more, we wanted to contribute more than simply an overview. Hence, we use the chapters in this book to delve into and interpret women's work from an architectural perspective and a gender-historical perspective. The following chapters are therefore structured around the work of selected individuals and associated themes. Drawing inspiration from the Finnish art theorist Katve-Kaisa Kontturi's book *Ways of Following* (2018), we have chosen to *follow* individual women and the events, buildings and places with which they have worked, investigating what these endeavours can tell us about how architecture comes into being through collaborations across genders and different forms of knowledge. As in Kontturi's book, in which she does not see art as works, we break away from a traditional understanding of the architectural work as a closed and elevated unit.[9] Kontturi specifically points out that creative work – in this case architecture – comes about because many forces, individuals and materials collaborate in a given context, one which is conditioned by historical, political and economic structures.

In line with international feminist researchers in architecture such as Lori Brown and Karen Burns, we examine not only these societal structures or individual persons and their specific works, but precisely the interaction between them.[10] The women appearing in this book have helped to define the societal development in Denmark and made concrete proposals for architectural contributions to the process. But given that many of their stories do not quite fit into the usual narratives of 'great' architecture or what a 'great' architect looked and acted like in the period, their untold stories give us the opportunity to take a fresh and alternative look at how we may understand the architect's work and distinctive contribution to society.

The situated approach which sees us follow and examine specific people, places and events means that the various chapters are different from each other. This reflects our perception of the feminist studies to which this book is indebted and within which it inscribes itself: we do not see them as a linear movement with clearly defined waves or unambiguous positions. Rather, we apply a focus on gender and historic justice to forge new connections across time, places and people, thereby contributing to a more accurate and fair understanding of the world.[11] By acknowledging ambiguity, paradoxes and multiple voices, as well as by including stories from the margins, we want to correct misleading patriarchal preconceptions and thus contribute to creating a more just and sustainable future.

Introduction

Where Are the Women in Danish Architectural History?

On 30 November 1936, seven women sent a telegram to architect Ragna Grubb with the words: 'CONGRATULATIONS ON THE BEAUTIFULLY EXECUTED WORK'. The seven women – Kirsten Westergaard, Sonja Meyer, Rigmor Andersen, Hilda Rømer, Andrea Norn, Ingrid Møller Dyggve and Gerda Schäffer – were, like Grubb, also architects in 1930s' Denmark. They had all studied at the Royal Danish Academy of Fine Arts' School of Architecture in Copenhagen, graduating a few years earlier. They wrote the telegram to their colleague Grubb to congratulate her on having just completed a large and prestigious project: a brand-new building for women in Niels Hemmingsens Gade in inner Copenhagen. The purpose of the building was to strengthen women's associations and networks across the various organisations which at this time dealt with the role of women in society, such as the Danish Association of Midwives, the Copenhagen Teachers' Association, the Danish Housewives' Associations and the Danish Women's Society. The building was equipped with offices and meeting rooms as well as a restaurant where women could meet across the various organisations and associations that all worked to promote women's interests. Known as Kvindernes Bygning – the Women's Building – it also offered accommodation for women arriving in Copenhagen from other parts of the country, and contained a hotel called Cecil. The building was planned, funded, built and decorated by the joint efforts of many people, especially women.

Having its wellspring in the activist women's movements in the late 1800s, the Women's Building in Copenhagen was closely linked to the period's major expositions of art, industry and crafts. At the World's Columbian Exposition in Chicago in 1892, part of the exhibition area was dedicated to women's work. This formed the basis for setting up the 'Woman's Building' in Chicago in 1893.[12] In corresponding fashion, an exhibition in Copenhagen paved the way for the creation of the Women's Building: the summer of 1895 saw the opening of *Kvindernes Udstilling fra Fortid til Nutid* (The Women's Exhibition from Past to Present), showing women's art, crafts and household items to a large audience.[13] The exhibition was a success, and the profits it generated were used, among other things, to establish the aforementioned building for women in Copenhagen.[14] In 1936, after decades of preparatory work, fundraising and scouting for the right site, the building was complete. It was a new type of institution in a Danish context: a house which gave women the opportunity to gather, organise themselves, get a roof over their heads in the big city and support each other in shared endeavours. Emphatically modern in its aesthetic, it stood out in its setting in a historic street, and a large sign on the façade left no one who passed by in any doubt: this was the Women's Building. The edifice was a slice of modern metropolitan life in the midst of old Copenhagen, heralding a new era in its form, construction, creation and function.

Ragna Grubb was commissioned to design the Women's Building after winning the design competition announced in 1934. The major task of designing and overseeing the construction of this building paved the way for her setting up a company in her own name – a big step for a young architect in Denmark in the 1930s. However, Grubb

Kirsten Westergaard (1901–1994) was admitted to the Royal Danish Academy of Fine Arts' School of Architecture in 1920. Prior to this she had attended technical school in Copenhagen. She was employed in the Municipality of Frederiksberg's department of architecture in 1923, where her assignments included working on the maintenance and expansion of Frederiksberg Hospital. Together with Sonja Meyer, she won an architectural design competition in 1927: their winning submission for a retirement home in Esbjerg was in the Neoclassical style. As part of her work for the Municipality of Frederiksberg, she designed residences for nurses and doctors at Nordre Fasanvej 79, which were completed in 1950. She was interested in issues pertaining to the needs and wishes of housewives, taking part in initiatives such as the 'Women's Meeting on the Current Housing Problems' in 1934.

Sonja Emmy Meyer (1898–1981) completed secondary school at N. Zahles Skole in 1918, and the following year was admitted to the School of Architecture at the Royal Danish Academy of Fine Arts. She had prepared for the entrance exam by taking classes from a painter. In 1927 she completed her degree, and that same year, together with Kirsten Westergaard, won an architectural design competition for a retirement home in Esbjerg, which was built between 1927 and 1929. She designed several private homes under her own name, including in Frederiksberg, Charlottenlund and Hørsholm. In 1939, together with architect Flemming Grut (1911–1987), she designed a large private residence at Østerled 17 in Copenhagen.

In 1934, the board behind the Women's Building initiative issued a design competition, which Ragna Grubb won. When the building was inaugurated, Grubb received a telegram from seven fellow woman architects congratulating her on the result. In the first decades after women were admitted to the Academy's School of Architecture, only a few of them completed the programme, but here we see a group of women supporting each other.

The Women's Building is located in Niels Hemmingsens Gade in Copenhagen. Inaugurated in 1936, it was designed by the young architect Ragna Grubb. Its purpose was to house a variety of women's organisations as well as a restaurant and hotel rooms for women visiting Copenhagen.

In 1927, the architects Kirsten Westergaard and Sonja Meyer won a design competition for a new retirement home in Esbjerg. The building was constructed over the next two years, evincing classical motifs with its strong symmetrical and harmonious façade. This was presumably the first time that two women had won an architectural design competition in Denmark.

was no lone pioneer. As the seven signatories to the telegram indicate, she was one of a number of women working as building architects in 1930s' Denmark, all of whom knew each other and who maintained a professional network. Nor was Grubb the first woman in Denmark to win an architectural competition. The architects Kirsten Westergaard and Sonja Meyer had already won first prize in a design competition for a retirement home in Esbjerg in 1927.[15] Similarly, Grubb was not the only woman to run an architecture firm in her own name at this time.* Architect Ingrid Møller Dyggve had established her own company in 1917, while garden architect Anka Rasmussen ran a design studio in her own name around the same time as Grubb.[16] What is more, several women would collaborate on various tasks. For example, Grubb won a competition in 1937 working alongside women architects Ingeborg Schmidt and Karen Hvistendahl, and she and Karen Hvistendahl designed a villa together in Frederiksberg, which was built in 1936.[17]

* We know that Gerda Schäffer designed a house in Fredericia under her own name in 1915, but we do not know whether she officially had her own studio. Several other women may have had their own architecture firm/design studios, but this cannot be confirmed.

Women were clearly in the minority within the architectural professions in 1930s' Denmark, but they were there. However, we often have to look in vain for traces of their work in the histories already written about Danish architecture in the twentieth century.[18] And if we look at the architects who have so far been presented in their own biographies and monographs, there is a clear dominance of male practitioners.[19] However, we know that women architects have made important contributions to Danish architecture right from the beginning of the twentieth century, and that they became more numerous over time. So much so, in fact, that today the majority of those studying architecture in Denmark identify as women.* Thus, the time is more than ripe for talking about how women have contributed – as architects and designers – to shaping, planning, organising and managing our physical surroundings. When architectural history books in Denmark are so heavily focused on men, we get a gender-biased and skewed picture of history. At the same time, we lose important knowledge about how architecture is created in a wider field of contributors.

* At the landscape architecture programme at the University of Copenhagen, women make up 79 percent of the students today. At the schools of architecture in Copenhagen and Aarhus, women make up 68 percent (Copenhagen) and 65 percent (Aarhus) of the students. All figures pertain to 2020.[20]

Recent years have seen an increased focus on the architecture and planning of the welfare state, both internationally and in Denmark.[21] Many people still live, work and spend their leisure time in the houses, institutions, public spaces, road structures, gardens and parks constructed with the rise of the Danish welfare state from the 1930s and the four subsequent decades. Planning for cities and rural areas in Denmark after the Second World War was in itself a huge and comprehensive project that reshaped many aspects of people's daily lives on different scales. Planning made it possible for the strong expansion

Ragna Grubb, Karen Hvistendahl and Ingeborg Schmidt on the terrace at Grubb's parents' house. The three women set up a studio together, and because Grubb's brothers had left home, her parents' house could accommodate the three women's professional set-up. After she married architect Christian Laursen (1902–1973), Grubb ran a studio from their home in Gentofte.

of urban areas to be controlled and managed along new infrastructural corridors that made room for collective and private mobility. Not least in the new suburbs that surrounded the larger cities, a key objective was to ensure easy access to green spaces for all citizens.[22]

The flat, extensive urban development paved the way for detached family homes with gardens, social housing developments accompanied by green areas, parks and recreational areas linked by bicycle and pedestrian paths, schools and other municipal institutions with generous outdoor spaces and sports facilities, as well as modern institutions such as hospitals, high-rise buildings and shopping centres. The general developments seen in Danish society during the construction boom after the Second World War up until the oil crisis in 1973 led to a comprehensive transformation of Denmark's demographic and economic structure, changing it from an agricultural society to an industrial society centred on cities.

This book is based on the hypothesis that the tremendous spatial and architectural transformation which was such a central part of the development of the welfare state in post-war Denmark was only

Hilda Rømer (1906–1964) was admitted to the School of Architecture at the Royal Danish Academy of Fine Arts in 1923, and by 1933 was a qualified architect. She and her husband, architect Paul Nyboe-Pedersen (1904–1991), worked together and designed several buildings in the Gentofte area north of Copenhagen, including the Dairy and Cheese Store for Irmas Fabrikker (1935) and private residences at Vældegårdsvej 22 (1930) and 59 (1947). Several of their houses were subsequently awarded prizes by the municipal authorities. Rømer was for a time chairman of the Danish Women's Society's housing committee.

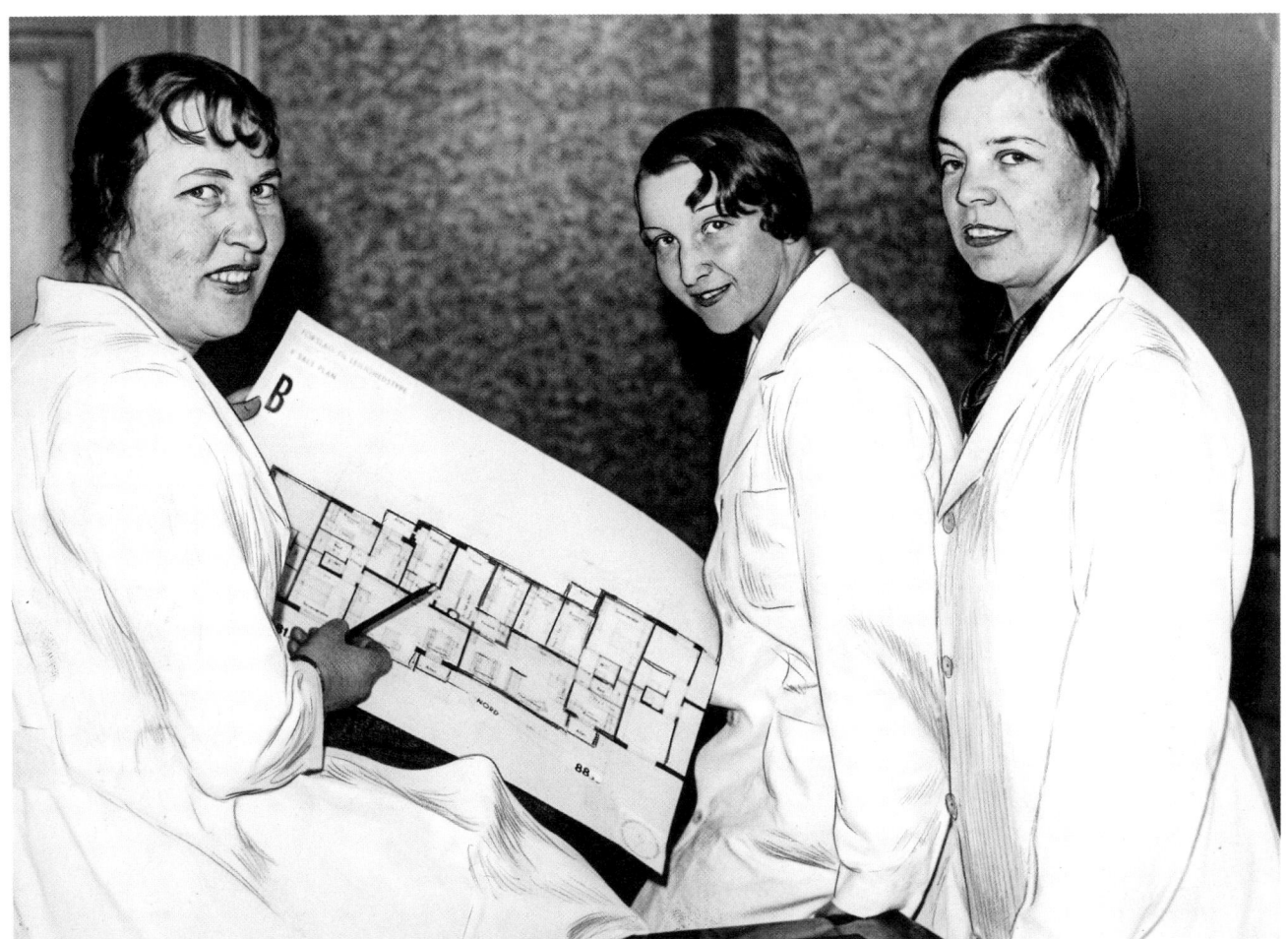

In 1937, architects Ragna Grubb, Karen Hvistendahl and Ingeborg Schmidt, working together, won the social housing association fsb and Privatbanken's design competition on the homes of the future. The newspaper *Aftenbladet* depicted them, looking very much like professional architects in their white coats, with their winning design.

In the post-war years, new schools, educational institutions and housing were built throughout Denmark. Across the nation, architects designed the physical settings of the emerging welfare state. The architects Karen and Ebbe Clemmensen designed a new teachers' college (now a high school) in Skive in the late 1950s. The buildings respond directly to the hilly landscape, and every classroom has a view of green areas outside. The design was particularly inspired by Japanese architecture.

Many post-war developments were designed as collaborative, cross-discipline efforts. One such project was the newly built Technical University of Denmark in Lundtofte, which architects Eva and Nils Koppel and landscape architects Edith and Ole Nørgaard worked on from 1958 to 1974. This collaboration has created a very special campus area where buildings, terrain and planting combine to form varied and distinctive spaces.

possible because different forms of knowledge and practice came together and mutually reinforced each other. Women have made different and important contributions to this development, and because their contribution has received little attention in architectural historical literature, we want to highlight, interpret and understand the significance of some of them here. Doing so can contribute to elucidating how diversity and collaboration drive complex processes of change, which is a well-known hypothesis championed in recent organisational research.[23] Women's contribution is an obvious place to start because it has been under-examined in Danish architectural history studies of the period.[24] When, inspired by the architectural historian Despina Stratigakos, we use this book to ask the question 'where are the women in Danish architectural history?',[25] we have found that a great many women have in fact contributed significantly to the development of architecture as well as to town and landscape planning in Denmark.

Rigmor Andersen (1903–1995) finished secondary school in 1922 and then studied drawing at a technical school. In 1923 she was admitted to the School of Architecture at the Royal Danish Academy of Fine Arts, graduating in 1930. While at the school, she studied under architect Kaare Klint (1888–1954) at the newly established department for furniture and spatial design. From 1927 to 1929 she worked for Poul Henningsen (1894–1967), designing lamps. Upon graduating, she worked with Kaare Klint at his design studio until 1939. While there she designed furniture, and in 1931 she was responsible for furnishing the student hall of residence for women, Kvinderegensen, in Copenhagen. Andersen designed several pieces of furniture under her own name, and from 1944 to 1973 she taught at the Academy's department of furniture and spatial design.

Do women create 'feminine' architecture?

Anyone trying to find something particularly feminine about any and all of the various forms of architecture and design addressed in the following chapters will look in vain. We do not set out to construct or support the idea that a particularly feminine aesthetic or theme connects the many architectural works created by women over the course of the approximately fifty-year period under scrutiny here. To take just one example, we can once again look at the Women's Building. Designed by a woman, the building was specifically created to accommodate women and women's organisations in keeping with what is often called the first wave of feminism, involving many advocates of women's rights in Denmark and other Western countries. But the Women's Building, in its expression and construction, does not correspond to stereotypical notions of a 'female' architecture – one which, for example, is particularly soft in its feel or design, or created based on empathic and motherly organisational principles.[26] Like so many other architects of her time, Ragna Grubb was interested in the modern, functionalist currents of the era as well as in the incipient industrialisation of construction brought about by new technologies and rationalisation. She was well-travelled and had an international outlook, as is evident from details such as her use of imported tiles for the façade.* The building's aesthetics are simple and typical of

* At the Women's Building, the use of imported tiles was a controversial decision which Ragna Grubb had to defend in Danish media. Materials produced abroad were generally frowned upon.[27]

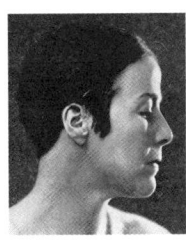

Ingrid Møller Dyggve (1890–1969) was admitted to the Royal Danish Academy of Fine Arts' School of Architecture in 1910, having previously attended classes at technical school in Copenhagen. She completed her degree in architecture in 1915. She worked at a design studio where the other architects included Carl Brummer (1864–1953) before setting up her own studio in 1917. Her practice covered a wide range of disciplines, from furniture to kitchens to private homes and holiday homes, including in Tibirke Bakker, where she and her husband, the architect Ejnar Dyggve (1887–1961), drew up a plan for the subdivision of plots in 1916, making the area one of Denmark's first planned holiday home areas.

the period's modernist ('functionalist') aesthetic, and it was technologically innovative for its day. The Women's Building was one of the first buildings in Denmark to have walls made with the use of reinforced concrete, and it was equipped with cutting-edge heating and ventilation systems.[28] A keen interest in construction was the very factor that prompted a young Grubb to want to train as an architect,[29] and her work can, by its example, help disprove the notion that all women have worked on the basis of a particularly feminine mode of expression or set of values. The building's inherent focus on women's conditions and interests made having a woman design the building an obvious choice, but then again, no one in the 1930s would regard the architect's gender as relevant if the issue at hand was a building for an organisation led by men which primarily looked after men's interests. The difference here, then, is that the question of gender is raised only when the matter at hand concerns women, who at this time still occupied a marginalised position in society's public life.

In its relationship with its urban setting, the Women's Building can also in no way be described in terms of gender stereotypical concepts of care and empathy. The project required the demolition of three early-eighteenth-century buildings, and the building's aesthetics as well as its gender-political purpose point to a desire to usher in a new

Before the Women's Building could be built, three older buildings, dating from the 1730s, had to be demolished. Ragna Grubb followed the entire process closely, taking several photographs of the demolition and the subsequent construction of the new building. Niels Hemmingsens Gade is a narrow street with several buildings from the eighteenth and nineteenth centuries, and today the functionalist building remains strikingly different from the surrounding properties.

In the foyer of the Women's Building, women could read the daily newspapers or talk with other women. The large, modern windows testify to Ragna Grubb's active use of new, industrialised technologies that enabled the creation of large windowpanes. With such choices, the women's organisations wanted to show that their work pointed ahead towards a new era, placing themselves in a setting radically different from the older architecture in the neighbourhood.

and better future, heralding new ways for people to live – and live together. A future where women took part in debating and resolving social and political issues on an equal footing with men. Entirely in line with the reform agendas of the time, we see here a desire to let modern architecture and technology actively contribute to creating better conditions for more people than just the ruling class of powerful, affluent men. Ragna Grubb was an influential and innovative architect who has left a lasting impression on the world but, like so many other women and architects, she subsequently slipped out of the public eye, and her work has not been featured in architectural historical literature. Neither Grubb nor the Women's Building appear frequently in publications,[30] meaning that she shares the fate of many of the other women addressed in this book whose work has, for various reasons, been under-examined in history writing.

The women who held leading roles in the organisations based at the Women's Building during its first years were typically from the middle and upper middle classes. They used the building to congregate and to help underprivileged women, but also to attain greater influence in society at large. Ragna Grubb and the seven women who congratulated her in the telegram all came from relatively privileged backgrounds.* The Women's Building was created during times that point ahead towards the Danish universal welfare model, which took shape in earnest after the end of the Second World War.[32] Shortly before the building was constructed, in 1933, a broad political majority in the Danish parliament, then called Rigsdagen, entered into the

* Their fathers' professions included: army captain, doctor, Supreme Court lawyer, public-sector payment supervisor, machine inspector and pastor. In their applications to the Royal Danish Academy of Fine Arts, only their fathers' occupations are mentioned, so unfortunately we do not know anything about their mothers.[31]

Gerda Schäffer (1884–1960) studied at Copenhagen's Technical School and spent half a year as a bricklayer's apprentice in the Danish town Odder before being admitted to the School of Architecture at the Royal Danish Academy of Fine Arts in Copenhagen in 1910. She is believed to be the first woman to design and build a building in Denmark under her own name – specifically a house located in Fredericia at Øster Voldgade 8, built in 1915. Gerda Schäffer oversaw the construction of several holiday homes in Tibirke Bakker, a rural area in North Zealand, but her primary focus was on designing and furnishing private homes.

Ragna Grubb (1903–1961) finished secondary school in 1921, having attended Nørre Gymnasium in Copenhagen. In 1922, she enrolled at a technical school in Copenhagen before being accepted at the Royal Danish Art Academy's School of Architecture the following year. She earned her degree in 1933, and the following year won her first architectural competition, having submitted the winning design for Kvindernes Bygning – the Women's Building – intended to accommodate a number of women's organisations in Copenhagen. She set up her own design studio in 1935. The Women's Building was inaugurated in 1936, and in 1937 she won the Privatbanken and fsb competition for future planning solutions together with architects Ingeborg Schmidt and Karen Hvistendahl. They realised their ideas in the development Kantorparkens Blok 7 between 1939 and 1941. Grubb also designed furniture, residences and holiday homes as well as factory buildings.

landmark Kanslergade Agreement, which is best known for ushering in social reform that included incipient state-organised redistribution policies which would later be firmly established and run by specific institutions after the war. During this period, Denmark saw the creation of a society where the state introduced a range of new institutions, especially in the areas of education, health and housing, that all let the question of 'the good life' take centre stage. This introduced legal regulations on welfare for all by virtue of an overarching policy that involved public institutions taking care of all citizens' needs from cradle to grave, regardless of income.[33]

The Kanslergade Agreement also paved the way for the first of several laws on support for construction projects – the so-called state loans – which especially prompted social housing associations to build several housing developments with regulated rents. This shows how the distribution policy of the modern welfare state begins to manifest itself in physical environments as far back as the 1930s.[34] The Women's Building arose out of a different and older distribution model where civil society in the form of affluent benefactors, foundations and organisations used private funds in the efforts to support various causes and help people they considered in need (and deserving) of aid.

Danish architects, urban planners, landscape architects and designers played significant roles in the emerging welfare state: they gave physical form to the new institutions created during the period. On a par with intellectuals, writers and other artists, they were seen to embody cultural movements and trends, making them prominent voices in the public exchange of opinion about which values should define the development of the welfare state.[35] Several women, such as Ulla Tafdrup and Anne Marie Rubin, were important voices in the public debate in their time. They contributed to discussions of what kind of society was to be built and how, thereby helping to articulate what 'welfare' is. As the literary historian Lasse Horne Kjældgaard has described, the concept of welfare was not a stable term in the post-war period; it had not grown out of a single, clear-cut ideological point of view. Rather, it was a nebulous concept discussed from different positions and changing notions of what it could and should mean.[36] These women did not take the floor to speak out *because* they were women, but if we look at their work through the lens of gender history, it becomes clear that special circumstances pertaining to their gender as well as to their professional capacities have contributed to the fact that their voices are heard to a far lesser extent, if at all, in the various subsequent narratives about the period. The feminist social scientist Anette Borchorst has pointed out how historical writing about the Danish welfare state has often emphasised the contributions made by men and has tended to portray women as passive recipients of welfare offerings through institutions and policies designed for them. As she points out, women have subsequently been increasingly recognised as active co-creators and significant players in the creation of the welfare state.[37] Our research contributes an architectural-historical perspective and concrete empirical material that underpins such an understanding of women as active co-creators of the welfare state. Thus, we do not strive to identify a particularly feminine way of being an architect. Rather, we examine women's contribution to the architectural professions from a gender perspective as well as through the lens of architectural history.

The people whose work we elucidate here can all be identified as women. In this book we consider them as a unified group on the basis of their gender identity, and we do so even though we know that only a few of them have had direct connections to each other, been avowed feminists, or otherwise shared similarities in their approach to being architects. However, many of the women addressed in this book do share one particular trait: at one point or another during their professional careers they have reflected on how their gender has influenced or affected their professional work or career path. We do not know of very many, if any, men within the architectural professions engaging in similar deliberations during the period. This fact in itself gives cause to ask about the significance of gender and of being a minority in the profession, for example as pertains to cultural stereotypes and the opportunities and limitations found in society as such. The question hints at a bias in the general perception of who worked as architects during this significant period within the profession in Denmark – and of what kind of work architects actually did carry out at the time.

Anka Rasmussen (1893–1977) was probably the first woman in Denmark to work as a garden designer. A trained gardener, she went on to supplement her studies in various ways, for example at the design studio of the garden designer I. P. Andersen. Rasmussen ran her own business which was focused mainly on the design of private gardens, including for residences in Frederiksberg and Copenhagen, and also on landscape gardening, while running a real estate business at the same time. In 1912, she was the first woman to join the Havearkitektforeningen (later the Association of Danish Landscape Architects), where she remained the only woman until 1945. She was editor of the trade journal *Havekunst* in 1931 and 1932 and published the book *Moderne Haver* (Modern Gardens) in 1929. She published texts about gardens for books in Sweden, Germany and Denmark. Anka Rasmussen was an expert on the iris species.

Structure and content of the book

By taking women's work as our point of departure, we establish a new historical understanding of architecture and urban and landscape planning from the 1930s to the end of the 1970s, a time when women became increasingly active in the labour market as paid professionals, in principle working on an equal footing with men. We not only shed light on unknown stories about forgotten women, but also contribute new perspectives on the work done by well-known women from the period. The women whose work we explore articulated their positions in texts, conversations, exhibitions, actions and unrealised projects

Andrea Maria Norn Nielsen (1888–date unknown) attended technical school in Copenhagen before being admitted to the School of Architecture at the Royal Danish Academy of Fine Arts in 1909. She completed her training in 1920, and in the same year received a travel grant. She worked at several different design studios, including with architect Sven Risom (1880–1971), and also designed furniture. She submitted an entry for the Women's Building design competition in 1934.

Erna Sonne Friis (1902–1990) travelled around the world with her father at the age of seventeen, a trip that would have a great impact on her professional work due to their many visits to gardens. Having completed secondary school at N. Zahles Skole in Copenhagen, she went abroad, visiting the United States, Switzerland and more, and in 1927 she went to Finland and stayed for eight years. Upon returning to Denmark, she enrolled at the Royal Danish Veterinary and Agricultural College and visited Britain over the course of her studies. She specialised in plantings, and her many gardens with innovative colour combinations were widely published in Denmark and Sweden. She was an active contributor to professional magazines such as *Dansk Havetidende*, *Haven*, *Anlægsgartneren* and *Havekunst*, created a large number of private small gardens and was a consultant on several large manor gardens in Denmark. She planned the crocus bed in the Kongens Have park in Copenhagen together with the head gardener at Rosenborg Castle, Ingwer Ingwersen (1911–1969). She also designed several spaces in the garden of the Royal Danish Horticultural Society in Frederiksberg.

as well as through the many homes, schools, swimming pools, parks, roads and landscapes they designed for public-sector and private clients. Their work still stands as concrete physical takes – conceived by women – on how modern people could and should live. The physical environments created during the period thus express different and often new ideas found in the emerging Danish welfare state – for example on what it means to be an individual, a community, citizen, woman, man, child or other identities. The book's chapters delve into the work done by a handful of individuals, while at the same time showing the diversity of their approaches and practices.

Chapter One, Visions, is about the layout of the kitchen and its relationship to the rest of the home's floor plan – a field rarely highlighted within the architectural profession. We focus on the work of the architects Gytte Rue, Rut Speyer and Ulla Tafdrup.

Chapter Two, Love, describes the gendered design philosophy behind the single-family houses designed by and for the architect couples Inger Exner and Johannes Exner, Karen Clemmensen and Ebbe Clemmensen as well as Rut Speyer and Eigil Hartvig Rasmussen.

Chapter Three, Growth, examines the planners Anne Marie Rubin's and Vibeke Dalgas's approach to urban and landscape planning, which points to alternative values as well as to more caring ways of working than have generally been in focus in the history of modern urban development.

Chapter Four, Alternatives, shows new aspects of the socially oriented positions in 1960s' and 1970s' architecture by delving into works created by Susanne Ussing and Anne Marie Rubin and the feminist working communities of which they were part.

Chapter Five, Collaboration, presents new knowledge about how an iconic piece of architecture, Kildeskovshallen – a sports venue and indoor swimming pool built in the late 1960s in Gentofte Municipality – was the product of a very special collaboration across gender and professional disciplines.

The significant decline in activity seen in the construction industry in 1970s' Denmark contributed to the rise and prominence of a number of social and counter-cultural movements, a development concurrent with a growing interest in issues of gender, participation, resource consumption, ecology and alternative forms of living. As part of what is often called the second feminist wave, women in Denmark established feminist initiatives specific to the field of architecture, such as Kvinder i Byggesektoren (Women in the Construction Sector, 1977),

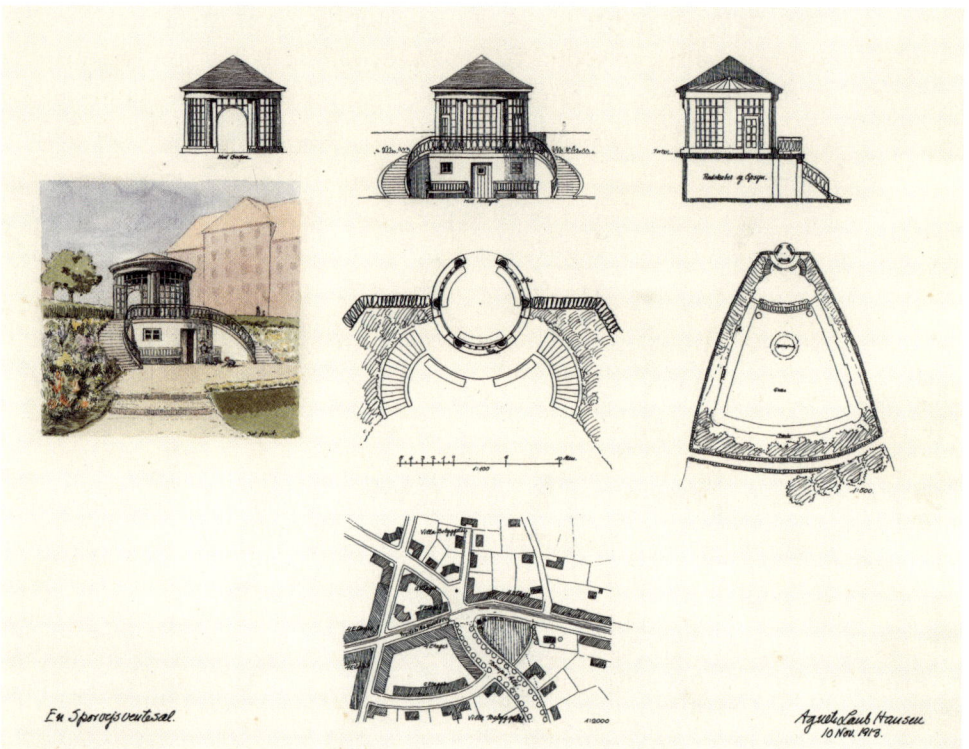

Agnete Laub Hansen was the first woman to train as an architect in Denmark. During her time as a student, her designs included a tram waiting room, shown here.

Kvindelige Arkitekter i Jylland (Women Architects in Jutland, 1977) and Nordiske Kvinders Bygge- og Planforum (Nordic Women's Building and Planning Forum, 1979–1985). At the same time, we see a growing number of women with or without formal architectural training getting involved in feminist collectives and in the first Danish self-proclaimed women's design studio, Thyra, which was founded in 1977.[38] We touch on examples of these initiatives in the postscript, which stretches further in time than the book's other chapters.

Becoming an architect

It is a well-known fact that for many years women were barred from training as architects due simply to their gender. The first woman to be admitted to the School of Architecture in Denmark was Agnete Frederikke Laub Hansen. When she first embarked on her education at the Royal Danish Academy of Fine Arts in Copenhagen in 1907,

Agnete Frederikke Laub Hansen (1886–1970) was admitted to the preparatory class of the Royal Danish Academy of Fine Arts' Model School in 1907 before passing the entrance exam to the School of Architecture in 1908. Before then, she attended classes at the Tegne- og Kunstindustriskolen for Kvinder (School of Drawing and Applied Art for Women). She obtained her degree in architecture in 1915 – making her the first woman architect in Denmark. Subsequently, she worked with her husband, fellow architect Henning Hansen (1880–1945) at his design studio.

Ester Claesson (1884–1931) was born in Sweden but moved to Denmark to attend the horticultural school Vilvorde in Charlottenlund, north of Copenhagen, from which she graduated in 1903. After graduating, she was first employed at the architect Paul Schultze-Naumburg's design studio in Germany. She later found employment with architect Joseph Maria Olbrich in Vienna at the artist colony Mathildenhöhe in Darmstadt, after which she returned to Sweden in 1913. In the early 1900s she was one of the most active garden designers in Sweden, building an extensive portfolio, and her work was published in leading international journals such as *Deutsche Kunst und Dekoration* in 1907 and *The Studio* in 1912.

women were not permitted to study architecture so she opted to study decorative painting instead. The following year, it became possible for women to apply for admission to the School of Architecture – which by then had been in existence since 1754, that is to say, for well over 150 years – and Agnete Laub Hansen immediately changed tack. She became the first Danish woman to complete her schooling as an architect, presenting her degree show project in 1915, the same year that the women of Denmark were given the right to vote for Parliament.[39] During her time at the Academy, she designed multiple projects, including a tram waiting room, a town hall in Dragør, a building for Kvindelig Læseforening (the Women Readers' Association) and a school.[40] Her final exam did not go unnoticed in the Danish media:

'We have our first woman architect. She is Miss Agnete Laub Hansen, who yesterday passed the Academy's graduation exam for architects. The young lady, who is the daughter of engine superintendent Holger Hansen and is engaged to architect Henning Hansen, has not received any vocational crafts training. The young lady attended technical school for a year and then went on to frequent the construction engineering class at the Academy. Eight other future women architects have attended the Academy at the same time as she, but Miss Agnete Laub Hansen is the first to pass the exam.'[41]

When women were allowed to enrol at the Academy's School of Architecture, the rules were also changed so that applicants no longer had to be fully trained craftsmen first. However, all students, regardless of gender, were still required to have technical insight and practical experience from a construction site, either a carpenter or a bricklayer. Here, Ragna Grubb is seen in her work clothes with colleagues at a construction site.

Agnete Laub Hansen was the first, but not the only, woman at the Royal Danish Academy of Fine Arts' School of Architecture; more joined them in the years that followed. Some did not complete their education. Several of the women stopped early on, and in some cases their files in the Academy's records state that they stopped because they were married, which does not seem to be the case for the men.⁴² Some of the women who did not graduate went on to work in the profession nevertheless. The same holds true of several men. The most famous example is perhaps the architect and professor Steen Eiler Rasmussen (1898–1990), who never completed his education yet became very influential and successful.⁴³ Similarly, not all of the women featured in this book have official graduation certificates from an architectural education. This applies, among others, to Ulla Tafdrup, who called herself a kitchen architect and crucially influenced the development of the modern kitchen. Others completed their education, but primarily worked outside of Denmark.

Ever since the Royal Danish Academy of Fine Arts in Copenhagen was set up in 1754, students wishing to enrol at the School of Architecture first needed a journeyman's certificate as a carpenter or bricklayer. In 1908, when women were admitted, this requirement changed: now, students had to have technical insight into construction from a technical school or by attending the School of Architecture's courses on building technology.⁴⁴ Well into the twentieth century, students were furthermore required to work on a construction site during the summer months. Architect and later professor Hanne Kjærholm recalls:

'At the time, we had a four-month summer holiday, during which it was mandatory for us to either apprentice with a craftsman or be a construction assistant on a construction site. I was apprenticed to the excellent local carpenter in Hjørring, where I come from.'⁴⁵

A similar requirement for practical training also applied for a long time at the degree programmes for garden architects. Students would generally attend a horticultural education programme at either the Royal Veterinary and Agricultural University or some other school, such as the horticulture school Vilvorde in Charlottenlund.* The horticulture programmes delved mostly into plant science and the cultivation of crops, but a few subjects focused on architectural treatments.* At the beginning of the century, only very few students from the Royal Veterinary and Agricultural University, regardless of gender, became garden designers.⁴⁸ Instead, the graduates from horticultural studies were found in nurseries or other professional roles within the field of horticulture. This also applies to the first woman

Previous spread: Women worked on equal terms with the men at the construction sites. Here Rut Speyer (far right) is laying bricks as part of her training. Presumably, she made the collage herself using photographs from the construction site and of her colleagues.

Vilhelmine Busck (1869–1954) was the first woman in Denmark to obtain a degree in horticulture. She did so in 1895, two years after the programme was established. During her studies, she was employed in the garden at Rosenborg Castle in Copenhagen. After graduating, she moved to the United States and in 1895 she became co-owner of the firm of Pennock and Co., Charlestown, West Virginia in the United States. She later moved to San Pedro, California, where she remained for the rest of her life.

* In 1968, the horticultural programme became known as 'Hortonom'. The international programmes with which women combined their horticultural training from The Royal Veterinary and Agricultural University include Swanley Horticultural College and University of California, specifically Berkeley's course on garden botany.⁴⁶

* For example, one item on the curriculum in 1910 was the study of 'The different garden styles and the most important principles for the construction of gardens of different types and sizes'. This was part of the subject 'Horticulture and the Cultivation of Ornamental Plants'.⁴⁷

Those wishing to become architects had to attend the Royal Danish Academy of Fine Arts, while becoming a garden designer could be achieved in several ways. The first woman to train at a Danish horticultural school and later work as a garden designer was Swedish: Ester Claesson. She studied at the Vilvorde school of horticulture and subsequently founded her own company. Claesson is believed to be the woman on the left in this picture, clad in white, attending a class on pruning fruit trees.

Anka Rasmussen designed several private gardens, and German, Swedish and Danish readers could familiarise themselves with her designs in international books about new garden design in the 1930s. In 1929, Rasmussen published the book *Moderne Haver* (Modern Gardens), presenting a number of new gardens in text and pictures.

Agnete Petersen was reportedly one of the first to inspect the area that would house the Louisiana Museum of Modern Art in Humlebæk together with its founder, Knud W. Jensen. She worked closely with the architects Jørgen Bo and Vilhelm Wohlert, and together they created a museum now widely renowned for its intimate interaction between buildings and landscape. In her design, Petersen preserved large parts of the existing planting and actively utilised the terrain.

Danmarks første kvindelige havearkitekt
har kirkegaarde og legepladser som speciale

Blandt de kandidater, som i aar er demitteret fra Det kongelige Akademi i København, var et lille hold paa kun fem. Men denne lille gruppe betegner en ny udvikling indenfor et specielt fag. De fem bestod eksamen som havearkitekter, og erhvervede derved et for deres stand meget betydningsfuldt diplom. Der var kun een kvinde paa holdet, frøken A g n ē t e P e t e r s e n, der i en aarrække har virket som anlægsgartner med et virkefelt, som strækker sig over det meste af Sjælland. Agnete Petersen er desuden tilknyttet institutionen „Socialt boligbyggeri" som anlægsgartner og konsulent.

Om sin nyerhvervede eksamen siger Danmarks første kvindelige havearkitekt: — Det har indenfor vort fag i mange aar været et stærkt ønske om at faa uddannelsen lagt i faste rammer, og eksaminationen er et skridt i retning af en beskyttelse af havearkitekttitlen.

Det er jo saadan, at enhver, der har haft med beplantning eller gartneri at gøre, kan kalde sig havearkitekt, og det kan naturligvis ikke være helt tilfredsstillende for dem, der har gennemgaaet den behørige uddannelse — lige saa lidt som det kan være tilfredsstillende for de mennesker, der har brug for en havearkitekt. Kunderne spørger jo ikke om at faa lov til at se eksamenspapirerne Ogsaa i anden retning er skolen en hjælp for havearkitekterne. Naar de har gennemgaaet uddannelsen paa Landbohøjskolen, der hovedsagelig lægger vægt paa det økonomiske havebrug, har der hidtil kun været den mulighed at søge ind paa tegnestue for at faa udvidet den side af uddannelsen, der gælder det æstetiske. Nu er der for fremtiden mulighed for yderligere et supplement paa Akademiet.

Historisk og nutidig opgave.

— Hvori har akademiprøven bestaaet?

— Vi har gennem de sidste to aar fulgt forskellige forelæsninger om arkitektur, byplanlægning og kunsthistorie, men det er et forholdsvis frit studium ... vi har alle haft arbejde ved siden af. Der var indstillet ni, men kun fem bestod. Selve den afsluttende prøve bestod af to opgaver: en historisk og en nutidig, som blev bedømt af et særligt udvalg, bestaaende af bl. a. skolens leder, professor C. T h. S ø r e n s e n, havearkitekt G e o r g B o y e, der er direktør for „Det kongelige danske Haveselskab", og lektor G e o r g s e n, Landbohøjskolen. Desuden har arkitekter, malere og billed-

Havearkitekt Agnete Petersen

huggere deltaget i bedømmelsen.

Som nutidig opgave valgte jeg at anlægge en kirkegaard i en storby. Kirkegaardsanlæg har altid haft min store interesse. Det er afvekslende. Der kan ikke gives bestemte retningslinjer for, hvordan man mener, et kirkegaardsanlæg bør se ud; det maa i hvert enkelt tilfælde indrettes i pagt med det bestaaende, da det jo i langt de fleste tilfælde drejer sig om udvidelser. Ogsaa gaardsanlæg en god opgave, idet det udformes uafhængigt af byggeri — saa der kan arbejdes mere i ro. Naar man har med boligkarreer at gøre, kan man først komme i gang, naar byggeriet er færdigt og saa skal havearbejdet helst være færdigt i en fart.

Plads til børnene, men ...

— Og børnene maa der i højere grad tages hensyn til

— Naturligvis maa man tænke paa dem ved havens anlæggelse — eller naar den lægges om. De er jo ikke altid lige hensynsfulde overfor haverne. Men der maa naturligvis holdes en vis hævd over anlæget. Det kan ikke nytte, børnene faar lov at gøre lige, hvad der passer dem — selv om jeg naturligvis godt kan se, det er fristende at spille fodbold paa den grønne plæne. I den retning er anlægene ved de nye ejendomme nemmest at have med at gøre. Det er for det meste unge mennesker, der flytter ind — enten uden børn eller med smaa børn, og saa faar anlæget ro til at komme i groning. Værre kan det kan være med nyanlæg ved de gamle ejendomme.

* Der er efterhaanden mange
* steder indrettet specielle lege-
* pladser, men det er jo sjæl-
* dent der, børnene helst vil
* være. En pæn, velindrettet
* legeplads har kun tiltrækning
* den første tid. Børnene skal
* stadig have noget nyt, der
* kan sætte fantasien i sving;
* der er jo ikke noget saa godt
* som en byggeplads for eks-
* empel, hvor de kan boltre sig
* med sten, bjælker og hvad
* der ellers findes saadan et
* sted.
* Det er en vigtig opgave at
* finde frem til en skrammel-
* legeplads, hvor børnene kan
* faa fuld beskæftigelse for de-
* penge, og haven kommer som
* bekendt i sidste række ved et
* byggeri. Dog er man fra man-
* ge sider begyndt at vise for-
* staaelse for sagen — der er
* rettet meget op efter krigen.

De offentlige stillinger

— De var eneste dame paa holdet — det er i det hele taget et fag, der ikke tæller mange kvindelige udøvere, skønt det synes at være et omraade, hvor det kvindelige instinkt nok skulle kunne gøre sig gældende, ikke mindst ved indretning af anlæg med legepladser ...

* Hvad muligheden for kvinde-
* lige havearkitekter angaar
* — ja, da de har den samme ud-
* dannelse som deres mandlige
* kolleger, skulle de jo have
* samme chancer, men vi kan
* nu ikke helt komme uden om,
* at der for eksempel ved be-
* sættelse af offentlige stillinger
* stadig raader noget af den
* gamle fordom, at man ikke
* skal have en kvinde til at be-
* stride en ledende post. Dog
* vil tiden vel nok ændre noget
* i dette forhold, og da de grøn-
* ne omraader i alle byer er i
* stadig udvikling, vil der blive
* stadig bedre muligheder for
* kvindelige havearkitekter.

The first woman to sit the Royal Danish Academy of Fine Arts' exam for garden architects was Agnete Petersen. Upon her graduation in 1955, the media hailed her as Denmark's first woman 'garden architect', even though other women had practised the profession previously. Petersen initially worked with garden designer C. Th. Sørensen (1893–1979) before undertaking her own commissions for the social housing association fsb, where she designed landscapes and outdoor areas for several social housing developments.

to graduate from the horticulture programme, Vilhelmine Busck. The degree programme was established in 1893, and she graduated two years later, in 1895.⁴⁹ In the years from 1900 to 1903 we find the first woman known to have trained at a Danish horticultural school and who later went on to become a garden designer: Ester Claesson from Sweden. Having studied at Vilvorde, she subsequently went on to found her own company and built up a large portfolio.⁵⁰ Looking back, she describes her time at Vilvorde and how she initially found it difficult to be the only woman – for example, she had to spend the night further away from the school than the male students. However, she also reports being given other and, in her eyes, better assignments than the men in her year. For example, she describes how the women students were allowed to work in a special part of the school's garden specifically because of their gender:

'Being allowed to work on the rockery, which was the apple of Director Nyeland's eye, was certainly considered a special privilege, and this work was usually handed over to us female students, who did not 'blunder' and were more careful around the director's dearly beloved plants, which were often rarities from foreign countries.'⁵¹

The first woman we know of who set up her own garden design company in Denmark was Anka Rasmussen. Her education consisted of various training programmes and courses on horticulture as well as employment with a practicing garden designer.⁵² Erna Sonne Friis, who became the next woman working in the profession in Denmark, also had a piecemeal education, studying partly at the Agricultural University in Copenhagen and supplementing this with international practice.⁵³ From the middle of the century we know of two women who both held regular degrees in horticulture: Agnete Petersen, who graduated in 1942, and Agnete Muusfeldt, who graduated in 1955. We will return to Muusfeldt in Chapter Five.* Agnete Petersen's prominent projects include the first garden plan for the Louisiana art museum in Humlebæk, and as a consultant for the non-profit social housing organisation fsb she designed landscape settings for housing projects that have constituted the backdrop of everyday life for thousands of people since then.⁵⁵

What was it like to be a woman and a student of architecture in early twentieth-century Denmark? How were women viewed and how did they see themselves? Those questions were asked by a teacher at Vilvorde, Anna Weber (1893–1993), around the same time as the Women's Building was being built. Seeking to encourage more women to pursue a career in gardening, Weber wanted to find out what it was like to be a woman in the gardening profession, and she

Agnete Petersen (1916–2000) obtained her degree in horticulture in 1942 and passed the exam on garden design at the Royal Danish Academy of Fine Arts' School of Architecture in Copenhagen in 1955. She prepared the first garden plan for the Louisiana art museum in Humlebæk and also designed several landscapes for public housing developments, some in collaboration with garden designer Morten Klint (1918–1978). Petersen later moved to England; whether she designed any gardens there is unknown.

* As of 1951, it was possible to take a supplementary course as an add-on to the horticultural degree programme, namely the exam on garden architecture offered by the Royal Danish Academy of Fine Arts in Copenhagen. Agnete Petersen sat the exam on 25 March 1955. In 1960, the horticultural degree programme included a specialist course focusing on social planning. The new subject arose as a result of the many new tasks associated with the welfare state, and it would later develop into the degree programme now officially known as Landscape Architecture.⁵⁴

The year 1964 saw the graduation of the first class from the new specialised course on landscape gardening (later landscape architecture) at the Royal Veterinary and Agricultural College. Front row, l. to r.: Jette Abel, Ulla Wicksell, Morten Falmer-Nielsen, Carl Aage Sørensen. Back row, l. to r.: Peter Thorsen, Kirsten Duus, Frank Pettersson, Poul Hagedorn, Professor Georg Boye.

In the early 1930s, Anna Weber, a teacher at the Vilvorde school of horticulture, set out to study what it was like to be a woman in the gardening profession. She conducted a questionnaire survey, using it as the basis for coming up with good advice for the women. For example, she encouraged them to join existing professional organisations and to take part on an equal footing with the men, seeking influence there instead of creating their own associations for women only.

set about it thoroughly. She conducted a questionnaire survey sent out to a hundred women and twelve men who worked in various nurseries – only one of whom was both a woman and a garden designer.* Anna Weber writes:

'When a young girl elects to become a gardener, it is very often out of an abiding love for flowers. The young girls who choose to become gardeners were brought up in homes with a garden. It is quite natural for women to find satisfaction in seeing how the living things they care for and look after sprout and grow into something beautiful and valuable.'[57]

The sentiments point back to a long-established tradition in the Western world of viewing flowers and gardens as a woman's domain.[58] That tradition may have helped make it more acceptable for women to follow the path of horticulture and garden design rather than looking towards architecture, a field stereotypically associated with masculine connotations and one where women are often rather more sparsely represented. The issue is also connected to cultural notions associating the woman's space with the realm of the domestic, the private, and the decorated, while the representative, public space

* The garden designer was probably Ester Claesson. Anna Weber received responses from eighty-nine women and ten men. These are conscientiously credited in the foreword, where she writes: 'Thanks to their great helpfulness, my little book can rightly be called: "The book with the 100 authors".[56]

Anna Weber illustrated her book with several photographs of women at work. She stated that the women responding to her survey preferred to dress in the same kind of clothes as men, for example in plus-fours or overalls, rather than the traditional dresses. Several of the women emphasised that men's clothes were more practical.

has traditionally been seen as men's domain.[59] Such notions have also contributed to giving women a greater role in interior architecture and design as a professional field, as exemplified by the work of Ulla Tafdrup, Grethe Meyer, Gytte Rue and Rut Speyer, specifically with regards to kitchens.[60]

On closer inspection, however, the realities of gender within the architectural professions are more complicated than binary gender concepts tend to suggest. This is evident, for example, when looking at Stephan Nyeland (1845–1922), the founder and long-time head of Vilvorde, who is described in the sources as an all-dominant father figure.[61] He was known among the students for expressing his love for flowers with great fervour and frequency, and this, combined with being a horticulturist himself, interested in caring for living life, means that in many ways he takes on roles that are often associated with the feminine in a traditional binary view of gender.[62] Concurrently with this, he took on traditionally masculine roles: as managing director, as the one responsible for finances, as expert, professional head at the school and as a writer of great social commitment. As such, he cannot be understood exclusively in terms of a binary opposition between the masculine and the feminine.

Similarly, the many women in the gardening profession to whom Weber's book lends voice cannot be described as fully adhering to a traditional feminine role. Several of those she interviews state a desire to work as hard as the men and on an equal footing with them, and several assert that they do not feel inferior to their colleagues who are men.[63] Weber reports that an 'overwhelming majority' of the women respondents to her survey preferred to go dressed in 'men's clothing', which means that they did not work in dresses but in plus-fours or overalls, simply because it was more practical.[64] Pictures in the book show women clad in trousers and wearing their hair up or cut short. Presumably not unaffected by the vitalist currents of the time, many of them point to the joy of working outdoors in the open air.[65] The men interviewed by Weber say that they are happy to have women as part of their working community, although a few note that it can lead to rather too much 'silliness and flirting',[66] which could be distracting. The book does not overtly address the idea that some might fall for members of the same sex. Others among the interviewed men express a concern which has often been a stumbling block in women's struggle for access to education and society as such: they suspect that women may take work from men in the nurseries, especially because some of the women 'work for slightly less pay'.[67] When more workplaces in the financially dire 1930s began to take on a greater number of women, a certain amount of tension arose.*

* 'Back in his day, Louis Pio, who was leader of the first socialist workers' union in the 1870s, believed that women and children did not belong in the labour market, partly because that made them competitors to the men. [...] When unemployment in the 1930s resulted in attacks on married women's right to a place on the labour market, this right was reaffirmed by the Social Democratic Prime Minister Thorvald Stauning'.[68]

The example of the gardeners shows that we cannot reduce the issue of gender to stereotypes about the 'masculine' and 'feminine' if we are to properly understand the context in which women entered the realm of architecture and thus also worked within the crafts. We need to nuance the narrative.

Weber's book ends with a piece of advice for women who want to enter the gardening and horticulture profession: 'absolutely do *not* create associations only for women – join the already established associations where the men are. And make sure, she writes, to be listed under 'your full name in membership lists', making it clearly visible that women have been present.[69] In doing so, she recommends a different strategy than the initiators behind the Women's Building, who believed it was important to form organisations exclusively for women.

In the following chapters, we will see that women in the architectural professions follow both of these strategies to gain influence in different ways and at different times: they form alliances with other women, and they work within the established system together with the men. Exactly what their gender has meant for their lives and work varies greatly. The opportunity to shed light on this diversity was a key motivation behind our choice to unfold this material across different periods, situations and biographies.

Privileged and disadvantaged?

Today, very little material can be found about the first generations of women at the Royal Danish Academy of Fine Arts' School of Architecture in Copenhagen, and so we know correspondingly little about what it was like to be a woman among the many men on these courses. However, a few scattered records remain. For example, in 1927 the newspaper *Nationaltidende* asked the architect Sonja Meyer what it was like to be a woman working in the architectural profession:

'But – she concludes – one of the most appealing things about the entirely excellent treatment we two young architects have received here in Esbjerg is that we have not for a moment held or been assigned any special position due to being women. We have never been regarded as "two young ladies who happen to be architects", but as "the architects Westergaard and Carstensen".'[70]

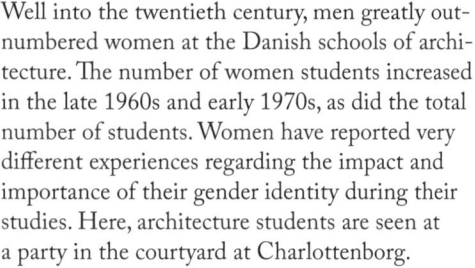

Hanne Kjærholm (1930–2009) attended the Tegne- og Kunstindustriskolen for Kvinder (School of Drawing and Applied Art for Women) from 1949 to 1950 and applied for admission to the School of Architecture at the Royal Danish Academy of Fine Arts in 1950. She was accepted and graduated in 1956. Two years later she founded her own design studio while also teaching at the Royal Danish Academy of Fine Arts. In 1989, Kjærholm was appointed professor of architecture at the Royal Danish Academy of Fine Arts – the first woman professor here. In 1953 she married furniture designer Poul Kjærholm (1929–1980), and in 1962 she designed their private home, while Poul Kjærholm designed the furniture for the house. In 1976 she won the design competition for a new art museum in Holstebro, a town in Jutland, which opened in 1981.

Well into the twentieth century, men greatly outnumbered women at the Danish schools of architecture. The number of women students increased in the late 1960s and early 1970s, as did the total number of students. Women have reported very different experiences regarding the impact and importance of their gender identity during their studies. Here, architecture students are seen at a party in the courtyard at Charlottenborg.

Karen Zahle (b. 1931) graduated from the Royal Danish Academy of Fine Arts' School of Architecture in 1959, having also attended classes at the École des Beaux-Arts and the École d'Urbanisme in Paris in 1957. She worked in the Ministry of Housing at the commissioner for town planning matters between 1961 and 1964. In addition, she worked at various design studios, including those of Anne Marie Rubin and Palle Suenson. In the late 1960s she began teaching at the School of Architecture, and between 1980 and 2000 she was head of the Laboratory for Housing Construction there. Zahle has published numerous articles on housing forms and gender and contributed to several exhibitions, including *La Femme Danoise*, shown for the first time at the Danish Cultural Institute in Paris in 1975.

The outlook was rather less positive ten years earlier, when the board of the scout association for young women, the KFUK (YWCA), were to select an architect to design a building for the association. In 1916, the board refused to let women take part in the design competition, a decision which did not go unnoticed in the media:

'It must feel like a slap in the face to all working young women to see that the board of K.F.U.K. has circumvented women architects, even denying them the opportunity to participate in the competition for the design of the young women's building, having limited itself to letting three selected male architects compete. [...] And when even a notable authority such as Professor [Martin] Nyrop recommends the young women architects, what responsibility can have weighed so heavily on the board[...]'[71]

From the beginning of the 1920s onwards, Danish media regularly encouraged women to train as architects. When doing so, journalists would also emphasise that women drew from a different wellspring of experience than men, and that those experiences needed to be brought into play in the efforts to raise the quality of Danish housing. In 1921, the newspaper *B.T.* wrote:

'We poor housewives curse the exalted Messrs. Architects and Craftsmen for having arranged and designed our homes and tool with such blessed impracticality; just imagine if our kitchens, our stoves, etc., had been devised by women architects and constructors who have first-hand knowledge of cooking, cleaning, etc. [...].'[72]

The number of women who applied to the School of Architecture and completed the programme grew steadily from the mid-1930s, and the generations from the time after the Second World War have been much more communicative about their student days. A common trait among the women at the Royal Danish Academy of Fine Arts' School of Architecture is that many of them emphasise how they were significantly outnumbered: well into the twentieth century, the majority of the students admitted were men. When the later professor Hanne Kjærholm applied for admission in 1950, there were several hundred applicants: forty got in, of which five were women.[73] Kirsten Sestoft enrolled in 1954, and in a subsequent interview she pointed out that being a woman among so many men had its advantages: '[...] you were noticed, feted, waited on – and girls were not used to be made a fuss of in ordinary family life. It was delightful'.[74] In an interview, Karen Zahle has explained that being a woman at the Academy was like 'being an exotic plant in a Danish bed',[75] and in retrospect describes life as a woman in the profession as one of being simultaneously 'shut out and shut in'.[76]

There can be no doubt that life was different for women attending the Academy in the middle of the twentieth century compared to today, partly because they were outnumbered. Like several other women (and men), Vibeke Dalgas got married during her time as a student, but she insisted on coming back and completing her degree after having become a mother, even though her family struggled to understand why.* Looking back, she concluded:

'My student days were for me, as for so many other young women at the time, an amputated youth. Holding full responsibility for a couple of children, the daily housework and so on, all remaining energy had to go towards the most essential part of the studies. All the amusing stuff, anything extraordinary had to be cut out. My role was most often that of a spectator and listener.'[78]

The experience of being immersed in a male-dominated and patriarchal environment was described by a group of women in the journal *Blød By* (Soft City) in 1981, as they investigated the distribution of women and men at the recently founded school of architecture in Aarhus,[79] where women were still a marginalised group in some ways.[80] This gives food for thought today, when issues of gender, diversity, marginalisation and unequal power relations continue to be important agendas in the architecture industry and in education. We hope that by becoming more aware of the importance of gender identity in this historical context – and by addressing, in this book, the importance of diversity for collaborations and innovative thinking – we will become better equipped to push the architecture industry in a direction that is more equal and equitable for people of all genders, bodies, ages, positions, backgrounds, class and more.

* 'Fortunately, I got rid of the burdensome housework, found a cheap place to live, was married very quickly, moved back into a proper flat and had a year off while I had my first child. But I wanted to return to my studies again, despite great outrage among my immediate family and difficulties with childcare'.[77]

Kirsten Sestoft (1936–1990) enrolled at the School of Architecture at the Royal Danish Academy of Fine Arts in 1954. She graduated in 1959 but began working in a design studio well before then, in 1956. For many years she worked as department manager at various architectural design studios. She was the first woman to chair the Council of Practising Architects, now the Danish Association of Architectural Firms, a role she held from 1983 to 1984.

In 1965, the Aarhus School of Architecture opened, and in 1981 a group of women described, in the journal *Bløactionsd By*, how several women found the school to be a male-dominated and patriarchal environment. In 1983, the editors behind the magazine continued the theme of women in architecture with an issue about what they called 'Women's Architecture'.

Chapter 1

Visions – A Revolution in the Kitchen

'We are going to live in entirely new ways',[81] *proclaimed the newspaper* Aftenbladet *one spring day in 1937. And new ways were needed. The housing situation in the cities was under pressure due to population growth, migration to the cities and the aftermath of the worldwide economic crisis in 1929. In Copenhagen, one finds examples of families with two parents and five children living in a single room of twelve square metres, with no bathroom and only access to a communal kitchen which they share with several other families.*[82] *With the adoption of the Housing Benefit Acts in 1933 and*

1938 respectively, it became possible for non-profit social housing companies to build new housing where the rent was affordable. Architects played an important role in this, designing many of the new homes in ways that helped raise housing standards for the population as a whole. At the same time, the design and layout of the new homes helped pave the way for new ideas about the role of women in the family and in the modern welfare state. The issue will be explored in this chapter, where we examine the work and various collaborations of Gytte Rue, Rut Speyer and Ulla Tafdrup.

The article in *Aftenbladet* was prompted by the publication of a new type of floor plan designed by architects Ragna Grubb, Karen Hvistendahl and Ingeborg Schmidt. In the spring of 1937, the trio won a major design competition issued by non-profit social housing organisation fsb (foreningen socialt boligbyggeri) and the Privatbanken. The specific objective was to create better housing conditions for the less well-off part of the population, especially for those families with many children who often live in miserable conditions in the cities.[83] The winning project breaks away with the previously prevalent bourgeois floor plans with their focus on reception rooms, not least a dining room that is left empty for much of the day.* The new design principles assert that the floor space available must be utilised differently, for example so that parents and children can each have their own bedroom.[84] The three architects also share the clear conviction that children of different sexes should not sleep together, so they make room for a boys' room and a girls' room. And by taking space away from the dining room, they expand the kitchen to fit in a dining table where the children can draw or do homework while their mother prepares food or washes the dishes.[85]

The three architects' winning project is mentioned in numerous newspapers, trade journals and weekly magazines, and September 1937 sees the opening of a major furniture exhibition in Tivoli in Copenhagen, where visitors can see a full-size model of the winning proposal. 'And it turns out that the three women architects, Ragna Grubb, Ingeborg Schmidt and Karen Hvistendahl, have completed the task brilliantly' is the verdict given by *Politiken*'s journalist, who hopes that the homes of the future will be built according to their guidelines.[86] The winning proposal presents a clear vision for how to plan and design flats in the future so that everyone, regardless of income, has access to good housing suitable for modern family life in Denmark.

Looking at the issue in a Nordic context, a landmark Swedish exhibition of architecture, arts and crafts, the *Stockholmsutställningen* (Stockholm Exhibition) in 1930 proved seminal in terms of presenting

Karen Margrethe Hvistendahl (1903–2003) was admitted to the School of Architecture of the Royal Danish Academy of Fine Arts in 1923 and graduated in 1932. In the summer of 1927, she worked as an apprentice mason under master mason Rasmus Sørensen, who was a 'specialist in reinforced concrete in all kinds of structures'. In 1937, with architects Ragna Grubb and Ingeborg Lange Schmidt, she submitted the winning entry in the bank Privatbanken and the social housing association fsb's competition for the home of the future. She and Ragna Grubb also worked together on designing a private property in Frederiksberg.

* In 1929, architect Henning Hansen and his project Solgården in the Østerbro district of Copenhagen initiated the first showdown with the bourgeois-inspired floor plan – especially prevalent in Copenhagen – which dictated that reception rooms such as living rooms/drawing rooms faced the street, while the private rooms and utilitarian rooms such as the kitchen were located towards the back courtyard. In Solgården, he took into account the light entering the flats. On one long side of the semi-open square complex, the living rooms face the courtyard, while the kitchen and bedroom face the street.

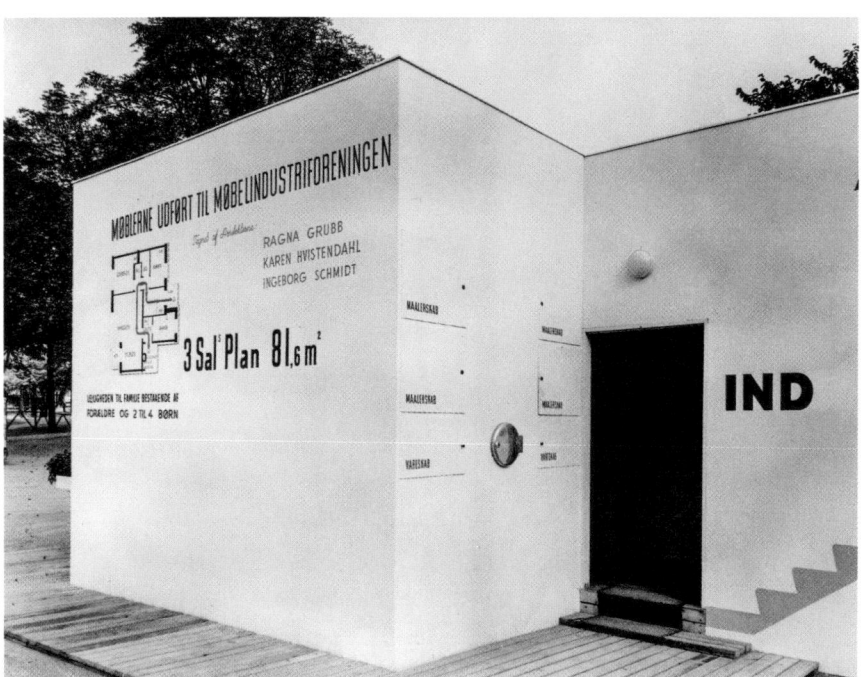

After Ragna Grubb, Karen Hvistendahl and Ingeborg Schmidt won a competition on designing the home of the future in 1937, a full-scale model flat was built according to their winning proposal. Presented as part of a furniture exhibition in Tivoli, the flat was arranged in accordance with their idea children of different genders should have separate rooms. Furthermore, the kitchen was expanded at the expense of a dining room so that the family could be together while the meals were being prepared.

For much of the twentieth century, much of central Copenhagen's housing stock was of poor quality, in particular kitchens and other sanitary facilities. Often the kitchens were small with poor ventilation or little to no access to fresh air or daylight. Even in newer housing developments from the 1930s, the kitchens were cramped, oblong rooms with room for no more than one person at a time, meaning that women were isolated from the rest of the family for much of the day – because women were almost exclusively responsible for the housework.

* See, for example, Lundevænget, one of the first so-called 'stokbebyggelse' developments in Denmark (the term denotes residential blocks placed with access roads to one side and recreational/green areas to the other), or Vestersøhus, one of the first examples of a project utilising the balcony-bay motif. Both are located in Copenhagen.[87]

and disseminating various ideas about architecture for the future as they manifested themselves in various European cities. Danish architects flocked to the fair, where they saw examples of new conceptions of rational interior design and the industrial manufacture of housing, but in the years that followed they were more interested in devising new kinds of development plans and a more modern architectural aesthetic than in investigating how the floor plan of individual homes could support everyday family life.* Thus, the 1937 design competition helped promote a new focus and bolstered the architects' interest in how they could design the most optimal setting for the family life of the future – not only for the upper echelons of society, but also for those who had modest financial means. The next twenty years would see major changes to Danish approaches to housing construction.

But how did architects find answers to the question of how the homes of the future should function and what they should look like? Several books have been written about Danish architecture from the so-called Golden Age in the 1950s[88] but little attention has been paid to those fundamental aspects underpinning the development of new residential architecture which are *not* mainly about aesthetics and design. For example, one finds few descriptions of the development of the kitchen as a room, or of the relationship between the kitchen and the rest of the rooms inside the home.[89] Surprisingly few, in fact, given that the kitchen was one of the aspects that underwent the greatest transformation and innovation in the development of residential architecture from the 1930s to the 1950s. This chapter shows that the budding scientific and far more methodical approach to architecture emerging during this period had a decisive impact – not only on the development of residential architecture where the kitchen and living room were combined to form a single room, but also on women's increased opportunities to work outside the home.

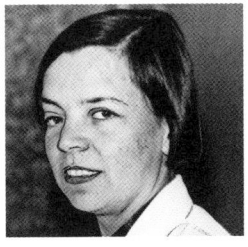

Ingeborg Lange Schmidt (1905–1986) applied for admission to the School of Architecture at the Royal Danish Academy of Fine Arts in 1923. Prior to this, she had completed secondary school and studied at technical schools in both Copenhagen and Roskilde. She ended her studies in 1933 without graduating. In her last year at the School of Architecture, she attended the department for furniture and spatial design. Together with architects Ragna Grubb and Karen Hvistendahl, she submitted the winning entry for the bank Privatbanken and the housing association fsb's competition for future planning solutions in 1937. They realised their ideas in the Copenhagen development Kantorparkens Blok 7 between 1939 and 1941. Schmidt worked for a number of years at Vilhelm Lauritzen's design studio.

At this time, in urban flats many of the everyday chores carried out by women took place in a kitchen set in a small, narrow and oblong room comprising approximately six square metres of floor space, separated from the rest of the home by a door. There was no room for more than one person to work there at a time, nor could the family eat in the kitchen. The countertops were low and the furnishings sparse, consisting of cupboards under the worktop and sometimes open shelves on the walls. Lighting conditions were often poor, and ventilation was done through a small kitchen window, if indeed there was a window at all.

In response to these conditions, architects began to envision the kitchen of the future offering much better working conditions in the form of larger rooms where there was room for the whole family to eat together, or even a fluid transition between kitchen and living room so that women were not isolated from the rest of the family when they prepared food and cleaned up. In the middle of the twentieth century, several architects articulated the idea that the kitchen should not only be a purely rational workspace but also a social space. The best-known example in this context is the French architect Charlotte Perriand's (1903–1999) open hatch connecting the kitchen and living room in the well-known residential building Le Unité d'Habitation by Le Corbusier (1887–1965) in Marseille, built from 1947 to 1952,[90] while the contribution made by Danish architects to this development has not yet been thoroughly investigated. The architects' work, then, was about much more than simply designing kitchen cabinets. They were concerned with finding the right location for each cabinet and its contents, pointing to a more rational way of working in the kitchen as well as to deliberations on where best to place the kitchen within the home.

Architects and politicians alike had many new ideas about the demands of modern life and what a home suited to those requirements should look like. When looking at the issue from a gender perspective, one crucial aspect is that women's physical, social and practical experience as housewives now began to be seen as a valuable source of knowledge for architects. Such interest testifies to a recognition of the kind of work mainly carried out by women in the home in the 1930s and 1940s, and of the importance of this work for the individual family as well as for society as a whole. Literature on twentieth-century architectural history has often presented Le Corbusier's supposedly universal scale of proportions 'l'Homme Modulor', which was presented as a yardstick for absolutely everything when developing new architecture suited to a modern life where technology and new ideas can set humankind free from all the hard work and harsh conditions of the past. The scale was based on a 1.75-centimetre male body extending its arm into the air, thereby measuring a total of 2.26 metres. In contrast to this, the trade magazine *Boligen* offers a very concrete example of how kitchens in Denmark should be developed on the basis of an average Danish woman's body of 164 centimetres. The Danish studies and surveys on the home and kitchen show that a great deal of resources and research is invested in *not* using a stereotypical masculine body but the female body instead as a yardstick for how the new homes should be designed.[91] Doing so is in itself an overlooked diversification of architecture and a way of making room for women's bodies and gender (albeit in a standardised form) that otherwise would have received no special attention in design processes. It follows, then, that this issue is key to a proper understanding of the transformation of society that these new housing

Ragna Grubb's, Karen Hvistendahl's and Ingeborg Schmidt's winning design from 1937 was partially realised in block 7 of the Kantorparken social housing development in Copenhagen from 1939 to 1941. While the flats were smaller than those suggested in the proposal, nevertheless they were of better quality than most of the housing stock in Copenhagen. Characteristic traits of the building are the large balconies and the green areas planned by C. Th. Sørensen's design studio. A kindergarten was added later, designed by architect Tutti Lütken.

developments represent. The development of the kitchen is based on women's experience and the proportions of the average woman's body, and new principles for interior design and production are developed on the basis of these experiences and measures. Those principles prove decisive in terms of launching extensive rationalisation and industrialisation of kitchen units and of construction as a whole, a process that gains serious momentum in the 1960s.

Generally speaking, the invisible work done by women in the home was not accorded great value, neither within the individual families nor in society as such. However, for the Danish architects – men and women alike – who took part in developing the new principles for the design of homes during this period, it became a guideline for residential construction for many decades to come. And it still leaves its mark on people's lives and homes today, because the one room that people in Denmark spend the most time in (and money on) is the kitchen.[92]

Ragna Grubb's, Karen Hvistendahl's and Ingeborg Schmidt's winning proposal from 1937 is thus not only interesting because of the new floor plans; it also points to how women really established themselves in the realm of architecture – not just as objects of scientific study, but as architects themselves. They were part of a new generation of women who, to a greater extent than before, graduated from the Royal Danish Academy of Fine Arts' School of Architecture. Taking their own experiences as their point of departure, these women set out to use their creative abilities as architects to make the work done around the home less time-consuming, enabling them to spend their time on paid professional work instead. Kitchen architect Ulla Tafdrup emphasised that her motivation for working with kitchen design was 'laziness'[93] and a desire to spend her time on something other than housework. Architects Gytte Rue and Rut Speyer compared poor kitchens to unproductive factories, pointing out that a failure to rationalise kitchen layouts would cost society money.[94]

Gytte Rue (1918–1993) trained as an architect at the Royal Danish Academy of Fine Arts' School of Architecture, but the date of her graduation is unknown. In 1944, she and Rut Speyer initiated a survey of Danish kitchens which later became part of the Joint Committee for Housing Studies' housing survey. She spent much of her career working as a journalist at Danmarks Radio (DR). She presumably began working there after the Second World War, initially participating in a few programmes on homes and houses before she left the world of architecture behind in the 1950s. In 1980, she helped found the association 'Women for Peace'.

Assembly-line work

The Danish architects' interest in improving housing conditions for all social groups was in line with what was happening outside the nation's borders. Since the beginning of the twentieth century, architects had been keenly interested in creating better homes, and the new residential developments that sprung up in Europe aimed to bring more natural light and fresh air into the flats and to provide access to green areas close to the homes.[95] Europeans looked towards the USA,

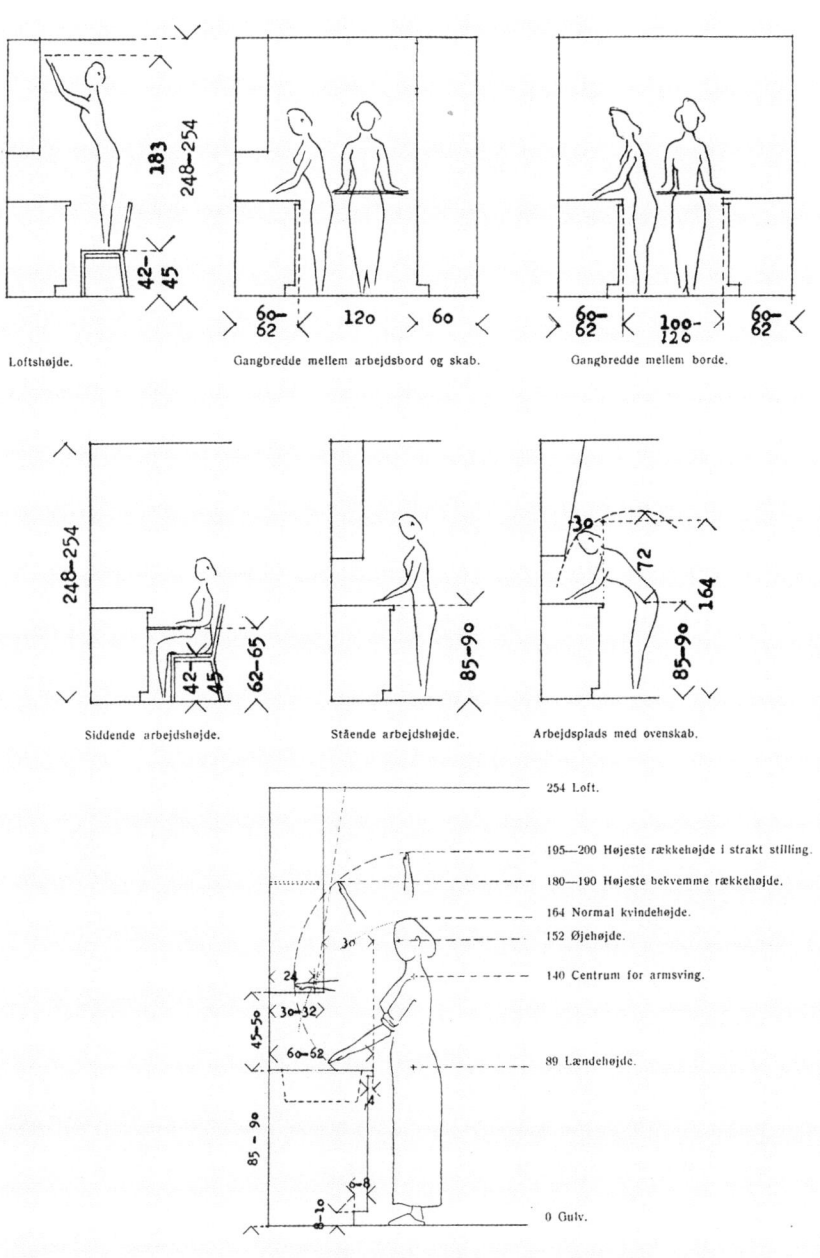

In the 1940s, the Franco-Swiss architect Le Corbusier developed 'l'Homme Modulor', a supposedly universal scale of proportion based on a man's body standing 175 cm tall. Much of Le Corbusier's work was carried out using this yardstick. However, a universalist male body was not alone in being central to the development of modern architecture. In 1951, the trade magazine *Boligen* provided an example of how kitchens in Denmark were developed based on an average Danish female body standing 164 cm tall, showing that the female body could also be a yardstick for new architecture.

where the American engineer Frederick W. Taylor's (1856–1915) efficient and productivity-boosting approach to organising work, developed in the early twentieth century, inspired changes. The new ideas about rationalisation were first applied to the factory as a workplace, and the home was next in line. Most households, both working and middle-class, stopped employing domestic workers during these decades,* and doctors produced new insights about the importance of health and hygiene issues in the home, prompting increased interest in arranging the kitchen in new and more hygienic ways.[97]

Some of the most pioneering ideas in the development of kitchens were formulated by the American Christine Frederick (1883–1970), whose book *Household Engineering. Scientific Management in the Home* (1919) compared kitchen work to modern assembly-line production. She mapped out various kitchen processes, recording the time and movements involved, and made drawings showing how a housewife could make her kitchen as efficient and rational as possible. In the following decades, Frederick's ideas were widely disseminated in Europe and the USA, especially when her book was translated into German in 1922, forming fertile soil for new approaches and methods.[98]

The focus on better living conditions and especially on more practical and efficient physical kitchen design grew in scope and intensity in Europe when the Austrian architect Margrete Schütte-Lihotzky (1897–2000) presented her take on a modern kitchen, known as the Frankfurt kitchen, at an exhibition in 1927 in Frankfurt am Main. Schütte-Lihotzky developed the kitchen for the many thousands of residential buildings that were to be built in the following years in the suburbs of Frankfurt. She was employed at the German architect and town planner Ernst May's (1886–1970) studio, which was central to the development of 10,000 housing units that, by means of standardisation and rationalisation, could provide affordable housing in response to extreme housing shortages. Schütte-Lihotzky was asked to continue the progressive movement she had launched in her earlier work in Vienna by creating a rationally designed kitchen that could ease the work of housewives and improve hygiene – and which could be mass-produced and thus made cheaply.[99] The kitchen was developed and designed on the basis of several studies, including surveys of the traditions for kitchen design found in different countries, and on considerations of how best to divide the kitchen work so that the work tools were placed where they would be used.[100]

In the same year that Schütte-Lihotzky presented the Frankfurt kitchen, the Danish architect Viggo Sten Møller (1897–1990), writing in the trade journal *Arkitekten*, requested a survey of the current

* At the end of the nineteenth century, industrial companies began to take over the production of everyday comestibles, which meant that households increasingly bought provisions instead of producing them themselves. Thus, many Danish families no longer required extra domestic help.[96]

Rut Speyer (1914–2003) graduated from the Royal Danish Academy of Fine Arts' School of Architecture in 1942. Prior to this she had attended classes at Aarhus Technical School, where she passed her exam with distinction in 1937. She worked as a bricklayer concurrently with her studies. Also in 1937, she and Bodil Krohn set out on a bicycle trip from Jutland to Copenhagen with a small detour through Sweden, where they looked at modern architecture. While still a student, in 1941 Speyer founded a design studio together with her husband Eigil Hartvig Rasmussen (1905–1980), but in 1950 she set up on her own. She designed several single-family houses, including at Hjortekærbakken in Kongens Lyngby north of Copenhagen, and helped design a few public housing developments. She also took part in designing the Atlas factory in nearby Lundtofte.

In 1927, on the basis of scientific studies, the Austrian architect Margrete Schütte-Lihotzky developed the so-called 'Frankfurt kitchen': a standardised kitchen intended for the many thousands of residential buildings that were to be built in the following years in the suburbs of Germany's Frankfurt am Main. The Frankfurt kitchen has since become world-renowned as an attempt to rationalise and modernise women's housework. It soon turned out that the modern kitchen was in fact not a particularly good workplace: it was too narrow. More work was required to create better working conditions for women in their own homes.

state of Denmark's flats with a view to improving housing conditions.[101] Before this, back in 1923, Karen Braae (1882–1962) – chairman of De Danske Husmoderforeninger (The Danish Housewives' Associations) – had called for greater interest in kitchen-design issues among the architectural profession.[102] Architect Ingrid Møller Dyggve was among those who heeded the call, working purposefully to improve living and working conditions, especially for women. As early as 1926, meaning shortly before the presentation of the much more well-known Frankfurt kitchen, she designed a so-called model kitchen for the Akademisk Arkitektforening (the Danish Association of Architects) based on the premise that the modern housewife should be able to manage without help. She presented her model kitchen at the exhibition *Dansk Bygge- og Boligudstilling* in Copenhagen.[103] In her work, she mapped out the most important functions of the kitchen and argued that a well-thought-out floor plan and solid furniture, as well as an emphasis on practical solutions as regards materials and lighting, constituted the best starting point for creating a rational and hygienic kitchen where the housewife could manage without too much effort and in the best possible time.[104] The architect Edvard Heiberg (1897–1958) was also interested in the international currents, and he used his own house (1924) at I.H. Mundts Vej 16 in Virum, north of Copenhagen, as a test object. He laid out his home in a new and more rational way by, among other things, inserting two hatches in the wall between the living room and the kitchen, thereby saving his wife many steps every day when serving the food. Instead of going from the kitchen through the corridor to the living room, she could simply hand the dishes of food through the hatch directly into the living room. Later, in the post-war period, Heiberg would play a decisive role in the development of a kitchen consisting of standardised units.[105]

The Joint Committee's housing survey

Despite several attempts to rethink kitchen design in the 1920s, no major breakthroughs occurred in Denmark during these early years. But the idea of a more scientific approach to improving housing conditions was not forgotten. Architect Viggo Sten Møller, who in 1943 had become director of the Landsforeningen Dansk Kunsthaandværk og Kunstindustri (the National Association of Danish Crafts and Applied Art),* succeeded in 1944 in gaining support for his idea of initiating a nationwide housing survey together with the Fællesorganisationen for Almennyttige Danske Boligselskaber (the Association of Non-profit Danish Social Housing Organisations) (today BL – Danmarks Almene Boliger).[107] They formed the Fællesudvalget for Boligundersøgelser (the Joint Committee for Housing Studies), which included representatives from the Statens Bygningsdirektorat (the National Building Directorate), Akademisk Arkitektforening (the Academic Architects' Association, for academically trained practitioners, now the Danish Association of Architects), Dansk Arkitektforening (the Danish Architects' Association, for architects with a tradesman background, now merged with the academics in the Danish Association of Architects), De Danske Møbelfabrikkers Handelsforening (The Danish Furniture Manufacturers' Trade Association), Centralforeningen af Møbelhandlere (the Central

Grethe Meyer (1918–2008) graduated from the Royal Danish Academy of Fine Arts' School of Architecture in 1947. While still a student, she became part of the team behind *Byggebogen* (The Building Book), being the only woman on the staff. For many years, *Byggebogen* was a key reference work used at Danish design studios and schools of architecture. In the same period, she also worked on the Joint Committee's housing survey; in 1949 she helped edit the book *Køkkenundersøgelse* (Kitchen Survey). In 1955, she began a five-year employment at the Statens Byggeforskningsinstitut (now BUILD, University of Aalborg), where she was responsible for several housing surveys and authored a number of publications. In 1960, she set up her own design studio and translated her theoretical and methodological knowledge into award-winning dinnerware and stoneware designs such as *Blåkant*, *Hvidkant* and *Ildpot*.

* From 1932 he was editor of *Nyt Tidsskrift for Kunstindustri* (later renamed *Dansk Kunsthaandværk*), where he advocated – in articles and in his editorial approach – a 'sober and rational direction' within the applied arts.[106]

Ibi (Elisabeth) Trier Mørch (1910–1980) was admitted to the Royal Danish Academy of Fine Arts' School of Architecture in 1932, graduating in 1944. During her studies, she worked at various design studios, including in Sweden from 1937 to 1940. She became good friends with architect Bent Salicath (1915–1973) and Grethe Meyer, and in 1949 they worked together as editors of the book *Køkkenundersøgelse* (Kitchen Survey, 1949). She designed the glass series *Stub* and *Stamme* (1959) for Kastrup Glasværk together with Meyer. She primarily worked with applied art, especially silver. Several of her works have been exhibited internationally and been purchased by museums.

Association of Furniture Dealers in Denmark), Snedkerlaugets Møbelsnedkerafdeling (the Carpenters' Guild's Furniture Joinery Department) as well as Statens Husholdningsråd (the Danish Home Economics Council).[108] Architect Bent Salicath (1914–1973) and M.Sc. in Economics Svend Haunsø (life dates unknown) acted as secretaries for the committee, which was initially financed by grants from all the member organisations as well as the City of Copenhagen and the City of Aarhus. Later, the National Building Directorate provided extra funding, as did several private foundations.[109]

The purpose of the housing survey was to obtain insight into lived life in the homes and to investigate what difficulties, if any, living in them might present. Viggo Sten Møller emphasised that the future development of Danish housing conditions and domestic architecture should be based on what he called objective information. This consisted partly in recording how residents had furnished their flats, and partly in interviewing the residents, asking them about what living in the flat was like, how they used the rooms, and which elements they would like to be different in order for their home to be optimally in keeping with their everyday life.[110] Initially, the goal was not to produce concrete proposals in the form of new specific layouts; rather, the results were to act as a basis for solving future problems that might arise.[111] The study originally included approximately 400 flats in Copenhagen, but was later expanded to also include some 250 flats in other parts of the country.[112]

In addition to Salicath and Haunsø, around thirty employees were involved in the interviews, registrations and measurements. Most of them were trained architects, and several of them were women, including Tutti Anthon (later Tutti Lütken, 1914–2012), Grethe Meyer and Ibi (Elisabeth) Trier Mørch.[113]

Concurrently with the launch of the Joint Committee's housing survey, which was supported by several recognised organisations and authorities, two young architects, Gytte Rue (twenty-six) and Rut Speyer (thirty), took it upon themselves to write a grant application to a Danish private foundation, Overretssagfører L. Zeuthens Mindelegat. The two knew each other from the School of Architecture and had not yet acquired much practical experience. Prior to enrolling at the Royal Danish Academy of Fine Arts in Copenhagen, Speyer had attended classes at Aarhus Technical School, and as part of her training there she spent six months in 1934 working at a master mason's firm.[114] She obtained her degree as an architect in 1942; we do not know when Rue graduated. In their grant application, they asked for DKK 1,000 to carry out a survey of modern kitchens in Copenhagen. They included the following point:

Optælling af Glasservice i Specialundersøgelsen (100 Køkkener)

Glasservice

Betegnelse	Findes ikke	Findes		Standard-udstyr[1]		Udstyr incl. Gæsteservice, højere Leve-standard[1]
	Antal Familier	Antal Familier	Antal Stk.	1–3 Pers., Antal Stk.	4–6 Pers., Antal Stk.	4–6 Pers., Antal Stk.
Vinglas	12	11	5–10	–	–	54[2]
	–	22	11–12	–	–	–
	–	12	13–19	–	–	–
	–	17	20–24	–	–	–
	–	10	30–39	–	–	–
	–	11	40–49	–	–	–
	–	5	50 og fl.	–	–	–
Vand(Øl)glas, daglige	10	9	3–6	6	10	8
	–	14	7–10	–	–	–
	–	49	11–12	–	–	–
	–	12	13–19	–	–	–
	–	6	20–24	–	–	–
Vand(Øl)glas, fine	91	1	7–10	–	–	18
	–	6	11–12	–	–	–
	–	2	13–19	–	–	–
Samtlige Vand(Øl)glas	4	8	4–6	6	10	26
	–	13	8–10	–	–	–
	–	52	11–12	–	–	–
	–	15	14–18	–	–	–
	–	8	20–24	–	–	–
Sodavandsglas	58	19	1–10	–	–	–
	–	19	11–12	–	–	–
	–	4	13–24	–	–	–
Snapseglas	18	15	1–6	6	6	18
	–	17	7–10	–	–	–
	–	36	12	–	–	–
	–	9	14–20	–	–	–
	–	5	24–36	–	–	–
Glasasietter	57	10	1–6	–	–	–
	–	27	7–12	–	–	–
	–	6	13–39	–	–	–
Karafler	49	33	1	–	–	–
	–	11	2	–	–	–
	–	7	3–9	–	–	–
Glaskander	52	34	1	–	–	–
	–	11	2	–	–	–
	–	3	4–8	–	–	–
Glasskaale	17	20	1–2	1	2	14
	–	31	3–4	–	–	–
	–	24	5–7	–	–	–
	–	8	8–20	–	–	–
Osteklokker	62	37	1	–	–	–
	–	1	2	–	–	–
Skylleskaale	99	1	1	–	–	–

[1] Disse Kolonner angiver det Antal, der fra husholdningskyndig Side anses for rimeligt.
[2] Heraf 18 til Rødvin, 18 til Rhinskvin og 18 til Hedvin.

In 1944, the architects Gytte Rue and Rut Speyer launched their own study of Danish kitchens, having successfully applied for DKK 1,000 in funding to do so. In 1945, their study became part of the work undertaken by the Joint Committee for Housing Surveys, where one of the key focal points of the architects' visits was to count the dinnerware in the home. In 1949, the findings of the kitchen survey were published in a book, including the results of such counts. This was the first time such an approach had been taken in Denmark, and Rue and Speyer thus introduced a new way of working in housing construction.

'In the most recent occupational census of 1939, it was found that 80% of married women are exclusively employed in their homes. The majority of their working hours are spent in the kitchen, which means that many millions of kroner are managed from here each year. An impractical factory equals reduced production or increased expenses, and the same applies to impractical homes.'[115]

Ideally, they would have liked to launch a more extensive study of housing conditions in Denmark, but since there were only two of them, they deemed such an undertaking near-impossible. Accordingly, their application focused solely on funds for carrying out a study on kitchens. Furthermore, they believed that their efforts were best focused on the kitchen because virtually all new buildings built in the 1930s had old-style kitchens. Only in a very few cases had Danish architects treated the design and function of the kitchen to thorough, rational treatment even though fellow professionals in other European countries and in the USA had focused on this issue for decades, rationalising the work done in the kitchen and, thus, its layout and design. The criticism of the existing Danish kitchens rested on the fact that they were often very small, narrow and deep – often less than two metres wide – which meant that the woman was isolated from the rest of the family while cooking. Even if her husband or children wanted to help, there was no room for them.[116]

Gytte Rue and Rut Speyer planned to visit approximately 300 kitchens to clarify what shortcomings they had, and furthermore aimed to interview the same number of housewives in order to obtain information on what improvements they deemed necessary to give women better working conditions in the future. The two architects emphasised the urgency, highlighting that the study should be launched as soon as possible so that the results could benefit the planning of the housing construction expected to take place after the end of the Second World War.* We do not know how Rue and Speyer, being academy-trained architects engaged in systematic investigation, conducted their visits to families in non-profit social housing developments, but an article in *Berlingske Tidende* from 1944 headlined 'Voluntary House Survey' gives us some insight into the proceedings when the Joint Committee's architects came to visit:

'We come from the Joint Committee for Housing Survey and would like to talk to you about your flat […]. The front door is respectfully opened, and two young architects enter to be greeted with smiles and handshakes. There is a hint of some tangy, soapy scent in the atmosphere. A couple of freshly washed children's heads, their hair neatly combed for the night, look out from the bedroom though a

* The application was accompanied by recommendations from the Danish Women's Association and professor and architect Palle Suenson (1904–1987) at the Royal Danish Academy of Fine Arts' School of Architecture, who both pointed out that such a study would provide essential knowledge for the future design of a standardised kitchen.[117]

As in other countries, Denmark saw widespread interest in improving the working conditions for women, specifically in terms of housework and cooking. Various organisations agreed that such efforts should be undertaken on a methodical and systematic basis, prompting the launch of the Joint Committee's housing survey in 1944. The participating architects, both men and women, visited several hundred homes, recording the ways in which Danish families had set up their homes and interviewing them about the advantages and disadvantages of their kitchens. The image shows several of the architects involved in 1944.

One of the key employees of the housing survey initiative and the editor of the resulting book *Køkkenundersøgelse* (Kitchen Survey, 1949) was architect Grethe Meyer. Around 1950, she won two design competitions. One of the winning proposals, a terraced house, was realised at the exhibition *Kvinde og Hjem* (Woman and Home) in Copenhagen in 1950. Here the many visitors, including Queen Ingrid, could see how Grethe Meyer, Poul Abrahamsen and Emanuel Johansen had arranged and distributed the common areas inside the house in a new way. The design of the house was based on lessons learnt from the housing survey.

door left slightly ajar. The master of the house turns the pipe like a rudder in his face and pulls a jacket over his shirt sleeves. He ushers the strangers into the best armchairs in the living room, just as he would usually host his parents or friends. Some polite courtesies are exchanged, offering information on the procedure, but these are neither formal nor strained, but quite natural and in a jocular tone. One of the guests moves freely around the home, measuring the furniture and recording its location on a pre-prepared plan of the flat, while the other asks the couple 129 questions […].'[118]

The visits paid by Rue and Speyer were probably not very different from what is described above, the one exception being that they did not tell the housewives in advance when they were coming to visit, because they were not interested in 'kitchens in their spick-and-span Sunday best'. They wanted to see how the kitchens functioned in everyday life, with all their faults and shortcomings – and, according to them, there were many of these. This was entirely due, they believed, to carelessness on the part of the architect, and even though some housewives stated that they were quite satisfied with their kitchens, the rooms were not 'functionalist in their design'.[119] The two architects based their investigation on a ten-page questionnaire they had prepared themselves, and in addition to interviewing the women, they also tested a completely new method which Rue explained as follows: 'Furthermore, we carry out […] a comprehensive inventory of tableware, kitchen utensils, linen and so on'.* This had never been done before in a Danish context, and the two women entertained high hopes regarding the usefulness of the statistics yielded from their count. It was a way of clarifying and highlighting what individual families actually needed to have in the home and how much storage space this required. For the interviewees, the experience may have been somewhat mixed; on the one hand, the initiative was about being seen and heard and about actively contributing to an improvement in housing conditions. Yet on the other hand, it may well have been rather overwhelming for a working-class family to have to host two well-educated women carrying notepads and surveying equipment, arriving unannounced in a home that was not prepared for such a visit. An example which serves to highlight that, amidst our greater focus on women in general, we should not forget that women are not a uniform group with equal opportunities, limitations and interests; issues of class and education have also played a role.

After visiting fifty families, the duo concluded that the kitchens were too small, that they were not placed in the optimum place in relation to the pantry, and that the lighting was too poor and the ventilation inadequate. Furthermore, the kitchen counters were too

---

* In an interview in the newspaper *B.T.*, Rut Speyer explained the problems associated with properly placing the few kitchen appliances women had access to: 'Meat and bread slicing machines also pose problems. Where to put them? My husband [architect Eigil Hartvig Rasmussen] has solved the problem for us by placing the bread slicer beneath one section of the kitchen table, which can then be swivelled around its axis and voila! – the machine is in front of me'. In the homes they visited they had seen rather less functional solutions. For example, they related how one home had a pull-out shelf for the meat slicer that could only be used if the cupboard door beneath it was open, so that the shelf rested on its edge. The problem was that every time the woman turned the handle to slice meat, she slammed her hand against the cupboard door. [120]

high when the working women had to sit down, and too low when they were standing.[121] Rue and Speyer were not only interested in the shortcomings of these kitchens – they also wanted insight into the housewives' own wishes, and here they discerned a clear trend. Virtually all the women wanted to have a refrigerator so that they could shop for several days at a time and thus save time. They also wanted to be rid of gas stoves and have an electric one instead, which made less mess – thereby saving them time on cleaning.[122]

The two architects did not complete their many interviews before their study was incorporated into the Joint Committee's housing survey, presumably in early 1945. At the same time, the Association of Non-profit Danish Social Housing Organisations provided extra funding so that the kitchen study could be even more extensive than the two architects had planned.[123]

The questionnaire used in this more comprehensive kitchen study was based on the one devised by Rue and Speyer, and the Joint Committee decided that only Copenhagen kitchens should be closely studied. The reasoning was that this would allow the staff to carry out a more in-depth and comprehensive investigation of the individual kitchens and continue to make comprehensive inventories of the individual families' kitchen equipment. Whereas the housing survey as a whole was a collaboration between both women and men, the kitchen study was different: 'The surveyors were […] women architects who were also housewives themselves'.[124] In contrast to the male architects, the women had concrete, physical and practical experience due to their gender, amassed during the hours they had spent in a kitchen. According to this logic, that made them better qualified for the task.

The study ran over a number of years, and along the way Viggo Sten Møller and Bent Salicath revealed some of the preliminary results in the trade journals *Boligen* and *Dansk Kunsthaandværk*, but also at *Forhandlinger paa den 1. nordiske Kunsthaandværkerkongres* (Proceedings at the 1st Nordic Craftsmen's Congress) in Copenhagen in 1946, where the architects exchanged knowhow and lessons learnt with peers from other Nordic countries. At the launch of the housing survey in 1944 and as work progressed, the Joint Committee had some contact with mainly Swedish but to some extent also Norwegian colleagues, partly to be inspired and partly to exchange concrete experiences.[125] Sweden was ahead of Denmark: Hemmens Forskningsinstitut (the Swedish Home Research Institute) had already carried out various kitchen studies for years and, on that basis, had developed new and more modern kitchens.[126] However, the Danish housing survey differed significantly from the Swedish one,

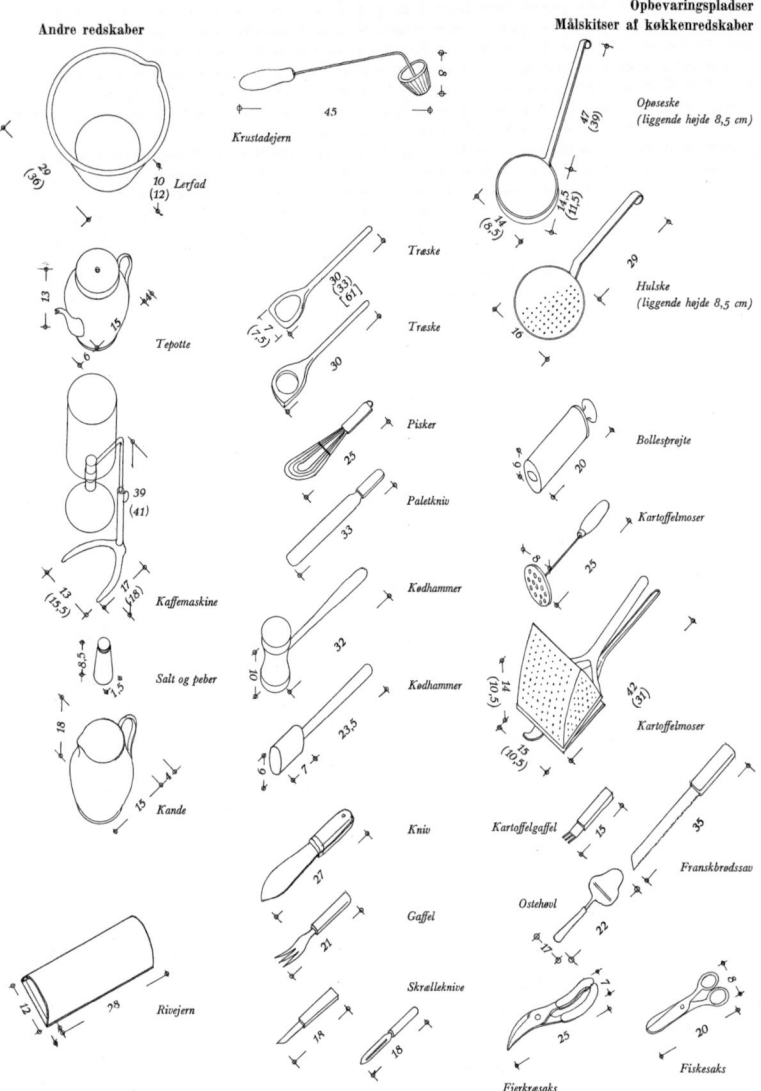

In connection with a competition in 1950 on 'Creating Kitchen Types and Standardising Kitchen Details', the architects Edvard Heiberg, Svenn Eske Kristensen and Bent Salicath published the book *Planlægning af køkkener i etagehuse* (Planning Kitchens in Multi-Storey Houses, 1950). The book was mainly based on the results of the Joint Committee's kitchen survey, but the architects also incorporated information yielded from the countless other studies of and experiments with kitchens done in the preceding years. The book included information on the measurements and sizes of various kitchen utensils so that architects could design suitably sized kitchen cabinets.

which had conducted only a few field surveys and was primarily based on experiments with different work processes in test kitchens, after which the authorities drew up types and standards for kitchens that could be said to meet certain minimum requirements.[127] By contrast, the Danish study was based on interviews and specific measurements taken in the participants' homes.[128]

The architects know best

The results of the large-scale housing survey were, for unknown reasons, never published in their entirety, but in 1949 the Joint Committee published a comprehensive book, *Køkkenundersøgelse* (Kitchen Study), in which the data from the surveys was processed out by architects Bent Salicath, Grethe Meyer and Ibi Trier Mørch and the economist Svend Haunsø.[129] The architects concluded that it was necessary to carry out studies pertaining to function and actual work and correlate these with the available financial and production-related possibilities – reflecting the methods used in Swedish research.[130] They thus concluded that the first major kitchen survey in Denmark could not stand on its own, and that the kitchen question needed to be approached from other angles, too.

The scientific, systematic study of housing conditions in Denmark would prove an important element in the further development of better housing conditions and not least the standardisation of construction. The starting point had been the entire home, but only the most specialised study focusing on the kitchen was published in a book format. The assumption was that by improving the kitchen housing standards in general could be raised while better working conditions for women could also be facilitated. The design competitions launched in 1937 by fsb and Privatbanken called for new types of layouts, and housing conditions for families took centre stage. This also applied to the Joint Committee's housing survey, but under Gytte Rue and Rut Speyer the focus shifted towards the women's specific situation because the kitchen was the housewife's domain.

Rue and Speyer pointed out that it was too expensive to have the majority of women in Denmark working under impractical conditions which made daily chores at home difficult and extended the time required to do them. Cooking and housework were regarded as comparable to work outside the home, and just as other work processes in society were rationalised – especially in factories – so too should domestic work be. They emphasised that this was not just a question of improving matters for women but for society as a whole, and they had a clear and definite notion that they could help 'ordinary' women by optimising how their kitchen were laid out and organised – even though several of the women interviewed had pointed out that they were quite satisfied with the kitchens they had. According to the two architects, they had only answered that way because they did not know any better.[131] Rue and Speyer listened to the women, and they observed them in their kitchens, but they also acted as professional experts who were best equipped to define the problem and find the solution.

The two architects were not the only ones interested in streamlining women's work in the home. As has been mentioned, Danish politicians were very keen to rationalise construction and property development at the time, a trend which was reinforced with the establishment of the Ministry of Housing in 1947. The ministry was initially mainly concerned with rationing the scarce materials available and making working hours as efficient as possible in the individual construction project, thereby increasing the overall amount of housing being constructed. But it was also interested in how women's workload at home could be lightened. Following a proposal from the Danske Kvinders Nationalråd (the National Council of Danish Women, now the Women's Council Denmark) and after consultation with the minister at the time, the Social Democrat Fanny Jensen (1890–1969),* the ministry set up the Committee on Collective Facilities in October 1948. The committee was given the task of investigating how the workload for the large number of mothers working outside the home could be lightened, partly by easing the domestic work and partly by giving the homes access to more collective amenities.*

In 1950 the exhibition *Kvinde og Hjem* (Woman and Home) opened in Copenhagen. Subtitled The Danish Women's Exhibition for Rational Housekeeping, it had Fanny Jensen as its honorary president. She pointed out why rational housekeeping was important:

'If we continue in the old way, housewives and self-employed women will eventually be completely exhausted by their very demanding work, so that the time left for the children is frittered away as a result of an overwhelming workload that could be managed in half the time if only the right rationalisation measures were carried out.'[133]

She also emphasised that rationalisation was not only in the best interest of individual women or families but equally much in the best interest of society in general. In 1954, the Committee on Collective Facilities presented its report, concluding that married women were

Ulla Tafdrup (1907–1996) attended boarding school abroad before she began attending classes at the School of Architecture at the Royal Danish Academy of Fine Arts. Although she was never formally enrolled, she became a kitchen designer. She began her career at the design studio of Hans Erling Langkilde (1906–1997) and Ib Martin Jensen (1906–1979) before setting up her own business. In addition, she was a kitchen consultant for the social housing association Dansk Almennyttigt Boligselskab from 1947. She contributed her specialist knowledge of kitchens to social housing estate projects such as Høje Søborg (1951–52), Søndergård Park (1949–51) and the Carlsro collective housing estate (1952–53).

* She was a minister without portfolio 'with particular regard to the interests of the home, home economics and children's needs and to the interests of self-employed women'. She had an office in the Ministry of Social Affairs and was to offer advice to other ministers within her area of responsibility.

* Collective facilities included, for example, kindergartens, playrooms, laundries, communal freezers, shopping facilities and playgrounds.[132]

increasingly active in the labour market and that this issue must be taken it into account when designing physical settings, especially in housing construction.[134] The report's conclusions were based partly on experiments and partly on literature, including a number of reports from a Swedish research institute. The section on kitchens, however, was predominantly based on Danish housing surveys, including the Joint Committee's kitchen survey and not least Ulla Tafdrup's efforts to bring about better working conditions for women in the home. As she noted eighteen years after her first marriage: '[…] as a newly married housewife, I [was] put into a kitchen. […] I quickly [discovered] all the unreasonable traits of my "workroom"'.[135] And after her career ended, she dryly stated in an interview that she 'was completely useless at housework, which was why I came up with clever ways to get the cooking and washing up done as quickly as possible'.[136]

Rational kitchen design

'[…] first take in the exciting dishwasher faucet which automatically mixes soap and water, and where the temperature can be regulated at the turn of a tap. Regrettably, it's no use putting it on your birthday wish list; it's an American invention and isn't sold here in Denmark.'[137]

In early 1953, the weekly women's magazine *ALT for damerne* presented Ulla Tafdrup's own kitchen in two successive issues, where, among other things, readers could see the American mixer tap she had brought home from one of her many study trips abroad. The description provided of the kitchen focused on the many rational and functional solutions that Tafdrup had implemented in her kitchen, the underlying idea being that she should save as many steps as possible during the day – and generally get the kitchen work done as quickly as possible, enabling her to spend her time on work outside the house instead. She had also moved the kitchen from its original and traditional location to the north, relocating it to a former small room to the south and east, thereby ensuring that it was better located in relation to the living room and thus closer to the rest of the family.[138]

It was not the first time that Tafdrup used her own kitchen as a laboratory for developing her ideas. In order to get a better handle on cooking as a young, newly married woman, she tore down the existing kitchen and installed new, German-made units – bought in Hamburg

En „krummeopsamler", nedfældet i den plastic-beklædte bordplade, er en af de små finesser, der er til stor hjælp for husmoderen.

Når køkkenet planlægges

De kan sikkert hente mange nye ideer fra denne anden artikel om Ulla Tafdrups idealkøkken. (Den første artikel fandtes i sidste uges nummer)

Af indendørsarkitekt Ellen Bisgaard

Stålvasken har sektorlås, som gør det muligt at lukke for afløbet uden prop eller kæde.

at klappe ned i passende strygehøjde. Underneden er der et skab til symaskinen og nederst en dejlig, dyb og lang skuffe, beregnet til lappetøjet.

Køkkenbordet har naturligvis plastic-belægning, som skarpe knive ikke kan ridse og varme gryder ikke brænde. Noget helt nyt er en nydelig, lille „krummeopsamler" i rustfrit stål, som er nedfældet i bordpladen. (Billedet øverst til venstre.) Når der arbejdes ved bordet med familiens madpakker, fejes radisegrønt, pølseskind og andet småt herned, efterhånden som maden ordnes, og det er uhyre nemt at tage samleren op og tømme den. Brødkrummerne går samme vej, og man risikerer ikke, at noget i farten drysser ud over gulvet.

Under køkkenbordet er der sørget for plads til tevognen, så den er hurtig „lastet og losset", og den høje køkkentaburet „bor" i rummet under opvaskepladsen.

En af de ting, Ulla Tafdrup er mest glad for, er den sektorlås, hun har i sin opvaskekumme (billedet lige under overskriften), og som gør det muligt at lukke for afløbet uden kæde eller prop. Det er efter hendes mening det ideelle afløb, der burde findes i alle vaske.

Til sidst er der blot at nævne, at der også er tænkt på hyggen i dette køkken, som trods alle moderne finesser er lykkeligt fri for det laboratorieagtige præg, man så ofte træffer på i vor tids „ønskekøkkener". Væggene i den del af køkkenet, hvor spise- og arbejdspladsen findes, har mønstret tapet, og ved vinduerne hænger ternede bomuldsgardiner i muntre farver. (Se også billederne på side 19 i vort sidste nummer.)

Over el-komfuret er der hylde til de daglige kogegrejer. Skuffer til mel, salt og sukker er indbygget i væggen, og røremaskinen (yderst til venstre) har plastic-hætte.

Strygeskab med bræt til at klappe ned, rum til symaskinen og skuffe til lappetøjet. Når tevognen ikke bruges, har den sin plads under køkkenbordet.

Tingene bør være dèr, hvor de skal bruges – det er en af hovedreglerne, når man planlægger et køkken, siger køkkenarkitekt Ulla Tafdrup. Derfor har hun anbragt kaffekanden samt kasserollerne til æg og havregrød på en hylde umiddelbart over sit elektriske komfur, hvor tingene hurtigt kan tages ned og stilles hen. Under hylden har skufferne til mel, salt og sukker deres plads. Og denne tanke: at spare så mange skridt som muligt, giver sig udtryk overalt i Ulla Tafdrups køkken.

I skabet til venstre for spisepladsen – der også er tænkt som arbejdsplads, når der skal ordnes tøj efter vask, foretages reparationer og så videre – findes strygebrættet. Det er lige til

---

One of the most influential women in the development of Danish kitchens was Ulla Tafdrup. She was everywhere in the media in the 1950s, including in the weekly magazine *ALT for damerne*, where her own kitchen was presented to the readers in no less than two issues in 1953. Her advice to women was partly based on numerous study trips abroad, from which she would bring back new knowledge and kitchen equipment. At the bottom right is the dishwasher faucet from the United States mentioned in this chapter, which was not available in Denmark.

In 1947, Dansk Almennyttigt Boligselskab (the Danish Social Housing Organisation, DAB) employed Ulla Tafdrup as kitchen consultant. Prior to this, she had worked with Hans Erling Langkilde and her husband Ib Martin Jensen, who designed several public housing developments, and her new appointment meant that she would now work with other architects. With Tafdrup on board, kitchens became a focal point in DAB's new housing developments. Depicted here is one of her kitchens for a social housing estate.

during the 'Bauhaus period'.[139] And the change in the kitchen layout led to the realisation that it was easier to manage a household when the physical framework was in good order.[140] Her public efforts to rationalise the kitchen as a workplace began in 1939 at an exhibition in Aarhus, where she proposed, among other things, that the kind of kitchen she regarded as old-fashioned could be modernised by placing the pots on the wall by the stove, putting them within quick and easy reach.[141]

It was by no means written in the stars that Tafdrup would eventually work on the development of the modern kitchen. Born as the daughter of a managing director, she grew up in an upper middle-class home north of Copenhagen where no academic demands were ever placed on the dyslexic young woman. She did not receive a high school education, instead taking the lower secondary school leaving examination. She was sent to boarding school in England and France, partly to learn the languages and partly to prepare her for life as a wife and mother in the upper echelons of society. She duly proceeded to marry a suitable man* and have two children; she had a maid to help with the housework – and according to herself she had no idea what to do with her time. Her ambition had always been to become an architect, and she began to clandestinely attend lectures at the School of Architecture at the Royal Danish Academy of Fine Arts. In her own words, she went on to visit the nearest architectural firm in Gentofte, offered her help, and a year later she was divorced and married to one of the young architects there, Ib Martin Jensen (1906–1979), who, together with his business partner, architect Hans Erling Langkilde (1906–1997), designed a range of projects which included housing developments for Dansk Almennyttigt Boligselskab (the Danish Non-profit Social Housing Organisation, DAB).[143] According to Tafdrup, it quickly became clear to Langkilde that she had a talent for kitchen design, and she was attached to some of the design studio's cases.[144] Shortly afterwards, she gave a lecture on Danish radio on her ideas for reforming kitchen set-ups. The broadcast was structured like a dialogue with a friend, and the next day the phone was ringing almost non-stop with new commissions.[145]

During the first years of her career, Ulla Tafdrup worked on Langkilde and Jensen's projects for DAB, but in 1947 the social housing organisation hired her to design kitchens for their new buildings and to advise on kitchen matters.* One of her first independent tasks for DAB was to design kitchens for the Mozartgård estate (1949) in Copenhagen, a development designed by architect Knud Thorball (1904–1980) which also came to form the basis for a more systematic and interdisciplinary study of kitchens. DAB's study of kitchens included a number of experiments in multi-storey apartments, and the results were published in the book *Vore køkkener. En forsøgsrapport* (Our Kitchens. A Report, 1951), which involved contributions from household consultant Bodil M. Begtrup (1902–1987), housewife Emilie Olsen (life dates unknown), civil engineer Jytte Kruse (life dates unknown), MSc in Economics Inger Bjørn Svensson (1911–2003) and architect Johan Pedersen (1902–1970).[147] The study timed the housewife's work in five different kitchens over the course of a week in order to ensure that 'human inaccuracy' did not influence the conclusions too much, and according to Tafdrup the time measurements clearly showed that some kitchens constituted better workplaces than others.[148] Housewife Emilie Olsen kept a diary during the proceedings, in which she included the following statement on kitchen countertops:

'The kitchen countertop must absolutely be the right height (90 cm was excellent); it is too tiring to stand at *low* kitchen counters. The kitchen countertop in type III was laboratory-stained, which

One of Ulla Tafdrup's first independent tasks for DAB consisted in designing kitchens for Mozartgård in Copenhagen, which was subsequently made the subject of a study. The results of the study were published in 1951 in the small publication *Vore køkkener* (Our Kitchens), which included accounts of the participating housewives' opinions on the different types of kitchens. The cover shows how a sub-optimal layout can generate a lot of extra work.

* In 1930 she married Hans Rottbøll de Neergaard (1897–1964). She was married a second time, to Ib Martin Jensen in 1940.[142]

* Besides DAB, the non-profit social housing organisation Arbejdernes Andels-Boligforening (AAB) initiated an experiment and an investigation into what a so-called hallway kitchen-diner might look like and how it worked in practice.[146]

VORE KØKKENER

En forsøgsrapport fra Dansk almennyttigt Boligselskab

I KOMMISSION: ARKITEKTENS FORLAG · KØBENHAVN 1951

One of the stands at the exhibition *Kvinde og Hjem* (Woman and Home) in 1950 belonged to DAB, focusing partly on kitchen design. The organisation presented the results of the kitchen survey as well as a number of their new housing developments, including the terraced houses Carlsro in Rødovre (1952–53) and Søndergård Park in Bagsværd (1949–50). However, the most prominent and visible element in the exhibition was a full-scale model kitchen.

might look a little drab and dark at first glance; but once you have tried for yourself how wonderfully easy it is to keep clean and how practical it is in use [...], you reconcile yourself to the black colour.'[149]

While DAB wanted to raise the quality of housing for future residents, Ulla Tafdrup took a broader aim. For her, the issue was about creating better working conditions for the many women who were in charge of the household, but also about rationalising their work processes so that they would have more time for other things, for example going to work outside the home and spending time on themselves or their children. She emphasised that 'men – in other words, the ruling part of society – must begin to consider homes and the heart of the home, the kitchen, as a productive workplace and as the first link in the chain called preventive care'.[150]

Tafdrup pointed out that it was no easy task to change many centuries of firmly embedded ideas and work processes in the kitchen. In a lecture at the Danish Society of Engineers in 1950, she explained that better kitchens not only require money and a more rational layout and arrangement, but also a shift in mentality among women as well as men. The more rational workflows could help save society a lot of money in the future, and domestic work should be considered a profession on a par with other professions.[151] That same year, at the exhibition *Kvinde og Hjem* in Copenhagen, the catalogue included an article about 'The work of the housewife from a national economic perspective'. Here it emerged that the Department of Statistics had carried out calculations which showed that the work done by housewives in their own homes in 1949 had a total value of approximately two billion kroner, while the total net national product – meaning the value of all the work done in Denmark – came to approximately DKK seventeen billion. The four largest occupations in Denmark were industry and crafts, agriculture, trade, the financial market and then housekeeping – despite the fact that the housewife did not get paid for her work. The two billion was probably a very conservative estimate, as an alternative calculation showed that Denmark's stay-at-home housewives at the time put in approximately 3,000 working hours per year (equivalent to eight to nine hours a day). This made for a total number of working hours of approximately 1.9 billion, and with an hourly wage of two kroner, you would arrive at a value well over twice the figure reported by the Department of Statistics. Furthermore, the calculation did not include the housework done by women who also worked outside of the home.[152] The figures made the economic value of women's unpaid work in the home very clear, highlighting that, from a societal perspective, there were major consequences to failing to ensure good conditions for domestic work.

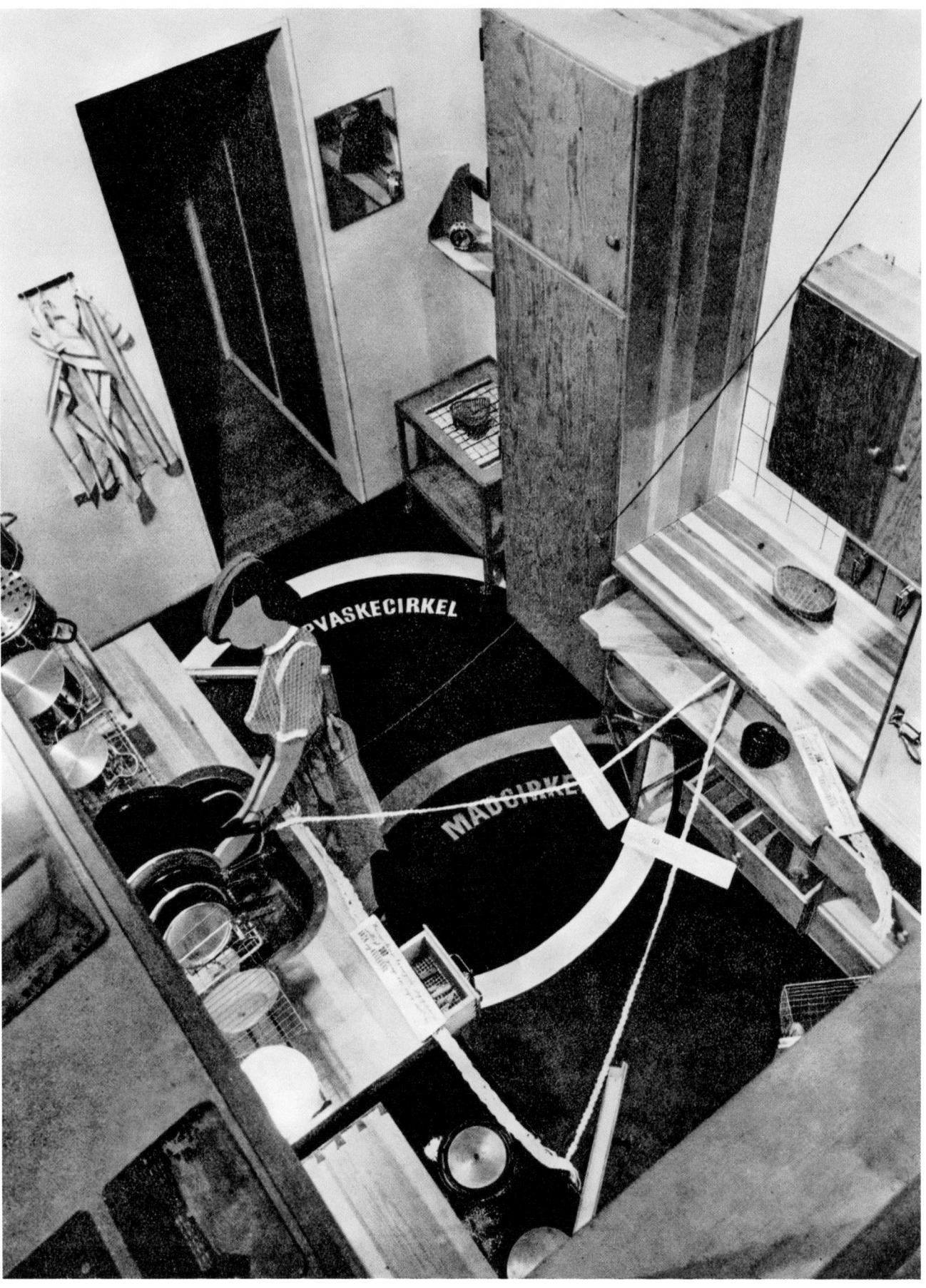

DAB's model kitchen at the exhibition *Kvinde og Hjem* (Woman and Home) manifested Ulla Tafdrup's guiding principle for furnishing a modern kitchen. A kitchen was to have three zones: one for cold food, one for hot food and one for washing up. By positioning kitchen cabinets and their contents as well as relevant installations according to this principle, the women could save countless steps and the workflows would become more rational, reducing the time spent in the kitchen. In 1954, the Ministry of Housing concluded that this was the best way to design a kitchen.

The exhibition had a board of representatives consisting of twenty-seven associations ranging from the Academic Architects' Association to the Danish Home Economics Council to the Danish Technological Institute. Ulla Tafdrup was not alone – there was growing and widespread societal recognition of the economic value of women's work in their own homes.[153]

'Everything in its place'

The majority of Ulla Tafdrup's own practice did not take place at the drawing board. Rather, she conceived a range of ideas and principles and communicated them in words. One of her guiding principles was a new way of organising kitchens which involved three zones: one circle for cold food, one circle for hot food and a washing-up circle.[154] The cold circle was located close to the pantry, where bread, butter, wrapping paper and cold cuts were kept. The circle for hot food was centred on the stove, above which she placed a cupboard containing flour, semolina and sugar, and with easily accessible glass drawers side by side with all the accoutrements required for sauces: ketchup, food colouring, spices, as well as tea and coffee. 'You will no longer have to dash to the pantry all the time – you can simply reach out and pick what you need.'[155] Based on the same thinking, all pots and pans were to be hung on the wall, thereby avoiding the hassle of bringing them out from the back corner of a low kitchen cabinet.[156]

The washing-up circle was by the kitchen sink, where there was often very little counter space, and here she inserted collapsible shelves, one above the other, making it – in her words – a piece of cake to arrange dirty dishes from a twelve-person dinner in a very confined area. A tall, collapsible kitchen chair could be pushed in front of the sink in an instant, ensuring that the work could be done sitting down. Tafdrup believed that this came close to being the ideal kitchen, but the task was not complete until electric ventilation and a refrigerator had been installed.[157] In the mid-1950s, the Danish Ministry of Housing highlighted the division of the kitchen into three zones, each with their own tools and installations, as the design that facilitated the best and most appropriate way to work. An example to be emulated.[158]

Another way of optimising work processes in the kitchen involved helping women to adopt new routines. To this end, Tafdrup prepared what she called 'Tables of Contents', which were handed out to all residents of DAB's new buildings when they moved in. She emphasised on several occasions that such help was almost as important as good

The terraced houses of Carlsro, built from 1952 to 1953 were part of a larger housing development with an eight-storey co-operative collective house and green areas. More than half of the residents came from small, scruffy flats in the inner city of Copenhagen with improvised gas stoves and lavatories in the backyard, so the move to the suburb with lots of fresh air, direct access to green areas and daylight flooding the home was a marked improvement.

furnishings. In collaboration with Rødovre Almennyttige Boligselskab (RAB), DAB built the first part of the collective housing development Carlsro in 1952 and 1953, specifically in the form of terraced houses.[159] In some of the houses, the layout was so modern that it caused a great stir among architects and, at the beginning, a certain amount of scepticism among the new residents.[160] Ulla Tafdrup had, working in collaboration with the other architects, designed a kitchen that was directly connected to the dining area, which was placed in the living room. In addition, there were open-plan solutions where the kitchens were located in the living room, a trait familiar from many homes today.

A surviving photo lets us look inside one of the shiny new and extremely modern kitchens at Carlsro. The room is narrow with kitchen cabinets along the walls, and daylight flows in from a skylight. There is an electric stove, and a dish drying rack hangs beneath the upper cabinets so that it does not clutter up the worktop. For hygienic and practical reasons, the wall behind the stove and kitchen sink is covered with easy-to-clean white tiles. Two women stand in the kitchen: Ulla Tafdrup and Inge Hansen, who has just moved into the first completed terraced house in the development, which stood ready in 1952.[161] Tafdrup appears in aspirational dress, a figure of authority sporting a half-length, fitted dark skirt, a crisp, white, partially see-through blouse and shoes with a low heel. She wears her hair up, and she is seen pointing to the kitchen counter while clearly explaining something to Mrs. Hansen, who is far more casually dressed in a floral dress and flat, practical shoes. Inge Hansen and her husband,

Ulla Tafdrup and Inge Hansen in the latter's kitchen in the social terraced housing development Carlsro in Rødovre. Tafdrup demonstrates the most efficient way of working in the kitchen. Hansen and her family had moved to Carlsro from a one-bedroom flat in central Copenhagen and lived there rent-free for a year in exchange for showing their home to potential future residents. The design of the houses caused a great deal of discussion, especially among architects, not least due to the kitchens opening up on the living rooms. Critics believed that this would create a bad smell throughout the residence, although the issue was mitigated by a skylight that could be opened.

Christian Hansen, were allowed to live in the house for free for a year in exchange for hosting an open house after a while, sharing their experiences and demonstrating to potential future residents how to make the best use of the home. The family had moved out of a three-room flat in central Copenhagen, bringing only a few personal belongings with them. RAB had paid for all their new furniture. Tafdrup helped Hansen buy new furniture and kitchen equipment and then decorate and organise the whole house – not least the kitchen.[162] Looking at this image, it is easy to imagine Hansen being told how to use the kitchen in order to make everyday life as easy and efficient as possible. Perhaps Tafdrup has already given her the small manual for the kitchen network, 'Alt paa sin rette Plads' (Everything in its place), in which Tafdrup has meticulously drawn an overview of which food items and kitchen utensils belong in which kitchen cabinet.[163] By adhering to Tafdrup's drawing, Inge Hansen and all future residents could make optimum use of the kitchens and manage their households in the most appropriate way.

Half of the inhabitants of Carlsro came from small, dark flats in inner-city Copenhagen, where they had gas stoves and shared lavatories in the yard. Moving to the bright, well-equipped and modern homes in Rødovre would have been a major change for these families. Tafdrup's instructions for housewives can come across as patronising and moralising, and some women may have taken umbrage at being told by an architect and middle-class lady how to behave in their own kitchen. For Tafdrup, however, it was a natural part of her professional identity: to her, her work simply included explaining how the new setting should be used. As she stated in several newspaper interviews, new habits were called for if women were to save time, and those habits did not just happen on their own.[164]

Several architects criticised the open-plan kitchen in Carlsro because they thought that letting cooking fumes enter the living room was unhygienic,* but as more and more residents moved in, they reported being very satisfied. As one housewife said:

'When you had visitors at the beginning, they would go, "Gosh – that's a rather peculiar kitchen!" – But I thought it was ever so practical, the whole thing about having a kitchen without a door, right, and then having the dining area directly opposite. You didn't have to go anywhere to serve the food, you know? I thought it was lovely. They were ahead of their time when they did this.'[166]

While such design approaches had already been seen in other countries, it was quite a breakthrough in Denmark when Ulla Tafdrup opened up the kitchen towards the living room. She advocated greater

* The issue had been addressed in the design: a glass plate was installed beneath the ceiling between the kitchen and living room, and the skylight could be opened to provide ventilation.[165]

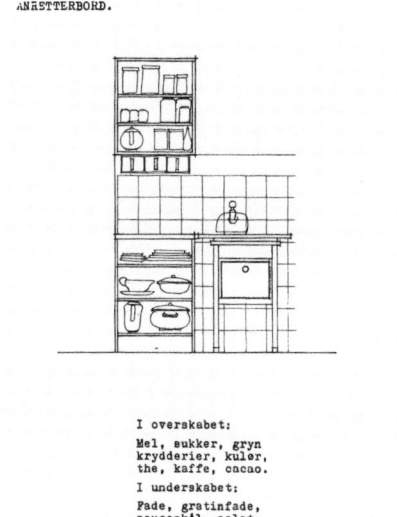
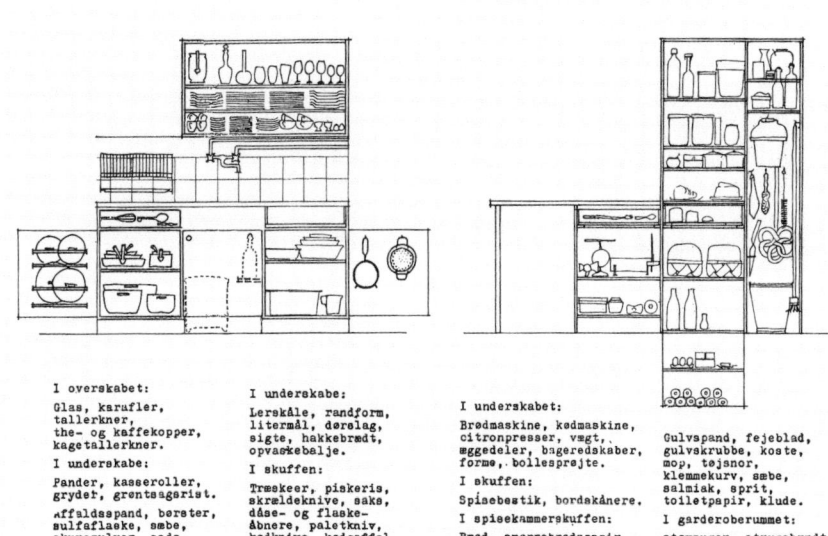

In the late 1940s, Ulla Tafdrup began preparing small overviews of how housewives should arrange their kitchen cupboards in the many new social housing buildings springing up. The drawing shows in detail where the flour, spices, pots, etc. should go in order to optimise the kitchen workflow. The design testifies to how the era's focus on rationalisation was not confined to factory assembly lines – it also extended to the home.

connection and coherence between the various rooms of the home so that the family could spend more time together. And if we think about the many recent renovations or new homes that have been built in Denmark in the past twenty years, we know that today it is perfectly commonplace to have your kitchen and living room in one – what is known as a kitchen-diner or open-plan living. While the kitchens in Carlsro were still relatively narrow and small, they point forward in time to the way we live today.

Exchanging ideas with the USA

Ulla Tafdrup's ideas regarding kitchen layout and design were greatly inspired by similar work in other countries. She was well-informed about the latest international trends, partly because she herself went on several study trips to, for example, Sweden as well as Switzerland where she participated in the first world congress organised by the International Union of Architects (UIA), held in Lausanne in the summer of 1948 under the heading *Architecture Faced with Its New Tasks*. Here she visited newly built residential areas with a view to looking at kitchens.* In the autumn of 1949, she went on a six-week trip to New York, Boston, Detroit and Cornell University in Ithaca, the latter of which had one of the era's leading research centres in

* She also visited Finland, Norway and the UK. In Switzerland she visited the Sonnengarten in Zurich by Karl Egender and Wilhelm Müller.[167]

Ulla Tafdrup contributed to some of the most innovative social housing developments in Danish architectural history, for example the Høje Søborg collective house (by Povl Ernst Hoff & Bennett Windinge, Aksel Andersen, Karen Sabroe and Grethe Forchhammer) from 1951. It transpires from the housing organisation's application for a government loan that they made significant changes to the design after Tafdrup and Sabroe were brought on board. For example, they added more collective elements, thus making everyday life easier for the women in particular.

the United States as regards the development of kitchens and rural living conditions.[168] From 1950 until 1955, an interdisciplinary research team developed the prefab Cornell Kitchen: based on scientific research, it had a rational and functional design.[169]

During her time in the USA, Tafdrup mostly stayed in the private homes of American families, giving her a first-hand impression of how their homes functioned in everyday life.[170] Travelling across the Atlantic was not without its challenges in the late 1940s, and the weak Danish krone in particular made matters difficult, but Tafdrup had helped Jewish families to the United States in the mid-1930s, and they now repaid her kindness.[171]

Greatly enthused by her trip to the USA, she was prompted to make the observation 'Oh, how old-fashioned a modern Danish kitchen is', compared to the average American kitchen. She noted that the American approach to interior design and living was markedly different than in Denmark, where 'cosy, homely *hygge*' was a major factor in how the Danes decorated their homes.[172] For Danes, the living room was the most important room, while for Americans it was the kitchen – certainly among the families that Tafdrup visited. She had noticed that when Danish families purchased an armchair, they liked to spend DKK 600 on good quality and design, while an American family only spent what corresponded to DKK 150, preferring instead to spend their money on the kitchen.[173] Despite the big differences, however, she believed that the Danes had much to learn from the Americans, and she concluded: 'Here in Denmark, a kitchen is modern if it has cold and hot water, electric cooking appliances and an oven, a refrigerator and – if it is fully up to date – a dishwasher'.[174] In the American kitchen, even more new appliances had entered the scene:

'In many places the overhead lights are fluorescent tubes, […] stopwatches and pressure cookers are used everywhere, and toasters which automatically make the toast pop out when it is done can be found in every American kitchen. The refrigerators have a special compartment set a certain temperature to ensure that the butter is never too soft or hard and always easy to spread. […] Among the other helpful appliances, we should note the stand mixers, which can be set for fast or slow mixing and kneading.'[175]

The Americans, on the other hand, could also learn much from the Danes, and they were particularly impressed by the use of exquisite types of wood and the fine joinery in Danish kitchens, of which Tafdrup brought pictures.[176] Tafdrup brought home a number of

Høje Søborg still functions as a collective house, and today the residents can have their evening meal in the restaurant. In addition, the building incorporates several other service functions: a 'concierge' accepts packages, etc., and when the building was inaugurated it was also possible for residents to hand in their dry cleaning or library books here. All flats have their own kitchen, but most of the kitchens are quite small – some are even placed in a cupboard in the living room, ensuring that they do not take up vital space in the small dwellings.

electric kitchen appliances to Denmark. Tafdrup's work, especially in the late 1940s and in the 1950s, was an important link in the development of the modern kitchen in Denmark – not only with regards to the interior design of the kitchen, but also in terms of ensuring a better connection between the kitchen and the rest of the home. In several interviews and lectures she emphasised that the housewife should not be isolated from the rest of the family, and that women should have the opportunity to work outside the home without being bogged down by a double workload. The woman was to enjoy a greater degree of freedom, and Tafdrup was part of a development where the kitchen gradually became the most important room in the home.[177]

One of the major concepts underpinning Ulla Tafdrup's thinking was rationalisation: a kitchen should be functional in its set-up, and the woman's movements and cooking had to be rational in order to save as much effort as possible, thereby freeing up time for other tasks such as paid work outside the home, which would benefit Danish society in general. Women were now subjected to an entirely new way of rationalising society, and at the same time many women actively contributed to this rationalisation in terms of their use of the kitchen and the placement of kitchen utensils and foodstuffs. Nothing was left to chance, and while many men could escape the widespread rationalisation efforts once they returned home from work, women were expected to adhere to optimised workflow edicts in the home as well. It was almost impossible to avoid the many admonitions: after all, you were handed instructions on how to use your kitchen before you had even moved into your new home. Things were not made any better by the fact that Ulla Tafdrup was very visible in Danish media, from weeklies to newspapers to trade journals. She was not the only one, either, and a review of the weekly women's magazine *ALT for damerne* from 1946 until the end of the 1950s unearths a great deal of well-intentioned good advice and normative descriptions of how a woman should behave and arrange her home. Readers were left in no doubt about how to be a woman in the 'right' way and what that entailed. Like her male colleagues, Tafdrup was eager to make everyday life easier and better for women, but their combined efforts also created a specific image of how to be a woman, which was presumably not always easy – or desirable – for everyone to adhere to. With the modern kitchen and new, more efficient habits came the freedom to work outside the home or to spend more time with one's family, but that freedom came at a price. The normative guidance and admonitions meant that the woman's individual freedom to choose for herself disappeared, and pre-existing inequalities within the family were cemented.

Everyday life

Looking back at what we have examined in this chapter, it can be said that the starting point for the overall work with kitchen design was the fact that, at the beginning of the twentieth century, housing standards were very poor for a large part of the population in Denmark. Accommodation was in short supply and whatever flats were available were often unsanitary, small and overcrowded. Politicians, non-profit social housing organisations and architects were growing increasingly aware of the need to do something about these conditions.

In addition to working with the layout of the kitchen and the placement of food and kitchen utensils, Ulla Tafdrup was interested in creating greater cohesion between the kitchen and the living room so that women would not be isolated from the rest of their families. The interconnecting rooms point to what we know today as a kitchen-diner or open-plan kitchen. The photo shows the interconnecting kitchen and living room in a terraced house in Carlsro.

A kitchen designed by Ulla Tafdrup in the late 1940s. The details include a pull-out tabletop underneath the kitchen counter, enabling users to sit down and work without straining their back. Note how the window is positioned to allow daylight enter the room.

Drawing inspiration from several international initiatives and from knowledge gathered abroad, the 1920s and 1930s saw several Danish architects call for a more systematic and methodical approach to the development of better residential architecture (and architecture in general). The argument was that a more rational and scientific approach was needed to raise the standards. Systematically collected knowledge was to form the basis for this new architecture. However, the first major Danish housing survey was not initiated until the Second World War, at the behest of the Joint Committee for Housing Surveys. The results of this study would play a significant role in the development not only of the floor plans of Danish homes, but also of the architectural disciplines more generally – and not least for the development of the modern kitchen with a completely new layout and a new, direct connection to the rest of the home. The overall results of the housing survey were never published. Only a small part of the study – the part that focused on kitchens, and one where the woman contributors had been of particularly great importance – was published. One argument for having only women conduct the kitchen survey was that they had first-hand experience with kitchen work as housewives. They thus supposedly had a special flair for the task – even though this included elements such as counting cutlery, which hardly calls for housewifely experience. However, the women conducting the survey also had to talk to the women who lived in the homes being examined, and in this regard it may have been an advantage to be a woman and to have personal experience of women's work in the kitchen. In the decades that followed, the major housing survey prompted several other studies where an interest in women's knowledge and their first-hand experience from their own lives was a central part of the basis used when architects planned new housing developments.

The existing specialist literature on Danish architectural history contains only very few descriptions of the many housing surveys that led to such striking development of Danish kitchens and housing architecture in the 1940s, 1950s and 1960s. Several books have been written about kitchen design, and the Joint Committee's housing survey is mentioned very briefly in Per H. Hansen's book *Da danske møbler blev moderne* (2006). Svenn Eske Kristensen, Bent Salicath and Edvard Heiberg's book *Planlægning af køkkener i etagehuse* (1950) is often highlighted as ground-breaking and an important step in the direction of better kitchens.

There can be no doubt that the latter book played an important role in disseminating the latest specialist knowledge, especially to the non-profit social housing organisations which at the time were behind a remarkable number of new housing developments. But by following the work and efforts of Gytte Rue, Rut Speyer and Ulla Tafdrup in reforming kitchen layouts through a scientific and methodical approach, we see that the history is far more complex than has hitherto been assumed, and that it involved significantly more people, disciplines and collaborations. It is obvious that the modern kitchen was the result of collaboration between many different people, not only in the sense of direct team effort, but also indirectly as various actors built on the experiences and knowhow of others. Svenn Eske Kristensen, Bent Salicath and Edvard Heiberg could not have written their book if Gytte Rue and Rut Speyer had not applied for funds to carry out a kitchen study, one where they were the very first in a Danish context to count and measure every piece of equipment and furniture in the homes of many families. Ulla Tafdrup could not have carried out her work without their contributions (nor those of several others), nor indeed without inspiration from her many trips abroad where she saw how others approached the issue in Sweden, Switzerland or the United States. While there, she also shared the knowledge arising out of Danish studies.

Women with different training, professional skill sets, backgrounds and knowledge have played a decisive role in the development of the Danish kitchen. It may very well be that back in their own day, these women were particularly affiliated with this area because of their gender. They played a dual role in the surveys conducted, acting simultaneously as women drawing on personal experience and as professionals. They also point to their own lives and experiences as part of their personal motivations. On the one hand, we are here seeing confirmation of the feminist point that 'the private is political' as women's professional identities are simultaneously shored up and limited by their gender. But on the other hand we also see that the women who contributed to the kitchen surveys knew how to let this duality benefit many other families and women – precisely because their work had an enormous influence on the ways of life made possible in the new housing developments.

Gytte Rue, Rut Speyer and Ulla Tafdrup – as well as a number of other architects such as Grethe Meyer – contributed new insights, experiences and knowledge to the overall efforts to develop the good home. They measured, analysed and translated their results so that the various elements of a modern kitchen could be placed more efficiently, thereby allowing women to spend less time in the kitchen cooking and cleaning. But at the same time, their approach to their fellow sisters was not unlike the one practised by many of their male colleagues. They were controlling and moralising, and for the most part they came from better-off homes and lived their own lives with a certain level of financial security. They used their creative abilities to promote greater freedom for women, but at the same time they restricted women's freedom by keeping them tethered to normative patterns about what it meant to be a woman and a housewife. This established an unequal division of labour in the home between the working and middle classes.

The fact that their significant contribution to the development of twentieth-century architecture and society has not previously been described in the history of architecture has to do with the tendency to consider only major buildings – such as mansions, town halls, museums and castles, designed by a very restricted circle of men – as proper architecture that merits writing about in literature on architectural history. Other fields have studied the history of the development of kitchens and other forms of interior design, but our focus here is on the architect's role in the efforts to change society – a role which is specific to the field of architecture in terms of designing the spaces and elements of homes, yet is also broadly collaborative and, not least, a place where the role and importance of gender becomes visible. For example, housing surveys – like floor plans and kitchen layouts – are a form of preparatory work that has rarely been emphasised in the history books. Nevertheless, these largely overlooked architectural practices had a decisive impact on the development of construction and architecture in the second half of the twentieth century, and not least for women's opportunity to engage in paid work outside the home. Furthermore, the discussion of the aforementioned women's contribution to the development of residential architecture reminds us that a broader view of architecture and who it is designed for is necessary. Their work focused on the woman and the family as a whole – not just on men or on powerful people or organisations. It was about creating physical settings to facilitate what they thought was the good life, and kitchens are an example of how all parts of the lifeworld were taken seriously. And women – who were the ones spending much of their lives in the kitchen – are taken seriously. A life is not only lived in the public reception rooms of the home, in a separate sitting room where guests come to visit. By connecting the living room and kitchen, and even opening them up entirely, as Ulla Tafdrup did in Carlsro, guests were invited into the family's everyday life, and the women became a visible part of the family as they went about their domestic chores. This work leads up to what we know today as the kitchen-dining room and open-plan living.

Chapter 2

Love – Three Houses Built for Women's Work, Family and Love Lives

In 1960, a recently subdivided building plot on top of a hill in Skodsborg, north of Copenhagen, is standing empty except for a low hill reminiscent of an ancient burial mound, accessed via a spiralling path that makes the hill resemble a giant snail shell surrounded by large linden trees. On this very special plot, in 1961, a young couple, the architects Inger and Johannes Exner, built a house for themselves and their young children as well as for their shared design studio. Placed low on the site, the house is a rectangular brick building set into the hill, which means that the façade towards the road comprises two storeys, while at the opposite end the house is one storey only, providing direct access to the garden.

A journalist from *ALT for damerne* visited the house shortly after the family had moved in, and described the property as a 'pencil case with many compartments'.[178] The house has approximately 160 square metres of floor space in total: on the lower ground floor facing the road, behind a modernist-inspired band of windows, is the couple's small design studio comprising approximately 30 square metres, while the family residence upstairs covers approximately 130 square metres of floor space in total. Aesthetically speaking, the house incorporates elements familiar from modern Scandinavian church building and modernist architecture: a mixture we also know from the couple's joint architectural business, and a style that finds expression here in a home created as the setting for the family's everyday work and love life.

In 2018, three years after Johannes Exner's death, Inger Exner created a website together with her daughter Karen Exner. The site documents the couple's lifelong working partnership. Inger Exner describes the couple's practice as 'special', occupying a position outside the familiar traits of Danish modernism of the period.[179] On the website, she relates how the couple often fought with and against the demands and wishes imposed by clients and builders. As a source of inspiration for the couple's distinctive profile and focus on church architecture, they point to Johan Exner, father of Johannes, who was a clergyman and launched a major undertaking aimed at protecting village churches throughout Denmark. Even though Johan Exner's approach to architecture is described as 'old-fashioned', he is also highlighted as a 'stepping stone' that helped establish and affirm the couple's joint success, as their many commissions for church construction and restoration were connected with Johannes Exner's work as a lecturer in restoration and the history of architecture at the Aarhus School of Architecture from 1965 onwards. From Inger Exner's descriptions on the website, we sense how the complementary nature of the Exners' expertise and personalities, which has been put forward as a distinctive trait of their professional collaboration, was conducive to their creative collaborations. In architect and writer Thomas Bo Jensen's monograph on the couple, for example, Johannes Exner is described as the firm's extroverted, charming and enigmatic, creative powerhouse, while Inger Exner is highlighted not only for her practical, administrative and empathetic qualities, but also as an important interlocutor and sounding board who could be sober and exact.[180] All this strongly suggests that the couple's differences were well-matched and

Inger Exner (b. 1926) graduated from the Royal Danish Academy of Fine Arts' School of Architecture in 1954. Between 1953 and 1955 she was employed by the architects Acton Bjørn (1910–1992) and Sigvard Bernadotte (1907–2002), before she and her husband Johannes Exner (1926–2015) set up their own design studio in 1958. Their first major assignment was Sankt Clemens Church in Randers, a town in Jutland, and they would go on to work extensively with church architecture. In addition to designing several new churches, they also oversaw the restoration of several existing buildings. They are particularly known for the reconstruction of Koldinghus, a medieval castle in Jutland.

In 1961 – after several years of preparation and applications for government loans – the architect couple Inger and Johannes Exner's own house in Skodsborg was finally completed. The site had presented difficulties because in one corner there was a burial mound surrounded by old lime trees. The burial mound was protected, which necessitated extra effort to place the house in the best possible way. Made of yellow bricks, the house contained the Exners' joint design studio as well as their private residence.

balanced and that their professional success cannot be separated from the combination of professional and personal qualities they possessed together. At the same time, the description also involves elements of gender stereotypes with the man cast as the extroverted artistic loner and the woman as an indispensable but rather more invisible and withdrawn player who primarily operates in the background – 'his better half', 'significant other' or 'the woman behind the man', as is sometimes said.[181] Seen in that light, the couple's biography becomes interesting, as does applying a gender perspective when examining the values and ethics underpinning their professional collaboration, not least in relation to the issue of equality and equal opportunities for men and women in the architectural profession. Inger and Johannes Exner both graduated upper secondary school from Randers Statsgymnasium in 1945, shortly after the end of the Second World War. A few years later, when they were both studying at the Royal Danish Academy of Fine Arts' School of Architecture in Copenhagen, their friendship blossomed into a love affair, and they were married in 1952. It was Inger who sparked Johannes's interest in the architectural profession, prompting him to change

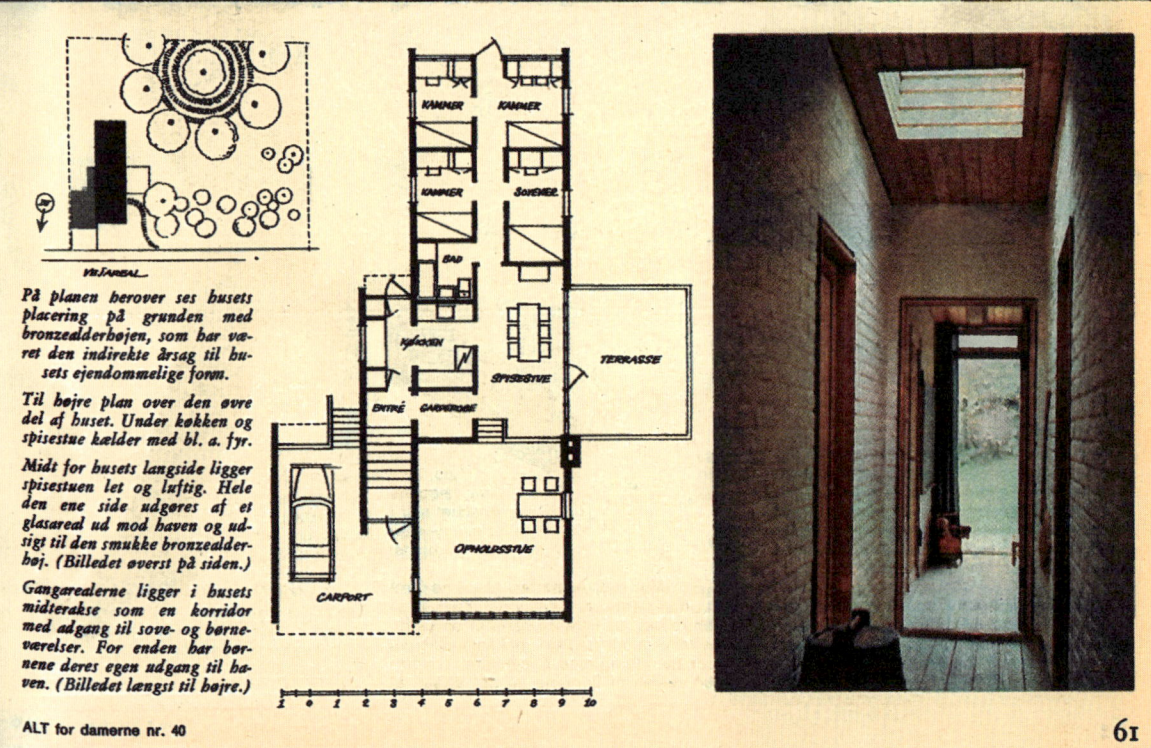

På planen herover ses husets placering på grunden med bronzealderhøjen, som har været den indirekte årsag til husets ejendommelige form.

Til højre plan over den øvre del af huset. Under køkken og spisestue kælder med bl. a. fyr.

Midt for husets langside ligger spisestuen let og luftig. Hele den ene side udgøres af et glasareal ud mod haven og udsigt til den smukke bronzealderhøj. (Billedet øverst på siden.)

Gangarealerne ligger i husets midterakse som en korridor med adgang til sove- og børneværelser. For enden har børnene deres egen udgang til haven. (Billedet længst til højre.)

ALT for damerne nr. 40

61

As was the case with the residences of several other architect couples, the Exners' house attracted a great deal of media attention. In the 1960s the weekly magazine *ALT for damerne* published an article about the residence, which the journalist described as a 'pencil case with many compartments'. Readers could see how the couple had decorated the house, which formed the setting of the family's everyday life and work. The architecture foreshadows the pioneering, modern church architecture for which they subsequently became known.

from studying agriculture to the School of Architecture where Inger was already enrolled. In 1956 they established a joint design studio,[182] which Inger Exner describes as having an intellectual outlook. For example, Johannes Exner was very involved in a theological discussion circle organised by his father, provost Johan Exner (1897–1981), who had campaigned for the preservation of Denmark's many medieval village churches for many years.[183] Shortly after the couple's fourth child was born, the family moved from the house in Skodsborg to Aarhus, where Johannes took up a position at the city's new school of architecture, and where they bought a large and somewhat dilapidated Art Nouveau villa, which would serve as the setting for the couple's joint work and family life for the next sixty years.

The couple renovated the house in Aarhus, giving it a coat of deep yellow plaster that provided contrast up against the decorative, symmetrical, slate-clad turrets. The house was set in a large, imaginatively laid-out, labyrinthine garden. It looked like something out of a children's book, a Pippi Longstocking fantasy compared to the much smaller, spartanly equipped, simple brick building they had built a few years earlier as a family home and shared design studio north of Copenhagen.

The private home as a manifestation of an architectural vision

With its simple forms and distinctive use of materials, room layout and interplay with the surrounding landscape, the house in Skodsborg manifests a special aesthetic which points ahead to the kind of church architecture and style for which the couple later became known. The elongated shape of the Skodsborg house with its raised living room is not unlike a nave. The modernist-inspired band of windows in the façade facing the road in the raised living room opens up on a magnificent vista of the treetops in the nearby Jægersborg Hegn, and the view from the small room presents an endless horizon of treetops rising up to meet an enormous, vaulted sky. In a house set in a depression at its site, this is a strong aesthetic device. In addition, the house is built out of materials familiar from both traditional and modern church construction. The floor of the dining room is Gotland marble, and the room's windows extend in long rectangular shapes

The Exner family did not stay in Skodsborg for long: in 1965, Johannes Exner accepted a position at the newly established School of Architecture in Aarhus. They moved into an older villa, renovating it on an ongoing basis. The architectural aesthetic was markedly different from the simplicity of the Skodsborg house. Here are ornate, slate-clad towers, old-fashioned windows and a large, maze-like garden. As with their previous home, the house in Aarhus was a combined setting for the couple's family and work life.

from floor to ceiling in a way that frames the mound in the garden to almost monumental effect. Overall, the house is built using a restricted range of materials and with a high degree of craftsmanship and precision, as is evident in the distinctive yellow-brown brickwork visible in the house's internal staircases and walls. The house's sleeping area is divided into very small rooms, or cells, for each family member, and we also find Kaare Klint's well-known so-called church chair from 1936 in the dining area.[184] Thus, one may say that the building was not only created as a house in which the couple's life together could unfold, a framework to be shared as a couple, a family and as business partners, but also as a dwelling that offered the possibility of privacy, contemplation and strong aesthetic experiences of the surroundings and of the space-defining elements within. With the house in Skodsborg, its architecture carefully thought through down to the smallest detail, the couple crafted a poignant framework for how one may live and work together as a couple, family and business partners. In this sense, the house can be interpreted as a joint effort to arrive at an idiom and a special form of architecture which uses modernist, architectural tools to point to ethical and metaphysical dimensions – a trait we later see unfolded in the couple's work with church architecture.

As the sociologist Eva Illouz explains, taking her basis from Marxist theory, any given love relationship can be seen as a relationship that in itself adds value for the individual even as it also carries with it limitations due to the ways in which emotions and passion are organised in society.[185] A love relationship reflects particular notions of gender as well as of financial realities, and this inequality is a particular focus of feminist theory which criticises marriage as an institution rising out of notions of capitalist ownership.[186] Unpacking the consequences of such inequality is not an end in itself in the discussion in this chapter; rather, we are interested in love as an organising societal force that leaves particular traces in the organisation and architecture of the home, as well as in relation to the opportunities that women and men in these relationships have for creative (co)work. We want to understand how the situation typical of women who have engaged in romantic relationships with architects with whom they have also worked can make us aware of particular inequality-creating structures associated with these women's complex gender, heteronormative and professional identities. The woman's work as an architect is here conditioned by 'love' as an organising emotional structure and as an institution associated with 'ownership' not just in the legal sense, but also as regards the properties that the women themselves help to design, live in and own. At the same time, we can say that the architect's creative work is itself a form of love – it is hardly surprising that motifs such as passion, suffering, obsession, commitment and perfection pop up in narratives about the dedicated architect. This means that the architect's creative energy connects her with something outside her own self, something in which she invests a part of herself.[187]

The Exner couple's house in Skodsborg is an example of a very special type of architecture: a single-family house designed by and for a couple where both were architects – and a house which was to contain not just a family home but also the couple's joint business. In this chapter we address several examples of such detached houses built in the post-war period in the Copenhagen suburbs, funded by government loans and created by and for heterosexual architect couples. We examine the significance of the material, financial and family-related opportunities and limitations for the women involved, specifically with regards to their ability to realise their professional

The Exner couple's house in Skodsborg had 160 square metres of floor space, of which 130 were devoted to the private residence and 30 to the studio, which was on the lower floor facing the road behind the long modernist band of windows.

dreams and ambitions. We can gain insight into the latter by interpreting the houses as products of and settings for several different forms of love. On a more structural level, we can also use these houses to consider how love in the twentieth century is shaped by social institutions and social relations, and how love as an emotion and as a social organising force circulates in spaces infused by inequality. The couples' collaborations are determined by their love lives as well as by the social organisation and conditions of working relationships, which are manifested here through the houses the women and their partners built as settings for their families and working lives.

The Exner couple's house in Skodsborg is thus an example of a property having been entirely customised for and by a couple who were married and had children as well as a joint business. In this light, it is telling that Inger Exner writes, on her website: 'Johannes devoted a lot of attention to his individual students. He was a firebrand, passionate about his work. It was perhaps more interesting to him than raising children. His students were his life's work'.[188] The duplicity inherent in this statement is to some extent associated with the kind of gender stereotypes that spring to mind when we think of the post-war era. Here, women are often seen as caregivers who carry out domestic work, and whose daily lives are sharply separated from those of the men, who work outside the home, meaning that they have easier access to taking on intellectually important positions in society. Indeed, Thomas Bo Jensen's monograph on the couple describes Johannes Exner first and foremost as an eccentric, intellectual creator and teacher – and then as a husband, father of four children and Inger Exner's professional partner. Inger Exner, on the other hand, is described as a robust, practical and empathetic person – the mother of four children.[189] Focusing on differences between the couple is, of course, closely associated with the many practical things that need to be managed and resolved in order for the couple's professional cooperation to be fruitful. One might say that enjoying a way of life and a way of working that needed to accommodate creative development, a successful business and time for contemplation on life's big questions came at a price. Inger Exner's own words point to this: she writes that her own life was very 'meaningful' but also 'hectic',[190] as the couple took an intensive approach to work, paying keen attention to every detail of a given project in the planning and execution stages alike. This thorough and, one can imagine, time-consuming way of working coincided with Johannes Exner's employment at the Aarhus School of Architecture and with the couple having to find the time and space required for everyday life in a household with four children.

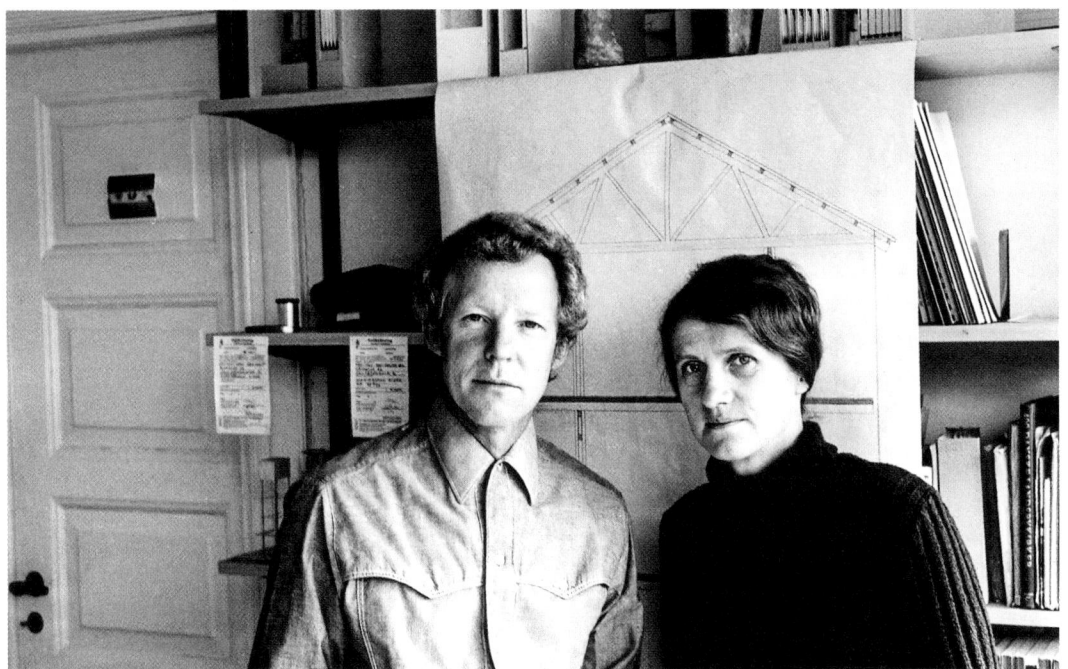

Inger and Johannes Exner knew each other from Randers Statsgymnasium, and while they were both students at the School of Architecture in Copenhagen, their friendship developed into a romantic relationship. They married in 1952. Later, they founded a joint design studio and worked together all their lives.

The story of the Exner couple not only points to a working relationship based on professional and personal reciprocity. It is also a story of a married couple who are in harmonious agreement in their life choices, and where architecture, everyday life and existential considerations merge in the design choices they made as a couple. Here one may say that the architectural idiom and spatial organisation developed for their house in Skodsborg illustrate the couple's deliberations on not just the *good* life (as we know it from the architecture of the welfare state more generally), but also about the *right* life, an ethical position. In the house in Skodsborg, a carefully thought-out understanding of life's everyday and practical issues is expressed in the house's meticulously considered spatial organisation, in the quality of the craftsmanship and in the monumental devices employed. Here one finds an architectural practice where the outlay in time and money that building an architect-designed, owner-occupied home

Inger and Johannes Exner's house in Skodsborg had relatively large common areas while the bedrooms were very small, almost like monastic cells. Despite the small scale, several children could still share a room: here we see the daughters Anna Mette and Karen's room, while the son, Hans, had a room behind the door on the left.

entails is associated with considerations about the right and proper way of life for a modern family where both mother and father work – and work together – in the same house in a suburb. The couple's joint practice is, then, underpinned by complex considerations, great effort and high standards, all of which perhaps contribute to why, towards the end of her life, Inger Exner looks back on a life she describes as both rich and meaningful, but also busy.[191] When Inger Exner writes about deep commitment, but also about challenges and struggles – not just regarding the couple's stance on architectural devices, but also in terms of the site and surroundings of a given project – she points to an inner conflict faced by many architects when their ideas have to be realised in a concrete context.

There are several reasons why building on the plot in Skodsborg required great architectural skill and effort. Not only does the protected, monumental, snail shell-shaped mound, surrounded by tall linden trees and complicated terrain, impose many restrictions on the architect; the site is also charged with historical significance, having formed the backdrop of one of Denmark's best-known – and most tragic – love stories. In the eighteenth century, the spiralling path winding up the sides of the burial mound was supposedly the way to a secret meeting place used by the then heavily pregnant Queen Caroline Mathilde (1751–1775) and her secret yet publicly known lover Johann Friedrich Struensee (1737–1772).[192] Johann Friedrich Struensee was Denmark's forward-thinking and powerful de facto head of state, a position he had gained through his work as physician to the mentally impaired absolute king Christian VII (1749–1808), and Struensee and Caroline Mathilde spent a great deal of time in the area, including at the nearby Frydenlund.[193] In the summer of 1771, Struensee had even moved the court to Hirschholm Palace in North Zealand. Caroline Mathilde gave birth to a daughter at the palace that summer, and the daughter was accepted into the royal family even though it was an open secret that Struensee was the child's biological father. The story goes that the very hill found on the Exners' plot, popularly nicknamed Mathilde's Hill, which also commanded a view of forest and sea back in the eighteenth century, was a meeting place for the two lovers. While the historical accuracy of this story must remain unverified, we can still indulge in imagining Caroline Mathilde on the spot in the early summer of 1771. Heavily pregnant, the queen wears an extravagant Rococo dress, having arrived by horse-drawn carriage or by riding through the countryside. She is now strolling up the spiral path of the hill to meet with Johann Friedrich for a secret rendezvous – unaware that this will be her last summer in freedom and as queen. A few months later, Struensee was executed for high

Previous spread: The house in Skodsborg has an elongated shape with a large window section and access to a terrace. The raised living room is reminiscent of a church nave, a trait which, alongside the use of solid materials such as brick and Gotland marble, points to the kind of architecture and style for which the Exner couple later became known.

treason and his body put on public display, while Caroline Mathilde was sent into exile without her children and died a few years later in the German city of Celle.

Given this historical reference, it seems reasonable to assume that the Exners engaged in serious deliberations in their work with the place. By building a family home in this particular plot, they created new meaning for and redeemed the place. The narratives unfolding in the life of a relatively well-to-do middle-class family – such as the lives led by the architect couples examined in this chapter – are mundane and undramatic, containing none of the tragic elements of the royal love story. And yet we will see that these everyday narratives are no less powerful in how they connect love, life stories and creative energy in the couples' work on designing and building houses created for their intertwined love, family and work lives.

Karen Clemmensen's regret

We know that many architects find their romantic partner and/or spouse among fellow practitioners of the discipline. In fact, the architecture industry is notable for its many romantic relationships. That holds true today,[194] and it held true for some of the most internationally famous couples of the twentieth century, such as Ray (1912–1988) and Charles Eames (1907–1978), or Denise Scott Brown (b. 1931) and Robert Venturi (1925–2018), who worked closely together.[195] And it held true in Denmark with well-known couples such as Eva and Nils Koppel, Elsebet and Kjeld Ussing, Karen and Ebbe Clemmensen and Inger and Johannes Exner, whom we have just met. The Clemmensens built their family home in the 1950s in a suburban setting around the Hundesømosen marshlands, a natural area in the affluent area of Gentofte. The neighbourhood grew rapidly during the period, and a large number of smaller single-family houses were built in the area, several of them by architects – so many, in fact, that the area reportedly went by the name 'The Architects' Marsh'. Eva and Nils Koppel built a house for themselves and their joint design studio back in 1941, and it was supposedly the Koppel couple who inspired Karen and Ebbe Clemmensen to buy a plot of land in the same area and build their home here.[196] In an interview, Karen Clemmensen has reflected not only on the importance of her gender for her career opportunities, but also on the importance of this house for her working conditions. Let us therefore take a closer look at the house and interpret its spatial organisation and genesis while focusing on the architect and woman who lived and worked here with her life partner.

Eva Koppel (1916–2006) applied for admission to the Royal Danish Academy of Fine Arts' School of Architecture in 1935 while still studying mathematics at the Polytechnic Institute in Copenhagen. At the School of Architecture she met her future husband Nils Koppel (1914–2009), and they both graduated in 1941. In 1943 they fled to Sweden, escaping the German occupation. Upon their return to Denmark they founded a joint design studio in 1946. Before then, they had designed their own house at Hundesømosen in Gentofte, north of Copenhagen (1941). In the post-war years, they designed several single-family houses. Later they were given larger assignments, in particular in and around Copenhagen, such as the Langelinie Pavilion (1958), the H.C. Ørsted Institute (1958–64), the Technical University of Denmark (1960–73) and the Panum Institute (1971–86).

Akademiets arkitektskole er næsten som et ægteskabsbureau

Forbløffende mange arkitekter danner par og samarbejder på fælles tegnestue

ÆGTEPARRET Karen og Ebbe Clemmensen har i fællesskab fået årets Træpris på 25.000 kroner. Det er der ikke noget nyt i, for det blev meddelt allerede i juni, men i næste uge skal prisen altså uddeles ved en højtidelighed på Blaagaard Seminarium i Søborg. Der er heller ikke noget nyt i, at et arkitekt-ægtepar vinder præmier. Det er snart så almindeligt, at arkitekter gifter sig og får præmieprojekter sammen, at det er lige ved at være påfaldende. Man spørger sig selv, om Kunstakademiets arkitektskole samtidig fungerer som en slags ægteskabsbureau.

Ganske vist hænder det også i andre erhverv, at kvinder og mænd med fælles kunstneriske og forretningsmæssige interesser finder sammen og driver en virksomhed, men næppe på noget område så udbredt som blandt arkitekterne.

Da arkitekt Karen Clemmensen i fjor fyldte 50 år, skrev avisernes, at hendes karriere på væsentlige områder var faldet sammen med hendes mands, professorens, og at det var sære naturligt, fordi de sammen havde drevet tegnestue i mere end tyve år. De har i fællesskab foruden Blaagaard Seminarium gennemført projekter som skole i Gladsaxe, svømme- og idrætshaller i Gentofte, Skive Seminarium, og de arbejder med færdiggørelsen af LOs Højstrup Højskole i Helsingør. De har sammen modtaget Bissens Legat og Eckersberg-medaillen. I 1952 tegnede de julemærket. Så langt tilbage som i 1946 vandt de en skandinavisk konkurrence, også i fællesskab.

Mindst en snes

Clemmensenerne er blot ikke det eneste arkitekt-ægtepar, som kan opvise et langvarigt og positivt samarbejde. Der er mindst en snes andre, som har fundet sammen på tilsvarende måde.

Eva og Nils Koppel hører til blandt de kendte. De har i øvrigt også sammen fået træprisen — i 1960, da den var på 10.000 kroner. Hun blev straks drillende kaldt Trækvinden. De fik prisen for blandt andet Langeliniepavillonen og Søllerød Parken, og de fik prisen overrakt i Byggecentrum, hvis hus de har tegnet.

Da Nils Koppel for 10 år siden blev udnævnt til kongelig bygningsinspektør og lykønsket med titlen, svarede han:

— Må jeg takke på min kones og egne vegne. Officielt er det jo kun mig, der er udnævnt — ja, men min kone og jeg arbejder altid sammen som en enhed. Hendes problemer er mine og omvendt. Så hvis man tror det er m i g, der er blevet kgl. bygningsinspektør, er det en misforståelse. Det er o s!

Sammen har parret vundet talrige arkitektkonkurrencer, og de har modtaget Eckersberg-medaillen og fået et diplom af Foreningen til Hovedstadens Forskønnelse. For øjeblikket samarbejder de om ombygningen af Statens Museum for Kunst og om den ny tekniske højskole i Lundtofte.

Da "Koppeline", som Eva Koppel kaldes, fyldte 50, erklærede hun, at hun ærligt måtte indrømme, at hun aldrig havde rørt en finger hjemme. Sammen med sin mand har hun arbejdet på tegnestuen fra de var unge — en overgang var tegnestuen hjemme — og hun betegnede det som meget inspirerende for arkitekter at arbejde parvis.

Umuligt at skelne

Tove og Edv. Kindt-Larsen er ligeledes et kendt arkitektpar, som har vundet mange præmier sammen. Det strækker sig fra projektet til Tivolis fornyelse for 25 år siden til Georg Jensen jubilæumsbestik for et par år siden. Man siger om dem, at det er næsten umuligt at skelne mellem arkitekt T. Kindt-Larsen og arkitekt E. Kindt-Larsen. De står begge inde for det vellykkede resultat, af skitser til nye stoffer, smykker eller korpusvarer. I mange år var de medarrangører af smedelaugets udstillinger i Kunstindustrimuseet, og i 1959 fik de laugets årspris.

— Jeg er ret langbenet og min kone er ret lille, sagde arkitekt Kindt-Larsen engang til Berlingske Aftenavis. Hvis en stol passer til os begge, plejer den at kunne passe alle. Der er rart at have målene i huset. Der er tider, hvor man inspirerer hinanden — og der er tider, hvor man næsten modarbejder hinanden og ikke kan komme af stedet. Så må man være så voksen, at man kan se det i øjnene og ikke kritisere, men vente på, at den anden kommer i gang.

Hanne og Poul Kjærholm er et eksempel på et arkitektægtepar, hvor hun i de første år foretrækker at passe hus og hjem — og når børnene er ved at vokse op, tager hun fat på arkitekturen næsten til den store guldmedalje. Hanne Kjærholm er lærer på Kunstakademiet hvor hendes mand er lektor. Hun tog afgang fra akademiet i 1956, og byggede straks et hus: familiens eget i Rungsted. Siden har hjem og børn lagt beslag på de fleste af hendes kræfter, men i år — 37 år gammel — deltog hun i en konkurrence om et teoretisk projekt i en lystbådehavn i Nivå — og vandt straks den lille guldmedalje.

— Nu føler jeg, at jeg kan overkomme det hele, sagde hun. Det skyldes ikke mindst, at jeg har fået betryggende hjælp til børnenes pasning de tre gange om ugen, jeg underviser på akademiet. Nu vil jeg gerne til at bygge — det må være vidunderligt at få realiseret sine tanker.

Med udlænding

Ditte og Adrian Heath beviser, at arkitekter møder hinanden andre steder end på Kunstakademiets arkitektskole. Han er britisk, hun dansk arkitekt, og de har boet i Storbritannien indtil for en halv snes år siden. Sammen har de vundet flere præmier for — typisk Danish Design i møbler.

Birte og Niels Rohweder vandt deres første fælles præmie i 1930 i en international schweizisk møbelkonkurrence. Det er også sket senere, men de har beundringsværdigt arbejdet hver for sig — hun som indendørsarkitekt, han for eksempel for øjeblikket med den ny Lindenborg Kro.

Jytte og Ove Tapdrup hører til den yngre generation og har fælles tegnestue i Esbjerg, hvor de for eksempel arbejder om byens ny domhus.

Gerda og Jørgen Hartmann-Pe-

Arkitekt-ægteparret Tove og Edv. Kindt-Larsen

Arkitekt-ægteparret Eva og Nils Koppel

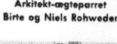

Arkitekt-ægteparret Birte og Niels Rohweder

tersen har signeret talrige af landets nyeste skoler. Præmier har de vist ikke vundet sammen, og han har jo også gennem årene været optaget af andre ting som for eksempel at redigere "Politikens At Tænke Sig" indtil 1965, og oversætte lystspil som Cranks. For øjeblikket arbejder ægteparret med de såkaldte Lille Louisiana i skoven ved Brøndbyerne.

Karen og Jan Eggen, der blandt andet har udført huse ved Furesøen, og Ege-Træppers moderne administrationsbygning i Herning, kan ligeledes nævnes.

Inger og Johannes Exner har skabt sig et navn som kirkearkitekter, og har i fællesskab vundet både danske og nordiske konkurrencer.

Bodil og Helge Fons lavede for nogle år siden arbejdstilsynets udstilling på Nørrevold, og har fået præmieret et hus i Gentofte. De arbejder i fællesskab med Køge Bugt-bycentret.

Karen Westergaard og Erik Jensen har beholdt hver sit efternavn,

Også min kone!

Edith og Ole Nørgaard har vundet præmier i flere konkurrencer, blandt andet en førstepræmie i fjor for bebyggelsen langs Københavns havn. Da der forleden var omtale i Berlingske Aftenavis af projekteringen af det kommende udenrigsministeriums, nævnte vi, at kgl. bygningsinspektør Eske Kristensen samarbejdede med Ole Nørgaard. Sidstnævnte bad os dagen efter meddele, at samarbejdet gjaldt E d i t h og Ole Nørgaard.

Inge og Jørgen Vesterholdt er ligeledes et arkitektægtepar, der har vundet præmier sammen. Han sagde engang efter en konkurrence:

— Jeg tror, det er en god ting,

men har vundet konkurrencer sammen.

Anne og Jørn Ørum-Nielsen har sammen vundet en svensk arkitektkonkurrence.

Elsebeth og Kjeld Ussing har udarbejdet projekter i fællesskab.

at mand og kone kan arbejde sammen om de arkitektoniske opgaver — de supplerer hinanden, o konen i huset siger meget fornuftigt om boligindretningen.

Inge Vesterholdt tilføjede:

— Vi er et godt team, og vi snakker arkitektur fra morgen til aften.

Traditionen for arkitekt-ægteskaber er gammel. Arkitektforbundets ældste kvindelige medlem, de 82-årig Agnete Hansen, var gift med arkitekt Henning Hansen, der blandt andet byggede Frederiksberg Rådhus. Hun blev akademis

---

The Exners and the other couples addressed in this book were not the only architect couples in twentieth-century Danish architecture. On the occasion of the Clemmensen couple receiving the Danish Wood Award in 1968, the newspaper *Berlingske Tidende* ran an article about how the School of Architecture in Copenhagen was virtually a marriage agency because so many architects met each other as students, became romantically entangled and often got married.

In the late 1940s and in the 1950s, several architect couples built homes for themselves by Hundesømosen in Gentofte. Eva and Nils Koppel had already built a house here in the early 1940s, and the area was nicknamed 'The Architects' Marsh'. The Koppels expanded their house several times as their design studio grew.

Among the other architect couples who built their own home close to Hundesømosen we find Elsebet and Kjeld Ussing. They designed their house in 1956, living there with their five children and running their studio from there. The house consists of three joined wings surrounding a terrace, which is further shielded by a high wall. The couple designed a number of social housing developments in the 1960s and 1970s, such as Korngården in Ballerup from 1961.

Herover: Lavt og elegant ligger arkitekterne Kjeld og Elsebet Ussing's hus højt på bakken på Ermelundsvej med en pragtfuld udsigt over Hundesømosen. Der er store vinduer og døre og dekorative skodder, som er behandlet med lysebrun solignum; indvendig lukkes skodderne med enkle glatte skabsdøre i glade farver.

Til venstre: Den nordlige ende af opholdsstuen. Loftet er af naturfarvet gran; skabet, af professor Frank fra Wien, er beklædt med olivengrønt læder. Lampeskærmene er japanske.

PLADS TIL FAMILIE MED FEM BØRN

AF BIRGITTE DE BOURBON   FOTO: MARIE HOLSTEIN

Elsebet og Kjeld Ussing er begge arkitekter: Ganske vist kniber det meget med tiden, men Elsebet Ussing deltager, så ofte som hus og børn tillader det, i mandens arbejde.

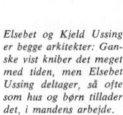

Den sydlige ende af den store opholdsstue. Kaare Klint's stilrene møbler står smukt på det gotlandske marmorgulv, lampen er tegnet af Poul Henningsen. På væggen et af Susannes arbejder.

Arkitekterne *Kjeld* og *Elsebet Ussing's* hus på Ermelundsvej er ualmindelig smukt placeret, højt på toppen af en bakke og med den dejligste udsigt over Hundesømosen. Det er bygget i en vinkel om en lille gård, der lukkes på de andre sider med et sort plankeværk og en høj hvid havemur. Her er intet loft og ingen kælder, og heller ikke noget pulterkammer, det nødvendige fyrrum er begrænset til det mindst mulige, således at man på det samme areal har fået ekstra meget plads til beboelse. »Det er først og fremmest bygget til at bo i, og sådan som vi kan lide det«, fortæller arkitekt Kjeld Ussing. Og her er på en gang både hygge og stil med flere smukke møbler af Kaare Klint og morsomme lave taburetter, som er tegnet af Kjeld Ussing og virker japansk inspirerede. I det hele taget giver hele indretningen en japansk fornemmelse, der er dekorative japanske bambuspersienner for alle vinduer, japanske lampeskærme og ude i den lille gård eller have Kjeld Ussings morsomme lave haveborg og bænke – det særprægede lille anlæg hensætter os flere tusinde mile mod øst.

Flere gange spurgte vi om en eller anden tings oprindelse, og hver gang var svaret det samme, at det havde et af børnene lavet. »Vi kan bedst lide kun at have vort eget,« smiler arkitekten, men det kan man også tillade sig med så talentfuld en familie. Der er 5 børn, 4 piger og en dreng i alderen fra atten til 6, de har deres egen afdeling i den sydvestlige ende af husets vinkel, medens tegnestuen og arkitektens kontor optager den nordlige del. Den store opholdsstue ligger i midten som et centrum, hvorfra man let har adgang til alt og alle.   *Fortsættes side 41.*

Elsebet and Kjeld Ussing's own house was featured in the weekly magazine *Tidens Kvinder*. The presentation focused on the architecture, the two architects and their family life. This was not peculiar to the Ussing couple; several other architect couples also appeared in Danish media at the time. The era saw keen interest in how to furnish the many new detached houses being built around the time, and architects were often seen as role models.

Karen Clemmensen (1917–2001) completed secondary school at Sønderborg Statsskole in 1935. Following this, she was an apprentice mason for a short time before enrolling at the Royal Danish Academy of Fine Arts' School of Architecture, graduating in 1942. While still a student, she and her husband, fellow architect Ebbe Clemmensen (1917–2003), took part in several design competitions, and in 1945 they founded their own design studio. The couple designed several large public institutions, including the Skive teacher-training collage in northern Jutland (now a high school) (1957–59), Blågård teacher-training collage and the Enghavegård school west of Copenhagen (both 1962–66) and designed in collaboration with professor and architect Jørgen Bo, as well as the swimming pool and sports facility Kildeskovshallen (1966–72) and LO-skolen (1967–69, extended 1973–75), a large complex for adult education, the latter two with architect Jarl Heger and landscape architect Agnete Muusfeldt.

From 1953 to 1954, architects Karen and Ebbe Clemmensen designed a home for themselves in the Hundesømosen area in Gentofte. Created to accommodate their private residence and design studio, the house was financed by a government loan. In order to have as large a house as possible, the couple chose to save on building materials, using unplastered aerated concrete for the outer walls. The house has 130 square metres of residential space plus the studio.

In 1981, when Karen Clemmensen was sixty-four years old, she was asked in an interview about the conditions and challenges she had encountered as a woman in the architectural profession.[197] In the interview, she explains how she met Ebbe Clemmensen as a student: they were married when they were in their third year of study, and in 1946 they founded a joint design studio. Karen Clemmensen relates that it was important to her not to lose out on career development opportunities as a young woman, and that the opportunity to work from home, not least after they had built their house with its own design studio in 1953, facilitated this. By the time the couple moved to the area by Hundesømosen, they had two boys. In the interview, she also reflects on issues pertaining to gender and the architecture industry. She explains that at the beginning of her career she took on many tasks that fell under the heading of what she terms 'women's areas' – such as kitchen and bathroom design, so-called flower windows (slightly projecting window frames) and furniture – but also that the scope of professional work slowly expanded and led to commissions which did not have specifically feminine connotations.[198] Furthermore, she reports that there were times when the workload had a negative impact on the family's life, and that both she and Ebbe Clemmensen were told off by their sons, who were concerned about their parents' health.[199]

But apparently what most frustrates Karen Clemmensen is that on the many occasions when journalists visited their home and design studio, she played the role of the perfect wife and mother. And not only that: she had personally and single-handedly ensured that the house was clean and tidy before the journalist's visit. What she presented to the curious eyes of the journalists, cameras and readers was a dream, a façade, rather than an honest presentation of how 'the home looked on an ordinary Thursday morning', the day before the housekeeper came. 'It would have been more honest towards my fellow sisters,' she continues, if she had been less focused on the outward appearance of herself, her family and her home.[200] Given that the pictures and descriptions from newspapers and magazines are the source material available to us today, we can use them to try to understand not only what kind of aspirational dream world Karen Clemmensen creates for the readers, but also which fractures and inconsistencies we might sense behind the glossy surface. By comparing these media images of the house and the descriptions of family life in it with analyses of the physical framework created by the home as architecture, we see a fundamental paradox: all the attention lavished upon the couple through the many journalists' exposure of their home and domestic life – as well as Karen's own investment in this utopian media image – was in all probability an important factor in promoting the couple's professional success.

Let us try, then, to imagine some of what we do not see in the pictures: during the small hours of the night before the journalist's visit, Karen Clemmensen is busy tidying up and arranging furniture and other objects in the home so that the interior will look great on camera and will impress the journalist and the readers. In 1954, for example, her efforts are a resounding success when the women's magazine *ALT for damerne* publishes a major article about the home and the family headlined 'A house full of sun, light and happiness'.[201] In the article, we see pictures of a smiling Karen Clemmensen in the process of handing her fair-haired, well-groomed and identically dressed boys what looks rather like an empty plastic plate through the serving hatch connecting the kitchen and the living room. The living room looks spick and span, neat as a pin, with fresh flowers on the coffee table. We also see images of a lush garden awash in summer sunlight, and a small group of children playing peacefully beneath an apple tree laden down with luscious fruit. Karen Clemmensen's frustration and regret must therefore revolve around the pressure the couple put on themselves in terms of succeeding in their work, and we may ponder whether this pressure is solely linked to their desire for success and recognition in the profession – focusing on professional and aesthetic development – or whether it also points

Elsebet Ussing (1915–1978) worked as a mason's apprentice before applying for admission to the School of Architecture. She attended classes at the Royal Danish Academy of Fine Arts' School of Architecture in 1937 and 1938, and in 1940 she founded a design studio with her husband, Kjeld Juul Ussing (1913–1977). Their designs include several commissions in and around Copenhagen, including their own house at Ermelundsvej 100, Gentofte (1956), the public housing developments Korngården (1962) and Grantoften (1974) in Ballerup, as well as the student accommodation Østerbrogården (1964–1968).

to a desire for the kind of financial success necessary to maintain the way of life they showcase, complete with mortgages and cars. Another issue obviously concerns the image of Karen Clemmensen as the perfect wife and mother, an image repeatedly paraded before the world in the many features from their home.* For example, the journalist from *ALT for damerne* writes:

'Karen Clemmensen answers the door. Blonde and blue-eyed, she is dressed in modern woman's "national dress", a jumper and skirt. She is an architect and has, together with her husband and fellow architect, Ebbe Clemmensen, built the house they live in. […] "The living room" must be the right term, because the entire main wing is in fact one single, vast living room. It is not at all easy to describe: it has so many subtle details and reflects much ingenuity that it is difficult for a guest to take it all in at once. The house and its people are a perfect match. She is witty and quick to respond, smiling and genuine in her demeanour, displaying a keen eye for practicality and expediency and for colour combinations. He is dark, sensitive, rather more hesitant, yet precise when the words do come in deliberate sentences, withdrawing whenever one tries to reach past the architect to reach the man'.[202]

This contrast of personalities is emphasised by the journalist's polarised psychological portrait of the married couple. Karen Clemmensen is described as an extrovert, talkative, intelligent and elegant woman, while Ebbe Clemmensen comes across introverted and professional, an artist and architect in one and the same thoughtful figure. The journalist would hardly have formed this impression entirely by chance. The interview appears carefully orchestrated, with Karen Clemmensen answering the door, smiling and well-dressed, and then proceeding to shows the journalist around while speaking in great detail about the many smart solutions she has integrated into the design, and which are primarily her work.

This is a highly developed, optimised and customised version of some of the more standardised kitchen solutions we have seen in Chapter One. The first stop on the tour around the home is the functional and expensively made kitchen with its many modern appliances and practical and time-saving solutions – such as the small built-in kitchen chute so that you do not have to carry the rubbish out of the house, or the little insulated cupboard where the delivery boy or the milkman can leave goods even when no one is at home. The cupboard can be opened from the road and from inside the kitchen, where it can be locked: a time-saving and practical device for someone who, like Karen Clemmensen, has a professional career to look

* *ALT for damerne* was not alone in visiting the Clemmensen couple. We find the house and home mentioned in the weekly magazines *Billed-Bladet* and *Se og Hør*, in the so-called women's section of the newspaper *Berlingske Tidende* and in more traditional media such as architectural journals and books. Nor was the house at Hundesømosen alone in being presented in the media. An earlier home, a terraced house by Mindelunden, also appears in both Danish and Swedish media.

Huset er ladet med SOL LYS og LYKKE

I denne uge har Dag Lénard besøgt arkitekterne Karen og Ebbe Clemmensen i deres dejlige hus, som de selv har tegnet, og som er blevet en meget fint afstemt ramme om deres hyggelige tilværelse med sønnerne Jens og Lars

Det lave hus er lukket ud mod vejen – ikke en „gnaven venden ryggen til", men blot en hyggen sig indadtil mod solen. Det er langt og smalt som et penalhus, opført i lette, lyse betonblokke, og med dørpartiet og garagens skydelem i de kanariske sangfugles solgule farve. For tidens mennesker må det være et ønskehus, og vi standser derfor og kikker indenfor hos de moderne folk, der bebor det ...

Karen Clemmensen lukker op. Hun er lyshåret og blåøjet og er klædt i nutidskvindens „nationaldragt", jumper og nederdel. Hun er arkitekt og har sammen med sin mand, Ebbe Clemmesen, der ligeledes er arkitekt, bygget huset, de bor i.

To hvidhårede, solbrune drenge, den niårige Jens og den syvårige Lars kommer barfodede og kvidrende i spring over græsplænen for at tage den fremmede i øjesyn. Jeg accepteres efter at have vist forståelse for, at den ældste af de „unge Clemmensener" er en

Sofapladsen ved kaminen med fyrretræsbordet og safaristolene er et yndet opholdsted — og der er ikke langt over til køkkenlemmen, hvor husets frue rækker servicet til sønnerne, der dækker bord.

„mexikaner", der optræder inkognito som postbud, mens den yngste forestår stillingen som postmester i „postkontoret" nede i havens legehus. Så får jeg lov at se hus og have.

Det er et yndigt efterårsvejr. Æbler og blommer strutter af kraft og rødmer af sundhed på den jadegrønne plæne. Huset har glasdøre, der fylder en hel væg, og som nu, da de står åbne, lader den milde, disede luft strømme ind i stuen.

„Stuen" må være det rigtige udtryk, for hele hovedfløjen er faktisk kun een stor stue. Den er slet ikke så let at beskrive, for den rummer så mange finesser og så megen hittepåsomhed, at det er svært for en gæst at overskue det hele på en gang. Hus og mennesker passer sammen. Hun er hurtig i replikken, smilende og realistisk betonet med sikker sans for det praktiske og hensigtsmæssige og for farvesammensætninger. Han er mørk, følsom, mere tøvende, men præcis, når ordene kommer i stilfærdig sætningsopbygning og med en trækken sig ind i sig selv, hvis man forsøger at nå forbi arkitekten og ind til mennesket.

Han lægger vægt på, at huset er bygget med henblik på at få naturen ind i stuerne, at overgang mellem hus og have så at sige ikke findes eller i hvert fald ikke mærkes, og at hvert lille glimt af solen, sommer og vinter, kan besøge familien i „Solbakkehuset"... Hun viser rundt. De to, som bor i det splinternye hus, er selvfølgelig meget optaget af deres hjem, og fru Clemmensen går foran mig, viser og forklarer, smiler og afbryder nu og da for at råbe noget ud til de to små „postmænd" i havehuset.

Huset har ingen entré, man kommer lige ind i det store rum med loftbeklædning af mørke fyrretræsbrædder. Køkken, opholdstue og tegnestue går i et. Køkkenet, der ligger til venstre for indgangen, vil begejstre enhver husmor. Ud mod stuen har det skydevæg, som kan trækkes for, hvis det ikke skulle være i præsentabel stand. Når der er lukket, er væggen et moderne maleri i forskelligt farvede felter. Et af felterne er et gennemtrækningsskab til al daglig service, så familien kan være behjælpelig med borddækningen, idet spisearrangementet, et teaktræsbord, omgivet af hvide, gustavianske stole, er placeret lige ud for køkkenet. De smalle farvefelter er gennemtrækningsskuffer, så man kan tage knivtøj og servietter ud fra begge sider. Køkkenbordet har affaldsskakt, og længst til højre er der indleveringsskab for varer, så mælk, smør og morgenbrød kan stilles ind i skabet udefra. Under køkkenbordet sidder en udtrækningsbakke, hvor børnene selv kan smøre deres mad, og en lille affaldsbakke, som brødkrummer, ostekorper og pølseskind børstes ned i. Skuffen til grydeskeer har perforeret metalbund, så trætøjet hurtigt tørrer, og ved vasken er der en praktisk opdeling, hvor opvasken skylles, vaskes og tørres. Her er også tørreskab til viskestykkerne.

Over komfuret er der elektrisk udsugning af mados, og i endevæggen en lille lem ind til stuens anden ende, så man let kan række en kaffebakke til gæster omkring sofabordet. Ved siden af lemmen og lige ved komfuret findes et særligt „sovseskab" med alle ingredienser til sovs, salat og krydrede retter... Det er svært at løsrive sig fra dette vidunderkøkken, jeg er blevet her længere end beregnet, og vi går derfor hurtigt gennem sidefløjen, der vinkelret lukker for nabohuset mod nord for ligesom hovedfløjen at åbne sig mod haven.

Arkitektparrets soveværelse har loggia ud mod drengenes havehus, og børnekamrene er indrettet til at „vokse" i. Der er reoler til legetøj og bøger og et rigtigt arbejdsbord ved vinduet. En opslagstavle gør det ud for dosmerseddel til ting, der skal huskes, og begge kamre har markisestribede sengetæpper med løbegange, hvori der kan stikkes et „kosteskaft", så tæpperne altid ligger

„Vi er så heldige, at vort arbejde er vor livsinteresse. Vi er lykkelige mennesker," siger arkitekterne Karen og Ebbe Clemmensen.

pænt glatte, når børnene selv har redt senge.

„Huset er bygget ud fra den forudsætning, at her hjælper alle hinanden," siger Karen Clemmensen. „Jeg har kun konehjælp to gange om ugen, og vi har derfor nøje udregnet hver enkelt lille praktisk foranstaltning, så alt, som H. C. Andersen sagde, 'kan være på sin rette plads'. Væggen i korridoren er forskydelig. Her har jeg alt mit linnedtøj, og her er to badeværelser, et med brusebad og et med kar, det sidste kan anvendes som vaskehus. Nedenunder har vi kælder med hobbyrum til børnene og viktualieog frugtkælder."

Inde i stuen sætter vi os på sofapladsen ved kaminen, Ebbe Clemmensen slår sig ned i safaristolen, og jeg kan omsider lade mine spørgsmål strømme ud...

„De er begge arkitekter og arkitektbørn?"

Det er husets frue, der begynder: „Ja, Ebbes far var Mogens Clemmensen, hans farfar Andreas Clemmensen, som blandt andet byggede Illum, Statens Seruminstitut og nogle kirker. De var begge arkitekter i København, og det var min far, Holger Mundt, også. Vi var kun to piger hjemme, og da min søster ville være læge, blev jeg altså arkitekt." Både Ebbe og Karen Clemmensens mødre er malerinder. Harriet Mundt maler mest landskaber, mens Augusta Thejll Clemmensen er kendt for sine portrætter.

„Hvorfra har De fået inspirationen til at bygge Deres hus sådan?"

Nu er det ham, der svarer: „Ideen eller inspirationen til disse 'åbne' enfamiliehuse er nok oprindelig japansk. Folk synes altid, de har det så herligt i deres sommerhuse, så hvorfor ikke forfølge ideen i helårshuset? Tiden er ikke mere til pretentiøs isolation. I gamle dage blev et hus bygget med en forside, der skulle tage sig ud for de vejfarende, i dag bygger man for at gøre det hyggeligt for sig selv. *(Fortsættes side 26.)*

„Solbakkehuset" er bygget med henblik på at få naturen ind i stuerne, så overgangen mellem hus og have mærkes mindst muligt.

after and is often away from home during the day. And the result proves enchanting for the journalist, who describes the kitchen as 'every housewife's dream'.[203]

Of course, the glossy surfaces of the kitchen were presumably cleaned with particular zeal for the occasion, and the family dressed and coiffed with extra care. We may reasonably ask what we would have seen if Karen Clemmensen had *not* done all the preparatory work necessary to show her house and family to their best advantage prior to the journalist's visit – what Rut Speyer and Gytte Rue would perhaps call 'kitchens in their Sunday best'. Would we see breadcrumbs on the kitchen table and the remains of a hastily abandoned morning meal, or perhaps loud, hungry children running through the house, trailing mud after having played with their friends on the banks of the nearby lake? Perhaps Karen Clemmensen did not always have the energy to smile quite so invitingly to everyone she met on her way? Of course, we have no way of knowing all this, but we can see that the journalist bought into what Karen Clemmensen herself described as a fantasy rather than a truthful glimpse of the family's everyday life. From the perspective of the history of women, it is particularly disturbing to note how the journalist describes Karen Clemmensen's complicated juggling of work and domestic life as perfect and entirely authentic, while we are allowed to see Ebbe Clemmensen as the mysterious, professional artist-architect who, in the psychologising portrait painted by this journalist, is allowed to separate his private self from his professional identity.

Previous spread: In 1954, the weekly magazine *ALT for damerne* published an article about the Clemmensens' own home under the heading 'A house full of sun, light and happiness'. In a later interview, Karen Clemmensen expressed regret that she had made such effort cleaning and tidying up before the journalists' visit. It made the house appear as an idealised dream instead of reflecting the realities of ordinary everyday life.

A property that also holds ownership over the woman

The property in itself is a material and physically significant framework, one which was created on the basis of a design philosophy informed by great ingenuity, as is evident in the many practical, customised solutions intended to help the housewife save time on the daily chores. We can see such thinking reflected in the design solutions Karen Clemmensen tells the journalist about, created especially for the house. They express a progressive view of family life where the children must also be involved in daily chores and routines so that everything goes as smoothly as a well-oiled machine.[204] This combination of family collaboration and appliances and devices is necessary to relieve the housewife, leaving her time for other activities. In Karen

The dining area in the Clemmensens' house is placed in connection with the kitchen, and, very unusually for the time, dining area and living room are merged into one. The view shown here is of the kitchen and the entranceway seen from the couple's studio, which was separated from the living room by a sliding door.

Clemmensen's case, that meant pursuing a career as an architect. There was no stay-at-home housewife in this house. Reflecting this, the children had special duties which Karen Clemmensen facilitated by incorporating customised design solutions that made it easier for the children to carry out the tasks assigned to them. One example is the bedspreads in the children's rooms: she sewed broomsticks into their sides, making it easier for the children to make the bedspread nice and smooth every morning before leaving for school.

A photo shows the couple working in their design studio while the large sliding door between the living room and the studio is open, offering a glimpse of the private part of the home. However, the

Karen and Ebbe Clemmensen in their studio with a view into the private living room. The open-plan connection between work and private life made it easier for Karen Clemmensen to work during the early years. When the design studio began to receive larger assignments such as Kildeskovshallen, it relocated to larger premises in Copenhagen.

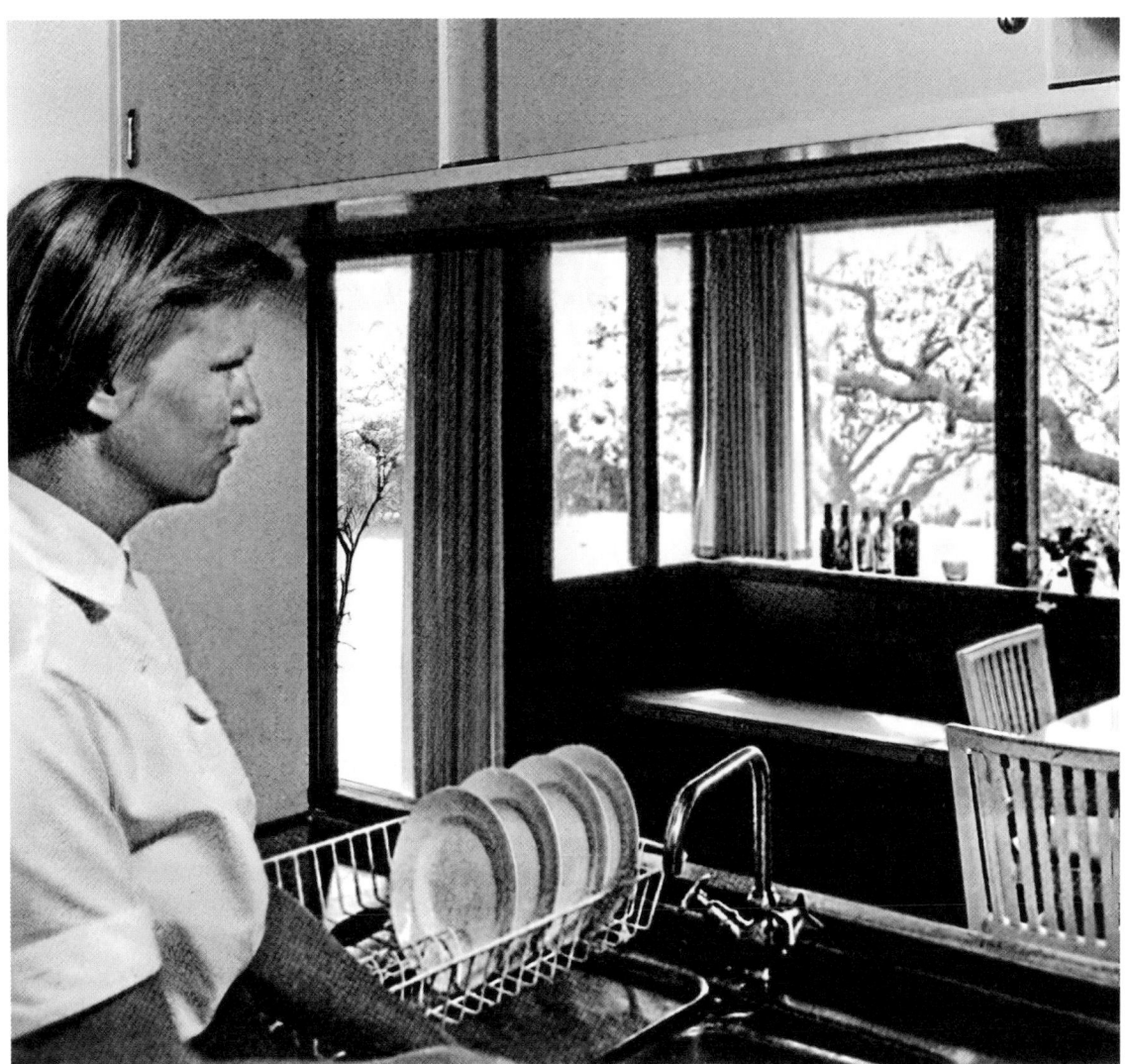

The journalist from *ALT for damerne* described the kitchen in the Clemmensens' home as 'every housewife's dream'; it was functional and boasted several practical and time-saving solutions. Towards the road it had a small built-in kitchen chute so you did not have to carry the rubbish out of the house, as well as a small cupboard where the milkman could put milk. The cupboard could be opened from outside as well as from inside the kitchen, where it could be locked. Part of the cupboard wall facing the dining area could be opened or closed, making it easy to serve up food and clear the table. In addition, the cupboards opened on both sides, from the kitchen and from the dining area.

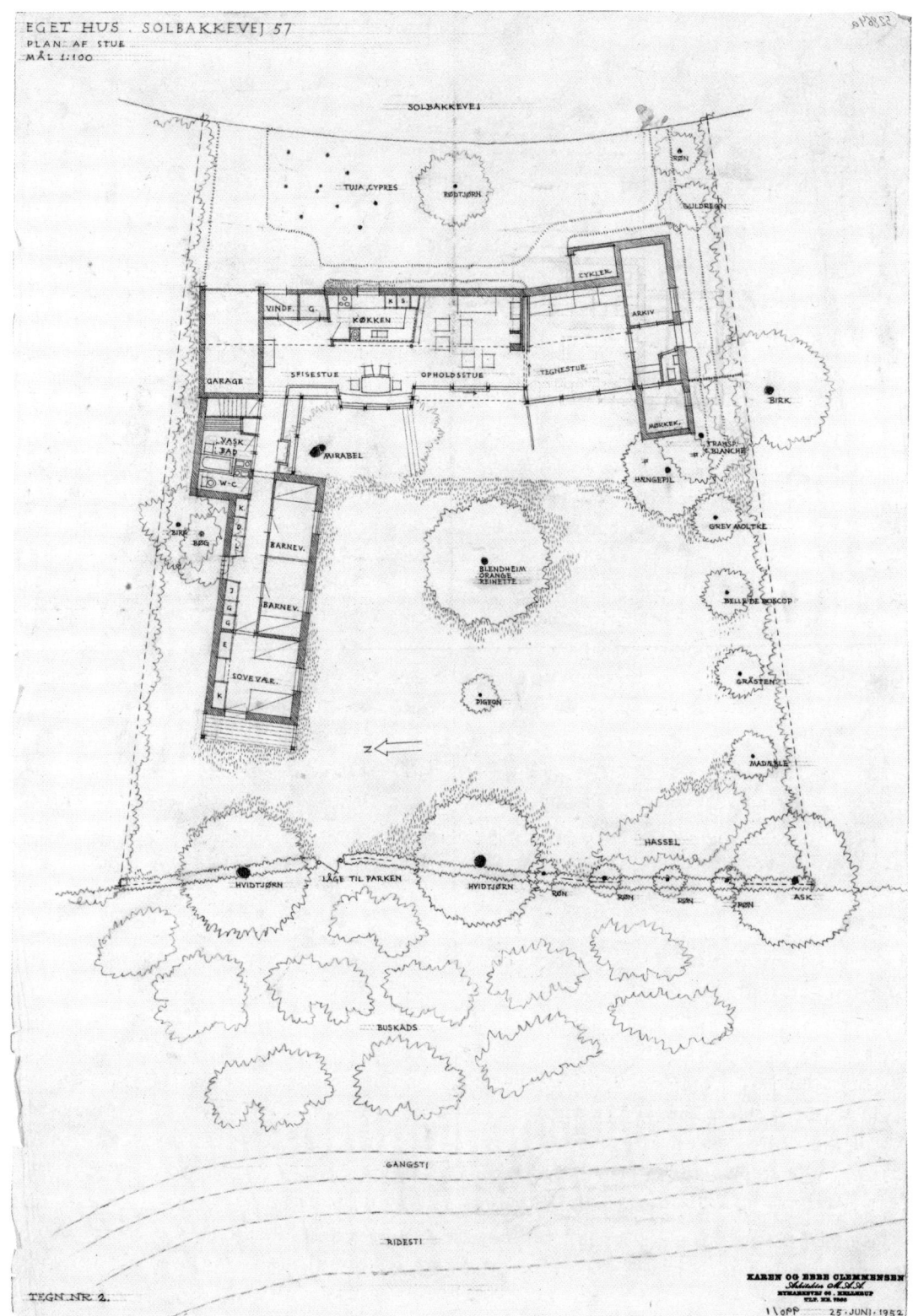

Floor plan of Karen and Ebbe Clemmensen's home, built in 1954 on a sloping site with direct access to the green area at Hundesømosen at the bottom of the plot.

separation between the domestic sphere of the house and the design studio, between the private and professional parts of the house, is not just a concept that makes sense on a floor plan. Or, to put it another way: the sliding door marks out more than just a visible architectural boundary; it also represents a boundary determined by financial concerns: the design studio is where money is made to maintain the family's modern, middle-class way of life in the next rooms. The separation is also governed by legal requirements: the couple were able to add more floor space to the house by including a professional office, all while still qualifying for a cheap government loan to build their home.[205] The sliding door makes a very concrete contribution to promoting equality between the sexes: according to Karen Clemmensen herself, the close proximity to the home made it easier for her (and thereby also for Ebbe Clemmensen) to achieve professional success. It not only enabled her to live out her dreams of having a career and making money for the family – it also enabled the professional collaboration between the two spouses to flourish. As such, the sliding door is also a symbol of an unequally distributed burden, one borne mainly by Karen Clemmensen, according to her retrospective reflections. With this reading in mind, we may consider whether, rather than viewing the house as a family home with a commercial part added on at one end, we should instead see the design studio as the central room of the house and the entire home as a showcase for the couple's work and skills: a calling card that gives the outside world insight into a fantasy where the architecture itself, the spatial organisation of the house and all the clever and time-saving solutions are tools which make it possible to live out the fantasy. At the same time, the place is also the setting for family life, keeping it barely visible from the public road outside the property, hidden behind the closed-off façade. And we know from Karen Clemmensen that, as soon as the cameras were turned off (echoing the realities of social media today), a much more emotionally rich and complex and by no means always smooth life unfolds behind the four walls of the home. If the home is a kind of stage or theatre, this family has been in charge of writing *and* directing the play while also conceiving and building the sets. The family members play the main parts, while the neighbours and the environment around Hundesømosen – where the children, as shown in the picture from the woman's magazine, play in each other's gardens or down by the marsh, and the couples in the area pay each other visits – are featured as supporting characters in a larger story about the good life in the new suburbs around Copenhagen.

It is, of course, an open question as to what extent the children's – and of course also Ebbe Clemmensen's – contributions to the household helped make it possible for a journalist to paint a picture of domestic perfection to the outside world, or whether that burden rested primarily on Karen Clemmensen's shoulders. It certainly transpires from the interview that while Karen Clemmensen spent a lot of time and effort experimenting with interior design and finding smart solutions to everyday problems, Ebbe Clemmensen spent his time creating an abstract, modernist sundial cast in concrete for the garden. So while many descriptions of their collaboration emphasise that the architect couple had a fluid and equitable professional partnership, we also see that their opportunities for unfolding their creativity take different forms and focus on different problems. Ebbe Clemmensen is shown to address more artistic problems as well as issues associated with construction, which cleaves very close to the familiar image of what an innovative, modernist mid-century architect would want to spend his time and energy on. His design philosophy is more abstract, and he can seek refuge in the well-established persona of the attractive, if somewhat distant, artistic architect. He is able to express his creative ambitions in areas where he is not required to deal with trivial matters associated with the organisation of everyday life, for example when constructing buildings or designing his marvellous sundial. In contrast to this, Karen Clemmensen's energy as a designer in relation to the house is largely directed towards issues associated with creating the kind of interior design and structure that lets the family lead the lifestyle deemed appropriate for a family of their social standing and class. At the same time, she is focused on finding smart solutions that help her avoid time-consuming housework – just as Ulla Tafdrup did, as described in Chapter One. If this life was not just framed but additionally made possible by the fact that the couple had invested in private property which had to be financed, the house can also be seen as a ball and chain that bound them, making it impossible for Karen Clemmensen to escape from the distinctive morality and normativity such a way of life entails. We are dealing here with a situation from which Karen Clemmensen cannot escape because the house itself is a co-creator of her success as an architect: the exposure the couple receives in the public eye because of their house helps her sell her designs and so ensures her success going forward. Even as it may help to secure income to pay off the mortgage, this dual bind is also central to her ashamed regret at having prompted guilt and shame in other women by pretending that the images presented in women's magazines are a true and accurate representation of life.

In the interview, Karen Clemmensen also reveals the price she paid for having created a house that could be run by a working woman with only minimal paid help.[206] It requires her to facilitate, organise and to some extent also carry out much of the housework herself. She becomes a project manager for the family. It is hardly surprising that this position was primarily the woman's job, given the norms and gender roles prevalent among Danish middle-class families in the 1950s. But the fact that she later looked back on that situation with regret indicates that in her own self-understanding she was first and

The Clemmensens' house at Hundesømosen comprises three wings, with the entrance, kitchen, living room and part of the studio located in the middle wing facing the road. The wing to the north contains the private rooms, and to the south were rooms used by the studio as archives and a darkroom. Although the house contained modern elements, the layout was quite traditional. The carefully thought-out relationship between the private and commercial parts of the house is an important point: it enabled the couple to qualify for a bigger loan and allowed them to build a larger house, but the design should also be seen as their attempt to carefully consider the relationship between their private and working lives.

foremost an architect, and that being able to realise her professional ambitions was an important driving force for her. The progressive and cooperative family format represented by the Clemmensens was not initially based on ideals of solidarity or reciprocity across genders and generations in the family; rather, it sprang out of sheer necessity for Karen Clemmensen. We are dealing here with a contradictory mixture of an extensive form of love and protection of the self's opportunity for creative expression, one which involves both individualism and self-sacrifice. Perhaps Karen Clemmensen had no other choice but to highlight the image of the perfect housewife so strategically presented to the journalists. Failure to do so would have created a rift in the overall image of domestic harmony and the fantasy of being able to have it all, a fantasy which the design of the home was created to make possible for Karen Clemmensen herself, and which she hoped could be instrumental in winning her more commissions, thus enabling her to develop her creativity and professional ambitions. Had she not made that choice, she would

Karen Clemmensen liked to paint watercolours, in this case an illustration of the living room before the house was built. To the left is a glimpse of the kitchen, showing differently coloured kitchen cabinets. In the finished house the cupboards were indeed given different colours, devised in collaboration with the painter Lisbeth Andersen. At the opposite end of the living room is the closed sliding door to the studio.

perhaps have moved too far away from the prevailing notions about how a proper woman of her social class should behave, thereby contravening the accepted norms among many of those customers and clients who could help facilitate the professional success of Karen Clemmensen and the couple. At the same time, the house is an important reminder that many people – and especially women – lived and worked in detached houses built with the aid of government loans and incorporating a business component. Karen Clemmensen was only one among many women. There were a lot of architects in the area around Hundesømosen, but around this time every suburb in Denmark saw the construction of houses where women lived and ran independent businesses – not only as architects, but also as hairdressers and the like. During this period, the suburbs were by no means the empty commuter towns they have later been reviled as. Not only did many homemakers (especially women) stay home during the day, carrying out unpaid work in the houses: the houses were also workplaces – for both men and women – meaning that they were not empty during the day.

We are now left with the question of whether it was even possible to design one's way out of the workload and standards expected of relatively well-to-do middle-class families such as the Clemmensen family, standards which demanded much from the housewife. The answer is probably: no, or not entirely. Karen Clemmensen's own description of the many hours of tidying and cleaning ahead of the journalists' visits is a clear indication of this. A diary entry from the early 1950s supports this interpretation: here Karen Clemmensen describes how she worked late into the night on an assignment for their design studio and did not finish until four in the morning. The next morning at eight o'clock she was visiting a construction site to keep an eye on a project currently being realised, and at noon she went back to the design studio and continued to work until five o'clock in the afternoon. Then the family packed the car, and Karen Clemmensen took her two boys to Tibirke in North Zealand to visit family in a holiday cottage. Here we may imagine the children playing in the garden in the bright evening hours before going to bed late. Karen Clemmensen describes a quarrel with one of the children, who did not want to sleep in the so-called little kid's bed he had been assigned, and states that it was difficult to get them to sleep. She also could not find any matches, and since there was no electricity in the house, she describes sitting on the bed with her children in the dark, having a very late supper of bread and apples before falling into a deep sleep. Perhaps it is little wonder that the children described their parents as workhorses and were sometimes concerned about their health.[207]

The Clemmensens' house has a closed-off feel towards the road, while a large wall of windows opens it up towards the garden. The carefully thought-out connection between outdoors and indoors was typical of this period's architecture.

A picture accompanying an article about the house in the magazine *ALT for damerne*. Here it is made clear why Karen Clemmensen feels that having a hatch between living room and kitchen makes life easier for the family: she demonstrates how she can easily give her children a bite to eat.

Of course, we cannot know whether Karen Clemmensen – with or without Ebbe Clemmensen by her side – would have had an equally successful career as an architect if she had challenged the prevailing standards of what was required of a good housewife, or made other choices as regards making her home a showcase for her skills. Even if she had shown her home to the outside world as it looked on a random Thursday morning to the journalist of a women's magazine, it is by no means certain that this would have promoted women's equality or liberation. However, looking at Karen Clemmensen's architectural endeavours through a gender lens, specifically with regard to the house she designed for herself and her family together with Ebbe Clemmensen, love becomes a concept that can help complicate our understanding of what made Karen Clemmensen's situation simultaneously privileged and infused by inequality at the same time. We are speaking here of love between man and woman as well as love within the family, for one's children and for one's immediate surroundings, shaped by a woman who is architect, wife, mother and housewife. This special multifaceted role gives Karen Clemmensen a platform from which she could use her skills as an architect and designer to come up with fresh ideas and create a framework for an everyday life enriched by smart solutions and high, aesthetic standards. But it is also a demanding and complex role that strives to weave together some of the ethical, moral and practical dimensions of life within a particularly gendered design philosophy: one we can now discern in the spatial organisation and interior design of the house.

Karen Clemmensen's professional work points to a particular ethic regarding child-rearing and the issue of personal integrity and freedom: here, there is no need for a housewife constantly hovering in the background, readily to solve all everyday problems. Rather, that role has been shared out between Karen Clemmensen herself, other family members, paid help from outside and, not least, the house as a machine for living in, where every detail has been carefully thought out to free the woman from domestic work. Yet at the same time it is also clear that such a moral imperative clashes with Karen Clemmensen's ambitions as a designer, and that connecting the two worlds places great strain on her. There is a price to pay, one which is partly associated with her demanding working life and partly with the property itself as a financial yoke that weighs Karen Clemmensen down – meaning that it in turn holds a form of ownership over her, even as she is financially and legally a co-owner of the house.

So how free is Karen Clemmensen really? The freedom she enjoys as a woman and as an architect is tied up in property, ownership and a special moral outlook associated with the era's perception of order and propriety. To some extent, then, Karen Clemmensen is trapped in the persona we see in the weekly magazines, the one who apparently can do it all. When she makes sure to fix her lipstick and smile sweetly at the camera, this comes across as a carefully rehearsed role undertaken because it gives her the opportunity to compete for the commissions she wants as an architect. Her professional dedication is, then, a form of love that brings her value, a professional identity and financial gain, but it is also a love through which she loses something of herself – or perhaps we may say that Karen Clemmensen deposits something of herself in the material structure and organisation of the house, if the house can be seen as a machine for everyday life that must function smoothly, especially for her own sake. It tells us something about what was seen as the right way of life for a relatively well-off, well-educated family of architects in Denmark in the 1950s, and about the price and the many binds, especially for women, such a life came with despite

Despite its relatively modest size, the Hundesømosen area has a lush feel. Detached houses can be seen in between trees and bushes.

the many freedoms and new horizons opened up with the period's increased prosperity and the new way of life being created in the suburbs. In the case of Karen Clemmensen, we can see how ownership over things, over other people and over one's own life flow together in the house in ways that are not unequivocally good or bad for her. The couple owns the house, but the building also holds a form of ownership over them, and especially for the woman this entails a high degree of invisible housework in order to maintain their way of life. All this points to deep-seated structures that cause inequality and an all-too-familiar objectification of women, even as Karen Clemmensen's work and life are characterised by a high degree of personal integrity and self-esteem due to her ownership over her own professional identity. Not because her practice as an architect targeted problems that particularly concern women, but because it originates in her desire for parity between men, women and children in an environment where architecture, people and things work together to create the good life for the family and to make room for several different forms of love – of architecture, of nature, between spouses and of children, manifesting itself in an everyday way of life where neither the big city nor nature is far away.

The many houses that Rut Speyer built

Love is a complicated concept. From the ancient Greeks we learn that there are many different forms of love and that they are not just about romantic feelings but that they can also be found in friendships or family relationships, can be an obsession or reflect a special empathy for the outside world. All these forms of love are found in Karen and Ebbe Clemmensen's house. Work as a passion is a form of love that as such has nothing to do with romantic relationships or erotic feelings. It is, however, a love which – just like the romantic one – can lead to a feeling of being connected with something else, and which can make the self and the world bigger. Yet it can also be limiting, claustrophobic and controlling – a love which can hurt.[208] The following story about the architects Rut Speyer and Eigil Hartvig Rasmussen, who lived together as a couple and parents, as a divorced yet cohabiting couple, and who would, especially in their young years, work together on various assignments, can also give us insight into the relationship between architecture and love. Like the example of Karen Clemmensen's family home, the couple's own house

Rut Speyer met her future husband Eigil Hartvig Rasmussen at the School of Architecture, and they founded a design studio together. In 1946, the couple – together with Bodil and Gunnar Krohn and Torben Miland Petersen – were commissioned to design buildings for the refrigerator factory Atlas in Lyngby-Taarbæk Municipality. The buildings have since been demolished.

Rut Speyer on a trip to Southern Europe when she was quite young. Together with her friend Bodil Krohn, she also set out on a bicycle trip from Aarhus, where they had both attended technical school, all the way to Copenhagen with a detour via Gothenburg to look at modern architecture. This took place just before they both began their studies at the Royal Danish Academy of Fine Arts' School of Architecture.

Bodil Krohn (1915–1979) enrolled at the Aarhus Technical School in 1934 together with Rut Speyer; both graduated in 1937. That same summer, Krohn set out on a bicycle trip from Aarhus to Copenhagen, where she was due to begin her studies at the School of Architecture. The trip was made in the company of Speyer, and before arriving in Copenhagen they visited Gothenburg to view modern architecture. Krohn graduated in 1940, and from 1945 she ran a design studio with her husband Gunnar Krohn (1914–2005). In 1946, together with Gunnar Krohn, Torben Miland Petersen (1909–1994) and Eigil Hartvig Rasmussen, she won a design competition launched by the machine factory Atlas in Lundtofte, north of Copenhagen. The factory was built between 1948 and 1952; it has since been demolished. In the post-war years, Krohn gave numerous lectures on modern urban development. She designed several private properties with her husband.

can become a key to understanding the conditions for women in the architecture industry during the post-war period, when extensive suburbs mushroomed around the big cities.

Rut Speyer was born in Aarhus in 1914 and graduated from the Royal Danish Academy of Fine Arts' School of Architecture in Copenhagen in 1942. In 1938, while still a student, she married the architect Eigil Hartvig Rasmussen with whom she established a joint design studio in 1941.[209] This joint professional work lasted in its formalised form until 1950, when Rut Speyer set up a design studio in her own name. As is described in Chapter One, Rut Speyer also worked with Gytte Rue on kitchen studies during this period. From 1946, Eigil Hartvig Rasmussen had worked closely with the architect Gunnar Krohn, and they founded the firm Krohn & Hartvig Rasmussen, which would later become one of Denmark's largest architectural firms under the name KHR. Gunnar Krohn's wife, Bodil Krohn, was also an architect, and the two married couples had previously worked together. In 1959, Gunnar and Bodil Krohn divorced. Rut Speyer and Eigil Hartvig Rasmussen did the same – but not until 1979, and they continued their cohabitation after the divorce.

Long before these upheavals in the couples' professional and private stories, Rut Speyer and Eigil Hartvig Rasmussen collaborated on single-family houses and on larger projects alike. For example, in 1944 they took part in a competition to design Denmark's first high-rise buildings at Bellahøj in Copenhagen. In a newspaper article in *B.T.*, the journalist described Rut Speyer as a young woman, wife and architect, who worked together with her older spouse and their at that time regular collaborator Torben Miland Petersen (1909–1994, known as Torben Helge Miland from 1962 onwards).[210] The team came second, and the journalist described the entire competition as a victory for youth. Just like Rut Speyer, the two winning architects – Tage Nielsen (1914–1991) and Mogens Irming (1915–1993) – were around thirty years of age, and the journalist lavished praise on this group of visionary younger architects who were to bring fresh ideas and vitality to the industry. In the interview, reference is made to a telephone conversation in which Rut Speyer joyfully reports that their team has won DKK 4,000 and that they are proud to have beaten some of the older, well-known architects who also took part in the competition. At this point in the interview Eigil Hartvig Rasmussen enters the conversation and passes on some more serious facts about the architectural qualities of the project, concluding with a remark on how the collaboration between the three architects has been happy and that the prize money and the recognition has reassured them that all their hard work has not been in vain.[211]

In 1946, the couple – together with Bodil and Gunnar Krohn and Torben Miland Petersen – obtained another major commission, having won a design competition for a large refrigerator factory for the company Atlas in the Lyngby-Taarbæk Municipality.[212] The project is an example of the local authority's visionary urban planning at this time. The municipality's population was growing at a rapid pace, and as is evident from its 1949 disposition plan, there was plenty of building activity of great variety, encompassing industry, institutions, non-profit social housing and single-family houses – all while aiming to preserve the area's great natural beauty. At the time, the Lyngby-Taarbæk Municipality contained green areas extending from Lyngby Lake by the large city centre in the west to the stream Mølleådalen in Brede and finally the forest of Jægersborg Dyrehave to the east, close to where the Atlas factory would be built. Smaller urban centres were being planned around the old villages of Lundtofte, Hjortekær, Fortunen, Virum, Sorgenfri and Taarbæk, involving ambitious (and partially realised) plans for excellent logistics connecting them to the main retail centre in Kongens Lyngby.[213] Where there had previously been fields, forest and small-scale agriculture, various residential areas and industries now sprung up, including a neighbour for the Atlas factory in the form of the Technical University of Denmark, then known as the Polytechnic Institute or Danmarks Tekniske Højskole, as the institution came to be called when it was built on plains of Lundtoftesletten in 1962.[214]

The Atlas factory was a large, modern assembly-line factory with housing for workers placed adjacent to the main building, and in the 1950s around 2,000 people worked at the factory. Thus, the place where the couple also lives themselves is a very mixed and complex town that includes working-class neighbourhoods, social housing estates, roads lined with expensive properties as well as smaller detached houses, schools, industry, shopping centres and magnificent natural and cultivated landscapes.

The Atlas factory was placed close to where Rut Speyer and Eigil Hartvig Rasmussen had built their first family home in 1942, shortly before the couple's two daughters were born. Their home at Lundtoftevej 267 was a 114 square metre house with a small design studio on the ground floor, commanding a view of the site's steep slope sculpted by Ice Age glaciers. When Rut Speyer set up her own design studio in 1950, all while Eigil Hartvig Rasmussen was making huge headway as part of the architectural elite of the time, she spent the next few years designing several single-family houses in the area. In 1952, the couple moved to a new and larger house which they had designed together.

The plot was on the plateau behind the slope on which their first house had been built. This house stood at the end of the cul-de-sac Hjortekærbakken, created in 1950 at the northern end of the neighbourhood known as Hjortekær. At this time, the neighbourhood was being developed with many single-family houses on land that had previously held orchards, nurseries and small farms, adjoining the Jægersborg Dyrehave forest to the east and bounded by what was to become the Elsinore motorway in the west. But Rut Speyer and Eigil Hartvig Rasmussen had not simply bought a new plot of land and designed a new home for their family. From a local farmer, they had bought the entire field on which the L-shaped road, Hjortekærbakken, and its adjacent plots came to lie. As these subdivided plots were sold off, Rut Speyer in particular was kept busy designing several of the single-family houses in the road, just as the couple had created the design of the road itself.[215]

The Hjortekærbakken road is distinguished by having a row of birch trees which reinforce the sense of being in a green area close to a forest. In addition, the pavements consist of just a single row of tiles with grass on each side, and parking is provided in spaces along the edges of the road.[216] The single continuous row of houses from numbers 19 to 23 provide a particularly clear idea of the vision the couple had for the road. According to one of the couple's daughters, the design points to Eigil Hartvig Rasmussen's fondness for Italian cities, constituting an attempt to transplant the interconnected rows of houses and bright colours of those medieval towns to a cool Danish suburban setting.[217] The very gesture of developing an entire road not only points to the couple's willingness to take risks, but also to a desire to work on a larger scale and to create coherent green environments for people to live the good life in. Rut Speyer and Eigil Hartvig Rasmussen were architects who created buildings, not urban planners, and they had worked within a scene of progressive, left-wing architects engaged in social housing projects. Perhaps we can say that they took some of the ideas about community and life in green surroundings familiar from low-rise social housing and blocks of flats set amidst parklands and applied them to an area dominated by privately owned single-family houses, where, by virtue of the unifying design of the road, they create a whole. That opportunity was available to them due to their financial resources and willingness to invest, and it also helped pave the way for the couple – together or only Rut Speyer – being commissioned to design several of the houses on the road. With all this, they merge ideas of community and the importance of a safe and well-designed neighbourhood with the life led in their own house – a house in a residential street in the suburbs among neighbours who all belong to a relatively well-to-do middle class; families who can

Aerial photo of the Lyngby-Taarbæk Municipality from the early 1950s. To the left is a wheel track which would later become the steep part of the road Hjortekærbakken, an L-shaped road which turns left into the area shown here as a mixture of trees – perhaps an orchard – and fields. At this point in time, Hjortekær is clearly an agricultural area with small nurseries, fields, stables and farm buildings. If you follow the road towards the right in the picture, you arrive at one of the entrances to the Jægersborg Dyrehave forest.

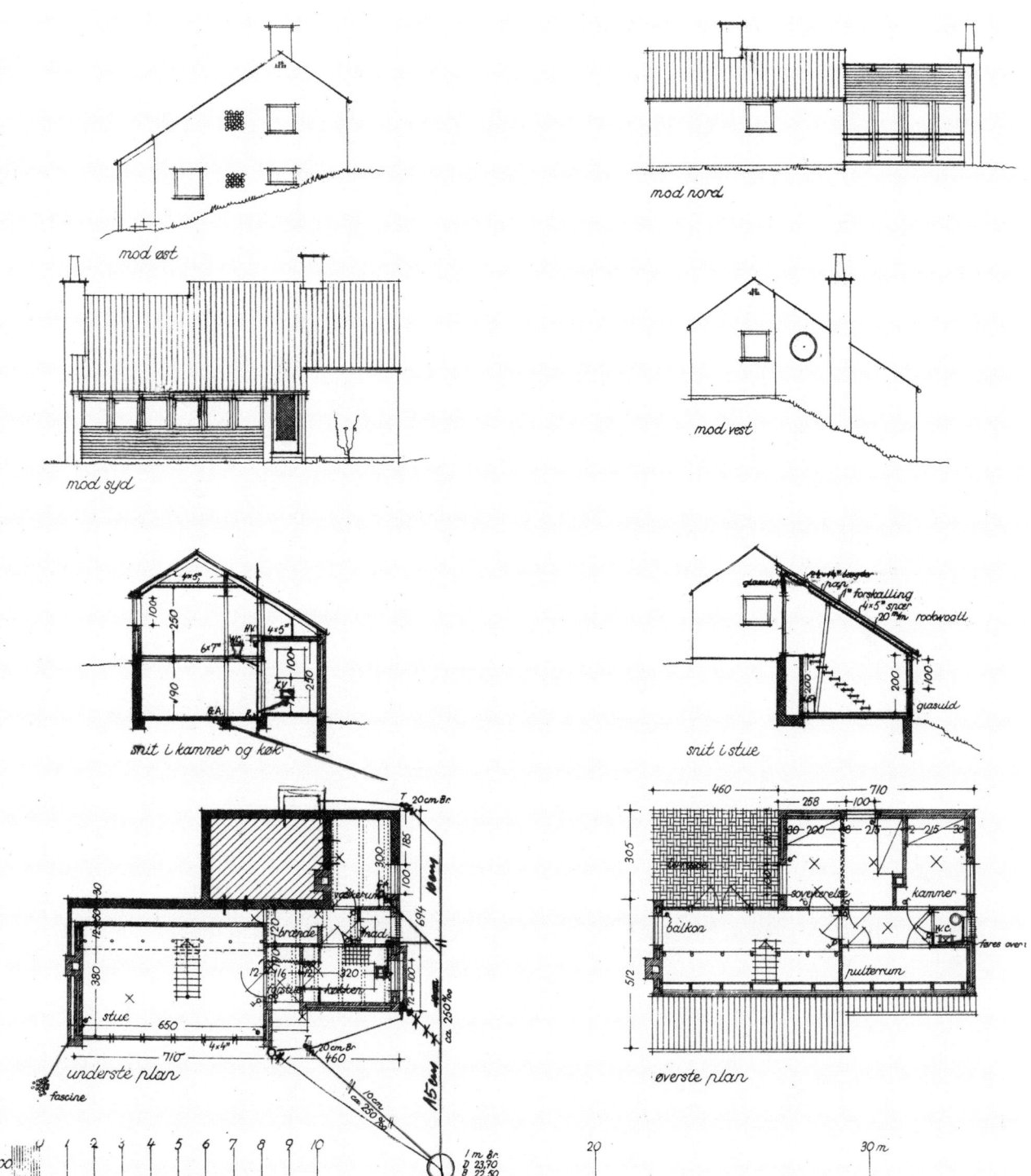

Rut Speyer and Eigil Hartvig Rasmussen designed several single-family houses, and like many other architect couples of the time they also designed their own residence. The first of their own homes was located on Lundtoftevej in Lyngby-Taarbæk Municipality on a steep building site. Completed in 1942, the house formed the setting for their family life and work for several years.

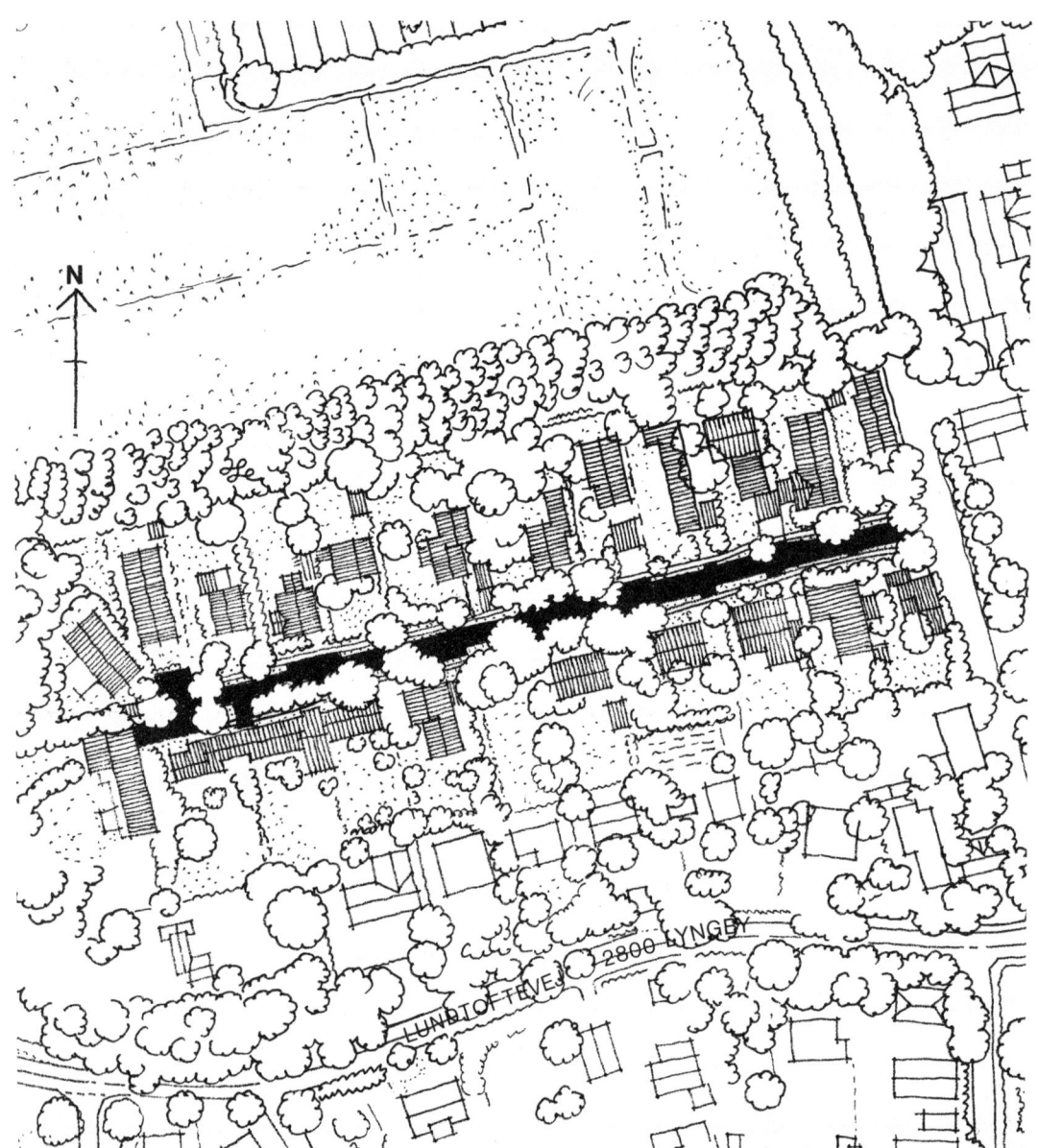

In 1952, Rut Speyer and Eigil Hartvig Rasmussen moved to their new house, which they had designed together, on Hjortekærbakken in Lyngby-Taarbæk Municipality. Having fallen in love with the place, they bought it from a local farmer and then subdivided the land into plots for single-family homes. Speyer designed several houses for the road. Their own house is at the end of the road, on the far left of the drawing. Their first property, built in 1942 on the slope north of Lundtoftevej, can be seen in the middle of the drawing.

The two architects bought the site at the end of Hjortekærbakken's cul-de-sac, where there were few neighbours. Their relatively large house formed a prominent end point to the road and encompassed a family home as well as their studio. The part of the façade facing the road as seen here is clad in wood painted black, while the left part and the rear are covered in horizontal bands of concrete plaster.

afford to buy and build an – often – architect-designed house in an attractive area close to Jægersborg Dyrehave. At the same time, the neighbourhood is located within a larger suburban context where different functions and community groups work and live within a short radius of each other.

The couple's own house on Hjortekærbakken was a large single-family house-cum-design studio, and it can still be seen at the end of the road through the row of birch trees – a monumental or at least significant end point to the road design. The house is 24 metres long facing the street, and the right-hand part is clad in black-painted wood, while the left part and the back are covered in concrete plaster applied in horizontal bands. On the garden side, the house has large, angled windows in the part designated as the design studio in the drawings; however, the space was reportedly in fact used as a living room.[218] At the rear of the house is a completely enclosed suntrap planted with trees, and no other houses are visible. The house is spacious, and despite its modern appearance and the modest materials used in its construction, it facilitates a bourgeois lifestyle with a live-in maid and also comprises a commercial section serving many different functions. The house has several entrances and staircases, ensuring that visitors to the design studio do not need to see the private sections of the house. Also, the maid has her own entrance. While Rut Speyer worked from the house at this time, Eigil Hartvig Rasmussen and Gunnar Krohn's firm had a large office elsewhere, comprising several departments.

The couple divorced in 1978 after forty years of marriage. Reportedly, Rut Speyer was unhappy that, as a married woman, she did not have the final say on her own tax returns, which were to be handled by the man within the patriarchal marriage structure of the time. In response, she divorced Eigil Hartvig Rasmussen – but they still lived together and remained a couple.[219] Speyer wanted financial independence, and the divorce should be seen in this light as a form of private-political feminist protest. However, the issue has made a considerable imprint on the biographies written about the couple: left unexplained, it arouses puzzlement within an otherwise logical course of life and overall narrative about a couple who lived out their calling as architects in different ways – together, separately and in collaboration with others. In 1980, at the age of seventy-four, Eigil Hartvig Rasmussen died as a result of a blood clot and in connection with a traffic accident on Hjortekærbakken.[220] After his death, Rut Speyer had no plans to leave Hjortekærbakken, but it was neither possible nor desirable for her to stay in the big house. The divorce had been a private protest against patriarchal economic structures, and it only constituted a break away from Eigil Hartvig Rasmussen in a strictly legal sense, not in their romantic relationship. However, his death prompted a division of the house and a subdivision of the plot, thereby making it possible to build a new house at the site.*

* In one of Rut Speyer's letters, she writes that she had to use all her abilities to get the municipal authorities to accept her idea of dividing up the land to make room for the new property.[221]

Rut Speyer built a new 112 square metre home for herself as a kind of extension of the existing house. She established a firewall some three metres inside the original 24 metre building, placing the entrance to her new house at that spot. The new house thus incorporated a small part of the old house, incorporating the entrance, utility room and a small study in the section that had previously been the couple's bedroom. In this way, she took part of the old house with her before it was sold on. Speyer stayed in her new house until shortly before her death in 2001.[222]

While largely unknown today, Rut Speyer was an important driving force in the suburban development of the Hjortekær district. She designed various types of buildings and infrastructure for the neighbourhood over five decades and, together with Eigil Hartvig Rasmussen, she invested in and established an entire environment around the Hjortekærbakken road.[223] Her own home was designed for a bourgeois way of life and to cater for the couple's independent business, while the neighbourhood as such and its style of architecture invited down-to-earth socialising across the often relatively small properties along either side of the road. Different and opposing threads thus intertwine in Speyer's life story: she was an architect who was both entrepreneur and investor, who lived a bourgeois lifestyle in a single-family house while socialist, modernist and feminist ideals infused her priorities and interests.[224] She and Eigil Hartvig Rasmussen were lovers, a married couple, divorcés and business partners, and perhaps they also competed against each other in their professional work. At any rate, they worked separately as well as together. When Eigil Hartvig Rasmussen and Gunnar Krohn joined forces, both of their spouses and former close collaborators were left out of the new company. And even though Eigil Hartvig Rasmussen and Rut Speyer can be said to have legally broken up with each other professionally and privately, given that their joint design studio and their marriage were both dissolved, they never left each other, and they stayed in the neighbourhood they had helped build from the ground up.

Love hurts

Discussions have often been heated in the world of architecture whenever the industry and its historians have looked for ways to describe the collective working style of the architect couples: a working style characterised by collaboration on creative processes between two individuals who work closely together while the same time engaging in a romantic relationship. One cause for controversy is the fact that it has been repeatedly seen that the man's story and deeds are primarily singled out for attention when their work is credited, described, assessed, rewarded and archived for the future. Just think of the group of Harvard students who, in 2013, tried in vain to have Denise Scott Brown's work count towards the Pritzker Prize awarded to Robert Venturi in 1991,[225] or of the exhibition *New Furniture Designed by Charles Eames* at MoMA in 1946, where Ray Eames's contribution was omitted.[226] We sense the contours of patriarchal hegemony in the industry itself and in architectural historiography, and the issue is not

After Eigil Hartvig Rasmussen's death, Rut Speyer wanted to stay at Hjortekærbakken, but the house was too big for her. She therefore subdivided the site, sold the large house and built a smaller house for herself. The new house was a kind of extension of the existing house, where the couple's former bedroom now became part of Speyer's new and somewhat smaller home. Part of the garden was also allotted to the new house.

just about the lack of recognition of women's work or how a range of special opportunities and limitations apply to women architects in the twentieth century, found in the mix of their professional and gender identity and in being both professionally and romantically involved with a partner. By focusing on the concept of love itself, we can consider whether there is something else at stake here, examining what it means for women's work and their self-understanding as architects when their creative work is undertaken in collaborative constellations between architects who are also couples in love. As we have touched on in this chapter, such collaborations have opened doors and opportunities for the women, but they have also entailed limitations. And they reveal much about the many collaborations that drive the architectural profession, and which turn out to be far more complex, interwoven and wide-ranging than is generally conveyed by the familiar narrative about the singular creative genius. By focusing on love and on the architects' own houses, we apply a different approach to the history of architecture and the architect's creative work that goes beyond regarding design as innovation created by dint of the sheer brilliance of specific individuals.

On a more structural level, and drawing on Eva Illouz's relational perception of love, we can point to love as a feeling that is made possible by and circulates in specific spaces, meaning that it also carries and contributes to creating and reinforcing structural inequalities. For Illouz, the relationship with the beloved brings increased value for the individual, but it also governs and conditions one's scope of possibilities and so entails various limitations – not least in light of the fact that love and passion in Western, capitalist society are organised around a binary and hierarchical understanding of gender.[227] Traditional feminist critiques of marriage as an institution growing out of capitalist forms of ownership teach us to understand and analyse the inequalities involved.[228] The house as property, ownership of things and ownership of the woman – of which Rut Speyer's protest divorce can be said to be an example – all also exist in our time. And in line with Illouz's interpretation, the readings presented in this chapter show how the home itself, as an architectural and spatial object, allows love, in its uplifting and restrictive forms, to play out between people, in relationships between people and things and between people and different passions or projects in which they engage. Our objective here has not been to search for the source of inequalities or injustices, but instead – by looking at couples who shared both romantic and professional love – to show how love itself is an organising force in society that has left an imprint on and is stimulated by the architecture that surrounds us.[229] Love, as a professional passion, helps to drive and produce creativity and transformation, a fact which, when focusing on

Rut Speyer in the garden behind the house on Hjortekærbakken, which she built for herself after Eigil Hartvig Rasmussen's death.

women in architecture as we do in this chapter, simultaneously works with and against their heteronormative and cisgender identities as parts of a relatively well-to-do upper middle class, all while offering a more nuanced understanding of what gender means to architecture. Striving to create both architecture and romantic passion can become restrictive, requires hard work and brings with it hurt, not least for women in a patriarchal society. However, both forms of love can also make the world bigger – they offer ways of approaching something outside oneself through complicated collaboration and a relationship with another person. This shows us that creating architecture also has to do with a particularly pronounced form of empathy for other people and the environment in which we live,[230] and it brings hope and opportunities for creating more reflected, caring and equitable creative practices for the architects of the future.

Chapter 3

Growth – Stories of a More Caring Approach to Urban Planning

It's a June day in 1967, at Hindsgavl Castle on Funen, and everything is carefully lined up for a pan-Nordic course on landscape management and planning in rural municipalities. Anne Marie Rubin, then widely acclaimed as one of Denmark's most experienced urban planners, is one of the keynote speakers, and her message is later reproduced in several newspapers: 'The frenzied, even panic-like expansion of the holiday home areas on our coasts has had unhappy, in some cases catastrophic consequences'.²³¹ Indeed, a great many holiday homes have been built as the nation has gradually recovered after the Second World War.* Anne Marie Rubin warns that if nothing is done, the holiday homes will 'consume'²³³ even more of Denmark's coastline, thereby taking up landscapes which ought to be accessible to the entire population regardless of income. Her conclusion, which must go down well with the many professionals present at Hindsgavl Castle on this June day, is that there is a dire need for urban planning to check and manage the developments.

Anne Marie Rubin is not alone in her concern. Three months before the conference at Hindsgavl, a car is on its way from Copenhagen to the small island of Nyord north of Møn. In it sit two young architects who, like Rubin, are concerned about the many new holiday homes and their impact on the coasts. One of them is design studio owner Vibeke Dalgas, who has brought along a young and freshly graduated member of her staff, architect Nina Rosenkjær, in order to help solve a completely new task – protecting the older buildings on Nyord and the unique landscape surrounding the small village on the island. There are plans to build 300 holiday homes on Nyord, and not all residents are pleased by the prospect of a stream of tourists every summer.

If one were to use a single word to sum up the Denmark in which the two urban planners we will follow in this chapter, Anne Marie Rubin and Vibeke Dalgas, worked and lived, that word would be growth. Never before had developments progressed so rapidly. From the beginning of the 1920s to the 1960s, the Danish population grew from just over 3 million to approximately 4.5 million.²³⁴ Policies on the organisation of the welfare society in Denmark were based on the ideas of the British economist John Maynard Keynes (1883–1946), which claim that continuous growth in the economy and in private consumption can create better conditions for everyone in society. The expectation was for developments to continue in the same manner and direction in the future, only faster. However, this logic of growth had begun to face criticism in discussions on economic issues, and in 1972 such criticism would manifest in the widely read report *The Limits to Growth*.²³⁵ Also, as we shall examine in this chapter, growth was not the only prevailing idea in 1960s' Danish urban planning.

In the 1960s, building activity in Denmark was higher than ever before. Extensive construction facilitated the rapid rise in population figures, consumption and the expected standard of living while in itself contributing to further growth. Denmark's built-up areas grew significantly in extent, scope and size.²³⁶ Planners and architects were

* It is estimated that by the end of the 1940s, Denmark had approximately 10,000 holiday homes. In 1966 that figure had risen to 100,000, and in 1974 it was 150,000.²³²

Anne Marie Rubin (1919–1993) completed her secondary school education at Holte Gymnasium, a secondary school north of Copenhagen, in 1936. She then worked as a mason's apprentice before being admitted to the School of Architecture at the Royal Danish Academy of Fine Arts in 1940. From 1943 to 1945, while a refugee in Sweden, she studied at the Kungliga Tekniska Högskolan (Royal Institute of Technology) in Stockholm and also worked at the Vattenbyggnadsbyrån –a design studio specialised in water towers, town planning and infrastructure. Graduating from the Royal Danish Academy of Fine Arts' School of Architecture in 1946, she went on to work at the Ministry of Housing until 1954, when she established a design studio in her own name with a succession of partners. The studio created town plans for a large number of municipalities throughout Denmark and had offices in Copenhagen and Herning. Rubin was an active voice in social debates, sat on several committees and was chairman of the Akademiraadet (The Academy Council which advises the Danish state on questions concerning art and architecture) from 1984 to 1987. Between 1968 and 1971 she was professor of urban planning at Nordplan in Stockholm and from 1974 at Aalborg University.

Frem med planerne
Foredrag holdt den 12. november 1965 på Øresundsrådets fritidskonference
Af arkitekt Anne Marie Rubin, DAL

In the 1960s, architect and urban planner Anne Marie Rubin gave several lectures in which she described the rapid construction of holiday homes along the coasts of Denmark as a growing problem, even calling them prospective slums and a cancer on the coasts. Here she appears at a conference on landscape development on both sides of the Sound where she, being one of the main speakers, highlighted the need for spatial planning in Denmark and in Sweden. To her right stands Hans Sølvhøj, director general of the Danish broadcasting corporation, and to the far right is Urban Hansen, Lord Mayor of Copenhagen. The man to her left may be the Swedish Minister of Agriculture, Eric Holmqvist, who was present at the conference, while the man on the far left has not been identified.

central players in this building boom and in the large urban expansions, and the discussions taking place among the professions were predominantly about planning new structures for the future, rather than about preserving, continuing and building on what was already there. One example of such an outlook on planning can be found in the writings of landscape architect Ole Nørgaard (1925–1978), who was one of the key planners in the urbanisation of the former agricultural landscape in Copenhagen's western region as directed by the regional plan for the Copenhagen region, known as *Fingerplanen* (literally 'The Finger Plan', also known as 'The Five Finger Plan'). In an article from 1969, he describes the decisive values underpinning the construction of one of the largest urban development projects in Denmark in the 1960s, namely in Albertslund, west of Copenhagen:

'Today, new urban areas are formed according to decisions based on a theoretical background: Copenhagen must be expanded along radial S-train lines, and the existing stations in Glostrup and Tåstrup are spaced sufficiently far apart for a new station to be placed in between them. This station must have a catchment area, and so we need to develop a new urban area in this particular spot. In the case of Albertslund, the landscape at the chosen spot was quite uninteresting […] – flat and dull.'[237]

Nørgaard's description presents urban development as a process that focuses on creating new cities and transport options for modern life in modern society, but which apparently has no interest in closely reading the local conditions, ecologies and historical structures, except by rejecting any notion that they might be of value for the city of the future.* However, there are important nuances which can be unpacked in that story. The planning of Albertslund in the 1960s also focused on preservation and on adapting the developments to existing qualities in the local agricultural landscape, for example the older villages and the course of the Store Vejleå river, which became the determining factor for the design of a large new park system.[239]

* However, later studies have shown that in Nørgaard's work on the landscape and town of Albertslund, account has been taken of certain historical conditions such as water, topography and more.[238]

Such nuances are not always visible in the available literature on architecture and planning from the period. For example, Arne Gaardmand's (1926–2008) acclaimed and widely read book *Dansk byplanlægning 1938–1992* mainly describes the 1960s by reporting on the development of new large urban plans and residential areas built by means of prefabricated modules.[240] In this chapter we take a closer look at examples of women's work in planning which challenged the one-sided focus on development and growth in architecture and planning in the 1960s. These examples show that the sharply delineated modern view of architecture which focuses entirely on the future and overlooks the importance of existing values was also up for debate in the middle of the century. During the period of great growth that gained momentum in the late 1950s and continued in the 1960s, one could also find planners who were concerned with combining development with conservation. They worked to preserve, continue and strengthen the existing characteristics of places – whether these mainly concerned historical, architectural, landscape-related or social qualities. We see this in professional circles working with conservation, where the 1960s saw a movement towards greater interest in large-scale perspectives and urban planning.[241] And we see

Much of the literature on urban planning in Denmark focuses on how architects envisioned new built structures for the future. Indeed, such issues were central when, in 1969, the landscape architect Ole Nørgaard stated that the landscape in Albertslund was uninteresting, and that the planning of the large modern urban areas thus took place on raw, flat land. However, closer inspection reveals that, in several cases, the planning undertaken maintained a keener focus on existing elements than we are often told. The picture shows how the placing of new modern residences in Albertslund takes into account the buildings and landscape of the older village of Vridsløselille.

The rapid overall rise in prosperity in 1960s' Denmark left visible traces in the form of new holiday homes emerging along the coasts. The number of holiday homes such as the one seen here increased with near-explosive force, prompting Anne Marie Rubin to warn against this trend which she, like other architects, believed would destroy the landscape and prevent public access to the beaches. The aerial photograph shows holiday homes and other buildings near Blokhus Strand in North Jutland, 1972.

this among urban planners such as Anne Marie Rubin and Vibeke Dalgas, whose work we will focus on in this chapter. Thinking of urban planning as continuations of what is there, as management, conservation work and as creating new connections and contexts in existing environments is particularly relevant today, where there is growing recognition of the importance of considering the biodiversity crisis and climate crisis within the construction industry – and greater awareness of the fact that there are limits to human growth and resource consumption.[242] The resource-intensive planning model employed by growth society, which involves building on a large scale to improve conditions for people, but which has devastating consequences for existing eco-systems, is not sustainable.

Each in their own way, Anne Marie Rubin and Vibeke Dalgas worked to develop methods capable of curbing the negative impacts of society's rapid growth and of strengthening the focus on incorporating valuable traits of existing urban and landscape settings in the work done by architects and planners. Their plans, analyses, articles and lectures have left an important imprint on the way Denmark looks today, and also on the way urban planners work. Even so, their work is only sparsely covered in the existing literature. A better understanding of their methods and positions, as well as of the imprint they have made on specific landscapes and cities, will provide a more accurate and nuanced understanding of the period, which in itself renders us better equipped for our future work with the vast physical legacy left behind by the massive construction activity of the post-war years.

The feminist thinker Joan C. Tronto's ethics of care can help us find a more caring way of acting in relation to the physical environment. She writes that in our present day, it is necessary to develop an understanding of architecture which is not focused on bringing new, beautiful objects into the world, but which 'is sensitive to the values of repair, of preservation, of maintaining all forms of life and the planet itself'.[243] According to Tronto, developing such new and alternative practices requires us to be aware of the 'life-sustaining web'[244] in which we are all inextricably spun, and through which all humans and other living beings are connected. The efforts to develop a more caring architecture, as advocated here, will benefit from an expanded and more nuanced understanding of how others have worked in the past, as well as from tracing some of the previous intimations of precisely such an outlook. Anne Marie Rubin and Vibeke Dalgas are examples of how, even during the modernist building boom, there were voices who criticised the rapid growth and not least the consequences of such growth for existing cities, landscapes and local environments. To understand these positions, we will here follow the work done by the two women and examine the life circumstances and chance occurrences that led to them both playing significant roles in the development of urban planning as a professional field in Denmark through the 1950s and 1960s. Next, we will learn about examples of planning works where their critical position becomes clear. And we will see them encounter one of the great challenges of the era, namely the demand for a rapid and extensive expansion of holiday home districts in local communities along the coasts of Denmark in the 1960s. Here they come up with different and yet comparable answers to the question of how best to work on the basis of what is already there – and how to balance development and conservation.

The road to becoming a key town planner

Anne Marie Rubin was born as the eldest daughter in a well-educated middle-class family. Her father was the renowned professor of psychology Edgar Rubin (1886–1951), and her mother, Hedevig Elisabeth Marie Thiesen (1891–1965), was a homemaker and in charge of the parties and gatherings arranged for the many well-educated personalities who visited their home. Discussions about science and culture were a pivotal feature of life in the family, which moved from a flat in Copenhagen to a villa in the affluent suburban area around the commercial centre of Holte north of Copenhagen in 1933. The Rubin family's Jewish background did not play any significant role in terms of either religious or cultural influence in the upbringing of the three daughters. However, as was the case for so many others, their background would suddenly take on fateful importance for the family during the Nazi occupation of Denmark, forcing them to flee to Sweden in 1943.[245]

Having enrolled at the Royal Danish Academy of Fine Arts' School of Architecture in Copenhagen in 1940, Anne Marie Rubin had to interrupt her studies when she fled Denmark. The fact that she came from a home with financial resources and a strong belief in education was probably a factor when, at the age of twenty-four, she left the rest of the family, who were in exile in Lund, to move to Stockholm with one of her sisters. Here she attended classes at the Royal Institute of Technology, where she studied until the end of the war in 1945, becoming part of a vibrant, cultural expat scene in Sweden which

Previously, only the wealthiest Danes had the money and time to take a seaside holiday, but the Holiday Act of 1938 and the growing general prosperity made it possible for a much larger part of the population to either rent holiday cottages or build their own. Here we see a summer day at Blåvand in 1961 – one of the areas along the West Jutland coast where tourists flocked every summer.

included many architects.[246] Alongside her studies, Anne Marie Rubin found work at Vattenbyggnadsbyrån – Sweden's largest design studio within the field of non-governmental hydropower plants.[247] The company specialised in water towers and infrastructure associated with water, and it had a town planning department. This would prove fortuitous: in the years after the war, town/urban planning would become a rapidly growing, but under-staffed, discipline in Denmark.[248] Since 1938, the adoption of a new Town Planning Act meant that all towns with more than 1,000 inhabitants were legally required to prepare so-called disposition plans,* but urban planning was not yet a prominent discipline on the curriculum of the Art Academy's School of Architecture.[250]

* According to the Town Planning Act, all towns with more than 1,000 inhabitants were obliged to draw up a town plan within five years of the Act coming into force. The town plan then had to be submitted for approval by the Ministry of the Interior and subsequently registered on all affected properties. However, due to the Second World War, several cities were delayed in their work on the plans.[249]

After the end of the war, Anne Marie Rubin resumed her studies at the Art Academy's School of Architecture, where she was one of four women among the seventy-nine students who graduated in 1946.[251] Her knowhow and the experience she had acquired in Sweden quickly made her a highly sought-after professional. As she wrote:

'During my time as a refugee in Sweden, I had the opportunity to specifically study urban planning issues, and it interested me so much that I continued to do so when we were able to return home. I discovered that very few people in this country were working with those particular problems.'[252]

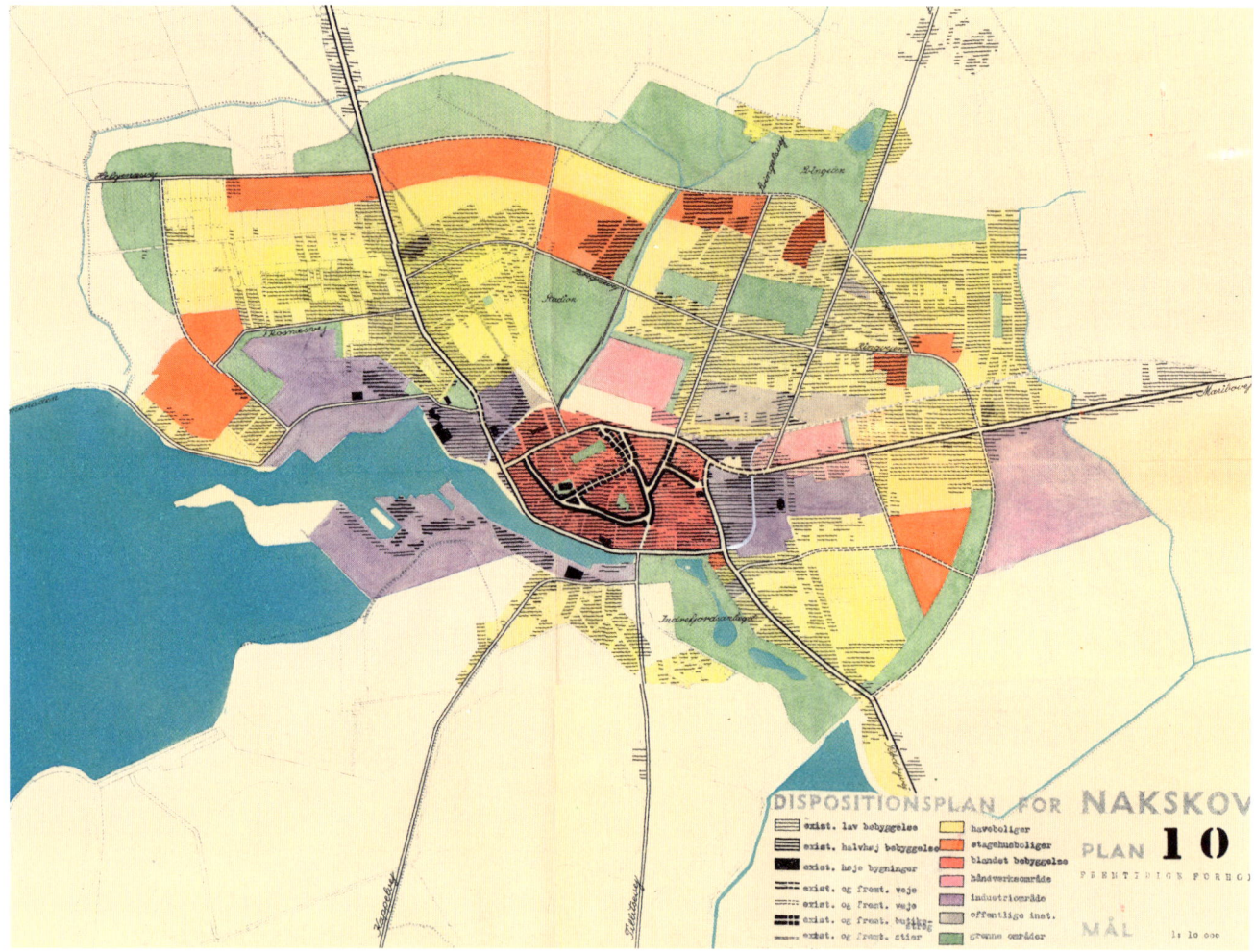

The town of Nakskov was quick to submit its statutory outline plan to the Danish Ministry of the Interior, but the state authorities rejected the plan and recommended that the town hire an urban planning consultant. In 1958, Anne Marie Rubin presented a new plan. This would later serve as an example of how to draw up an urban plan in which some of the older houses and roads were preserved while at the same time adding a new bypass, thus making room for the many new cars.

In 1949, she began working at the barely two-year-old Ministry of Housing's department for town planning matters, or, as it was called, with the 'commissioner for town planning matters' – often simply known as 'den kommitterede' / 'the commissioner', meaning the highest ranking official within the field.[253] Here her duties were commenting on, qualifying and approving the municipal authorities' many new disposition plans. These plans represented a major planning task that involved recording existing conditions as well as prescribing future developments to the physical setting. The majority of the municipalities did not yet have their own planning staff in the years after the war, so the involvement of 'the commissioner' was seen as particularly important.[254] Rubin thus took on a central role in the approval of town plans in several municipalities. Concurrently with her regular work, she also began to prepare a few town plans in a consulting capacity, for example for the Varde Municipality in Western Jutland.[255] Based on her experience and with a keen eye for the growing need for urban planning advice for the municipalities, she set up her own design studio in 1954. Here she worked with a succession of partners and employees, although the public most often referred to it as Anne Marie Rubin's design studio or simply as Anne Marie Rubin.[256]

Anne Marie Rubin quickly became an important player in Danish urban planning, and from the beginning of the 1960s onwards she was publicly known as a professional with solid experience.[257] One of the many cases which landed on the desk of the Ministry of Housing's commissioner for town planning while she worked there was a disposition plan for Nakskov – a town on the island of Lolland. Drawn up by the municipality's own urban engineer in 1942, the plan was initially almost exclusively a road plan.[258] 'The commissioner' rejected the plan and asked the municipality to bring in an urban planning consultant.[259] Soon afterwards, Rubin, who already knew the area from previous processing at 'the commissioner's' department, was asked to review and transform the plan at her own design studio in collaboration with the municipality and with the traffic planner and civil engineer Anders Nyvig (1914–1986) as a consultant.[260]

The disposition plan for Nakskov would be the first of its kind in Denmark. It dealt with issues that many other enterprising market towns in Denmark faced at the start of the 1960s. Across the nation, towns and cities seemed to vie with each other to see who could, in the shortest time possible, transform the town centres with older houses into a modern city that met the era's demands for large supermarkets, plenty of retail trade and parking for the growing number of cars. In several places, this prompted the demolition of older houses worthy of preservation, and entire neighbourhoods disappeared.* The disposition plan for Nakskov responded to the expected growing number of cars which would put great pressure on parking in the historic centre. The distinctive feature of Nakskov's plan was that it protected the old streets and squares against large parking areas and major roads.[262] Instead, the approach roads to the city were connected by a new circulation street giving access to new parking spaces, from which you could walk to the shops and other destinations. The disposition plan was based on a thorough analysis of the existing conditions and

---

* For example, parts of the neighbourhood around Borgergade-Adelgade in central Copenhagen were demolished from 1942, and after the Second World War the rest of the houses in the historic district disappeared.[261]

urban areas, and it became the basis for the decision to preserve the main pedestrian shopping street and the harbour with its old warehouses. The plan for Nakskov became a model for the many other municipalities which also had to develop disposition plans in the years that followed, and it was often highlighted as a good example in lectures and on courses including the City Planning course taught at the Art Academy's School of Architecture.[263]

In the years that followed, Rubin worked on a steady succession of such disposition plans, and as a journalist wrote in 1968, she received commissions from all over Denmark: 'The tracks lead through Herning and Sakskøbing, Korsør and Nykøbing M. and out into the open country on the west coast and in North Zealand'.[264] Herning Municipality in particular became a close collaboration partner: her design studio prepared plans for Herning for almost two decades, and for a long period it had a separate branch there.* Concurrently with her urban planning work, Rubin taught at the Art Academy's School of Architecture for a few years, and in 1968 she was appointed professor at a new Nordic planning programme, Nordiska institutet för samhällsplanering in Stockholm. In 1974, she took the chair as professor of community planning at the new Aalborg University Centre, where she joined several fellow professionals in building the university's architecture and planning programme.[266]

* Anne Marie Rubin's studio was a consultant for the Municipality of Herning from 1959 to 1988.[265]

The holiday homes are coming – and the town planners respond

With the adoption of the Holiday Act in 1938, all workers in Denmark were guaranteed two weeks' paid holiday.[267] Large sections of the population now began to enjoy their newfound leisure time on the coasts, which had become a popular holiday destination among the affluent upper class back in the eighteenth century.[268] The growing economic prosperity gave a significantly larger part of the population the opportunity to either buy or build holiday homes, including working families and others with lower incomes. In a relatively short time after the Second World War, the number of holiday homes in Denmark grew at unprecedented rates. In some places they were laid out together as part of a total development, but often they were simply placed where it happened to suit the individual family best, where it was possible to subdivide plots, or where it seemed expedient for other reasons. Subdivisions of agricultural land for holiday home

In 1951, Anne Marie Rubin was the first woman architect to receive the Royal Danish Academy of Fine Arts' minor gold medal. She was awarded the medal for a project on the island of Mors: the design of a mining town where the town plan and buildings were all adapted to the existing landscape.

areas all over the country created opportunities for quick incomes for landowners who owned properties in areas where urban growth had passed them by as well as for many others involved in the real estate trade. As some critical voices observed, such subdivisions could be 'an easy way out for resolving everyday structural problems'.[269]

The new holiday homes sprang up along coasts all over the country: on the west coast of Jutland, on Funen, on Zealand and not least on Lolland, Falster and several of the smaller islands in the region. Many saw the process as a competition where the object was to snatch up the good views and the good plots before others did, and in the early 1960s one could, quite tellingly, read the following advertisement in *Berlingske Tidende*: 'Last chance to buy one of the few remaining much-coveted beach plots along Denmark's beautiful coasts! Simply get in your car and drive out onto the A1 highway. After 40 minutes of driving, you will come to a sign pointing to our sales office'.[270]

In 1967, Anne Marie Rubin notes that no less than 100,000 holiday homes have already been built in Denmark and, believing that growth will continue to accelerate if unimpeded, she estimates that in the next thirteen years leading up to 1980, the nation will see a fourfold increase in the number of holiday homes.[271] In the 1960s, she gives several lectures like the one at Hindsgavl Castle and writes articles in which she argues, in a polemical tone, that the development of holiday homes in Denmark should be regulated.[272] In a widely published lecture given at a conference for town planners in the Øresund region in 1965, she uses an expression familiar to her from the discussion in Britain, calling the many new holiday homes 'the cancer of our coast'.[273] Several other voices in society were also critical of the development, including architect and professor Kaj Gottlob (1887–1976), who wrote in 1970 that 'the West Coast is being destroyed by holiday homes'.[274]

Building on beaches had been forbidden in Denmark since 1937. A revision of the Nature Conservation Act from 1917, in which the Social Democratic Prime Minister Thorvald Stauning (1873–1942) is said to have been particularly keenly interested, stated that no construction was allowed within 100 metres of the beach.[275] However, many failed to comply with this provision, and conservationists wanted to extend the 100-metre line. The Danish Nature Conservation Act has historically been driven by a dual – and in practice at times conflicting – ambition to preserve natural values on the one hand and to make natural areas accessible to the public on the other.[276] In the discussions about the holiday home boom in the 1950s and 1960s, one of the key questions was how the coasts could be preserved as a public space accessible to all citizens of the welfare state. Another key concern was to preserve aesthetic values in the coastal landscapes, which meant that holiday homes were regarded as a problem in some circles. Conversely, one may also see the rise in holiday homes as a process of democratisation that made it possible for people from different walks of life to enjoy their own holiday resort.

Anne Marie Rubin did not believe that nature conservation measures in themselves were the answer to the growth scenario in which Danish society found itself.[277] Instead, she called for planning that could combine conservation and development. And, being a planner herself, she wanted professionals in control of the development. 'At the moment, no one is really equal to the task of managing it [the holiday home boom], so one is very happy to be brought into the picture,'[278] she said in 1959, two decades before the adoption of a new Town and Country Zoning Act that would give Danish authorities greater control over zoning and the subdivision of plots in rural areas.[279]

Onsdag 2. august 1967 — AKTUELT

De allerfleste af de områder i Nordsjælland, der for tiden udvikler sig som sommerhusområder, vil om nogle år blive inddraget til helårsbeboelse

Sommerlandet som storby-slum?

Der tages alt for lidt hensyn til, at disse områder skal være fremtidens forstæder med helårsbeboelse, siger kendt arkitekt – Her har vi orden i tingene, siger sognerådsformanden i Vejby-Tibirke, der har 2419 indbyggere – men 30.000 sommergæster

Er vi ved at skabe nye slumkvarterer ved vore kyster? Eksperterne har peget på en uheldig udvikling på en række områder, og hele problemet vil i aften blive gjort til genstand for en reportage i fjernsynet.

– Slum kan være flere ting, men vi er ved at gøre mange af de fejl, der er begået på Nørrebro og Vesterbro, om på en ny måde, sagde arkitekt Anne Marie Rubin til AKTUELT.

– Hus forbi her! sagde sognerådsformand Niels Peter Nielsen, Vejby-Tibirke, en af de kommuner i Nordsjælland, der for tiden har mangedoblet indbyggertallet som følge af sommergæsterne.

– Vi må gøre os klart, at problemerne ved vore kyster ikke kan være et anliggende blot for den pågældende kommune, siger afdelingsarkitekt Hugo Marcussen fra boligministeriet. Vore kyster, navnlig den jyske vestkyst, skal være rekreativt område for befolkningen i store dele af Europa. Med de seneste lovgivningsbestemmelser – navnlig landsbyggeloven – må vi have mulighed for at bringe udviklingen ind i faste rammer.

I sommerlandet
– hele året

Anne Marie Rubin har selv stået for planlægning af store sommerhusområder, bl.a. 2-3000 grunde ved Lollands sydkyst.

– Der var sket alt for meget i sommerlandet, før der for alvor blev plan i udviklingen, sagde arkitekten i sin udtalelse til AKTUELT. Vi må se hen til, at de allerfleste af de områder i Nordsjælland, der for tiden udvikler sig som sommerhusområder, om nogle år vil blive inddraget til helårsbeboelse. Når sådan noget sker, vil en sådan bydannelse på mange måder være tilbagestående og uden mulighed for at skabe alle de faciliteter, der ellers anses for nødvendig i et moderne bysamfund.

Jeg tænker på den måde, man spreder bebyggelsen ud over landskabet med mange små ensartede parceller, der ikke tager hensyn til menneskers forskelligartede behov og ikke engang står på højde med de forstæder, der nu under navn af soveby udvikler sig i Københavns nære opland. Udviklingen vil blot betyde, at forstæderne rykker så langt ud som de kan komme, og der vil for alvor blive tale om sovebyer, for folk har ikke mulighed for at foretage sig stort andet.

– I hvilken retning må bestræbelserne først og fremmest gå?

– Man bør navnlig sørge for, at der fortsat er landskaber ved kysten, der holdes fri for bebyggelse. Skal sommerlandets boligområder udvides, må det ske i baglandet. Men først og fremmest bør man tænke på, at disse områder i mange tilfælde vil udvikle sig som storbyforstæder og skal rumme mange tusinde helårsbeboere.

Byen skal dække disse menneskers behov for sociale, kulturelle og andre institutioner. Og det bør tages i betragtning allerede i dag ved den planlægning, der er i gang. Ellers vil de boligområder, der er under udvikling, slet ikke komme til at stå på højde med den boligstandard, der ellers hersker til den tid.

– Jeg må bestemt afvise, at man i vort område kan tale om slumkvarterer, siger sognerådsformand Niels Peter Nielsen, Vejby-Tibirke, en af de kommuner i sommerlandet, der har den største invasion for tiden. Der er lagt en meget nøje plan for udviklingen, og de huse, der bygges, er af en betydelig standard – og sanitære installationer og lignende bliver meget nøje overholdt.

Kommunens folketal er pr. 1. juli 2419 – men antallet af sommerbeboere drejer sig om mellem 25.000 og 30.000.

– Har sommergæsterne skabt en udvikling, som det kan være svært at følge med i.

– Vi har i alle tilfælde haft tid til at forberede den, siger sognerådsformanden. Vi har haft sommerbeboere her siden 1894, og vi har københavnergæster, som har fejret 60 års jubilæum hos os.

Store problemer

Alle bestræbelser går i alle tilfælde ud på, at der kommer ordnede tilstande i den meget betydelige udvikling, der er i gang i sommerlandet, siger afdelingsarkitekt Hugo Marcussen, boligministeriets kommitterede i byplansager. Der er i løbet af få år gjort et meget betydeligt indhug i områderne navnlig ved de sjællandske kyster, men lovgivningen, ikke mindst den nye landsbyggelov, har givet myndighederne mulighed for en fornuftig regulering. At de relativt små kommuner, der pludselig har fået den store invasion, har fået betydelige problemer at kæmpe med, er givet, men i de gældende retningslinjer er der taget skyldigt hensyn til både de økonomiske og tekniske problemer.
-mail

TO DAGES NORDISK DRØFTELSE

Den nordiske økonomiske politik efter Norges og Sveriges ansøgninger om optagelse i fællesmarkedet samt den fremtidige organisation af fællesnordiske U-landsprojekter er emnerne for Nordisk Råds økonomiske udvalgs møde i København fredag d. 11. og lørdag d. 12. august. Rådet har i øvrigt modtaget et forslag om et nordisk samarbejde på det skattevidenskabelige område fra folketingsmændene Henry Christensen (V) og Jørgen Jensen (K) samt den finske rigsdagsmand Joha Rihtniemi. Forslaget sigter direkte på oprettelsen af et nordisk skattevidenskabeligt forskningsråd med sekretariat til at varetage kontakten mellem nordiske skatteforskere og udenlandske skattevidenskabelige organisationer.

Den store invasion har givet de relativt små kommuner betydelige problemer at kæmpe med

The 1960s was a period of economic growth in Denmark, and the increasing prosperity prompted the construction of many new holiday homes close to the water. The development was addressed in numerous newspaper columns and features, making it clear that not everyone was equally enthusiastic about this expansion and its impact on the coasts. Anne Marie Rubin, described in this newspaper clipping as a 'well-known architect', was a prominent voice in the debate: she warned that the rapid expansion showed such a dire lack of planning that the new holiday home areas would decline into slums in the future.

Lolland: an island poised between growth and preservation

Anne Marie Rubin used planning as a management tool while working with specific projects all over the country.* The most comprehensive of all was the plan for Lolland's south coast. Here, in 1964, she prepared a unified and coherent holiday home plan together with her employee and later design studio partner, architect Ole Gerstrøm (1934–2009).[280] Known locally to this day as 'the Rubin Plan', it was the result of a new form of regional cooperation between nine parishes, meaning that it has certain traits in common with the more widely known 'Finger Plan', which was also a regional plan (1947). The plan for the coast of southern Lolland extends across 40 kilometres from the Albuen peninsula in the north-east down to Hyllekrog near the town Rødby in the south. The local county council launched the initiative for regional cooperation and prepared a preliminary outline. The council then contacted Rubin's design studio to have a cohesive development plan drawn up.

The low-lying coastal stretch on the south coast of Lolland had historically been used as summer pastures, but the area had been increasingly cultivated in connection with the agricultural reforms in the nineteenth century.[281] As a result, the area had several farms surrounded by corn and beet fields, lined by the poplars so characteristic of Lolland. The year 1872 was a landmark one for the area. A large storm surge hit the coast, and the water rose to over three metres above its usual level, causing extensive damage. The locals subsequently joined forces to build a dyke to secure the low-lying areas. As part of the dyke project, an entire fjord, Rødby Fjord, was drained – an undertaking that spanned decades, and which was completed with the construction of several drainage channels in the area by the former fishing village of Kramnitze, which became home to one of the largest pumping stations in Northern Europe. This newly dry area, which was not very suitable for agriculture, was among the sites where several holiday homes had been built in the middle of the twentieth century. In 1964, Anne Marie Rubin and Ole Gerstrøm counted a total of 620 holiday homes in the area, some of which adhered to current planning regulations while others were illegally built.[282]

* Examples include Vejby Strand, North Zealand, Husby Strand and the West Coast.

Vejby Strand in north Zealand is one of the first holiday home developments for which Anne Marie Rubin carried out the planning. She did so in 1958 together with architect Claus Bremer. The plan places the holiday homes in the low-lying areas, allowing the green and the landscape with its views towards the horizon and the sky to take centre stage.

* The zoning plan was prepared by Maribo Country. The inspection trips were undertaken on 12 February 1964 and 4–7 May 1964.[286]

The number of holiday homes in the areas was expected to rise, partly because more local residents from Lolland wanted to own one, and partly because of the hopes of attracting tourists from what was then West Germany.[283] The purpose of the plan was to oversee a controlled development to ensure that the area remained attractive, partly by ensuring that there would still be open spaces accessible to the general public despite the development of new holiday homes.[284] The issue of publicly accessible areas was central for Anne Marie Rubin, who stressed the importance of ensuring that the recreational value of the coast should not be 'reserved for those who came first'[285] – that is to say, privatised by the construction of holiday homes – but should be a common good for all, regardless of income.

More than anything, however, her argument seems to be an aesthetic one: future developments were to uphold and continue the qualities of the local landscape. To this end, it was essential to make a comprehensive analysis of the existing landscape, which Rubin and Gerstrøm did by studying maps and existing planning regulations and documents as well as by undertaking two study trips to the area. Here they went on long walks to 'reconnoitre' the south coast in the light of a more general zoning plan which was already available.* The following year Rubin appeared on a national television broadcast dedicated to the plan for Lolland's south coast, explaining what the two gleaned from their trips:

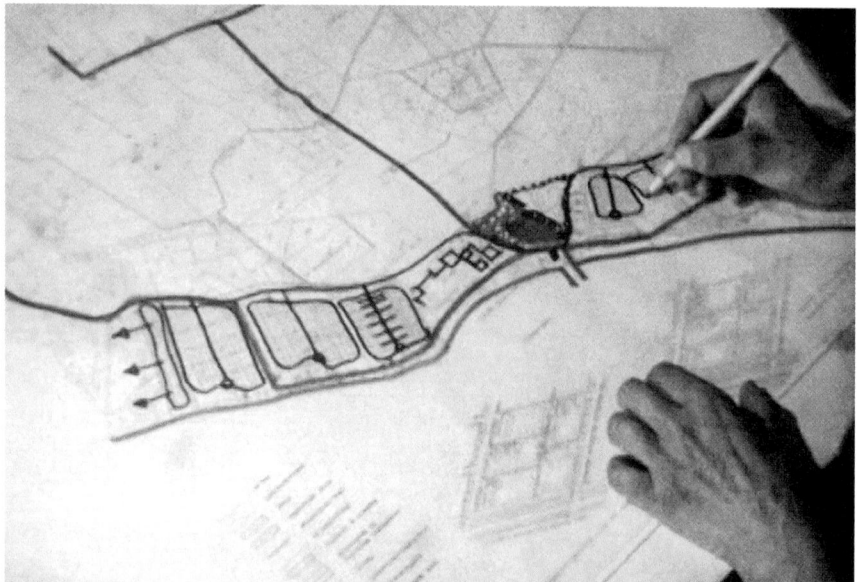

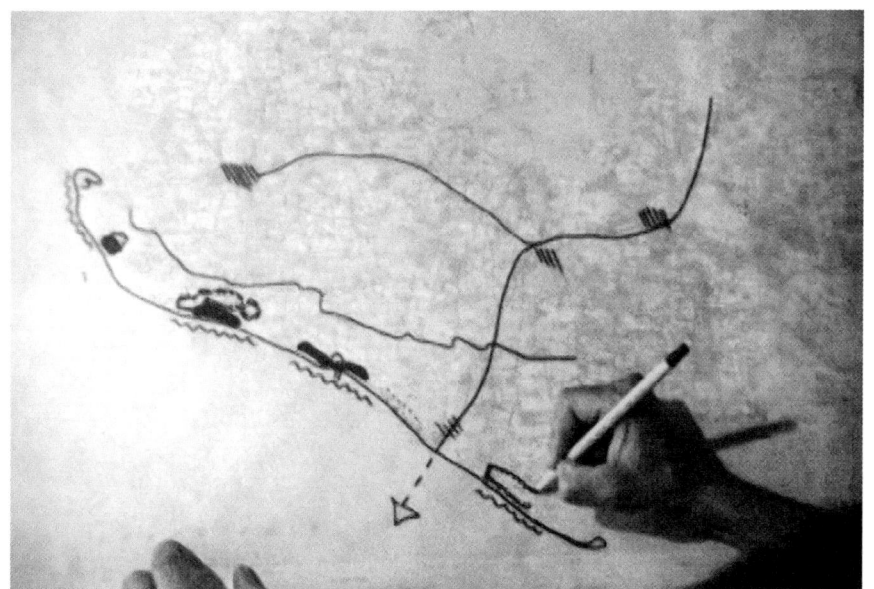

Clips from a thirty-minute national television broadcast dedicated to the plan for Lolland's south coast. Accompanied by jazz music, Anne Marie Rubin explains the principles of the plan as she draws it out on tracing paper. By the light of an iconic architect's lamp, she talks about the excursions she undertook in the area with Ole Gerstrøm: 'When you first arrive on Lolland, you think it's all flat and uniform, but when you inspect the coastline from one end to the other, you will discover that many issues apply here and that there are many values which merit preservation.'

Anne Marie Rubin was concerned that the Danish coasts should not be privatised by the building of holiday homes; instead, she wanted them to remain publicly accessible and a common good for everyone, regardless of income. In the plan for the coast of South Lolland, the best bathing beaches have been carefully recorded, and the planning was done on the basis that they should remain open to everyone.

'When you first arrive on Lolland, you think it's all flat and uniform, but when you inspect the coastline from one end to the other, you will discover that many issues apply here and that there are many values which merit preservation.'[287]

The clip shows Rubin seated at a large table full of plans and translucent paper while she explains the plan for South Lolland, point by point, to the Danish viewing public. The footage cuts between scenes of rural Lolland, accompanied by jazz music in the background, and close-ups of the professional planner, lit by an architect's lamp, who lays out the plan and says: 'The most important thing of all is to consider the landscape conditions'.[288]

Anne Marie Rubin and Ole Gerstrøm presented their analysis of the landscape in a systematic survey as part of the plan they submitted to the municipalities on Lolland. Here they show how the planned new holiday home areas were to be developed while taking as their starting point 'existing towns and road networks plus possibilities for sewerage and water supply'.[289] In other words, new holiday home areas are placed adjacent to existing towns or road connections, on sites where sewerage and water supply can be installed. Next, the plan shows a thorough analysis of the structure of agriculture and soil quality in the area. To this end, Rubin and Gerstrøm have consulted with others, including the crop consultant Holm Hansen from Sakskøbing.[290] The analysis concludes that the dammed-in areas at the former Rødby Fjord are sandy and less suitable for agriculture, and so may be used for holiday homes instead.*

* Furthermore, the plan recommends that 'in the detailed planning, efforts should be made locally to balance good and less good land and to try to form natural and suitable borders between the holiday home areas and the surrounding agricultural land'.[291]

Rubin and Gerstrøm also examine field boundaries and the types of landscape in the area, highlighting several local features of interest which, they believe, should be preserved and strengthened. Each area in the plan is registered based on its landscape qualities. An important focal point is the characteristic poplar borders, which in the flat landscape can resemble forest edges when seen from a substantial distance. Rubin emphasises this point when presenting the plan to Danish viewers.[292] They incorporate the motif of tree-lined areas and hedgerows, plus the planting of new forests and thickets of poplar and pine. Another important aspect is the beaches that lend themselves well to leisure and bathing; these are carefully registered and are presented as 'South-West Lolland's greatest asset'. Where there are good beaches, the largest number of new holiday homes will be built – and these are often areas where there are already holiday homes. The Saksfjed nature area is an existing nature reserve, and this is taken into account in the plan, which also highlights the old harbour of Kramnitze as being of significant value and worthy of preservation. While there have been local proposals to involve the police in removing illegally built summer houses, Rubin and Gerstrøm state they believe that the houses should remain so that the families who have already built houses here will not have to leave them.[293]

The plan envisages the formation of a centre at the pumping station and the Kramnitze harbour. Due to the existing buildings and the site's inherent nature as a point of convergence – a meeting place – in the landscape, they designate this area to hold the largest number of holiday homes. Year-round residences and other facilities are also intended to go here. Moreover, a holiday town for the organisation Dansk Folkeferie is to be built here – a resort where working families and other people from various income brackets can take a holiday without owning a second home, and where a sense of community is a key factor. A hotel is planned in the eastern section of the area. The holiday town is indicated in the plan as an urban structure that appears to be made out of standard prefabricated concrete elements, forming small, identical houses arrayed in direct extension of each other and linked by communal spaces. The plan has many features

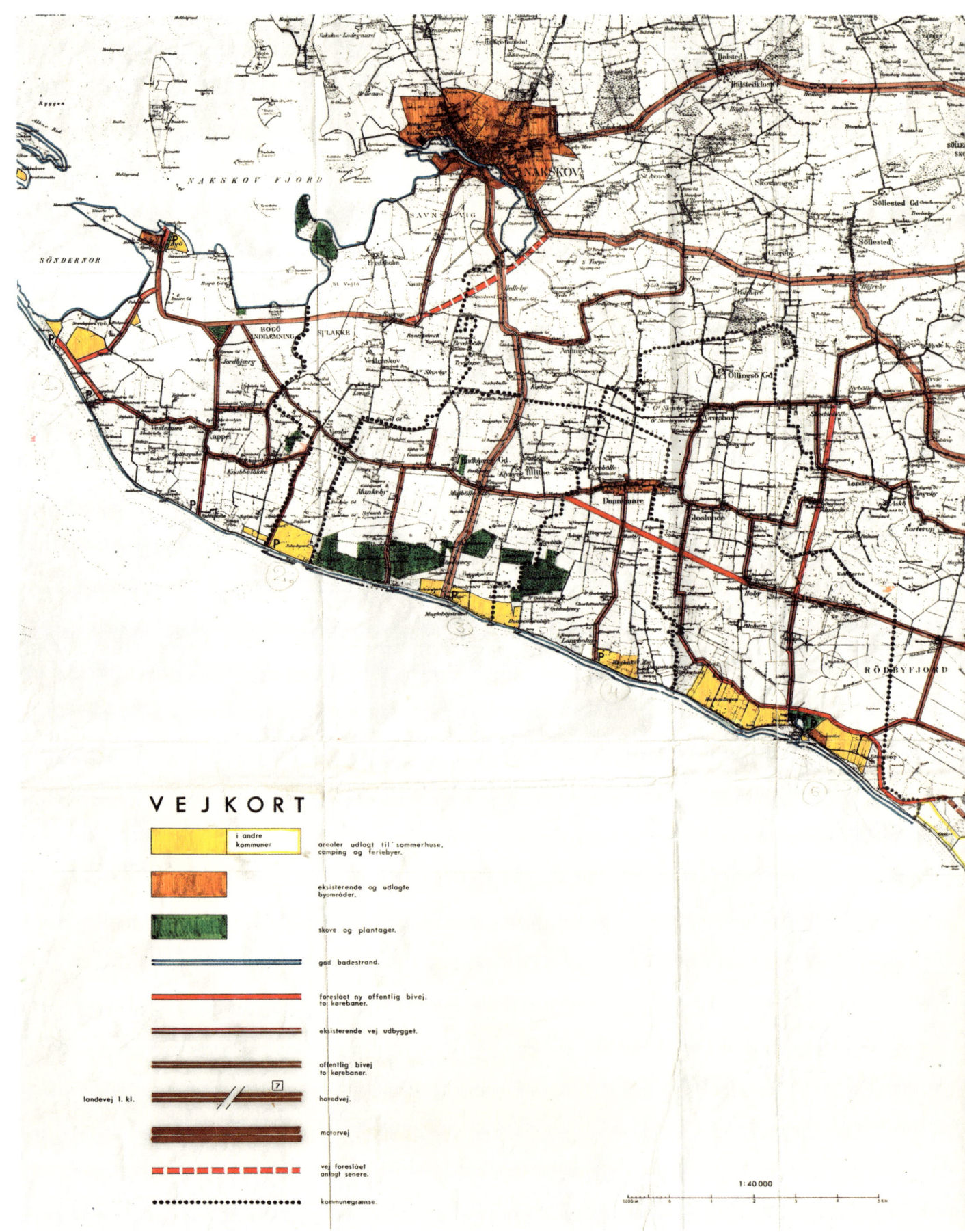

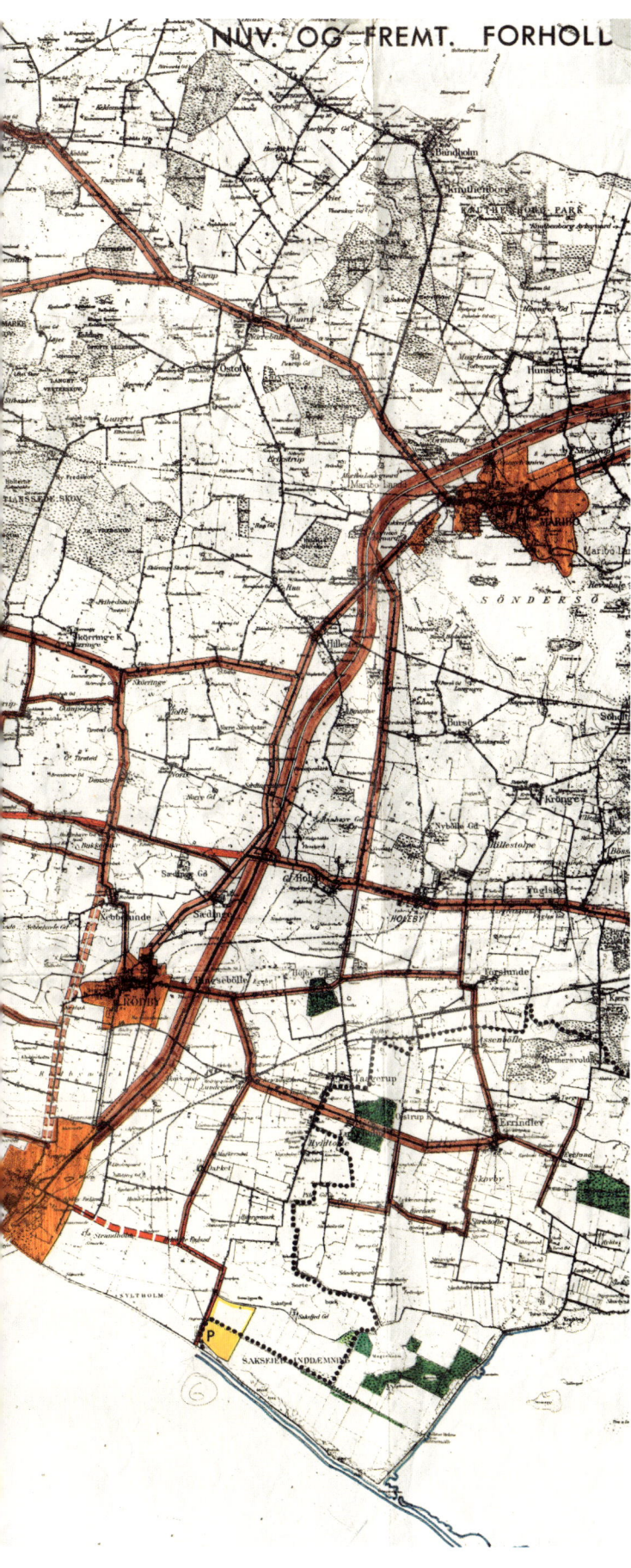

Anne Marie Rubin and her employee Ole Gerstrøm drew up a coherent plan for a forty-kilometre stretch on the south coast of Lolland. Their assignment was to provide a comprehensive proposal on how the area could be developed to accommodate more holiday homes, creating a plan which took into account landscape values and local conditions. The coastline, the green, forest-like plantings and the agricultural areas between the individual cottage areas were kept clear, remaining like pearls on a string along the entire long stretch of coast.

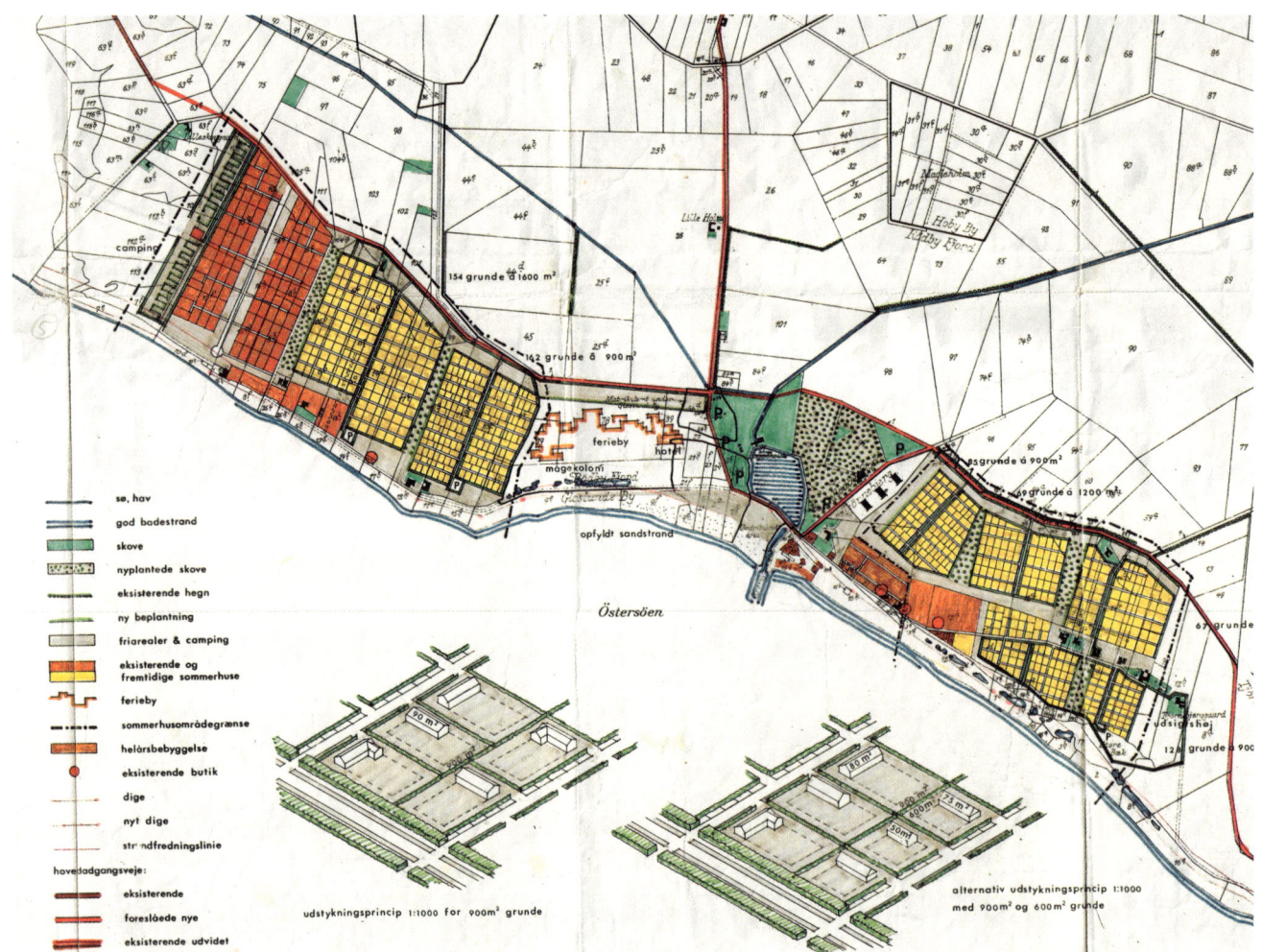

Section of the overall plan around the fishing hamlet of Kramnitze and the existing buildings found there when Anne Marie Rubin's studio drew up a plan for the coast area. According to the plan, a holiday centre was to be built here, but it was never realised. A number of holiday homes were built, incorporating large greens as shown in the plan.

in common with the holiday town that Anne Marie Rubin and her then-husband and former design studio partner, Claus Bremer (1919–1983), built for Rødhus Klit in North Jutland in 1960 – a development also created for Dansk Folkeferie.[294] The resort at Kramnitze is to be a densely arranged complex located within an open landscape setting popularly known as the Seagull Colony, and here Rubin and Gerstrøm propose filling in the area to create a new sandy beach down towards the coast and to augment the planting around the small lake by the pumping station. In addition, Kramnitze is to have a convenience store in the summer and other shared amenities for holidaymakers.[295] The idea is for the settlement to be at its densest by the small harbour, becoming increasingly spread out the further one goes east and west.

Large parts of the plan have left marks on the landscape along the coast of South Lolland that are still legible today. We can still see the plots subdivided for holiday homes as well as the greens laid out between them. Most importantly, we see where *no* construction was done. The coastline has been kept clear, as have the green forest-like plantings and agricultural areas between the individual holiday home areas, and these are now arrayed in a neat row along the entire long stretch of coast. However, the building boom on South Lolland never grew as extensive as had been imagined in the 1960s, and the island never got as many holiday homes as projected. Another part of the plan that was never realised was the year-round settlement which had been a point of contention since 1964.[296] Furthermore, the holiday resort at 'the Seagull Colony' was never built[297] – even though there was support for this project in 1975, when the area had been merged into a single, larger municipality, Rudbjerg. Its municipal architect Laust Ørnsholt (1924–1974) had drawn up a plan for 350 holiday flats located at the site proposed by Rubin's design studio. However, a local city council member, Kaj Stryhn, feared that the new 'concrete silos along the beach' would 'ruin the beach for local residents and spoil the countryside'.* Ever since the mid-1960s, this issue of striking a balance between expansion and protecting the coast has been central to the debate on Lolland – and it continues to be so to this day as the bridge between Germany and Denmark across the Fehmarn Belt currently under construction creates new, but related, discussions about how landscape qualities can be preserved and upheld while plans are made for increased tourism and the possibilities for local growth and development in South Lolland.[299] The Rubin Plan let the emphasis on having and preserving open, recreational areas determine where new holiday home areas should be built – in conjunction with a corresponding awareness of existing road systems and buildings. In this sense, the plan has certain similarities with the much more comprehensive Finger Plan for the Copenhagen area, which also took its point of departure in infrastructural systems and the need for green, recreational areas as a guide for determining where new developments should be built.[300] However, the Rubin Plan is drawn on a smaller scale than the Finger Plan and deals more directly and concretely with the design of buildings and landscape features such as trees, hedgerows and sight lines and the interaction between them. It is also very much based on fieldwork

---

* Here, mayor Kaj Lassesen states that the Rubin Plan 'is now twelve years old, and there is much to change'.[298]

which involved a close reading of the existing landscapes – a reading that takes an appreciative view of, for example, the existing beaches, forests, tree-lined fields and hedgerows. The plan particularly excels in this site-specific reading of the landscape and existing buildings, and so enables us to arrive at a more nuanced picture of 1960s' planning in Denmark. Anne Marie Rubin's enthusiastic lectures and articles as well as her concrete plans, as exemplified here by the Rubin Plan for Lolland, indicate that the period saw planners take several different approaches to resolving the dual challenge of enabling rapid societal growth on the one hand and creating a framework for – and accommodating resistance to – such rapid growth on the other. Thus, in the construction boom of the 1960s we also find a focus on striking a balance between facilitating developments and retaining existing qualities.

In this context, Rubin's comprehensive and ambitious regional collaboration in Lolland seeks to create an approach to modern planning that is responsive to existing qualities in the individual local environment – an approach which was applied in even greater detail by the younger Vibeke Dalgas, to whom we will now turn our attention. Around the same time as Rubin was drawing up her plan for South Lolland, Dalgas was hired to prepare a future plan for the island of Nyord near Møn. Here, too, there was a wish to subdivide agricultural land to create plots for holiday homes but the small island community was divided as to whether this is a good idea or not. The solution would prove to be quite different than on Lolland.

A history of urban planning – and of women

'When, in my third year as a student, I was supposed to have gone on the major mandatory trip to southern Europe to study the history of architecture, I had to decline due to my family obligations (even though I had never been abroad). I was summoned to see the dean, Poul Kjærgaard, and I was crying my eyes out. It was decided that I would solve another task instead'.[301]

Looking back in 1997, Vibeke Dalgas recalled the above situation from her time as a student at the School of Architecture in the mid-1950s, when she encountered one of the consequences of being a young, recently married woman with children. After her conversation with the dean, she was, in her own words, 'sent to see Professor Peter Bredsdorff', and he encouraged her to work with the island and the village of Nyord near Møn since she had to spend the summer holidays with her husband's family there anyway.[302] Her efforts were not to focus on a single building but rather on the entire village, the objective being to identify the characteristic traits of the village and its connection with the surrounding countryside. Her conversation with the architect and urban planner Peter Bredsdorff (1913–1981), who in addition to teaching at the School of Architecture had spearheaded the work on the vast Finger Plan,* was 'the most inspiring conversation I had had with a teacher at the Academy', as she later stated.[304]

* Peter Bredsdorff was head of the City of Copenhagen Regional Plan Office (Egnsplankontor), which had prepared *Fingerplanen*, published in 1947.[303]

Vibeke Dalgas grew up in Holbæk. Her mother was a trained home economics teacher and, in her own words, a 'bluestocking' – that is, among those keenly interested in the fight for women's rights at the beginning of the twentieth century.* Vibeke Dalgas's father was a civil engineer and worked for the Holbæk County Road Administration. In 1952, having completed her Higher General Examination (equivalent to sixth form/high school) with mathematics and science as core subjects, Dalgas applied to the School of Architecture at the Royal Danish Academy of Fine Arts. The proportion of women students there had only increased slightly compared to Anne Marie Rubin's day: Dalgas was admitted as one out of nine women in her year.[306] She embarked on her studies without knowing much about architecture nor, for that matter, about urban planning.

* When Vibeke Dalgas's mother met her future husband, she had a job and her own car. Upon their marriage she became a stay-at-home housewife and never entered the labour market again.[305]

During her first year of study, she met her future husband. They were married in 1953, and the first child soon followed. Vibeke Dalgas's role in the family was the reason why she could not join her fellow students on the mandatory study trip to Italy and Greece, as mentioned above. However, her absence on the trip and her family situation were also the very factors that steered her towards the field of urban planning. The one thing that in many ways burdened her with a double workload and impeded her opportunities to follow her studies here became a catalyst for her further work.* Her encounter with Peter Bredsdorff and the work assignment about Nyord shifted her focus away from architecture understood as individual buildings towards the field of urban planning, which would become the focal point of the rest of her studies – and of her entire career. Here she worked with the existing traits and qualities of villages and market towns, examining how a range of different and conflicting demands for conservation, change and renewal could be met with planning as a tool.[308] She and fellow student Stefan Ott (1928–1997) were the

* During her first year at the school of architecture, Vibeke Dalgas lived with a family in Hellerup where she helped with the housework morning and night in exchange for board and lodging. On wash day, she had to miss classes to help out.[307]

As a student, Vibeke Dalgas could not take part in a three-week study trip to Southern Europe because she had young children to look after. Instead, she was encouraged to investigate the island and the village of Nyord, where she was to spend a holiday with her family. She prepared a report on the place, describing, in text and drawings, the typical traits of the island and its settlements as seen here.

first two students to have an assignment on urban planning approved as part of their graduation process at the School of Architecture. At this time, the academic regulations did not allow prospective graduates to submit projects that were 'only' about urban planning, but she managed to get it in there, as she herself put it.[309]

After graduating from the School of Architecture in 1958, Dalgas worked as a town planning consultant for the Hillerød Municipality. However, a merger with two adjacent, smaller municipalities and the resulting restructuring meant that the administration had too many town planning consultants. Instead, in 1966 she set up her own design studio* with Hillerød Municipality as one of her clients.[310] Like Rubin, she used her experience and her network from the public administration sector as a basis for her private business practice. Based on her years in public service, it was clear to Dalgas that, on certain points, her view of planning differed significantly from that of several of her colleagues. In 1963, urban planning consultants Skaarup and Jespersen and ICP and traffic engineer Anders Nyvig had presented a comprehensive plan for Hillerød which included a four-lane road

* The design studio was called Vibeke Fischer Thomsen because she had taken the surname of her first husband. In 1983 she reclaimed her maiden name, Dalgas.

along the historic and idyllic Slotssøen lake. The road was part of a street system that was supposed to relieve pressure on the centre, creating pedestrian streets and additional parking spaces along the newly constructed distributor road, in much the same way as Rubin had planned for Nakskov.[311] Their proposed intervention, however, would have a drastic impact on Hillerød's older castle and market town environment, and Dalgas was of the opinion that urban planning of this kind was 'far too heavy-handed, rational and governed by financial concerns. The qualities of the existing environment were not given sufficient consideration'.[312]

Like several other architectural companies at the time, Dalgas's design studio was relatively small, employing up to ten people at a time. In addition to being a practising urban planner, Dalgas was an active writer throughout her career, and she was the initiator of the establishment of the Byplanhistorisk Udvalg (the Committee on Town Planning History) in 1982, which still publishes *Byplanhistoriske noter* (Notes on Town Planning History) under the auspices of Dansk Byplanlaboratorium (the Danish Town Planning Institute). She wrote strictly professional articles as well as more personal pieces reflecting on what it was like to be a woman in the male-dominated world of architecture and urban planning.[313]

Concurrently with the practical work undertaken at her design studio, Dalgas taught at the School of Architecture's town planning department from 1967. She chose to move to the restoration department in 1972, and taught urban renewal and conservation planning there until 1988, when she was given a chair as professor at Lund University.[314]

Nyord – an island community under pressure

One of the design studio's first tasks was to carry out a study at the island of Nyord. In the early 1960s there were discussions about creating a permanent link to adjacent Møn. Construction on the bridge began in 1966. At the same time, there were plans to issue official nature conservation orders for areas at Møns Klint, Ulvshale and Nyord, which experts had identified as those most worthy of conservation in the Sorø and Præstø Counties.[315] The upcoming bridge, the potential conservation status and the difficulties of engaging in profitable, modern agriculture* on the island meant that one of the

---

* During these years, Danish agriculture underwent a transformation from small-scale agriculture to large-scale industrialised agriculture, which required larger amounts of land than before, and this was difficult to find on the small island.

landowners planned to sell his land with a view to subdividing it into plots for 300 holiday homes. However, concerns regarding the disappearance of the island's large natural areas and the prospect of many tourists arriving with the arrival of the bridge prompted the Ministry of Culture to act. They asked the Conservation Plan Committee for the Sorø and Præstø Counties to initiate proceedings with the aim of giving the whole of Nyord protected status. Doing so would put an end to the development plans, and the cause received support from the Danish Society for Nature Conservation and the National Museum of Denmark.[316]

The prospect of the area being assigned nature conservation status met massive opposition among the majority of the island's landowners, which consisted partly of permanent residents and partly of people from Copenhagen who used the older houses as second homes. The island was under the auspices of the Stege Landsogn (a small, rural municipality), and the local authorities were also opposed to the conservation plans. However, they assured the media that even without nature conservation measures in place, the plans to divide up land for holiday home developments would be stopped.[317]

However, not all of the island's residents were against the conservation plans, nor did they welcome the idea of having 300 holiday homes in the backyard. The small island community was torn between the forces of development and conservation. Reflecting this, the residents wanted a closer study of the many different issues facing them before a decision was taken on the matter of conservation. The residents set up a local island committee and, together with De Samvirkende Danske Landboforeninger (The Cooperative Danish Farmers' Associations), approached the Fonden for Bygnings- og Landskabskultur (the Foundation for Building and Landscape Culture) to have such a study prepared.*

The active involvement of the foundation and the islanders is an example of the many associations, organisations and initiatives that were set up in Denmark and in a number of other European countries in response to the countless demolitions of older buildings and the construction of the many new holiday home developments in rural areas in the 1950s and early 1960s.[319] Vibeke Dalgas did not work alone but engaged in close collaboration with a range of stakeholders, including authorised experts and local associations. In Denmark, the nationwide Foundation for Building and Landscape Culture was established in 1964 and it became one of her key collaboration partners. Indeed, the foundation had a major impact on the development of conservation planning in Denmark. Its purpose was to provide or mediate grants

Vibeke Dalgas (b. 1933) was admitted to the Royal Danish Academy of Fine Arts' School of Architecture in 1952. Upon graduating in 1958, she was employed by Hillerød Municipality, where she worked as a town planning consultant. In 1966, she founded her own design studio, and alongside her work as a design studio owner she taught at the School of Architecture, initially in the town planning department and later, from 1972, in the restoration department. In 1988 she was appointed as professor at Lund University. Her design studio specialised in urban planning, and she contributed to developing new ways of approaching urban planning with a focus on conservation.

* The local island committee consisted of two farm owners, one of whom was a 'sognefoged' (parish executive officer) and the other a retired fisherman.[318]

One of Vibeke Dalgas's first tasks was to prepare a conservation plan for Nyord, based on a major survey of the island's characteristics. The well-preserved village had crooked streets with older plantings and trees, as well as a mixture of three- or four-wing half-timbered farmhouses and fishermen's cottages built out of brick. The village also had a small harbour and a distinctive octagonal church, seen here on the far left.

and expert advice for the preservation, maintenance and restoration of old houses.[320] It did not focus solely on the preservation of single houses, devoting equal attention to urban environments, parks and natural areas, which were a growing theme in conservation discussions in Denmark and several European countries in the middle of the twentieth century.[321] Nyord was one of the foundation's first major cases – and one which specifically concerned the conservation of a natural area as well as a village community with older buildings.[322]

After an initial visit to the island, the chairman, architect and professor Palle Suenson, stated that 'in our foundation, we are just as interested in the present with a view to the future as we are in the past'.[323] The statement raised hopes among the local island committee that the study would aid the efforts of those opposed to conservation measures.[324] In addition to being interested in Nyord, the foundation wanted to shed light on some of the more general problems associated with the future development opportunities for Denmark's small islands, with Nyord acting as a concrete example. Several of the Danish small islands faced major social problems as a result of the growing urbanisation. While large areas in Denmark experienced strong growth, the islands faced dwindling business and employment opportunities and unprofitable agriculture. As a result, many moved away from the islands, causing a deterioration in communal facilities and fewer or no shopping opportunities.[325] The study was intended as a starting point for learning how existing qualities – in terms of the countryside and older buildings alike – could be taken care of in the future while also facilitating development in ways that would meet the different needs of the residents. The questions were: Which wishes regarding conservation should be accommodated before the planned development and renewal was launched? And which qualities of the local architecture and landscape were important and should be carried into the future?

At this point, the foundation was only two years old and did not have much practical experience to draw on as far as investigations of smaller urban communities outside the market towns were concerned. Still, an expert committee was set up to take overall responsibility for the survey. The interdisciplinary committee reflected the many different interests at stake in the small island community and, in addition to representatives from the foundation itself, included members of various interest organisations, representatives of the public administration and expert committees.[326] The committee did not carry out the hands-on part of the study itself. Vibeke Dalgas's design studio was hired, via the foundation, to carry out this aspect of the proceedings.[327]

In 1966, few Danish design studios specialised in both planning and conservation, and truth be told Dalgas's newly established design studio did not have much concrete experience from similar tasks either. However, she knew about Nyord from her studies at the School of Architecture, so she was not starting from scratch.[328]

Many suggestions for the future

On an early spring day in March 1967, Vibeke Dalgas and her young colleague architect Nina Rosenkjær set out for a three-day reconnaissance trip to Nyord. Prior to making the nearly 150-kilometre trip from Hillerød to Nyord, they make careful preparations and are now ready to map the characteristic traits of the island and village alike.[329] They bring along forms of their own devising. Here they note the age and function of the buildings, the materials and colours of the façades and the roof material. Having mapped the entire village,

In the late 1960s, when Vibeke Dalgas and her employee, architect Nina Rosenkjær, came to Nyord, they not only met a well-preserved village; the rest of the island was also well preserved, and the cadastral map shows that the distribution of land had remained largely unchanged since the eighteenth-century land reforms. Each farm had between eight and ten plots of land as well as a small area of arable land and a larger area of meadow. The arable land was closest to the village.

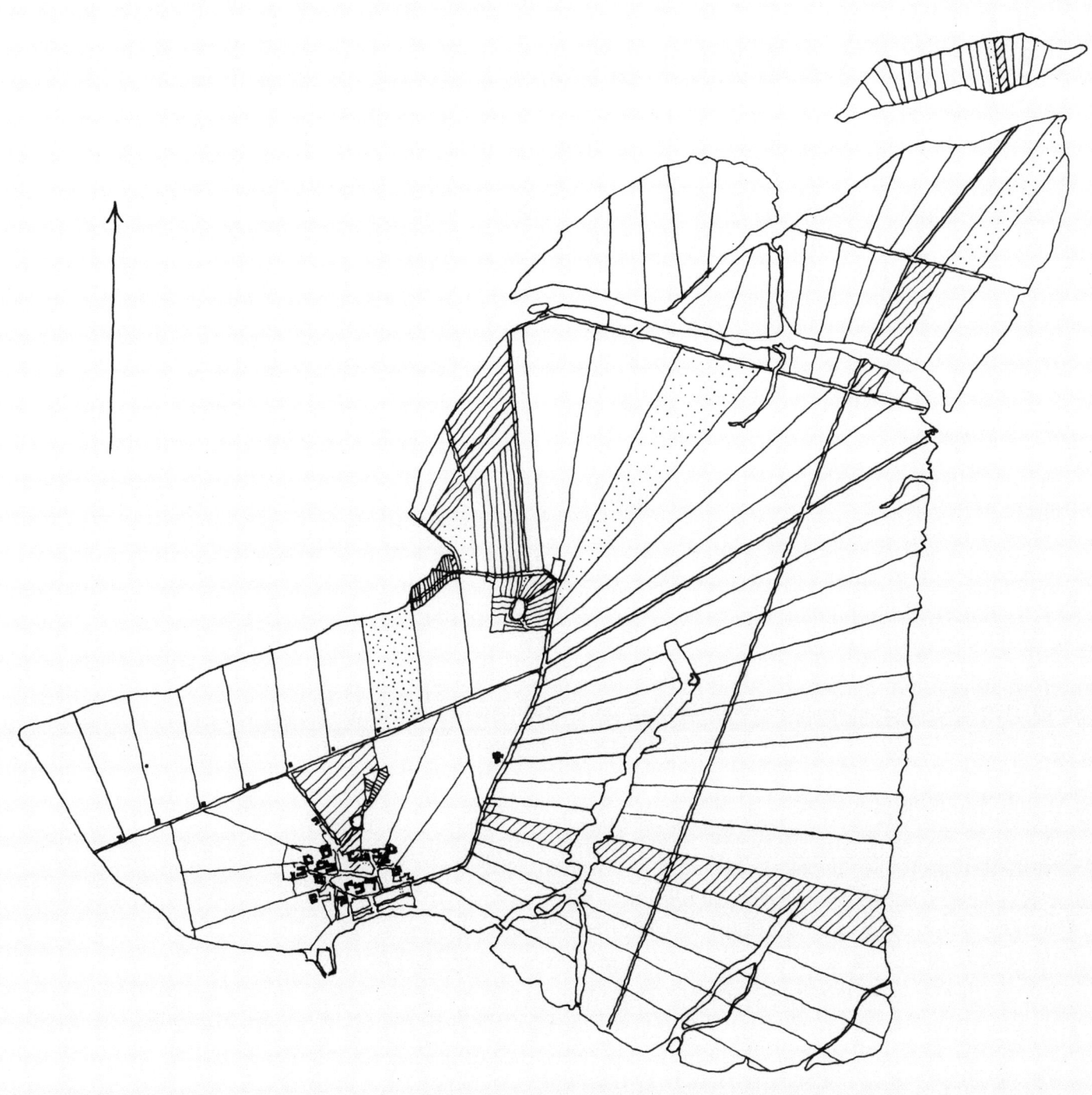

they go on to assess the architectural quality of the buildings as well as their structural condition, quality and age. While ambling along the winding village roads, they also carry out a 'planting reconnaissance', making a record of every tree – large and small – and of hedgerows, hedges, stone walls and other walls.³³⁰ In addition to the hastily scribbled notes and observations in their various forms, they document the village and the landscape by means of photographs. Bare trees, joined-up nineteenth-century cottages with scattered plantings in front, glimpses into the courtyard of a thatched-roofed, half-timbered whitewashed farm, the entrance to the small harbour, the clear boundary between buildings and agricultural land, wheel tracks between barren, brown fields, flat, vast meadows, the beach and an endless horizon. They capture the island's distinctive traits and qualities. Back in the design studio, they prepare an 'environmental value' map, marking out what they regard as the most valuable street sections and areas in the small village.³³¹

The Foundation for Building and Landscape Culture published the results of the design studio's work in *Øen Nyord* the following year, in 1968, stating that the design studio had solved the task with what they called

'a broad elucidation of the factors and conditions pertinent to an assessment of the island's current problems and future potential. The main emphasis is therefore on describing its development history in order to clearly outline the connections to the past and in order to identify some of the issues and conditions that may prove decisive for the future.'³³²

The study applied a characteristic approach insofar as it treated the island as a whole, one that had evolved over many centuries, and the design studio investigated how various factors had influenced this development. They did not restrict themselves to only looking at the island's buildings, for example by registering them and then identifying which buildings were eligible and suitable for preservation. Nor did they sketch out a new road through the village city without regard for the existing buildings. Instead, they mapped out spatial contexts, connections and relationships over time. They considered many aspects, including how the island's natural setting and landscape had governed the main occupations among its population over time, and how the village had been placed at the most expedient site because the natural conditions had been taken into account at the time. They pointed out that historical occupations such as agriculture, fishing and pilotage in the narrow and dangerous waters around the island had influenced the design of the houses in the village, which comprised a mixture of larger three- or four-wing farms and smaller fishermen's houses.³³³

Nina Rosenkjær (b. 1939) enrolled at the Royal Danish Academy of Fine Arts' School of Architecture in 1958 and graduated in 1964. Having specialised in urban planning, shortly after her graduation she began working at Vibeke Dalgas's design studio. Throughout her working life, Rosenkjær has focused on urban planning while also doing graphic design work for what was then Frederiksborg County. Furthermore, she has been active within the Danish Society for Nature Conservation. She is the daughter of architect Ragna Grubb.

Based on their survey, the design studio prepared several different development models for the future of Nyord, illustrating what each model would require in terms of changes to the building stock and within the village as a whole, as well as its impact on agriculture on the island. Given this background, the design studio then put forward possible scenarios for the consequences each of the different models would have for the island as a whole.

The interdisciplinary Nyord committee focused on four different models: (1) the island of Nyord as an agricultural island, (2) Nyord as a year-round town, (3) Nyord as a summer town and finally (4) a combination of the other three models. In December 1967, the committee reached the conclusion that a partial town planning statute should be drawn up based on model 4, which was to provide opportunities for both year-round and summer residences in the village. This is to say that no agricultural land was to be sold off as holiday home plots – the scenario that had initiated the entire investigation. In order to strengthen the integrity of the village environment, they would also take steps to have the most valuable buildings listed.[334] As regards the rest of the island, it was agreed that the open landscape should be preserved and that an agricultural statute should be drawn up. If, in the future, there was a desire for the construction of larger agricultural buildings outside the village, permission could only be granted if the location could be approved by the conservation authorities based on an assessment of the impact on the landscape as well as on considerations for the farm business. Finally, it was widely agreed among the committee members that the meadows should be protected, after which they should still be used for grazing, haymaking and reed cutting.[335] In the mid-1970s, a decision was made to protect Nyord Meadows. The protected areas make up approximately 80 percent of the island's area.[336]

Conservation and development

After the publication of *Øen Nyord* (1968), Vibeke Dalgas's design studio drew up a draft for a Partial Town Planning Statue No. 1 for Nyord Town, Møn Municipality, which the municipality adopted in 1973. The Town Planning Act from 1938[337] made it possible for a municipality to make demands on landowners and homeowners through either an outline plan ('dispositionsplan') or a partial town planning statute, which was more detailed than an outline plan – and which broadly corresponds to the present-day district plan ('lokalplan') in Danish zoning management. A town planning statute could cover

In March 1967, Vibeke Dalgas and Nina Rosenkjær went on a trip to inspect Nyord. They brought forms of their own devising to help them record the houses and plantings and rate the elements in terms of conservation merit. The four photographs, originating from their trip, clearly show how the village is an enclave surrounded by farmland and the sea.

a single block of flats, an entire neighbourhood or, as in Nyord, an entire village, and they were drawn up when a municipality had special wishes regarding the use of a building/development/area or special requirements regarding location or design.*

The urban planning statute for Nyord set out the framework for the conservation and thus also for the development of this unique and well-preserved island with its clearly demarcated and defined village, which had remained largely unchanged for over 200 years. It contained guidelines on the use of the area, road conditions, subdivisions, the extent and location of future developments, and the external appearance of such developments as well as fences and plantings. The urban planning statute covered the whole of Nyord village including the harbour, and in the future only detached one-family homes could be built within the area. The primary use of these buildings was to be residential, albeit with the option of setting up businesses in existing buildings to serve tourists and local residents. In addition, the statute also allowed the presence of smaller businesses with a natural connection to the place. The main bulk of the statute consisted of a description of the scope, location and outward appearance of future developments. Any new building in the village must take into account the existing ones and adapt itself to its surroundings in terms of height, length and depth, and in order to obtain a building permit, the building must 'in its essential features, proportions and details have such an outward form and appearance that, when viewed in conjunction with the other buildings in the area, a good overall effect can be achieved'.[339]

The Nyord study is an example of how architects, or in this case urban planners, can take a heterogeneous view of the place they are working with. Vibeke Dalgas and Nina Rosenkjær did not see Nyord as a fully finished place, with nothing more to be done, but rather as a place undergoing ceaseless change – infused by the past, the demands of the present, the residents' relationships with the place and their wishes for the future. In their work with Nyord, they took on a different role than the one generally associated with architects or planners. Like Anne Marie Rubin and Ole Gerstrøm, they chose to not only carry out their work by remaining in their studio, drawing lines on a piece of paper; instead they set out to personally inspect the buildings and landscapes they had to design for, applying an appreciative look at what might, at a cursory glance, look quite ordinary.

They, like Rubin and Gerstrøm, formed a relatively more holistic view that went far beyond identifying individual buildings or natural areas as suitable for listing and conservation, singling them out from the rest. At Nyord, the task was more about conservation and involving

* A town planning statute had to be submitted for a public hearing, and landowners could object to the proposal. The Ministry of Housing had to approve town planning statutes before they could be registered. A partial statute had far-reaching legal effects and could have a major financial impact on landowners.[338]

local stakeholders than was the assignment Rubin and Gerstrøm had carried out in Lolland. Dalgas and Rosenkjær also had to listen to the residents' many different wishes and hopes for the future, examine the site's history and landscape, look out for connections and highlight potentials. Based on their holistic view, they drew up potential scenarios for the future in which the traits and qualities identified in their survey were taken into account. Dalgas's and Rosenkjær's work involved forging a connection between past, present and future. They did so while maintaining an ongoing dialogue with the island's residents, local politicians and fellow professionals. And their work did not end when the study was completed. It continued for several years afterwards when the design studio acted as a consultant for the municipality on matters concerning Nyord after the approval of the urban planning statute. The partial town planning statute established the framework for future developments, upholding the preservation of existing values as an essential element, and this way of looking at a place would inform more of the work done by this young design studio in the years to come.

In the years after the Nyord committee was set up, the Foundation for Building and Landscape Culture – working in collaboration with Vibeke Dalgas's design studio – took part in several studies of other small islands which had what the foundation called 'distinctive conditions in terms of their natural setting and human settlements'.[340] The island of Ærø was one example: here, heated local discussions about the traffic conditions in the main town of Ærøskøbing prompted a major study of the town's conservation problems. Once again, the study was to help combine conservation and development, although it quickly became clear that the problems were different from those found on the islands of Nyord and Strynø, with which the design studio was working concurrently.[341] Rather, the problems on Ærø were comparable to those of several other market towns in Denmark. Besides the construction of holiday homes, one of the most visible signs of the era's almost explosive growth was the growing traffic, which prompted the construction of new roads as well as the extension of existing roads – as we have seen in the example of Nakskov. In several market towns, this led to the demolition of many older buildings worthy of preservation, and entire historic districts were destroyed.[342]

The problem was familiar to every municipality in Denmark, and in Ærøskøbing the discussion revolved around whether it was a good idea to build a new road, known as Marstalvejen, along the harbour, thereby destroying parts of the older town and waterside environment. The question was whether an alternative could be found that would show greater consideration for what was already there. In 1971, on the basis of a major survey to register the town's listed

Vibeke Dalgas and Nina Rosenkjær used their records to create overviews and maps of the village and the island of Nyord. Here is an overview of the houses and plantings in the village, showing the number of three- and four-wing farmhouses still found there in 1967. The architects concluded that the dense, closed-off village had always formed a marked contrast to the open countryside surrounding the settlement.

and preservation-worthy building and subsequent analyses, the design studio prepared a combined conservation and outline plan for Ærøskøbing, the first of its kind in Denmark.[343] In a new departure from usual practice, the document contained provisions and guidelines for both conservation and development, and in the coming years the design studio prepared more conservation and outline plans for other smaller and larger towns, for example for Strynø (1970), Roskilde (1971), Stenlille (1972), Aakirkeby (1972) and Rødekro (1984).

A characteristic trait of the design studio's work was that development and conservation were not as incompatible as one might well have been led to believe from the public discussions of the day. On

In order to develop a conservation plan for the island of Nyord, it was necessary to form a clear overview of the building stock in the village. Here, Vibeke Dalgas and Nina Rosenkjær have recorded the colours and surfaces of the houses. They investigated how many houses had red or yellow brick walls, and how many were whitewashed either white or yellow. Their forms were based on careful and detailed records, which they translated into easy-to-understand illustrations.

the contrary, the studio set out to take its starting point in what was already there, carrying out thorough inspections and registrations to identify the most important qualities of the given area. Only when steps had been taken to preserve them was it time to think about development. In Dalgas's own words, the objective was to create 'human-friendly' surroundings.[344] Towns that were pleasant to live in and visit, where everyone could see history reflected, and which were easy to navigate – and not only by car.[345] Dalgas's work shows strong signs of being inspired by Peter Bredsdorff's views on urban planning, and she has, on several occasions, emphasised the great impact which her meeting with Bredsdorff, and not least the many years of collaboration with him, has had on her outlook on planning.* According to Bredsdorff, a planner should distinguish between what is typical of a town and what is special and specific, to thereby gain an individual understanding of each particular city. By knowing its history, it was possible to reconcile the demands and planning of a new era with the city's history and identity.[347] Vibeke Dalgas stands on the shoulders of Peter Bredsdorff, and we can see connections to Anne Marie Rubin's work, but at the same time she has contributed significant and innovative ways of working to the world of Danish urban planning. The many assignments carried out for the Foundation for Building and Landscape Culture were important for the development of a method for working with conservation in planning. The foundation and its chairman Palle Suenson had many international partners, with whom Dalgas became acquainted, and she was inspired by how they worked with conservation analyses, registrations and methods – and not least, how all the different requirements had to be balanced in future planning.[348]

Like Anne Marie Rubin, Vibeke Dalgas has openly and repeatedly criticised Danish urban planning of the post-war years, stating that the planners were too focused on function and finances and did not pay sufficient attention to the existing physical framework and spaces.[349] The preservation of city centres and village communities was important to Dalgas, but it was not a matter of preserving things to stop time. There needed to be room for development, too – just not at the expense of historical values and the human scale. The design studio's work focused on planning and development for what she regarded as particularly sensitive urban areas and landscapes. Its philosophy was that established cultural environments were an asset that planners and politicians must take into account in future development.[350] Over a number of years she developed a method that was more considerate and complex than much other planning carried out at the time, which in many cases saw architects and urban planners demolish or clear out the older districts and then build new ones that did not pay any heed to their surroundings. She relates: 'We would see plans that focused exclusively on traffic and did not care at all about how to treat the landscape and physical forms of the town'.[351]

In 1979, she condensed the many lessons learnt from drawing up conservation plans, teaching at the Royal Danish Academy of Fine Arts and carrying out assignments for the Foundation for Building and Landscape Culture in the first booklet published in the Danish Planning Agency's series *Kommuneplanorientering*. Her contribution on conservation planning, *Bevaringsplanlægning* (1979), was a collaboration between her design studio as represented by employees Peter

* Peter Bredsdorff taught his students the importance of understanding a city before working with it. A city's history and topography must be respected. Bredsdorff urged his pupils to immerse themselves in the architecture, life and society of each given place to establish firm foundations for their further work. [346]

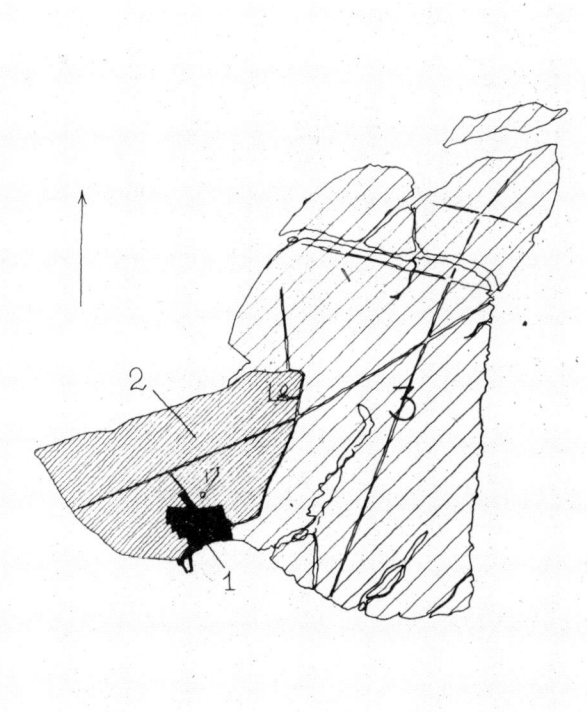

Based on their inspection tour in March 1967 and the subsequent follow-up, the architects drew up four different scenarios for Nyord's future for the consideration of a large committee consisting of various organisations, local authorities and residents. The original issue was whether land should be subdivided for holiday homes, but after the thorough preliminary work it was decided that large parts of the landscape should be protected countryside (areas 2 and 3), while a partial town planning statute would be prepared for the village and individual buildings would be recommended for listing.

Forslaget består i, 1) at der udarbejdes en partiel byplanvedtægt for landsbyen, støttet af enkelte fredninger, 2) at der udarbejdes en landbrugsvedtægt for agerlandet, og 3) at engene fredes. Målestok 1:20.000.

Tuxen, Mette Nørgaard Pedersen and Dalgas herself, the Planning Agency as represented by Edmund Hansen, Henrik Hvidtfeldt and Erik Dencker and the Conservation Agency as represented by Bent Rud and Torben Olesen.[352] The booklet unfolds how research that involves a registration of historical, architectural and environmental qualities can be carried out before the municipality in question embarks on preparing a conservation district plan. It comprises descriptions of typical older urban areas and settlements in Denmark as well as a description of how places worthy of conservation can be registered and rated, and which preliminary studies were deemed necessary to carry out conservation planning – an institutionalised approach to combining planning and conservation.[353] Anne Marie Rubin's design studio also carried out some of the early conservation plans, including a conservation district plan for Veddelev near Roskilde Fjord in 1973.[354]

This is to say that Vibeke Dalgas's design studio helped to develop a method for how Danish municipalities could best care for their historic town centres and environments – and then communicate this method to the nation's various design studios and municipalities via state authorities.* It is worth noting, however, that the guide came about as a collaboration between a private design studio and two public authorities responsible for urban planning and building conservation, respectively, testifying to the fact that this was a complex area which required co-operation across the ministries' specific areas of responsibility. Conservation and development are linked, and both involve collaboration across professions, sectors and gender.[356]

> * The design studio was also often consulted on ministerial reports, draft legislation and guidelines. In addition, it contributed to the development of the public process procedures regarding planning both before and after the new Municipal Planning Act was introduced in 1977.[355]

The development of methodological tools for carrying out conservation planning in the municipalities points towards the development of one of the most widely used methods for recording conservation values in Danish municipalities: the SAVE method (Survey of Architectural Values in the Environment). Developed in the late 1980s by the Danish Planning Agency, the tool facilitated a voluntary and gradual systematic mapping of conservation values in the nation's municipalities, which was documented in the so-called municipal atlases – later cultural heritage atlases, and also designated 'preservational atlases' in the international version of the tool.[357] The SAVE method remains the most widely used method in the Danish municipalities' designation of buildings worthy of preservation, and it is based on several decades of work on developing methods to integrate conservation into urban planning. Questions regarding development and conservation considerations, as well as which values – and to an increasing extent also *whose* values – should apply in that balancing act remain highly topical today.

Why are there no famous preservation architects?

In 1971, art historian Linda Nochlin asked why there have been no great women artists, and inspired by this, architectural researcher Jorge Otero-Pailos has asked why there have been no well-known restoration architects.[358] In a similar vein, we may well wonder why Anne Marie Rubin's and Vibeke Dalgas's important work with urban planning has received so little attention in the history of architecture or urban planning. Their extensive work has contributed to shaping not only professional discussions but also actual towns and landscapes. Both have also helped develop new approaches with a greater focus on site and conservation than what is usually conveyed in the established narrative about urban planning during the 1960s' time

Today, Nyord appears as a well-preserved village community with listed and conservation-worthy houses surrounded by older green belts and a protected landscape. The work carried out by Vibeke Dalgas and Nina Rosenkjær represents an alternative narrative about urban planning in the 1960s – one where Nyord was seen neither as a place devoid of value, nor as stagnant. It was and is a place in a state of ongoing change, which requires a special eye for already existing values when developing for the future.

of growth. Such approaches are highly relevant in our present day which call for more caring approaches to architecture and planning, and where there is growing recognition of the fact that we must find new principles and ways of organising society instead of exclusively prioritising economic and consumer growth – a new way of thinking that will have major consequences for how we organise the physical spaces around us in the future.[359] In this context, writing new histories that expand our picture of the positions taken by planners during the great transformation of Danish society in the decades after the Second World War can pave the way for a rethinking of practices today, when we sorely need a comprehensive transformation in light of the many challenges linked to climate, biodiversity, inequality

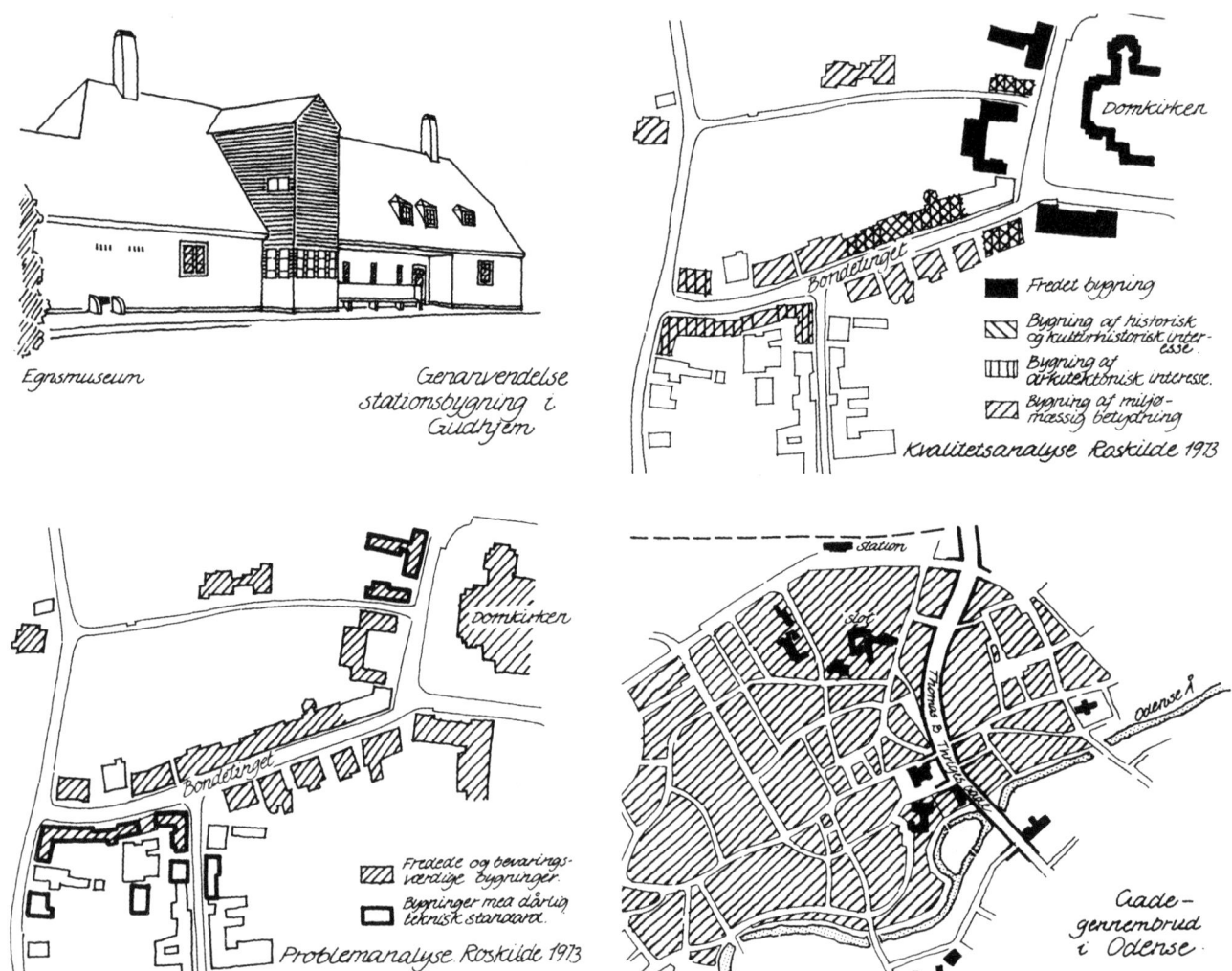

Nyord marked the starting point for developing new methods for working with existing cities and buildings. In the early 1970s, Vibeke Dalgas's studio drew up Denmark's first-ever combined outline and conservation plan, specifically for the town of Ærøskøbing. In 1979 the studio was part of a collaborative effort collecting lessons learnt in a publication on conservation planning that included guidelines for the municipalities. This work led to the development of the SAVE system, which remains fundamental to how many Danish municipalities work with protected buildings and built environments.

and sustainability issues. It is therefore absolutely essential for architects and planners to be able to work *with* rather than *against* the landscapes that are already urbanised, as well as the forms of life that unfold here. As Joan C. Tronto writes, we need to develop an architectural practice that connects people, buildings and ecological systems – one which does not reiterate a purely anthropocentric relationship with nature and with all life.[360]

Returning to Otero-Pailos's question about restoration architects, we can follow up with the question of why the planners who worked with site-specific and conservation-oriented approaches as early as the 1960s are not more widely featured in architectural historical literature. One of the answers is probably that among many architects, and concurrently among architectural historians too, there has been an unusually keen focus on developing something new and on leaving a clear and significant mark on the built environment – and that is also the narrative that has been passed on in the literature.[361] Preserving and enhancing what is already there rarely leaves a visible imprint in the form of clear design statements. Otero-Pailos even describes restoration architecture as a self-effacing practice which is often more about letting the historic building come into view than about designing something new.[362] In such work, the architect can easily be perceived as an invisible hand (and so an oft-forgotten hand), even though restoration architecture, urban planning with a conservation outlook as well as site-based landscape development are very much interpretive, creative and future-oriented endeavours that involve a wide range of choices.[363]

Arriving in Nyord today, it is hard to see evidence of an architect's hand, but nevertheless the place has been shaped by the work of Vibeke Dalgas and Nina Rosenkjær and their inventory and interpretation of the place. The same can be said about South Lolland's open, undeveloped green areas and the stretch of beach which Anne Marie Rubin and Ole Gerstrøm investigated in their fieldwork, interpreted and subsequently went on to make plans for. The starting point of their work is an analysis of the landscape, recording what is already there. They point to where one could develop and meet today's needs for holiday homes and recreational areas. And they combine consideration for the existing landscape with the construction of new holiday homes, roads and a new, modernist resort. Dalgas and Rosenkjær take the same point of departure but in their practice the conservation aspect becomes even more clearly visible as an independent piece of analytical work, which is translated into formalised environmental value atlases and conservation town planning statutes.

Like our protagonists in this chapter, Anne Marie Rubin and Vibeke Dalgas, several of their male colleagues have worked with public administration and the intersection between development and conservation – and these, too, appear only rarely in literature on architectural history.[364] Like so many other countries, Denmark sees a general development towards a stronger connection between conservation and development from the late 1960s onwards. Architects, historians, legislators, researchers, local citizens, associations, public administration employees and more have worked to forge a connection between development and conservation. One of the results is that today, citizens and visitors in Denmark benefit from coasts free of holiday homes and can still enjoy preserved older buildings and neighbourhoods in the former market towns.[365] A typical trait of conservation planning is that the local physical features are seen as a quality. In the rural context addressed by Dalgas, this includes elements such as willow fences, older village houses, marketplaces and a fishing hamlet. The discipline is different from traditional building conservation, where national or even international significance is mainly assigned to large monuments and buildings. Another characteristic trait is that the urban planners we have addressed here do not think in terms of sharply delineated opposites, such as, for example, a distinction between the conservation of nature and cultural heritage, which is otherwise often indicative in a conservation context.[366] To work from a premise of paired opposites is based on an unproductive outlook on the land that is particularly problematic in light of today's challenges with the biodiversity and climate crises, which require us think beyond the imagined and historically constructed split of nature and culture .[367] In the work done by Anne Marie Rubin and Vibeke Dalgas in the 1960s, we see intimations of such an interconnected view of, for example, the growing conditions of plants, water systems and human needs, even if the concept of 'natural values' is, in their work, more closely associated with the human aesthetic experience of nature rather than with the idea of plants and animals as having value on their own terms. Thus, the two architects' planning is basically anthropocentric in its orientation.

The differences between Anne Marie Rubin and the younger Vibeke Dalgas can be attributed, among other things, to changes over time – both within the architectural profession and more generally in society. The mid-1960s see a confrontation with existing social norms and values as well as more specifically with the idea of the architect or urban planner as the supreme expert whose opinion is the only one that matters (see Chapter Four). In the 1960s, Rubin is still able to act in the role of expert, didactically explaining the plan for Lolland to the general public on the only Danish TV channel extant at the

In South Lolland, you can still see the large greens which Anne Marie Rubin and Ole Gerstrøm planned for the new holiday home areas. Large lawns framed by dense shrubberies and trees make the area seem green and open despite the large number of holiday homes.

time. Even so, both she and Ole Gerstrøm invite collaboration with local stakeholders and listen to many kinds of experts, although they do not devote the same attention to local residents as will later be the case in the coming decades of urban planning in Denmark.

Dalgas worked in a different context, one characterised by greater local interest and mobilisation right from the outset. This holds true on Nyord, where the local residents initiate the entire investigation, and in Ærøskøbing, where there is also great local interest in the work, attracting media attention and several public meetings in the town. The Nyord study thus shows aspects of what is always at stake when, on a planning scale, you build something new in an existing environment; a range of different interests, viewpoints and attributions come into play, and these cannot be pinned down in essential truths. Rather, the issues must be resolved through negotiation and consideration. By applying an expanded understanding of the history of modern urban planning, we can see models for more caring ways of creating spaces than the familiar outlook on the architecture of the period, which is based on thinking that celebrates economic and urban growth and which has created some of the problems we face today. On the basis of such an extended history, we can create future ways of acting in cities and landscapes, aware of the fact that anthropocentric perspectives and a myopic insistence on growth are not compatible with the necessary green transition.

Chapter 4

Alternatives – A New Architecture for a New Society

During two warm summer months in 1977, audiences flocked to the exhibition Alternative Architecture *at the Louisiana Museum of Modern Art in Humlebæk. Here visitors explored drawings, models, films and slide shows showing a wide range of different buildings and settlements: from Buckminster Fuller's airy domes and Paolo Soleri's experimental town Arcosanti to examples of new 'marginal architecture' created by American hippie communities. In the museum's large park, visitors could sit in a small house built from an* old wooden boat, or walk along a model of the façade of a colourful block of flats. The critics were enthusiastic, seeing the spectacular exhibition as a welcome contrast to the standardised residential buildings which were increasingly regarded as 'human-unfriendly housing environments'.[368] The exhibition catalogue reflected the criticism of modern architecture and urban development which had been growing increasingly pronounced, arguing that the type of architecture that arose out of the 1960s building boom had failed on many counts, including in terms of resource consumption, ecology, social communities and aesthetics.[369] The main purpose of the exhibition, however, was not to criticise but to show that it was possible to build differently and thus promote alternative ways of living and, ultimately, a better society. It was not only a matter of introducing new forms and meanings in architecture, but – as museum director Knud W. Jensen (1916–2000) stated in the introduction to the catalogue – of focusing on the fact that a new generation was now in the process of redefining 'the very tasks of architecture itself'.[370] That ambition seems highly topical today, a time in which architecture is closely interwoven with construction industries and urban development processes that are strongly driven by financial concerns, while the increasing recognition of the current biodiversity and climate crises highlight the necessity of us being able to imagine alternative futures.

The exhibition was an important contribution to the reorientation that took place in international architecture in the 1970s. It showed how architects sought new, dynamic, community-oriented and socially inclusive ways of working. Meanwhile, liberating forces strove to dismantle patriarchal power structures through social movements such as student protests, hippie culture and – increasingly – feminist activism. This also found expression in several exhibitions, for example the well-known *Women in American Architecture* from 1977: here, American feminists created an exhibition dedicated to women's architecture as a response to the many exhibitions which – without declaring themselves 'men's exhibitions' – showed the work of men.[371]

Alternative Architecture was not a women's exhibition; quite the opposite. Among the many named architects behind the more than 240 exhibits, we find almost only men. The underlying idea seems to be that men's architecture is the norm, while women were seen as the exception. Nevertheless, the two parts of the exhibition that attracted the most public attention were wholly or partly made by women. We will now examine this self-declared alternative architecture by following two of the women behind these two exhibition parts, asking what kind of alternative realities they sought to establish through their architectural works. Here we see that they both strove to create

In 1977, the exhibition *Alternative Architecture* opened at the Louisiana Museum of Modern Art in Humlebæk. The exhibits included a full-scale model of the façade of an unusual multi-storey building. Designed by architects Susanne Ussing and Carsten Hoff, the project aimed to show an alternative to the industrialised architecture of the 1960s. In this approach, architects were to have an initiating and advisory role, while it was up to the individual residents to develop their own homes, for example by adding bay windows, greenhouses, stairs and extra rooms in response to changing needs and opportunities.

alternative ways of making architecture, wishing to free themselves from restrictive power structures and values in society in order to stimulate more liberating and fair ways of living. At the same time, they sought to foster new ways of positioning themselves that were different from those found in the established architectural world and in the societal structures in which they were, however, also inextricably entangled, for better or for worse.

The critique of modernism in Denmark is often told by way of the contributions to the debate made by architect Jan Gehl (b. 1936) – with growing attention also being paid to psychologist Ingrid Gehl (b. 1940). They combined environmental psychological studies with analyses of everyday architecture, but were less oriented towards issues of gender and participation as the voices we will hear here.[372] At the same time, the historiography of postmodern architecture, which would set new agendas in the wake of modernism, is often – in Denmark as in several countries in Western Europe and America – centred on those architects, mostly men, who focused on issues of form and meaning.[373] The work done by Anne Marie Rubin and Susanne Ussing offers new perspectives on the feminist and socially oriented critique of modernism and of the architecture developed in the late 1970s. Among other things, their contribution to the exhibition *Alternative Architecture* points to the fact that several feminist positions were formulated at the time, each addressing issues of gender, social justice and diversity in different ways. Finally, we will look at a project that has so far not received attention in history writing – a project from the 1960s in which Anne Marie Rubin explicitly addresses global power structures as well as the structural inequalities that the racialisation of people entails – questions that remain topical today.

The (quite literally) biggest attraction at the *Alternative Architecture* exhibition was a full-size model of an experimental non-profit social housing block by Ussing + Hoff, meaning that it was created by the design studio run by the architects Susanne Ussing and Carsten Hoff. The other exhibition project which also attracted a great deal of attention even though few people will be familiar with it today was a room with photographs and texts describing the then-new Freetown of Christiania, where young squatters had lived for six years since they first occupied the area in 1971. This part of the exhibition was made by professor of urban planning Anne Marie Rubin and photographer Gerda Tosti Nielsen (1928–2020). Here we will follow the two architecturally trained women behind these exhibition projects, namely Susanne Ussing and Anne Marie Rubin, each of whom was a significant voice in Danish architecture and society in the years around the time of this exhibition.

Susanne Ussing (1940–1998) was trained as a potter at the Kunsthåndværkerskolen in Copenhagen in 1959 before studying architecture, graduating in 1963. Together with her partner in life and work Carsten Hoff (b. 1934), from 1968 onwards she worked on a range of exhibition projects and installations, presenting them under the name *Atelier Cyberspace* and, later, as Ussing + Hoff, the design studio they ran until the end of the 1970s. Ussing was a co-founder of the feminist magazine *Land og By* and contributed to several actions on gender and art. Prominent exhibitions include *The Children's Exhibition* at Louisiana in 1978, the group shows *The Women's Exhibition XX* in 1975 and *på vej* in 1980, as well as the solo show *Susanne Ussing – Works 1957–87* in 1987. Ussing continued her prolific artistic production until her death, creating decorative commissions, ceramics, drawings, sculpture, installations, land art and more.

The full-scale façade mock-up was hung on scaffolding. The project attracted great public interest and became an emblem of the *Alternative Architecture* exhibition.

Poster for the *Alternative Architecture* show at the Louisiana Museum of Modern Art. The exhibition showed a large collection of projects by contributors ranging from well-known international architects to American hippie communities and the Freetown Christiania commune in Copenhagen. The idea was to show that the widespread new, standardised and industrialised architecture was not the only way to build, pointing to alternative ways for architects to contribute to a better society.

The Women's Exhibition XX at Charlottenborg in Copenhagen was one of the 1970s' most significant art exhibitions dedicated to women. On show here were sculptures and picture series dealing with motherhood and birth, and a vast heart created by Susanne Ussing and Lene Adler Petersen welcomed visitors at the entrance to Charlottenborg, the Royal Danish Academy of Fine Art's exhibition venue set in a Baroque palace.

Neither Ussing nor Rubin designed large, eye-catching buildings that have been adopted into the canon of architectural history. None of them wrote long books about their architectural positions. Nevertheless, they both formulated alternatives to what they perceived as the current norms of the day, partly as regard the design of specific spaces and partly as regards ways of practicing architecture.

Ussing was a trained potter before she graduated as an architect in 1963, and she subsequently engaged in a wide range of collaborations as a curator, artist, activist, shop window decorator, architect and much more.[374] From the end of the 1960s and for the next decade, she worked with her life partner Carsten Hoff on a series of projects leading up to and culminating in their contribution to *Alternative Architecture*. Throughout her adult life she also maintained an artistic practice – alone and with others – and it is in this context that we see some of her earliest efforts to challenge established institutions by introducing feminist agendas and creating new alternative spaces rooted in women's lives.

Women and women's world take over new spaces

In 1975, *The Women's Exhibition XX* (*Kvindeudstillingen XX*) opened at Kunsthal Charlottenborg in Copenhagen – an exhibition made by and for women as a reaction against the male-dominated exhibition practice found at the established art institutions. *The Women's Exhibition XX*, in which Susanne Ussing joined other writers and visual artists as initiator, curator and exhibiting artist, attracted a great deal attention at the time and has subsequently become regarded as one of the first and most significant European women's exhibitions in the 1970s.[375] As was seen in much feminist art of the 1960s and 1970s, the artists featured at *The Women's Exhibition XX* brought up themes connected to women's lifeworld and everyday existence: here were sculptures and picture series about motherhood and birth, and a huge heart welcomed visitors at the entrance to the monumental mansion which is home to Charlottenborg, then and now one of Copenhagen's most influential art venues. Susanne Ussing's contribution included a range of sculptures whose soft shapes were reminiscent of rounded body parts, with a pair of women's panties seemingly casually draped

The Women's Exhibition XX, shown at Charlottenborg in 1975, was the result of an intensive collaborative effort where a large group of women came together to organise, curate, disseminate and exhibit art created by women in one collective exhibition. Susanne Ussing is at the top, sixth from the left. The others in the picture, bottom l. to r., are: Anne Behrndt and son, Marianne Larsen, Eva Weis Bentzon, Kirsten Dehlholm, Annelise Bock, Mette Aarre, Kathrine Hedward, Gertrud Skot-Hansen, Else Kallesøe, Hanne Fokdal, Pernille Kløvedal, Alice Møller Christensen, Line Storm, Birgitta Faber, Eva Bjerregaard, Kirsten Brand, Birthe Dalland, Vibe Fly, Bergliot Ragnars, Helen Lait Kluge, Torild Kristiansen, Kirsten Christensen, Inga Lyngbye, Kirsten W. Rasmussen, Hedda Matthesen, Susanne Mertz, Pernille Clausen, Anne Arentz, Lene Adler Petersen, Alice Kalsø, Birgit Pontoppidan, Hanne Lise Thomsen, Susanne Ussing, Sonny Foltmar.

Susanne Ussing and Carsten Hoff in the process of installing a *Sensory Spaces* exhibition. To create the amorphous room elements, they experimented with letting polyurethane foam expand and find its own shape – thereby relinquishing some of their own creative control. The way in which the space was created was driven by the idea of liberation. For Ussing, the *Sensory Spaces* series was a political project linked to the life worlds of women.

In the exhibition series *Sensory Spaces*, Susanne Ussing experimented with new shapes and spaces aimed at setting people free – encompassing such aspects as their imagination, experiences, notions of gender and their ways of using space. Here, the installation included a series of amorphously shaped cushions made of soft fabric that could be moved around freely, inviting visitors to lie down. These were surrounded by long, white plastic tubes inflated with helium. The tubes resembled long tentacles through which each visitor had to find their own way.

* Carsten Hoff states that the concepts for the *Sensory Spaces* were entirely Susanne Ussing's, while he contributed to the further work on them.[376]

on top. The very fact that a group of women took over a venerable and traditional art institution like Charlottenborg and filled it with themes pertinent to women's realm of experience was new – and a clear feminist statement.

Ussing's early spatial experiments also saw her striving to bring elements from women's world of experience into established art institutions. In a series of installations called *Sanserum* (Sensory Spaces) for which she developed the ideas and to which Carsten Hoff contributed in the late 1960s,* she introduced new forms and themes with her spatial design. Large organic shapes hung from the ceiling or extended across the floor. In line with her oft-stated demands for freedom and free expression for the individual, the *Sensory Spaces* did not prescribe a single, specific way of exploring them, instead exerting a more general appeal to the body and the imagination.[377] In an exhibition from 1970, a series of amorphously shaped cushions made from soft fabric could be moved freely around by visitors. In between the cushions were long white plastic tubes, some of them floating up against the ceiling because they were inflated with helium, others hanging down like long tentacles. Each visitor had to find their own way among them. An exhibition at Grønningen employed other experimental techniques, such as letting polyurethane foam expand and take shape inside plastic bags. In these experiments with form, Ussing deliberately and actively surrendered some of her shaping power to the materials, thereby pointing ahead to ideas later found in new materialism and feminist art theory.[378]

The *Sensory Spaces* had a certain kinship with furniture designer Verner Panton's (1926–1998) experimental furniture, rooms and environments from the 1960s and early 1970s, which also combined a series of richly inventive, organic forms in ways that blurred and dissolved the space. While Panton was preoccupied with the aesthetic encounter between body and space,[379] Susanne Ussing had a more overtly political aim with her experimental space. She wanted to make people more aware of the physical, bodily impact that architecture has on us humans, pointing to the need for alternatives to the uniformity of 1960s architecture.[380] She believed that left-wing thinkers were too often blind to the fact that materials and light have a strong effect on people, and that creating different forms of architecture can therefore have a liberating effect for inhabitants. Furthermore, in an interview in 1982 she describes that the choice of a given material also involves a gender aspect:

'There is a definite difference between men and women as regards materials and their use. Women have been surrounded by soft and hard materials in a completely different way from men. They have felt and experienced fabrics and materials in very different ways by, for example, looking after children, doing the housework, sewing and so on. They have inhabited a completely different material world.'[381]

The point conveyed here is not that women have a different innate aesthetic than men but rather that the cultural and physical experience of being a woman in post-war Denmark brought women into contact with a different material world, one that was linked to their experiences as a gender:

'I myself take a very direct approach in my work with materials. I work as myself in relation to them, engaging with them with the sense of engagement and empathy which is necessary if you want to do anything at all. Male artists must have the same empathy, but I have to assume that my starting point different. I have worked a great deal with organic materials and with organic ways of building things where you make changeable, malleable things by doing it a certain way with your hands.'[382]

This perception of materials is a central trait of the *Sensory Spaces*. What is more, these experiments with space see Ussing take on the role of an architect, surrendering some of her own control over the materials and what the visitors do, instead letting the materials govern the form and leaving the spaces open to different interpretations, individual expression and physical interaction by way of the body.

Radical participation in response to masculine architecture

A drawing from 1975 reflects Susanne Ussing's feminist critique of modern architecture and its value systems. *Barsebäck by Evening Sunlight* shows the then brand-new nuclear power plant located on the Swedish side of the Øresund as she saw it from her window in the old fishing town of Taarbæk north of Copenhagen. Right from the outset, the Barsebäck power plant attracted many protests, and in her 'diary of drawings' series Ussing recorded how she saw the new nuclear power plant. Like much of her work, most of these drawings are now lost due to a fire at her workshop in 1984. As is stated in a catalogue for a major exhibition held at some point after the fire: 'Only one shelf escaped the flames – it was thrown out of a window'.[383] The conflagration has caused Ussing's artistic production, already quite ephemeral insofar as it consisted largely of exhibitions, experiments and temporary installations, to become even more hidden from view for us historians.

One of the Barsebäck drawings still accessible to us today because it has been reproduced in several books shows the sun reflected in the water near the nuclear power plant with its two characteristic towers.[384] The phallic figure reflected in the water can hardly be overlooked. In this way, the drawing serves as a visual example of how Susanne Ussing forges a connection between markers of masculinity and the problems she associates with modern, industrial society. This is in line with a vein of feminist critique also seen in other architects of the period,[385] and with the concept of hegemonic masculinities, which emerged in gender research a few years later.[386] The criticism associated masculine symbols – in this case a phallus – with an oppressive use of power, exercised by men (if not all men) against women, minorities and other living beings.

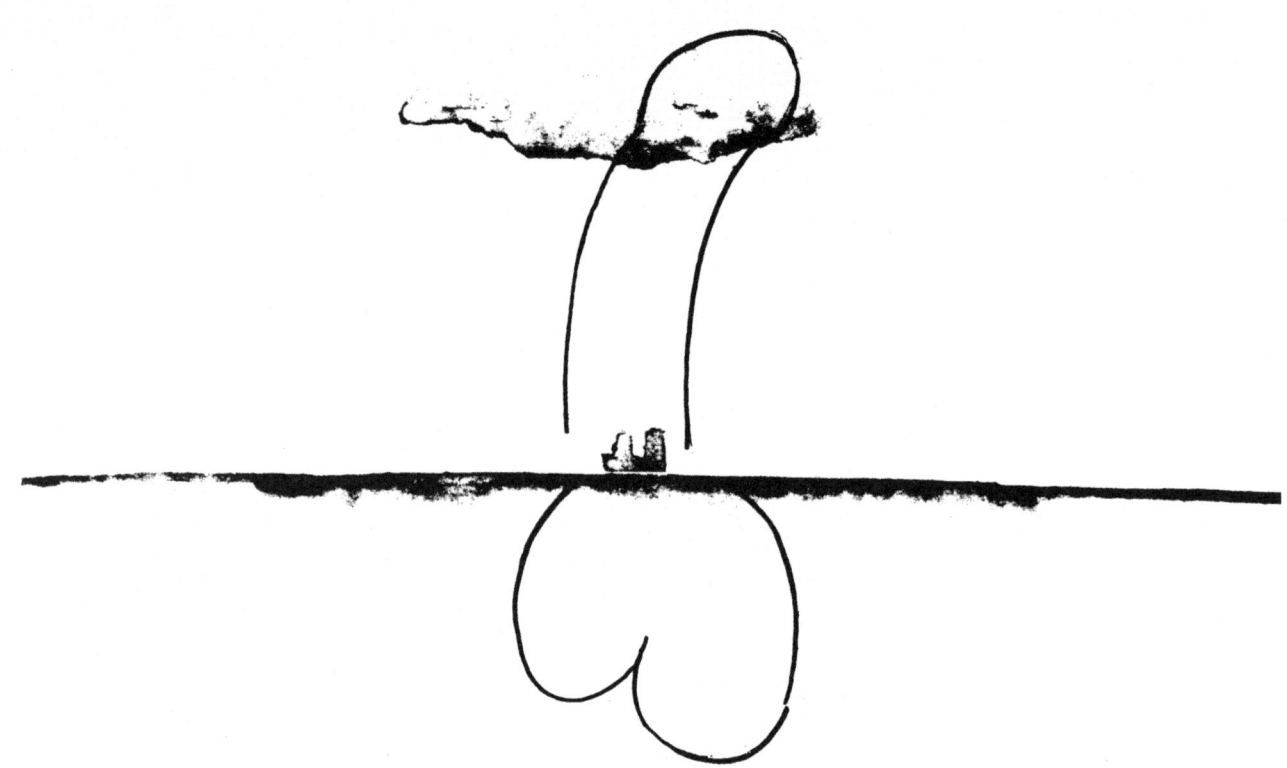

Barcebäck i aftensol S.U. 1975

Susanne Ussing was highly critical of the era's architecture and the value systems on which modern, industrialised societies were built. Her position is evident from this drawing. Made in 1975, *Barsebäck by Evening Sunlight* shows the then brand-new nuclear power plant on the Swedish side of the Sound, and the phallic form in the reflection can hardly be overlooked. For Susanne Ussing, modern architecture was very much infused by stereotypically masculine values.

The modern architecture against which Susanne Ussing, Carsten Hoff and several other architects rebelled was a result of sustained efforts to rationalise and not least industrialise building elements. This prompted the creation of thousands of flats arranged in uniform blocks, positioned with the aid of cranes on tracks, appearing as standardised concrete elements set on a uniform green carpet. Here is an example from Ballerup created by Ussing's parents, the architects Elsebet and Kjeld Ussing, just after it was built in the 1960s.

Susanne Ussing later described her own practice as a resistance to and rebellion against the dominant forms of architecture she observed at the time, prompted by the general growth and building boom of the 1960s (see Chapter Three). In particular, she was strongly critical of the many housing developments being built for thousands of people and which, as a result of the industrialisation of the construction sector were all designed at a desk, fuelled by a strong focus on rationalisation and quantity over quality. She, alongside many other critics of modernism, believed that it was now time to find alternatives to such alienating developments with no true relationship to their sites[387] – alternatives which she also linked to a critique of dominant power structures in society. She was a harsh critic of 'the prefabricated kind of construction represented by the old men – which is what I call those who make the decisions'.[388] On her own and in her collaboration with Carsten Hoff, she strove to engender alternative roles for architects that were not subject to the patriarchal structures of society, and which sought to escape hegemonic masculinities and oppressive power structures. It is in this light that we should view the project they showed at the Louisiana exhibition – a project that pointed back to their work from the early 1970s, which we will now introduce.

Liberating yet disappointing camp experiments

The story of Ussing + Hoff's Louisiana project begins with an architectural experiment created for and at the Thylejren encampment and festival in 1970. This and their subsequent joint projects were the result of such close collaboration that it makes no sense to single out Susanne Ussing's individual contribution. The Thylejren camp was organised by Det Ny Samfund (The New Society), an association of young people with an interest in developing alternative ways of living. They bought a piece of land in Frøstrup in north-Jutland and invited anyone who wanted to contribute to show up unannounced, live in the camp and help co-create its experimental lifestyle during the scheduled five-month duration of the festival. The exact activities at the camp would be made up as the participants went along, but the overall objective was to develop alternative models for society as a whole.

At the Thylejren encampment and festival in 1970, Ussing + Hoff made a range of cheap, easy-to-use building materials available to the camp participants: fishing nets, tarpaulins, chipboard and chicken wire, as well as corrugated cardboard folded using a special technique. Ussing + Hoff saw the Thylejren project as a model for the development of alternative, more open and participatory ways of building, serving as a basis for new and better ways of living together. Susanne Ussing recorded a film showing how the project developed along the way, and how she herself, together with Carsten Hoff and their children, had set up places to sleep, eat, play, climb, store things and enter into wider communities.

Ussing + Hoff's contribution consisted of a physical structure in which camp participants could settle and arrange themselves as they wished during the three months' duration. The shape of the complex was only sketchily planned in advance, and it would be changed along the way to respond to local weather conditions and the participants' activities. A sign at the entrance clearly indicated the open-ended, inclusive nature of the project: 'The Scaffolding Houses. Anyone is welcome to take part in this housing experiment. Anyone can arrange themselves as they like in the scaffolding. Bring your own ideas and materials, or use ours'.[389]

Ussing + Hoff provided a range of cheap building materials which would be easy to work with for the people who were to live in the temporary structure. They included fishing nets, tarpaulins, chipboard and chicken wire, as well as corrugated cardboard folded using a special technique.[390] Ussing + Hoff saw the Thy project as a model for the development of alternative, more open and participatory ways of building. This was in keeping with an approach taken by many architects from the 1960s and 1970s who strove to develop 'flexibility', 'open systems', 'organic growth' and 'participation'.[391] For example, the two Danish architects were keenly interested in the work of the Franco-Hungarian architect Yona Friedman (1923–2020). Back in 1958–62 he had developed the idea of the *Ville Spatiale* – an alternative city based on a kind of skeleton structure in which residents were to develop their own homes and everyday environment without the aid of architects.[392] However, the concept remained at the idea stage and was, unlike Ussing + Hoff's camp projects, never carried out.

Executing the experiment in practice also brought the realisation that things do not always go as expected. Susanne Ussing and Carsten Hoff became frustrated when people began using other materials that were not in keeping with the aesthetic direction laid down by the architects.[393] And the architects' ideas about the community which was to emerge and unfold at the site were challenged along the way. Looking back today, Hoff remembers that an anarchist moved into the camp who, apart from raising a single black flag, was not very interested in communicating with anyone else, let alone in participating in the community.[394] Was this a form of individual exercise of freedom that could be accepted in the experiment, which was after all based on an expectation that people would contribute to the social community? The lessons learnt from the alternative summer camp were food for thought.

Most of all, however, Ussing and Hoff were disappointed at the low turnout. Several camp guests only came to look at the proceedings or stayed for a few days without taking part in the collective, experimental construction projects. Others built something themselves, but in places that were more sheltered than Ussing + Hoff's structure, meaning that their structures were further away from the windswept coast. One visitor wrote:

'As far as I remember, the weather was bleak and overcast, the wind blowing across the open heath towards the A11 highway where Hoff's and Ussing's peculiar scaffolding with some ragged bits of plastic fluttered and roared in the gale, while tough individualists dug in to survive. The rest of us were sheltered behind the fir trees in De Gamles By and only felt the rush of the wind when we ventured out to the music venue.'[395]

With barely concealed disappointment, Ussing and Hoff reflected:

'The fact is that there was no real need for the activity we had planned. The self-built construction taking place at the site could not be accommodated within our project, because outside of it you could do whatever you wanted. Why would anyone voluntarily choose to be limited? [...] Nothing became of the model in itself because it did not channel the construction activity that was actually taking place. Engaging with the project required an awareness that this was a model situation, a study for something outside society. That is why those who went along with it were mostly architects.'[396]

However, their disappointment with this particular experiment did not put an end to Ussing + Hoff's work with participation. They launched more experiments where they tried to strike a balance between a sense of responsibility for the common good and individual liberty, between aesthetic and social coherence and community on the one hand and users' freedom of action on the other, or between the architects' own action and withdrawal. Building on the lessons learnt in Thy, Ussing + Hoff chose a different approach at a later summer camp at Vejlø outside Næstved in 1973. Here they assumed a role as architects where they encouraged participation to an even greater degree than in Thy. They chose materials which they believed would provide greater durability and make for a better aesthetic whole: upright mahogany posts on which roofs, floors and so on could easily be added. They then devoted their energy to building a large communal kitchen and common room to bring together the various campers. This time they did not want to direct or control how people should build, and they left the choice of materials entirely open. They therefore withdrew even more than in Thy. They left the camp and came back only for a brief stay once a week to observe how the experiment progressed over time. This time they were much more satisfied with the

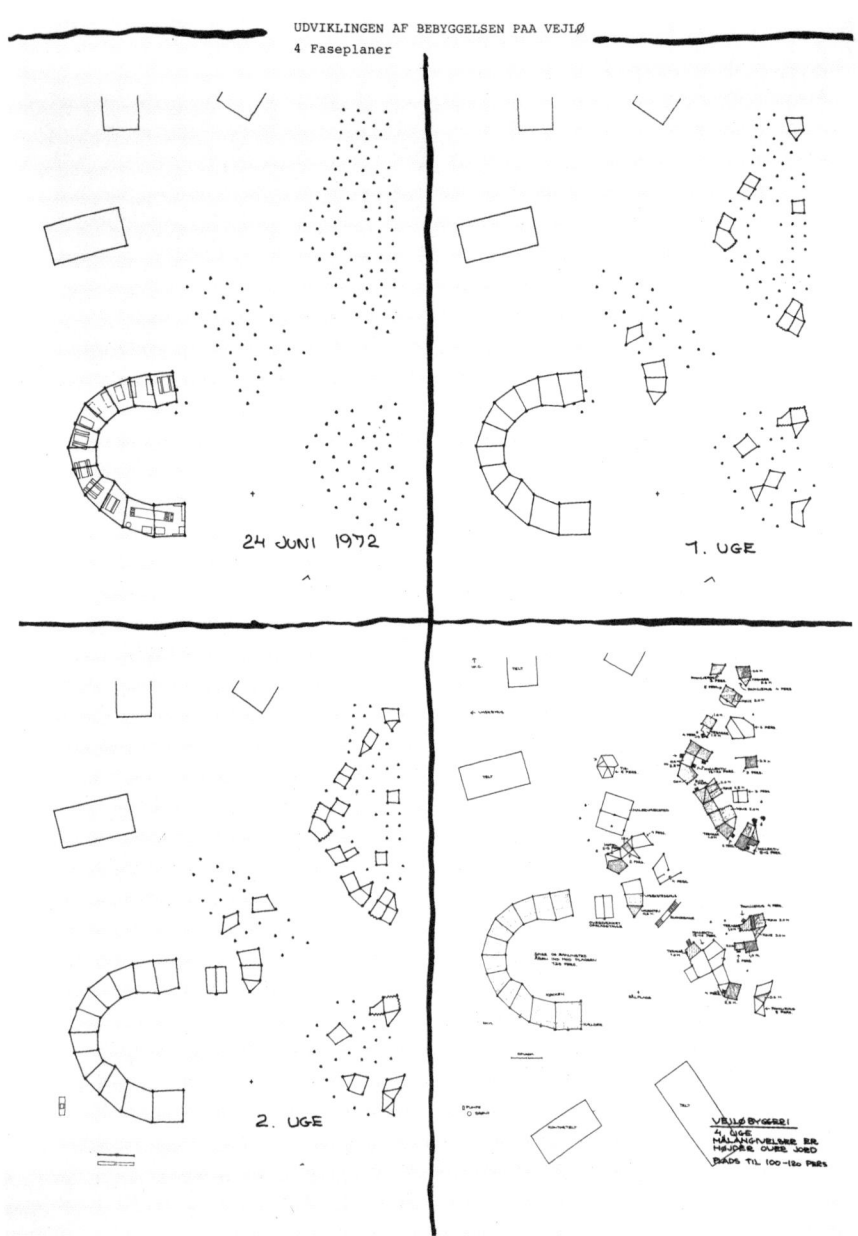

Based on their experiences as architects and participating observers at Thylejren, Susanne Ussing and Carsten Hoff continued to work with the ideas of participatory architecture, including at a camp at Vejlø near Næstved in 1973. Here they devised another scaffolding structure inviting people to continue building as they wished. Ussing and Hoff chose to play a background role as architects: they did not design any forms or spaces for the project, opting instead to document how the camp participants used the structure. Photographing the developments week by week, they also created drawings of how people built on top of the structure of wooden posts set up by the architects (marked as dots on the plan). They then charted how people gradually set up tent-like houses. Ussing subsequently published the drawing and the collage seen here in the feminist journal *Land og By*, of which she was co-editor.

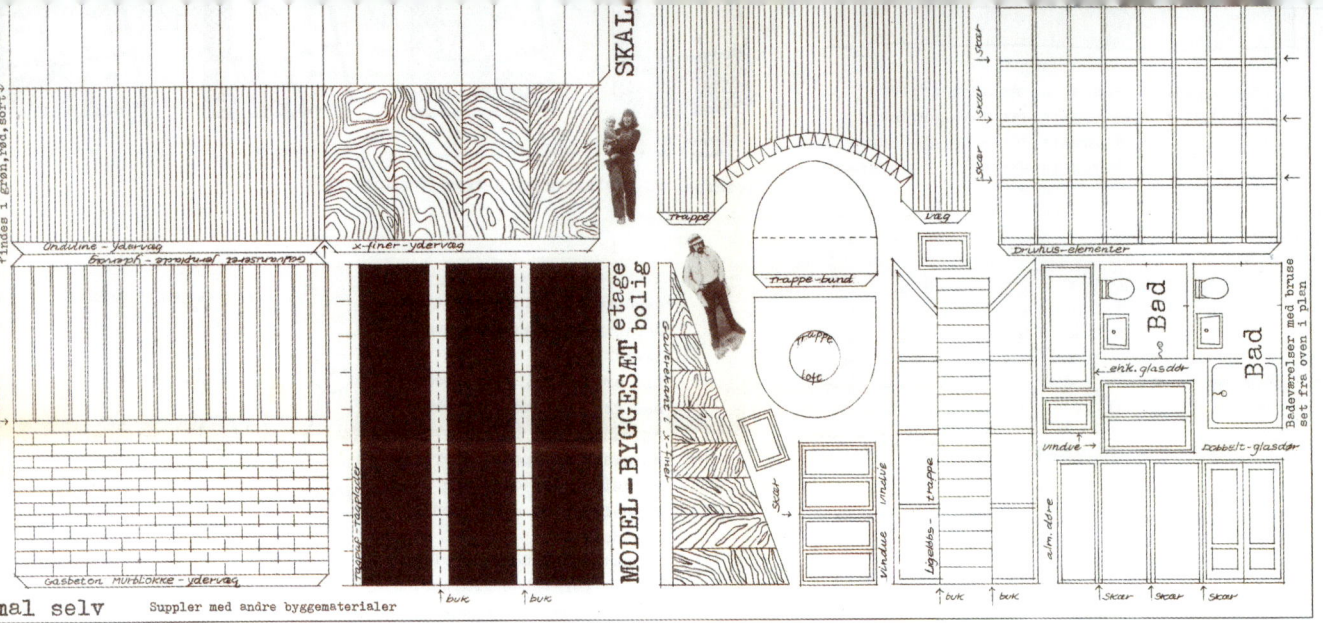

"Landskabet skal have en karakter der hele tiden kan skab[e] menhæng af visuelle og kropslige oplevelser i nærmiljø[et] sammensat både rum/form/størrelsesmæssigt."
"Landskabet er formet så det giver varierede, men forståe[lige]..."

"Boligselskabet udarbejder et byggesystem af LETTE elementer, så vidt muligt eksisterende, men suppleret med det, som mangler."
"... for at kunne indleve sig i byggesystemets muligheder for at tilfredsstille de individuelle behov, udleveres til de potentielle beboere en planche af pap eller plastic, der indeholder en udstanset skalamodel af byggesystemets enkelte elementer."

"Projektet repræsenterer udgangspunktet for et laboratorium, hvor bevidste boligforsøg sættes igang, analyseres og danner basis for byggeriets videre forløb".

"Grunden lejes, mens husene ejes. Spekulation er ikke tilladt, men egen arbejdsindsats honoreres ved videresalg."
Ejerformen er et middel – et middel i bestræbelserne på at bedre beboernes muligheder for at øve indflydelse på udformningen af deres bolig og øvrige nærmiljø, og for at udfolde sig inden for disse fysiske rammer.

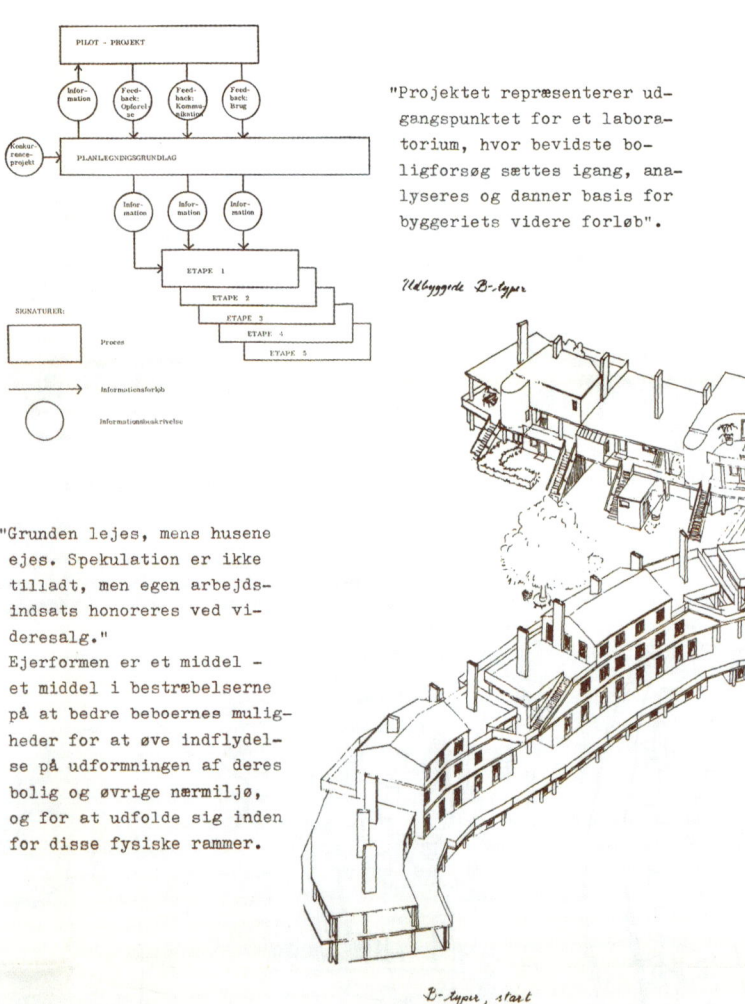

"Dette projekt beskæftiger sig med spørgsmålet om planlægning contra individuel frihed, udfra den betragtning at miljøfattigdommen i etagebolig-områderne bl.a. skyldes, at individet ingen indflydelse har på udformningen af sin egen bolig eller på de fælles omgivelser. Man har ingen udfoldelsesmuligheder, aktiviteter får ikke lov at opstå på frit initiativ, dels er der ikke plads afsat, dels lægger den stive arkitektur ikke op til den slags. Man bliver fremmedgjort fra sine omgivelser, selv de meget nære, man bliver isoleret fra sine medmennesker, til trods for at man bor i tætte bysamfund."

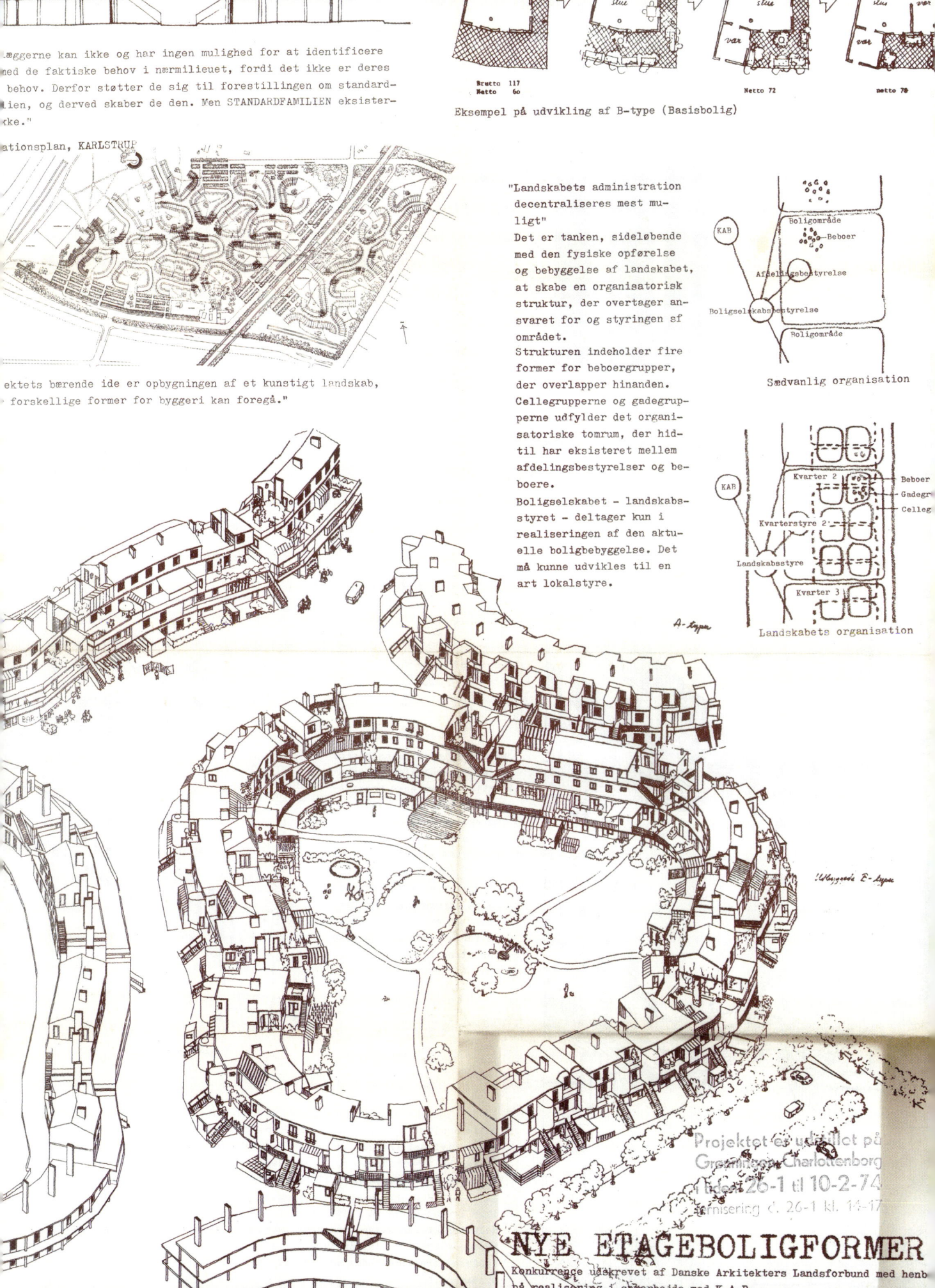

outcome. Acting as ethnographers, they made field notes, for example in the form of a floor plan and in a series of photographs, recording how people settled in, developed and built the structure over time.

Ussing + Hoff's work was characterised by a method whereby they would launch experiments and then learn from the experience. They questioned their own role as specially trained experts, and they tested the various positions they could adopt in their collaboration with people in temporary on-site experiments. They wanted to democratise architecture by incorporating many forms of knowledge, including those of future residents, while at same time retaining a responsibility as designers – a balance that several architects at the time tried to strike.[397] This shows that they were very aware of the tension between freedom and control, between process and form, and between individual and community, without resorting to simple binary either-or versions. Susanne Ussing later published a series of photos from the Vejlø experiment in the feminist magazine *Land og By*, of which she was one of the founding editors.[398] We can see their project as a feminist act – an attempt to set all people free from patriarchal structures. They sought to disrupt the established hierarchy of knowledge and power which unequivocally casts the architect in the role of expert vis-à-vis those who will later live in and use the architecture. Instead, they aimed to highlight the importance of situated knowledge from a user's perspective.

Greater freedom for residents and for architects

Frustrated by the norms, rules and established structures that applied in the field of architecture, Susanne Ussing and Carsten Hoff wondered if their only 'real political options as architects' resided in finding other ways than working within 'the existing system and with its methods'.[399] Yet they also benefited from these structures, networks and established institutions. The Thylejren project was supported by Danmarks Nationalbank's Jubilæumsfond of 1968, where their former professor at the Royal Danish Academy of Fine Arts' School of Architecture, Erik Herløw (1913–1991), sat on the board. In 1973 they won a major design competition in collaboration with the design studio run by Susanne Ussing's parents, Elsebet and Kjeld Ussing, as well as architect Sven Sture Müller (1931–2022) and

Previous spread: Materials from the winning submission for a 1973 design competition on new types of multi-storey buildings. Created by Susanne Ussing and Carsten Hoff along with architects Elsebet Ussing, Kjeld Ussing and Svend Møller and engineer Povl Egon Malmstrøm, the project experimented with new urban forms and with flexible principles of construction that gave residents extensive scope for shaping their own housing. A cardboard construction kit enabled residents to build small-scale models to assist them in developing their own home. The project also included detailed guidelines on how decentralised decisions about construction and management could be made by the individual resident groups.

their collaboration partner, the well-established engineer Povl Egon Malmstrøm (1917–1985).[400] This was shortly after the launch of the better-known design competition for low-rise high-density housing issued by the Danish Building Research Institute in 1971, in which Ussing + Hoff had also participated, but the task in 1973 was to create a new form of multi-storey non-profit social housing that 'diverges from general modern construction on essential issues'.[401] The contributions had to be flexible to changes over time and enable 'greater freedom to choose one's own lifestyle' for the future residents.[402]

Drawing on the radical form of participation that had characterised Ussing + Hoff's camp experiments, their competition proposal consisted of nothing more than a three-storey concrete structure and a modular system of vertical channels to which water, sewage and electricity could be connected; everything else was left entirely up to the people who would move into the building. However, to help future residents with issues such as room layout, walls, stairs and surfaces within the raw structure, the proposal included a template which prospective residents could cut out and use to build models from, thus enabling them to try out various options. The submission also provided thorough and detailed outlines of funding options, suggesting that residents could join together in groups and co-finance the buildings in ways that were far less centralised than established non-profit housing developments in Denmark. The architects offered to contribute technical support, advice on organisation and other assistance to the residents. In the second phase of the competition, a plot of land was set aside in Karlslunde, south of Copenhagen, where the social housing association KAB was to build the winning project.[403]

While the project was never realised, the architects used the *Alternative Architecture* exhibition in 1977 as a welcome opportunity to make their proposal publicly known and give it renewed topicality. Ussing + Hoff exhibited it in the form of a model in a glass display case and a large full-scale model of one of the three-storey façades in the garden outside the museum. The exhibition at Louisiana showed the dream scenario for this housing project: differently coloured dwellings placed on top of and next to each other, with additions such as garden trellises and chairs, an extra staircase and a turquoise-painted door that appeared to have been recycled from an older house. The total effect conveyed the impression that the residents had added various elements gradually – an extra room here, a greenhouse there – as new needs and ideas arose. These additions suited the recycling and vernacular aesthetics of the time, and their hodgepodge feel shared certain similarities with the Freetown of Christiania's caravan buildings in Børneengen or its converted barracks known as Psyak.

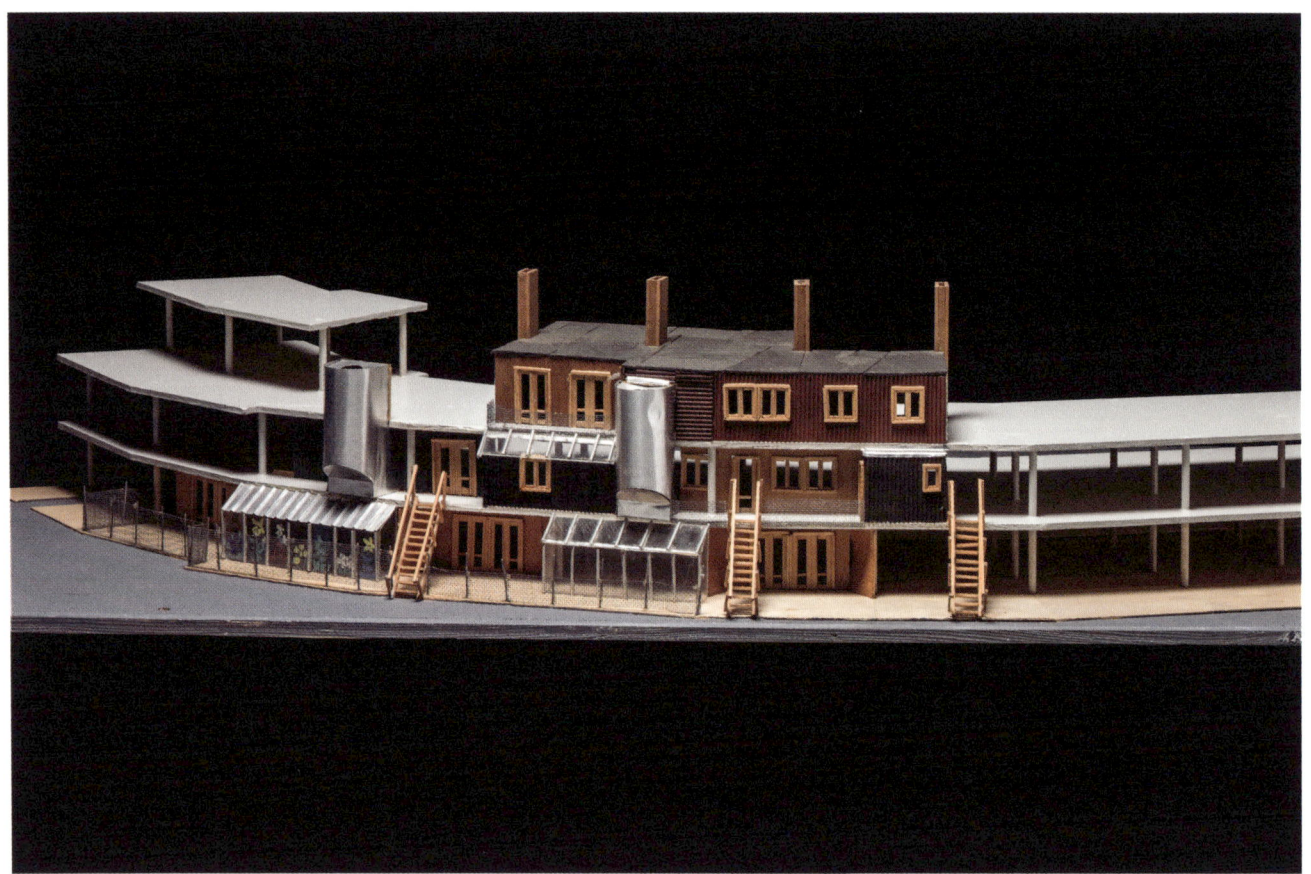

The winning project for the design competition on new types of blocks of flats was never realised, but it did receive a lot of attention. At the *Alternative Architecture* exhibition at the Louisiana Museum of Modern Art, visitors could see a life-sized mock-up of the façade as well as this architectural model. It demonstrates the fundamental principle of making a basic structure available and then letting residents create their own dwellings in keeping with changing needs and opportunities.

However, Ussing + Hoff's ideas about new ways of living in blocks of flats never reached the construction stage. According to the two architects, this was because the Danish social housing sector and the municipality were unable to sufficiently rethink their administrative and economic structures to facilitate the project's alternative ideas about participation and development over time.[404] Similar ideas about participation were found elsewhere in that time in countercultural experimental projects as well as established institutional construction, such as Ralph Erskine's (1914–2005) housing development Byker in Newcastle, Britain, and in some housing developments in Denmark – although these were less radical than Ussing + Hoff's submission for the multi-storey housing design competition.* Their ideas about

* Farum Midtpunkt and Tinggården are examples of Danish social housing from the 1970s created by architects who knew about Ussing + Hoff's projects, and where several design decisions were left to the residents. In the early 1970s, the Danish social housing sector saw the development of comprehensive resident democracy.

empowering residents to create their own living environment were not just utopian alternatives; they contributed to setting new agendas, and they were entangled with other movements stirring within the field of housing construction at the time, as is evident from the competition directions. Their efforts were partially supported by centrally located individuals, institutions and structures, meaning that they were simultaneously in opposition to and closely affiliated with established power structures in society and in their professional field.[405]

Creating a voice for yourself as a woman

Susanne Ussing repeatedly expressed the view that the conditions, norms and structures of construction stood in the way of developing the kind of cities and housing that she believed necessary. In 1980, she described how, a few years earlier, she had said her final goodbye to architecture as a practice: 'Having recognised my own powerlessness in the face of the dominant power structure, I no longer see, given what I can do, any other options than taking on the role of artist'.[406] To her mind, the alternative architecture practice she had developed together with Carsten Hoff had proved impossible to realise within the established system, and for that reason she could not continue working in the profession. Her sense of being outside the established field of architecture reflects a conception of architecture in which the construction of durable and obviously designed buildings was – and often still is – central. Within such an outlook on architecture, the alternative forms of practice with which she and Hoff worked – including exhibitions, temporary installations, experiments with participatory processes, design proposals that contributed to setting new agendas, and texts about architecture and the city – are not seen as equally valuable as the act of designing buildings which are clearly designed entities.

Ussing experienced other structural limitations associated with the general approach to architecture while still a student at the School of Architecture. In an interview in 1974, she described her time as a woman at the school in these terms: 'It was difficult. My voice, for one thing. It was too reedy, too light […]'.[407] She had similar experiences later in her working life when carrying out negotiations with 'the men in [the social housing company] KAB' who wanted to build Ussing + Hoff's winning proposal for the design competition on a block of flats. In such negotiations, she noted, it was obvious that 'a man seems to inspire greater trust [...]',[408] and so it often fell to Hoff to take the lead in conversations with clients. In a television interview from 1977, we see them standing together in front of their mock-up façade at Louisiana.[409] Susanne Ussing is looking directly and purposefully at the interviewer, both hands planted firmly in her front pockets. The interviewer is a man, notably older than the two architects, and he often passes the microphone directly to Carsten Hoff, for example when he asks how a project like this can be realised in technical and practical terms. Later in the broadcast, Ussing receives the microphone when the interviewer, in a slightly lighter tone than usual, asks how future neighbours will resolve potential problems in such a collective building. Showing great confidence and faith in the project, Ussing replies that when neighbours speak to each other, they are usually able to resolve things. Probing the question, the interviewer asks: 'What if water from the upper tenant's roof drips down into the flat of the tenant below?' Here, Hoff takes the floor again, describing the technical solutions and explaining how joint guidelines must be drawn up, and so the subject seems resolved. Ussing is the only one in the clip who is interrupted, and she does not get to speak as much as Hoff. While she appears self-confident and idealistic, she also meets resistance in the conversation – seemingly as a result of patriarchal notions about the man being the most trustworthy expert in matters regarding the technical and financial feasibility of the project.

Perhaps in such situations Susanne Ussing recollected her mother, the architect Elsebet Ussing, who was married to fellow architect Kjeld Ussing. The two had shared a design studio in the home where Susanne Ussing grew up. In an interview, Ussing states that she regards her mother as someone 'who was once a fine architect, but then got a husband who had to have his dinner first, and five children who had to have clean clothes every day – and that killed her career'.[410] Not wanting to end up the same way, Susanne Ussing insisted on being able to work on her own terms. As a ceramicist, she did not want to make 'lamps and all these little cups that girls indulge in, there are enough of those already. No, I wanted to make big, beautiful sculptures that you can really get to grips with'.[411] Here we find her poised between wanting to carve out her own space and still being subject to the constricting expectations associated with her gender.

Ussing and Hoff describe their collaboration as a close and 'equal partnership'.[412] People who worked with them describe how Ussing came across as the most visionary of the two, while Hoff – who was a trained carpenter before becoming an architect – was the practical

Susanne Ussing came across structural barriers and stereotyping due to her gender on several occasions, but at the same time she was a strong voice in public debates and engaged in a substantial artistic practice, creating significant projects. Thus, she found herself poised between asserting herself and being subject to the confining expectations linked to her gender. Shown here is her sculpture *In the Glass House* at the Ordrupgaard museum, in which a woman appears to be simultaneously confined, strong, and capable of breaking through the ceiling at any moment.

one that 'made it all happen'.[413] In an interview in 2022, Hoff describes Ussing as a 'courageous' artist who, unlike his own young self, dared to 'go all the way'.[414] Hoff has continued his architectural work through publications, exhibitions and smaller buildings ever since. Susanne Ussing died in 1998, and in recent years her artistic production has attracted renewed interest, manifesting in a number of exhibitions.[415] She is represented in major art collections, while several of Ussing + Hoff's plans can be found in private archives.[416] Hoff has created a website featuring Ussing's work, and he has helped to present and make her material available to several publications and exhibitions.[417] In this way, he continues to be her companion even after her death, tending to her legacy in a caring role that marks a departure from gender stereotypes where women are generally more often associated with such dissemination and archiving work than men.[418] The collaboration between Ussing and Hoff shows that values traditionally associated with the feminine and the masculine do not necessarily have to be attached to the female or the male body, as each of them has taken on multifaceted roles. Susanne Ussing's significant voice as part of feminist initiatives in social debates, her role as developer in her collaboration with Carsten Hoff – and her experience of not being taken as seriously as her male collaborator – all testify to some of the conflicting expectations and opportunities associated with her gender at the time. While it is well-known how the American architect Robert Venturi initially received the acclaimed Pritzker Prize without any credit being given to his life-long collaborator Denise Scott Brown (see Chapter Two), Ussing + Hoff were jointly awarded two of Denmark's most prestigious awards for architecture back in the 1980s, namely the Nykredits Arkitekturpris (1988) and the Eckersberg Medal (1989).

When historians of architecture have addressed twentieth-century women and their collaborations, their accounts have often emphasised specific types of collaborations. We mainly find women as collaborators of a better-known architect who is a man, such as Lilly Reich (1885–1947) and Ludwig Mies van der Rohe (1886–1969) or Charlotte Perriand (1903–1999) and Le Corbusier 1887–1965).[419] Recent years have seen a growing interest in women's collaborations in the feminist collectives which appear in the late 1970s and continue into the 1980s, such as Matrix in the UK, BIG in Sweden and others.[420] By telling Susanne Ussing's story, we become able to see how a single person can move across such collaborative relationships, being part of a number of long- and short-term creative communities that might even change along the way. One of these communities consisted of the other artists and writers with whom she created *The Women's Exhibition XX*.

One of Ussing's collaborators, the author Birgit Pontoppidan, later described how the women involved in the feminist magazine *Land og By* and *The Women's Exhibition XX* convened and worked together: everything was very informal, with no appointed leaders nor any minutes taken of meetings.

They were partly, but not entirely, the same group of women who made up the editorial staff of the feminist journal *Land og By* which Susanne Ussing had helped start. And all this happened concurrently with her collaborating with Carsten Hoff in their design studio and living with him as a couple. One of Ussing's collaborators, the writer Birgit Pontoppidan (b. 1942), describes how the women met up to work on *Land og By* and *The Women's Exhibition XX*: 'Everything was informal, there was no leader, no one wanted to take the minutes […]. There was an unstoppable energy that flowed from phone to phone'.[421] Pontoppidan notes that the women met in 'Susanne and Carsten's basement',[422] and we can imagine the young artists undertaking their loosely organised, collective work at a large table covered with cups, pens and sketch paper, perhaps with Carsten Hoff or their children interrupting them along the way.

Although Ussing became involved in several feminist initiatives over the years, she did not identify with one specific women's movement or group. In the introduction to a catalogue for a major solo show of her work in 1987 – a text we must assume she read before it was printed – it is stated that: 'To her, simply being a woman did not necessarily equate absolute solidarity with all women'.[423] So even though she would work exclusively with women in certain contexts, this does not necessarily signify that she was concerned with women's communities across class divides and global inequalities. Nor does it mean that she thought it was always relevant to work in women's communities. When Ussing was invited to curate an art exhibition in 1978, she made a point of including both men and women in the work.[424] The trait is typical of her practice, which does not fit easily into one specific group identity and category. Rather, as an architect and artist, she seems to engage in a ceaseless exploration in terms of working methods, themes and positions.

Learning from everyday life in squatted spaces

Besides Ussing + Hoff's mock-up façade, the parts of the *Alternative Architecture* exhibition which attracted the most attention were those associated with Christiania.[425] In this context we find Anne Marie Rubin, who was older than Susanne Ussing and already well established in the realm of Danish architecture when the exhibition took place (see Chapter Three). At this time, Rubin was professor of community planning at Aalborg University, where Gerda Tosti Nielsen worked in an administrative capacity. Tosti Nielsen had previously been a member of the Danish Parliament, was a professional photographer and involved in various women's associations. The two women, both of whom had powerful voices on the Danish cultural scene, had become interested in the controversial Freetown commune of Christiania and were now presenting it to the Louisiana audience.

Since 1971, squatters had begun settling in the former military barracks in Bådsmandsstræde in central Copenhagen, partly as a protest against the city's extreme lack of housing and partly out of a desire to create an alternative community and foster different ways of living. By moving into the abandoned military buildings and transforming them into homes and communal spaces, and by using caravans and mobile site huts as the basis for their building activities, the Christianites, as they eventually called themselves, created a social experiment which they later proclaimed a Freetown with its own rules, institutions and administration. For example, Christiania developed its own processes on how to develop and manage housing, communal houses, roads and green areas.[426] Located on state-owned land, the commune stood apart from the surrounding society and its institutions, yet was closely connected with and dependent on those factors. Christiania was due to be cleared when Rubin and Tosti Nielsen began to document the settlement as part

Byplanforslaget måske for ombudsmanden:

Tusinder protesterer mod Christiania-plan

Arkitekten, professor Anne Marie Rubin, Ålborg Universitetscenter, finder det så påfaldende, at Københavns magistrats byplanforslag for Christiania nøje svarer til et tidligere udarbejdet ideforslag fra Kooperativ Byggeindustri, at hun kræver spørgsmålet opklaret, og hun venter at sagen havner hos ombudsmanden.

Anne Marie Rubin gjorde allerede for nogle uger siden officiel indsigelse mod byplanforslaget, idet hun henviste til, at der ikke var tale om planlægning, og at det er i strid med ånden i byplanloven. Indsigelsen blev samtidig sendt til ombudsmanden, som har sendt den videre til planstyrelsen til udtalelse. Ombudsmanden har ingen muligheder for at gribe ind og tage en sag op, før alle øvrige klagemuligheder er udtømt, men Anne Marie Rubin venter ikke, at planstyrelsen under miljøministeriet vil give hende ret i alle klagepunkter. Derfor vil hun igen gå til ombudsmanden.

Den kvindelige professors indsigelse er kun en blandt adskillige tusinde, der er nået frem, før indsigelsesfristen udløb i går.

Protesterne kommer fra mange tusinde enkeltpersoner og fra en lang række arkitekter, byplanlæggere, foreninger og sagkyndige organisationer.

Kontorchef Henning Frederiksen, direktoratet for stadens bygningsvæsen, havde ikke det nøjagtige antal opgjort i går.

Men der er ingen tvivl om, at magistratens byplanforslag er det, der er mødt med den mest massive protest her hjemme.

Et gennemgående træk er, at de protesterende anser kommunens plan for at være et alibi til at rydde fristaden.

Og i den forbindelse kan udfaldet af Anne Marie Rubins supplerende indsigelse blive interessant. Hun spørger nemlig, om der i virkeligheden foreligger en formaliseret aftale mellem magistraten og KBI om, at kommunen skal følge KBIs idéforslag. Derved vil byplanloven være krænket, idet en sådan fremgangsmåde må betragtes som værende illegitim, siger hun.

Proceduren i kommunen er nu, at indsigelserne skal behandles i direktoratet og forelægges borgerrepræsentationen. Men selv om et flertal i borgerrepræsentationen fastholder den hidtidige plan, er den ikke godkendt. Det er miljøministeriet, der har det sidste ord at skulle have sagt. blue

Arkitekt, professor Anne Marie Rubin spørger, om der eksisterer en formaliseret men illegitim aftale om bebyggelsesforslag

---

In the 1970s, a number of architects fought for the continued existence of the Freetown Christiania commune, the best-known being architect and professor Steen Eiler Rasmussen. Anne Marie Rubin also used her influential voice as a professor to defend the experiment as an alternative form of architecture and urban development, presenting her arguments via the press.

* In addition to the *Alternative Architecture* show at the Louisiana museum, Anne Marie Rubin and Gerda Tosti Nielsen also exhibited their Christiania project at the Arkitekturmuseet in Stockholm in 1977.

of the teaching of urban planning students at Aalborg University in 1975. At the time, Christiania's approximately one thousand inhabitants were primarily young people – a mixture of left-wing activists, artists and members of the student movement – as well as people with social challenges and substance abuse behaviour. There were also children there, and the not-unproblematic conditions faced by these young inhabitants during the first years of this adult-oriented project of liberation have later attracted considerable criticism.[427]

At the exhibition, Rubin and Tosti Nielsen presented Christiania partly through a series of slides projected onto the museum's brick walls, and partly through short texts.* They showed street scenes and everyday situations in spaces where military architecture met psychedelic murals and recycled materials. One image shows a section of a street façade. In front of it are several long-haired, jeans-clad young people watching life in the street. A bicycle is propped against a wall near a front door, haphazardly placed. Green branches extend into the image of this seemingly idyllic environment. The photographs capture how people have improvised things as the need arose. A few boards can become a bench, a bicycle does not need a bicycle rack. This is how the alternative urban space of Christiania comes across through Tosti Nielsen's lens. The photos often show close-ups of social situations in buildings

Gerda Tosti Nielsen used her camera to show how the young squatters transformed the former military architecture at Christiania into new forms of housing and communal spaces based on alternative aesthetic ideals.

In 1971, squatters took over the former military barracks in Bådsmandsstræde in Copenhagen and founded the community that would later become the Freetown Christiania. Created in protest against Copenhagen's housing shortage, the action also reflected a desire to create a place where people could pursue alternative lifestyles. Architect Anne Marie Rubin and photographer Gerda Tosti Nielsen documented the site in connection with a course for urban planning students at Aalborg University in 1975 and later showed photographs of Christiania at the 1977 exhibition *Alternative Architecture* at the Louisiana Museum of Modern Art.

* Anne Marie Rubin was a friend of Christopher Alexander and visited him in California on several occasions.[428]

and communal spaces. With an implicit reference to the American Christopher Alexander (1936–2022), who was both a trained mathematician and an architect, and a weighty voice in the 1970s' international criticism of modernism, Anne Marie Rubin writes*:

'[…] just as in mathematics you sometimes have to choose a point outside the system in order to understand what is going on within the system, these images from Christiania may perhaps tell us something about the environmental problems within our general social system.'[429]

She describes Christiania as an alternative, but not as an isolated experiment disconnected from the rest of society. Rather, her argument is that architects ought to learn from Christiania in their practice within established society, for example by studying and photographing everyday scenes in the city – a method she considered necessary in order to generate knowledge about how spaces and places change over time. Being a middle-aged professor, she was perhaps not typical of the people you would generally meet on the streets of Christiania in the mid-1970s. Nevertheless, she visited the commune several times between 1975 and 1977. Of the two, Tosti Nielsen was the one who spent the greatest amount of time at Christiania: she settled there for several months, writing field notes and taking photographs. Rubin drew up the aims and methods of the research and, through texts and lectures, placed the resultant images within the context of architecture and urban planning.

By the time their photographs and texts were exhibited at the *Alternative Architecture* show at Louisiana in 1977, large parts of the Danish architectural world had already defended Christiania and opposed the idea of building municipal developments at the state-owned Bådsmandsstrædes Barracks. The best known example is Steen Eiler Rasmussen's book *Omkring Christiania* (1976), which reprinted the protests that he and a large number of architects, landscape architects, engineers and other professionals had put forward in various newspapers and other contexts, opposing the municipality's plans to build large housing complexes on the site.[430] In the book, the authors primarily delved into issues associated with legislation, fire regulations and urban planning, while Anne Marie Rubin and Gerda Tosti Nielsen set out to record the physical and social spaces that had arisen in Christiania. The two women's most important contribution consisted in reading Christiania as a form of alternative architecture and urban development by focusing on what Rubin called 'the environment for living in itself, the concrete physical framework and how it lends itself to living, working and self-expression'.[431] In that sense, they contribute to the more widely known studies from the 1970s of what happens to buildings and urban environments after they are built – prepared by architects such as Robert Venturi, Denise Scott Brown and Philippe Boudon (b. 1941).[432] Like the work done by Susanne Ussing and Carsten Hoff, the study by Rubin and Tosti Nielsen helped change our understanding of the people who live with and use buildings – moving away from seeing users as passive recipients to being active co-creators of the architecture. Their objective was to bring about a shift in the hierarchy of knowledge, one that could forge closer ties between the squatters' experience and authorised architectural expertise.

Anne Marie Rubin described Christiania as a place that could contribute to rethinking architecture and urban planning procedures because the residents there engaged in 'direct and active interaction' with their town.[433] For her, Christiania was a welcome alternative to the bureaucratisation of ordinary urban planning, with which she had struggled in her own practice. The issue has not become less relevant with time:

'Here we see very little distance from need (for example for a place to live) to idea and imagination (thinking about what it might be like) to action (you do it) – rather than the long and winding road taken through the usual planning and construction procedures where the "end" resident only figures sporadically in the process during debates, citizens' meetings, in needs analyses, etc. – and later in residents' and tenants' associations, environmental groups and so on.'[434]

Furthermore, Rubin, who spent much of her adult life as a divorcee without children, believed that one of the key strengths of Christiania was that the place offered alternative forms of housing that looked beyond the normative nuclear family. Here, in addition to nuclear family homes, she also saw a mix of large and small collectives for residential and production purposes, and she took an interest in their communal spaces for living and workshops.[435] As far back as the 1960s, she had pointed out the importance of offering diverse housing to form the framework for many different forms of life. Referencing the feminist Barbro Backberger (1932–1999) from the Swedish women's network Grupp 8, in 1966 Rubin criticised how 'cities are currently being planned by people with the patriarchal family institution as the only ideal for cohabitation'.[436] This is to say that she not only addressed some of the issues concerning freedom and individualism that we also find in the work of Ussing + Hoff, but she also specifically turned her attention to women's housing and living conditions. This creates a link between her and other contemporary feminists' work with the city, not least the urban historian Dolores Hayden's widely read *What Would a Non-Sexist City Be Like?* from 1979.[437]

Like Susanne Ussing, Anne Marie Rubin was not directly associated with specific women's movement groups, but she worked with feminist issues in various other ways. A few years before her death in 1993, she reflected on what being a woman in the architectural profession had meant to her. She wrote that at times it had been difficult to gain access to various professional circles, and she emphasised the need for women to support each other.[438] Like Ussing and an increasingly large number of feminist architects (see this book's 'Afterword'), she believed that there was a need to include women's knowledge in urban planning in order to get rid of excessively rational and quantitatively oriented approaches. Rubin pointed out that the contribution made by women consisted in promoting everyday perspectives in urban planning, as we see in her and Gerda Tosti Nielsen's study of alternative everyday spaces in Christiania, and she believed that cities should be able to accommodate personal expression and provide opportunities for meeting across different needs, wishes and backgrounds. The latter had also been the objective of a much earlier project in which she had sought to show ways to fundamentally change not only gender inequalities but also inequality-creating racialisation by proposing a radically different way of living.

The personal as a political showcase

In August 1967, the Danish newspaper *Aktuelt* reported that Anne Marie Rubin had met up with a very special client to discuss a new project. While the project aimed to accommodate an alternative lifestyle, the starting point was markedly different from Christiania and the Danish summer camps that Ussing + Hoff would later work with in the 1970s. Another newspaper article also reported on the undertaking and showed a picture of a standing Rubin together with the famous client, who is pointing to a large plan on a drawing desk; both women are studying the plan with avid concentration. The illustrious client was Josephine Baker (1906–1975), best known for her dance performances in revues in Europe in the 1920s. The newspaper articles presented a project the two women were working on together under the auspices of Anne Marie Rubin's design studio. The plan in the photograph shows Les Milandes, a château that Josephine Baker had bought in the Dordogne region of France in the 1950s. Rubin had been brought on board to draw up a plan for expanding the area, and she tried to raise money in Denmark to realise the expansion, which she would carry out together with her employees Dan Christensen (dates unknown) and Ole Gerstrøm.

Baker had been active in the civil rights movement in the United States, where Martin Luther King, Jr. and others fought for basic human rights for people subjected to racism, discrimination and even lynching. She wanted to make Les Milandes an example which showed that people of different cultures and religions could live together and respect each other, forming an alternative 'world village' that could offer a model for a better world.[439] Baker embarked on establishing this community by adopting twelve children from different parts of the world. The children were meant to represent all world religions and different cultural backgrounds. Together they were to become a family or, as she called it, a 'tribe' in all the 'colours of the rainbow'.[440] Baker thus staged herself as the guiding light of a

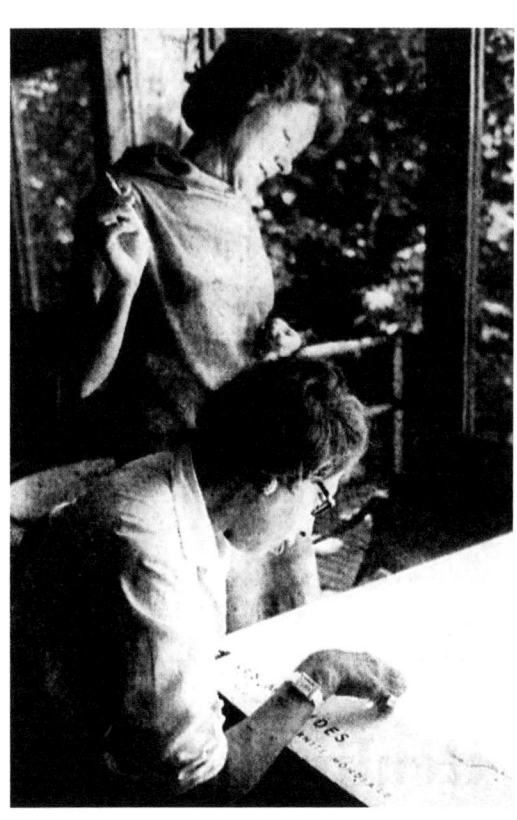

Anne Marie Rubin with American-born French performer Josephine Baker, known not only for her dancing in revues in Europe in the 1920s but also for her work as a civil rights campaigner. Here she is shown working on an alternative project for an anti-racist 'world village' at the castle of Les Milandes in Dordogne, France. With this image, Rubin and Baker's collaboration on a plan for expanding the area was presented to Danish newspaper readers in 1967.

new peace-loving family, decades before superstars such as Madonna (b. 1958) and Angelina Jolie (b. 1975) created large families through transnational adoption. Here, there was a far greater focus on spectacle and staging, on creating images of a new anti-racist community rather than on the structural conditions underlying global inequality. As historian Matthew Pratt Guterl points out, Josephine Baker's family project rested on a strong belief in the symbolic power that can reside in alternative environments; this is not so different from Anne Marie Rubin's idea that in urban development it is necessary to establish 'a point outside the system' – certainly when such alternative points or locations are staged and showcased in a carefully edited narrative. This narrative stood in stark contrast to the harsh reality of the United States, where Baker had spent her childhood. Matthew Pratt Guterl writes how this was noted at the time:

'At a moment when [...] black activists were struggling, literally, just to get a seat on the bus, [newspapers reported that] there was Josephine Baker, living in a castle – a historic building [...] that once housed [...] Napoleon Bonaparte.'[441]

Josephine Baker's intention with Les Milandes was to show that people of different cultures and religions could live together and respect each other, thus forming a model for a better world. She adopted twelve children of varying nationalities based on the idea that the new family, the 'rainbow tribe', could contribute to fighting global, structural inequality and racism. Yet, despite these good intentions, the project seems to have focused more on spectacle and the power of example than on the interests of the individual child.

Anne Marie Rubin designed the extension of the castle, devising buildings where paying guests could spend the night and take part in discussion clubs, sports and various cultural activities. The plan took into account the curving terrain and the historic building structures; the château was located on the upper plateau facing the river, and she compares it to the Acropolis, a reference which clearly reflects her academy training where Greek architecture was part of the canon.[442] There were plans to place an amusement park at the foot of the hill; this was intended as a meeting place in the same way as the agora had been in ancient Athens.

Despite the efforts made by Rubin and others to obtain support from charitable organisations in Copenhagen, she could not raise the necessary funds to complete the project. Josephine Baker was in deep financial trouble at the time and later had to sell the castle. Rubin's involvement in the project testifies to her international outlook and to the many transnational connections to which she contributed. The utopian project of the 'world village' at Les Milandes was – like the later Christiania commune and Danish summer camps – an attempt to show and realise other ways of living. The objective was not to create self-contained experiments or places completely outside the norm, but rather to create models for how the established society and established ways of building and living could move in a different direction. And Les Milandes, like Christiania and the summer camps, was inextricably linked with established society, partly through ties of financial support. And like Christiania, Les Milandes has also been criticised: it was an amusement park where staging and spectacle had a high priority, while the well-being of the children seemed less central.[443]

Nevertheless, the project expands our understanding of the many versions of 'alternative' architecture to which Danish architects contributed from the late 1960s onwards. In contrast to Susanne Ussing's projects and Anne Marie Rubin's reading of Christiania, Les Milandes was less about participation, and it used the nuclear family as a model: the patriarch, understood as the centre and authority of the family, was now a woman who served as matriarch and creative driving force for the area. The most radical aspects were about overturning hierarchies between cultures and global inequalities. With her great commitment to the project, Rubin expands our understanding of the architecture of the post-war Scandinavian welfare states – which we are used to hearing about in terms of its egalitarian ideals within the borders of the nation-state – to also include global and racial issues, albeit within a very privileged framework that does not provide any answers to deep structures of injustice.

Gender, participation and collaboration

Susanne Ussing's and Anne Marie Rubin's projects, which range from a spectacular 'global village' in a French castle to self-built communities and exhibition spaces in Denmark, were to a very great extent about making the lifeworld of women visible and about carving out a space for themselves as women in the world of architecture. They were interested in a project of emancipation which, by articulating and presenting alternative forms of living, would leave behind patriarchal structures that limited the opportunities available to individuals and communities, to architects and other citizens regardless of gender, and, in the case of the Les Milandes project, also regardless of skin colour and ancestry. And they wanted to move away from hegemonic perceptions of what has value and whose knowledge counts in the design of cities and buildings. With the projects discussed here, both Ussing and Rubin wanted to point to possible new paths, leading through the power of example by designing alternative projects. The alternative environments were not seen as isolated bubbles, but as proposals and examples of what was needed to change the established society, pointing in a better direction. In the course of working with these alternatives, each took part in the established art and architectural scenes of their day, and they received support from the welfare state and charitable foundations, meaning that they were dependent on established institutions and professional networks within the field of architecture.

The fact that both Susanne Ussing and Anne Marie Rubin came from a relatively privileged social class, being born to well-educated parents by the standards of the day, certainly also played a role here. Each had access to a network of influential people, possessed cultural capital and had the opportunity to take personal risks. Nowhere near all women from all walks of life would have been able to break through the glass ceiling the way they did – going from feeling ignored due to having a soft, female voice to becoming some of the era's most significant players on the cultural scene. While their visionary building projects did not always reach completion, nevertheless – by testing, publishing, exhibiting and discussing alternative projects – they became significant voices in 1970s' architecture, art, society and culture in Denmark.

Ussing's and Rubin's stories exemplify the wide range of ways in which architects active around 1970 developed feminist positions – sometimes clearly articulated, other times more implicitly. They did

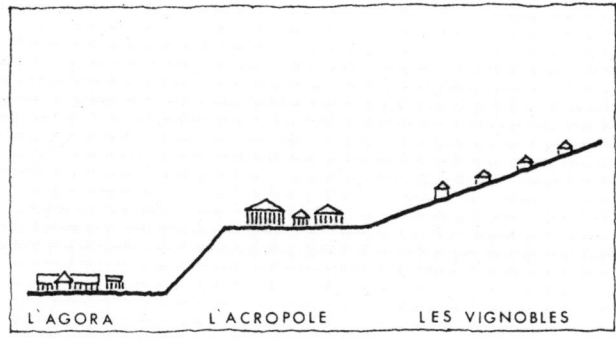

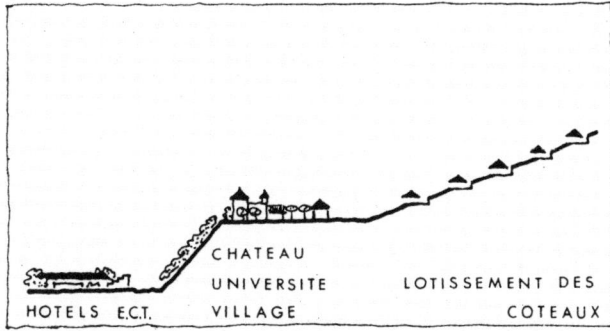

Les Milandes af i dag kan sammenlignes med det klassiske Akropolis og Agora. På snittet øverst ses Akropolis med det nedenfor liggende Agora og de ovenfor liggende boliger i bjergene. Snittet nederst viser Les Milandes med slot, højskole og landsby med de nedenfor liggende hoteller, forlystelser etc. og de individuelle boliger i vinhaverne på bjergsiderne.

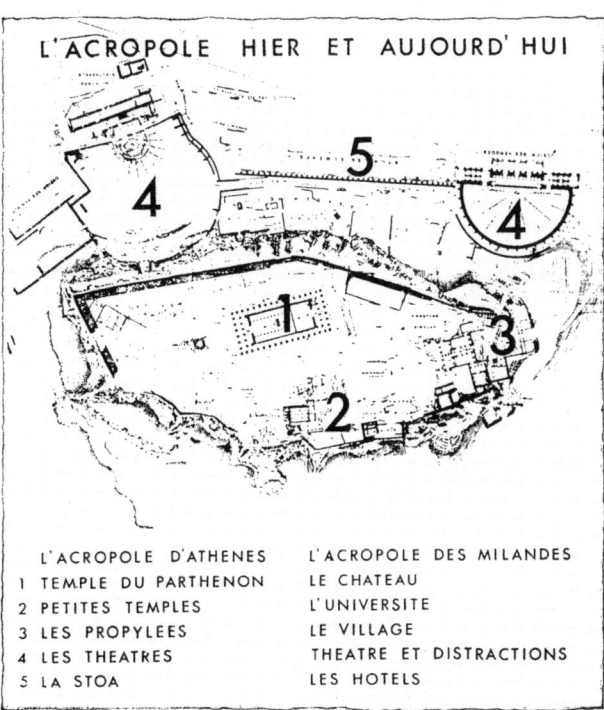

På planen af Akropolis angiver tallene: 1, Parthenon-templet. 2, de små templer. 3, Propylæerne. 4, teatrene og 5, Stoa'en. Disse kan sammenlignes med Les Milandes: Slot, højskole, landsby, teatre og underholdning samt hoteller.

Anne Marie Rubin's proposal for an expansion of Josephine Baker's Les Milandes was presented in the trade journal *Arkitekten*. The Danish architect had designed a new cultural venue complete with visitors' accommodation as part of the expansion of what she described as a world village. The plan has clearly taken into account the curving landscape and the historic buildings. The castle itself was on the upper plateau facing the river, and Rubin compared it to the Acropolis.

so in short- and long-term collaborations with feminist groups, with architectural partners and employees, with an activist woman as a client, with fellow citizens, through the use of certain materials and in other collaborations. Recognising such intertwined collaborations points to abundant possibilities for exploring different architectural practices in the future, cutting across gender and restrictive power hierarchies, and across past oppositions between expert and amateur – all in an effort to create the diverse and fair living environments we need. By reflecting on the challenges associated with developing new roles as architects, Susanne Ussing and Carsten Hoff revealed some of the inherent difficulties of such an endeavour, thereby initiating a reflexive and iterative practice. Reflecting on what at first glance looks like failure, and taking the position of the ethnographer and photographer who learns from what happens after a project is launched, remains equally relevant today – a time when the many intertwining crises associated with our environment, climate, social inequality and biodiversity all require us to handle uncertainty and change in our future housing and urban development.

In 1977 – the same year that *Alternative Architecture* brought new forms of building culture into the halls at Louisiana – a participant at the large *Women in American Architecture* exhibition in New York is reported to have said that 'architecture is, next to men, the most oppressive force in our society'.[444] Of course, stating that 'men' and 'architecture' were oppressive forces in themselves was intended to provoke. A rather more nuanced approach is taken by some of the era's architectural experiments already considered in this book: while critical, they also define and present alternative and feminist spaces that seek to do away with all forms of patriarchal structures and injustice in order to set the individual free – regardless of their body, gender and position in society. The multifaceted positions they developed cannot be pigeonholed as belonging to one particular movement; they are far less clear-cut and exclusionary than the above statements about men and architecture. Susanne Ussing and Anne Marie Rubin and their collaborators' projects were aimed at radically changing patriarchal hierarchies and values, without resorting to binary notions about architecture or men. Their strategy of showing examples of different ways of living depended on staging, spectacle and media attention. At the same time, it carried some of the transformative potential that many are looking for today, when we need to explore other imaginaries and create alternative futures to resolve the crises we face.

Chapter 5

Collaboration – A Story About how Architecture Comes into Being

You arrive at the indoor swimming pool from the foot of a small hill. The first thing you see from the car park if you arrive by car or bicycle is a dense, forest-like planting of deciduous trees, bushes and dark-green hedges. And where the ground is covered with reddish fallen leaves in the autumn, ground-cover plants light up among the tree trunks in yellows and purples in the spring. The swimming pool itself sits on a plateau behind dark-red, heavy brick walls with no windows at eye level, and you approach the main entrance through

Built between 1966 and 1972 in Gentofte, the Kildeskovshallen complex comprises an indoor swimming pool and sports centre as well as a public park. The buildings were designed by architects Karen and Ebbe Clemmensen, while landscape architect Agnete Muusfeldt designed the landscape. The complex is considered a masterpiece of Danish architecture, and the buildings were some of the youngest ever to be listed in Denmark, being added to the conservation list as early as 2000. Not until 2019 did the conservation authorities expand the scope of the listing to include the landscape.

a dim, covered passageway covered with burgundy tiles. If you walk around the building – or if you arrive by foot from the other side of the facility – you get a completely different impression. Here you walk through a small forest towards a large open lawn with a few large trees, and you will be able to see how the pool's transparent glass façades and columnar structure interact with the tall trees that surround the building. These are some of the angles from which the well-known building complex known as Kildeskovshallen has often been photographed.

Kildeskovshallen is a centre comprising an indoor swimming pool, a sports centre and a public park. Built between 1966 and 1972 in Gentofte Municipality north of Copenhagen, the centre is often described by architects and architectural historians as a unique, iconic building. It was created by the architects Karen and Ebbe Clemmensen.[445] In 2000, Kildeskovshallen was listed under the Danish Building Conservation Act as the (at that time) youngest listed building in Denmark ever: just a few decades after the sports facility was built, it was regarded as such an important piece of architecture that it had to be protected and preserved for posterity.[446] It is, however, worth noting that when listed, Kildeskovshallen was considered exclusively as a building – an approach entirely in line with general practice in Danish building preservation at the time.[447] The listing covered only the buildings (and the 'Sun Lawn') even though the way one arrives at – and so perceives – Kildeskovshallen is not just an experience created by a building made of brick, concrete, glass, steel and tiles. Trees, shrubs, grass and plants play a key part too,[448] and it would be more accurate to say that the various natural elements, indeed the entire landscape and topography around the building complex, act as co-creators of an overall spatial and architectural experience. As we will argue in this chapter, the landscape and thus the landscape architect's work is inextricably linked to the building in which architects and engineers, for their part, worked together to reflect the surrounding trees and incorporate them into the building's aesthetic. In addition, the landscape architect's work with the trees on the site played a decisive role in making the architects' designs and overall vision a reality.

In 2019, almost two decades after Kildeskovshallen became a listed building, the Danish Agency for Culture and Palaces extended the scope of the protection to include the 'Kildeskovshallen centre complete with its outdoor wading pool, associated stairs and walls as well as the immediate surroundings to the north, east, south and west, including the "Sun Lawn" with its encircling wall to the south of the centre (1966–72 by Karen Clemmensen, Ebbe Clemmensen and landscape architect Agnete Muusfeldt)'.[449] The new listing included a range of elements that had previously been regarded as separate: building and landscape. Shortly after it was first listed, Kildeskovshallen was expanded with the addition of an extra swimming pool and other functions, and these obviously had to take into account the building's protected status. With the new and expanded listing, the operation, care and any future extensions of the place – of which some are currently on the drawing board – must now also address the interaction between building and landscape.* New and substantial demands are imposed on our ability to interpret and understand relationships between landscape and buildings, between outside and inside, when several different professional design practices need to be considered. It forces us to develop a more complex understanding of the other elements besides architectural design that affected how the building complex came into being.

The conservation of building and landscape thus prompts a renewed awareness of the different professions that have worked together to create the total impression formed by the place, one where the interior, building and landscape engage with each other in a direct interplay. Taking Kildeskovshallen as our point of departure, we will show how such a process of becoming may be infused by negotiations, synergies, varying interpersonal skills and opposing, potentially conflicting positions that, when they come together, can mutually reinforce each other. This story about Kildeskovshallen is a more complicated narrative than the one found if we simply focused on the architects' vision or the building's form alone, but it is also an example of how we can arrive at a more nuanced and truthful picture if we broaden our view to consider more than just architectural practices pertaining to buildings and include other professional fields too.

Kildeskovshallen not only arose as a result of collaboration across different disciplines, but also across genders. In addition to architects Karen Clemmensen and Ebbe Clemmensen,[451] both the landscape architect Agnete Muusfeldt and the engineer Knud Bergholt (1921–2006) from the firm Chr. Ostenfeld and W. Jønsson played a significant role in the preservation and development of the existing landscape, the erection of the building and not least the spectacular construction. Many other forces also appear in this collaboration: municipal, administrative and political protagonists, landscapers, craftsmen and more. Here we will follow the above-mentioned design professionals to gain insight into their collaboration and its impact on the final project.[452]

The fact that cooperation between different professions was important for the Kildeskovshallen project is evident from a diagram drawn up in 1966 when Karen and Ebbe Clemmensen hired the architectural firm Møller Larsen and Zehngraff to oversee the construction of the

* The principles for expanding the facility were drawn up by Ebbe Clemmensen in collaboration with Gentofte Municipality, but the design studio entasis was behind the actual expansion. The same design studio drafted proposals for the expansion in 2021.[450]

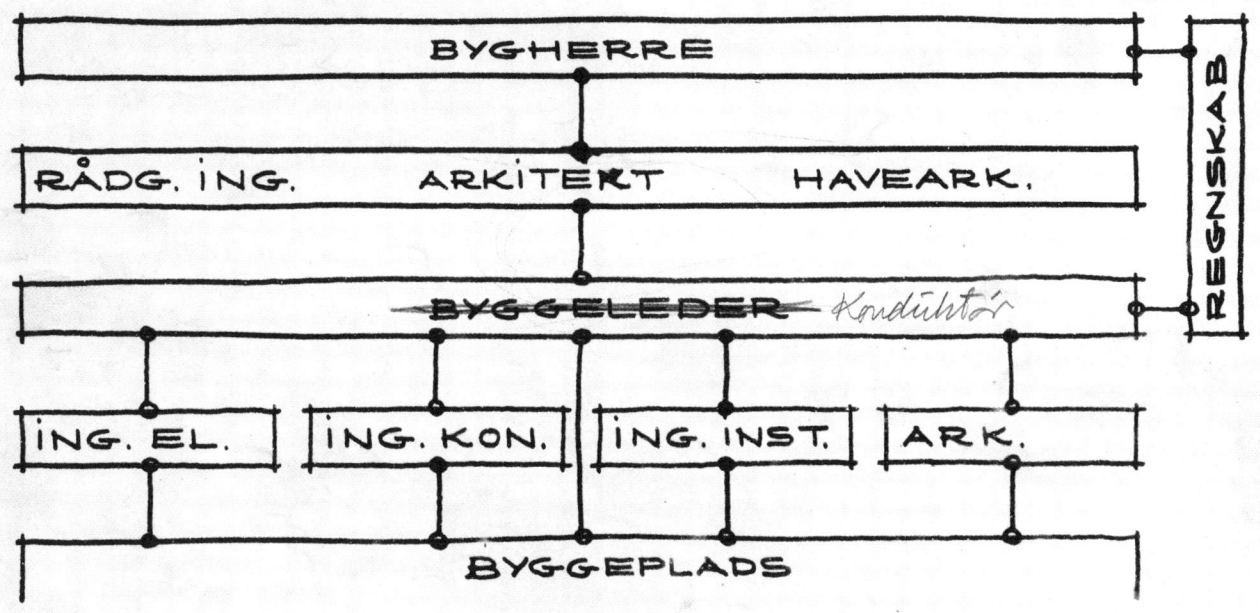

Organisational chart showing the various parties involved in the construction of Kildeskovshallen. Drawn up in 1966, the chart testifies to how cooperation between different professions was key – both here and in other construction projects. No single architect created the complex; it has many authors, plural.

Regardless of how you arrive at Kildeskovshallen, the surrounding landscape greatly shapes the overall experience of the building's architecture. The venue was built on a wooded site, part of which was preserved. As a result, extensive planting was already in place when the swimming pool was opened in the late 1960s: a marked contrast to other developments of the era where it could take years before the planting reached maturity.

swimming pool.⁴⁵³ At the top of the organisational chart is the client, which in this case was Gentofte Municipality, and on the line below the consulting engineer, architect and landscape architect are listed as equal parties in the project. The diagram shows that the question of who is the author of the complex requires an answer in the plural.

When Agnete Muusfeldt presented the complex to readers of the magazine *Landskab* in 1971, the headline ran 'Sports halls in the Kildeskoven forest'. Here, the focus is shifted away from the building to the forest that was there before work on the Kildeskovshallen centre began, and as a landscape architect it was Muusfeldt's job to respond to and create a future for the existing planting. The forest was designated as a 'fredskov' (forest reserve),* which imposed particular restrictions on new construction in the area. In addition to crediting the client Gentofte Municipality, the two architects and the engineer, Muusfeldt also credits landscape architect Rasmus Jacobsen, with whom she must have worked closely.⁴⁵⁴ In other words, our awareness of the collaborations that created a place such as Kildekovshallen depends on the eyes that see and on whose story is told, and in the following we will first outline the architects' articulation of the project's main idea (for more about the architects, see Chapter Two), then consider their collaboration (and clashes) with the engineer, and finally we will investigate the landscape architect's contribution. When combining these elements, a picture emerges of how different types of professional skills intertwine in the project, and the significance of their being based on different, but complementary, design and work philosophies.

Being a building complex built with modern materials and new technology on a big budget, Kildeskovshallen is an example of the growing prosperity and the changed living conditions for which Danish architecture formed a framework in the 1960s. As a public sports and cultural venue, it is an example of the welfare state's aim to give all citizens the opportunity to lead healthy and fulfilling lives – and architecture established a physical framework for lived life with well-thought-out, architect-designed public buildings. These were built using modern materials, yet they also incorporated elements of high-end craftsmanship, and in addition to housing special functions – in this case a swimming pool and sports hall – they also acted as backdrops for leisure time in parklands, socialising, dining and more in rooms furnished with designer furniture and modern art. However, to our mind the remarkable thing about Kildeskovshallen concerns not only the building's iconic architecture and the quality of its execution. Rather, we are interested in how the fundamental idea behind the design of the complex can only be fully understood if we let the interaction between the various professional contributions

* In Denmark, forest reserve areas must always remain forested and are protected against clearing, felling, cattle grazing, etc.

Agnete Muusfeldt (1918–1991) obtained her degree in horticulture from the Agricultural College in Copenhagen in 1946. Before that, she spent four years as an apprentice gardener. From 1946 to 1948 she worked at the design studio run by the Swedish landscape architect and garden designer Helfrid Löfquist (1895–1972) and Danish colleague Sven Hansen (1910–1989), following which she set up her own design studio together with her husband Erik Mygind (1916–1978). They designed outdoor spaces for new public housing developments in several municipalities west of Copenhagen. In 1961 Muusfeldt set up her own design studio. One of her main clients was Rødovre Municipality, for which her designs included the Schweizerdalspark and several road plantings. She also devised landscapes for a large number of high schools, hospitals and schools. In 1982, she was made an honorary member of the Association of Danish Landscape Architects, where she sat on the board between 1961 and 1963. She contributed to the education of landscape architects and was an active contributor to trade journals such as *Haven* and *Havekunst*. She was editor of the latter between 1958 and 1961.

come to light. The question of what makes Kildeskovshallen inspiring and important for posterity extends to more than the simple fact of being an example of beautiful, high-quality architecture. We believe that a better understanding of the collaborations that went into its creation gives us a more solid basis for deciding how such a building complex should be managed, preserved and developed in the future. What is more, the Kildeskovshallen project can provide us with a key to aid our understanding of the wider urban developments in Denmark from the period, which are often based on a close connection between buildings and landscapes, indoors and outdoors, as well as on spatial connections that cut across different scales. Kildeskovshallen prompts reflection on how architecture is created. It also prompts reflection on the ethics and the often complex design philosophy that underpins the complex as an example of the kind of public architecture gifted to Danish society during this period. We see here a special interplay between a general boom in construction, a strongly pronounced welfare state ideology and a keen appetite for public-sector construction. These different perspectives involve different forms of skill and knowledge all focused on a specific task while cutting across conditions such as gender, skills, technologies, materials and distinctive site-specific conditions.[455]

The idea and the architects' vision

The population of the Gentofte Municipality grew rapidly in the first decades of the twentieth century, and the local politicians held a keen wish to expand the available sports venues for the enjoyment of local residents. One of the biggest projects was the new Gentofte Stadium for various sports designed by architect Arne Jacobsen (1902–1971), who won the design competition in 1936. The Gentofte Stadium was completed in 1942, but was only partially realised, and the projected swimming facility was never built.[456] In January 1961, the municipality offered the architects Karen and Ebbe Clemmensen, working with the engineering firm Chr. Ostenfeld and W. Jønsson, the sum of DKK 100,000 to draw up a preliminary project for an indoor swimming pool and sports hall at Gentofte Stadium.

The architects and engineer presented their outline to the municipality in April 1961, and even at this early stage their programme is quite close to the final project in terms of the architectural volume of the halls.[457]

Agnete Muusfeldt was keen to preserve some of the trees around Kildeskovshallen, but she also removed vegetation that was not healthy. Her vision for the area was for it to be seen as a place in constant flux, where visitors would always find flowers and plants of various sizes and stages of growth.

In 1961 Karen and Ebbe Clemmensen were asked, along with the engineering company Chr. Ostenfeld and W. Jønsson, to draw up a design proposal for an indoor swimming pool at Gentofte Stadium. This model represents the first stage of the project. In December 1961, the municipal authorities decided that the architects should prepare a new proposal for a different building site. This project became what we know today as Kildeskovshallen. It differed from the first incarnation, particularly in the fact that trees did not play such a prominent role in the original complex. That changed with the new, forested site and the involvement of landscape architect Agnete Muusfeldt.

It is worth noting that in the preliminary project, trees do not play an important role in relation to the architecture – they had not yet taken on the prominence they would have in the final project. In the preliminary project, the trees are represented as a stylised, avenue-like row of trees that encircles the complex, but in the actual Kildeskovshallen they not only fill the grounds due to the dense forest-like growth – they also make a clear imprint on the facility's architecture.

By this point the Gentofte municipal council had agreed that the stadium site was not the right place for a new swimming and sports hall,* and in December 1961 the municipality paid the Clemmensen couple an additional DKK 25,000 to rethink the project for a location in the Kildeskoven forest close to the Bernstorffsvej train station, the site where the swimming pool would eventually be built. It was completed in 1972.[459]

The new building site, Kildeskoven, had been acquired by the municipality in 1956,[460] and it offered a completely different set of conditions. It was a large plot of land with gnarled, densely growing deciduous trees. Interestingly, the Clemmensen couple's business archives include a small text, almost a poem, written by the architects, which reads rather like a kind of site analysis as well as an attempt to set a direction for the project. Importantly, the vision evoked in the poem is not a fully formed, clear-cut recipe for how the buildings should look – rather, it describes an atmosphere where you get a sense of what it will be like to visit the swimming pool with the

* The municipal authorities decided to move the venue to Kildeskoven because the first location was not ideal. Quite simply, it did not have enough space for any possible later additions, such as a venue for handball. The municipal council were pleased with the first project from 1961, both in terms of size and design, and so decided to retain the architects and move the facility to a larger site where the surroundings would not limit the scope for expansion. The Kildeskoven site was also at a more central location, close to the Bernstorffsvej train station.[458]

sounds of splashing adults, yelling children and glints of sunlight in the water through the large glass facades.[461] The poetic text also describes the landscape qualities of the place and points ahead to how the many trees in Kildeskoven would prominently influence the architectural aesthetic of the final project. All proposals for new architecture, landscape architecture or planning constitute an attempt to imagine something that does not yet exist, something that belongs to the future. And this is how we can read this poem: as an invitation into a vision of a future immersive experience created in an interplay between landscape, architecture and construction. The Clemmensens' poetic statements became the basis for the collaborative ethics behind Kildeskovshallen, one where the architects invite other disciplines and skill sets to take part in the project as co-creators. As they say:

'THE IDEA

A forest —
with a clearing —
with an expanse of grass and four pools.
Protective screens to the north.
Above them three hovering levels —
Penetrated shielding structures.
The grass level and the four water levels —
Rising in a spiral —
From south to west to north to east.
Light falls through the trees —
Reflected by the grass and the water —
And makes the grid structure come alive […]'.[462]

By describing their project idea in the form of a poetic text, the architects activate mood-setting qualities that speak directly to all their collaborators' imaginations, dreams of the future, professional skills and willingness to not only work together, but also to work on the special terms and conditions set by the site. The poem is therefore in itself a meeting place and starting point for future collaboration; it can rally the collaborators around a special vision, and it can also encourage awareness and acceptance of the different elements featured in the design. Elements which are not just site-specific, but also have to do with all the human senses, pointing to the different types of skills and professional knowledge required to work with the project as a unified totality.

In addition to this, the architects' vision is manifested in a series of watercolours, presumably painted by Karen Clemmensen.[463] The watercolours also evoke the special atmosphere which the architects

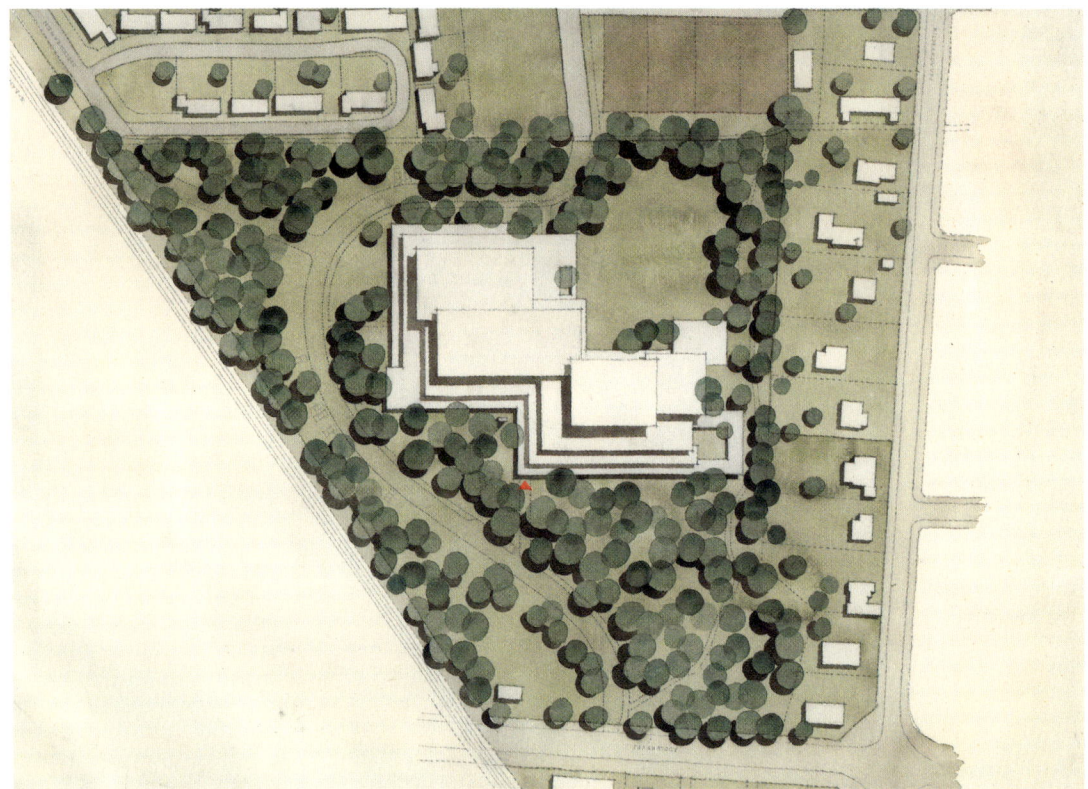

The presentation material for Kildeskovshallen included a plan of how the complex would be positioned within the existing planting. Clearly the team intended to preserve many of the trees.

want the future site to have, and they show the interaction between the building and the trees of Kildeskoven in a stylised form, engaging in a reading of the qualities of the place. While the poetic text was probably mostly a creative tool in the architects' own internal work, we know that the watercolours were presented to the municipality: they are part of the architects', engineer's and landscape architect's revised project from 1963, where they appear as illustrations accompanying the project text.

The watercolours present the future Kildeskovshallen as architecture characterised by a distinctive interplay between the structure of the building and the trees as pre-existing elements that create and define space at the site. The building's aesthetics enters into a meaning-making interaction with the trees, which are shown here as uniform, elegant shapes in the landscape – a far cry from the dense, wild-growing

In 1963, the architects, engineer and landscape architect involved in the Kildeskovshallen project presented their revised design for the new site to the local authorities. The text and calculations were supplemented by a series of watercolours, one of which is shown here. The building's architecture is characterised by interaction between the building's structure and the trees already found on the site, where they contribute to defining the space.

Kildeskovshallen's swimming pool comprises three separate pools, clearly demarcated by three different ceiling heights. What they all have in common is their close contact with nature: the large expanses of glass and the slender columns offer an almost unobstructed view of the trees. In this corner of the space, the light is almost dark green in the summer, and the atmosphere is dense and forest-like. In other parts of the venue, visitors enjoy unobstructed views of the large lawn and the atmosphere is light and airy.

deciduous forest found at site before the landscape architect Agnete Muusfeldt and the team gardeners began working on it. The trunks almost look like part of a pattern, a repetition of a motif, and the trees appear to be in a spring or summer state with dense crowns of uniformly light green leaves. The building's columns, appearing in series in various sections of the façade, mirror these rows of trees and echo the tree trunks. The interaction between the building and the trees is reinforced as a visual motif in the final project, and a picture of the columns inside the indoor swimming pool shows how their Y-like shapes echo the trees found at the site. This simple aesthetic in which tree trunks are reflected in the building's columns and design is made possible by the innovative technical contributions made by the engineers: a contribution which was instrumental in realising the architects' vision. Yet, as we shall now see, the collaboration was not without its hiccoughs along the way.

Conflict and compassion – the stuff of which cooperation is made

The engineer Knud Bergholt's work on Kildeskovshallen is described in an article in *Ingeniørens Ugeblad*. Here, the journalist refers to a lecture on construction given by Bergholt to his colleagues.[464] Held at the Dansk Selskab for Byggestatik (the Danish Society for Structural Engineering) in 1970, one year after the centre was completed, the lecture focused on the technical aspects of Kildeskovshallen. We know that in this lecture, Bergholt had a story he wanted to tell the architects: Karen and Ebbe Clemmensen were invited to the lecture. When they were unable to attend, they were sent Bergholt's manuscript along with a number of slides he borrowed from the architects.[465] Based on the lecture, the journalist concludes: 'The collaboration between architect and structural engineer must be established at a very early stage and be characterised by openness in order for a fruitful interaction between architectural and constructive viewpoints to unfold.'[466]

The method of construction used for the indoor swimming pool was innovative and untried at the time, requiring various technical tests. Carrying out an actual stress test of the structure had not been possible, but a storm in the autumn of 1967, when the building was

The swimming pool under construction. The inspiration from the trees at the building site and the building's connection to its surroundings are clearly evident.

still under construction, proved the sturdiness of the structure. In his lecture, Bergholt describes that working on Kildeskovshallen had been a very difficult process, which involved special compromises in relation to the engineering work. He speaks in great detail about the load-bearing structure that Karen and Ebbe Clemmensen developed for the project, and which they called 'tightrope walker on a string'.[467] He describes the grid structure of the ceiling as a non-load-bearing structure – a quite surprising revelation given that the repetitive modular construction of the complex with a 2 x 2 metre structure is so important for the entire visual impact of the building. The ceiling consists of a series of load-bearing beams held together by the transverse bars attached to the downward-facing tips of the 'pyramids' in the ceiling, which thus have a partly structural and partly ornamental function. These transverse beams gave the project its nickname – 'tightrope walker on a string' – because visitors to the swimming pool were to imagine a tightrope walker proceeding from one side of the building to the other. The aesthetics of the structure is characterised by a tension between the light and almost filigree-like metal structure and the enormous weight it must support and hold in place.

Bergholt explains how this task was solved partly by having the structure welded by highly skilled and painstaking craftsmen and, later, having it thoroughly analysed and checked in a complex, high-tech process that involved radioactive material and ultrasound equipment. The approach demonstrates that here we find ourselves in a transitional phase between more traditional, craft-based ways of working and a high-tech, industrialised construction industry: a tension also observable in the many artisanal details in the building's masonry, which here co-exist happily with the use of concrete and modern high-tech installations. In light of the eventual triumph of their collaboration – the building's design was quickly recognised as iconic even in its own day – it is interesting to note Knud Bergholt's rather dry comment on how a metal lattice structure would not have been an engineer's first choice in a damp environment like a swimming pool.[468] Clearly, he was not fully convinced of the feasibility of the roof structure. We may then well ask what problems he encountered in his collaboration with the architects. Bergholt himself describes the situation as follows:

'We find here the entirely legitimate contradiction inherent in the fact that the two parties approach the construction design from two very different points of view: the architect views the matter from the perspective of form and proportions, the engineer on the basis of statics and technology. This contradiction requires a great deal of mutual understanding in order for the result to be harmonious in the broadest sense.'[469]

In his lecture at the Danish Society for Structural Engineering, Knud Bergholt points to a dilemma which led to professional tensions and misunderstandings between architects and engineers in this particular project. However, the collaboration also prompted more long-term afterthought for Bergholt, causing him to describe a fundamental conflict which is rooted in opposing professional positions:

'The crux of the matter is that the architect wanted (and was given) such great geometric freedom in the construction of the grid structure that the system had to be subjected to an extra static constraint (I am alluding here to the reinforced beam layer in the roof surface) […] static clarity could have been achieved by omitting the bends in the sides of the pyramids, but this would be detrimental to the overall visual impact of the structure.'[470]

The structure used for the swimming pool was innovative and untested, requiring close cooperation between architects and engineers. Knud Bergholt, who was lead engineer, later gave a lecture about his interaction with Karen and Ebbe Clemmensen, emphasising how important collaboration had been for the finished result. The complex ceiling in particular had required extensive dialogue, balancing structural issues against the overall aesthetic vision behind the complex.

We are left to imagine the engineer's tone of voice during the lecture, including what he emphasised and how. In any case, the carefully considered and technical formulations of the lecture reveal deeply rooted professional dilemmas which point to an internal conflict in Bergholt himself in terms of the overall ambition to find sound and simple engineering solutions to the requirements put forth by the architects. What seems to particularly bother Bergholt is the architects' wish to have a quite specific and unusual pyramidal construction to create a sense of aesthetic lightness, because in his eyes this particular design leads to a loss of mathematical, constructive clarity. A similar position can be observed in the journalist's own comments in the article from *Ingeniørens Ugeblad*, which unsurprisingly takes the engineer's point of view: 'In structures determined by pure statics, geometry and statics meet without making demands on each other. Greater freedom for one side will always require coercion for the other.'[471]

267

The completed swimming pool at the Kildeskoven site with its spectacular ceiling structure above the large swimming pool. In the background you can see the diving pool, and under the lower ceiling is the children's pool.

Here, that dilemma manifested itself in a paradox in the realisation of Kildeskovshallen's architecture and the architects' vision: after all, striving for mathematical clarity also speaks to notions of beauty and is therefore perhaps not so far removed from the ambitions the Clemmensens set up for their work. They wanted to create a building that speaks to all the human senses, and whose structural make-up is part of the aesthetic and design instead of being hidden away behind plaster or concrete. The root of the conflict must therefore lie elsewhere than in the trivial idea of a conflict between practical engineers and the architects' pursuit of beauty. It may be that we are dealing with a conflict about what kind of beauty is worthy of striving for. Here one might argue that building design was headed for a more playful postmodernism, moving away from a stereotypical modernist understanding of architecture where 'less is more', where the building's structure is emphasised rather than hidden behind the stucco or ornamentation familiar from historicist architecture, and where one often works with an architectural style that is, in principle, detached from time and place. Although Kildeskovshallen does not effect a break with modernism as such, we can say that the question of unity has partially receded into the background in favour of collisions, fragmentation and unexpected aesthetic impulses, as exemplified by the improbable static effects of the structure. Furthermore, the building complex has, with its site-specific ethos, been created in such a situated interaction with its surroundings that it points away from the notion of a universal modernism. Kildeskovshallen was created for and with the Kildeskov forest.

If we turn once again to the diagram in which the landscape architect, architect and engineer stand side by side in the hierarchy, we see that the architects still occupy the central position, serving a connecting role. They have formulated the project's poetic vision and may also have had the last word in the collaboration. From the engineer we hear that the static and constructive clarity of the building has been compromised, without, in his eyes, being legitimised by the kind of satisfactory negotiation and dialogue that would have brought together the different professional perspectives and mutually reinforced the core focus of everyone involved. In his lecture, Bergholt calls for a new kind of process for future constructions, one where architects and engineers sit down together right from the early idea phase and strive to understand each other better by visualising their thoughts and any oppositions they have and encounter. As he writes:

'We engineers could learn a great deal from the architects' work with models. In all likelihood, the engineering profession's big mistake in collaboration is that we often rely on calculation results and implementation difficulties without demonstrating the issues in a clear, concise way. If we have not understood each other, nothing has been achieved.'[472]

Interestingly, Bergholt does not just see this in terms of a desire for a more pleasant work process and better cooperation; he also regards it as a matter of ethics in terms of how different professional groups should act. He particularly emphasises the importance of broader cooperation in a society characterised by strong growth and development in the construction industry, and believes that such cooperation is necessary if we are to achieve what he calls 'environmental value', which we would perhaps today describe as sustainability, implying a position that incorporates issues of value and ethics alike.[473] Bergholt encourages all 'busy architects and engineers' to take the time necessary to establish a good dialogue and a well-founded collaboration. We may conclude that, at least from his point of view, the Kildeskovshallen project was not quite successful in this regard.

Aerial photograph from 1954, showing the forested Kildeskoven site in the upper right corner. The architects' original idea was to place the venue in a park-like setting but Agnete Muusfeldt, wanting to maintain a forest-like feel instead, decided to keep the tall old trees. She saw them as something other than the serial formal elements highlighted in the architects' watercolours and went on to create a range of very different landscape experiences at the site.

Despite their disagreements along the way, the architects and engineer worked closely together to make the innovative and demanding structure a reality. But what did the landscape architects contribute to that process? We know that Agnete Muusfeldt was brought on board the project as a landscape architect in 1962, and that her work with the trees on the new building site, at which we will now take a closer look, was crucial to ensuring that the architects' design vision and the engineer's structure truly came into their own.[474]

Listen as the trees grow and the cranes build a new world

The Kildeskoven forest was densely overgrown when the decision was made to build the swimming centre here. As the name suggests – 'Kilde' means 'spring/source', 'skoven' means 'forest' – the place was formerly home to a spring, but by this time the ground was dry. Writing about the project, Agnete Muusfeldt describes how what she found at this place when work was about to begin was a forest, yes, but not a healthy one. The soil was parched, and the trees had not been thinned, forcing them to grow too tall too quickly, leaving them thin and overly close. It was, she describes, a mess of self-sown hardwoods, ash, linden, maple, beech, oak and elm trees, some of which were up to eighty years old.[475] Being a forest plantation, the area was subject to conservation regulations, which meant that the municipality had to apply for permission to cut down trees to make room for the new facility.[476] The architects' idea was to place the sports halls in a park-like setting: the watercolours show large open lawns that constitute a clearly man-made landscape with opportunities for sunbathing and other recreation. A calm, green surface interrupted only by trees that interact directly with the building complex: this was the primary impression formed when looking up at the transparent façades of the halls from the Sun Lawn. Muusfeldt refused to create a park in the former Kildeskoven area; instead she wanted to preserve many of the existing trees, a plan which required thorough registration, much deliberation and detailed planning. The desire to maintain the overall forest feel with tall, old trees suggests that Muusfeldt saw the trees as something other than the serial formal element accentuated in the architects' watercolours highlight, and her work was what made it possible to create very different landscape experiences on the site, ranging

Agnete Muusfeldt joined the project as a landscape architect in 1962, and when the local authorities decided to greenlight Kildeskovshallen in 1963, she embarked on thinning the tree population to let the trees get used to stronger winds, preparing them for when part of the forest would later be felled. She also took steps to protect the trees against damage before the construction cranes arrived.

from the Sun Lawn's magnificent clearing with beautiful, old solitary trees to the wilder, dense deciduous forest at the edge of the plot. When visitors approach the venue from the footpaths or from the car park, the experience is quite different from entering via the Sun Lawn. Here, you will either come via forest paths leading up to the clearing, or navigate the somewhat dark, labyrinthine walk up to the main entrance.

Muusfeldt relishes the forest as a living place comprising many species that interact in an ecosystem. She is interested in the aesthetic experiences that can be achieved by working with the temporality of the forest, not just by virtue of what the old trees can add to the site, but also via a forward-looking strategy for replanting, ensuring that the forest can always be a work in progress, as well as through work with the changing seasons and with ground covers that provide colour in the spring months. All this requires a lot of preliminary work.[477] Muusfeldt thus sees Kildeskoven from a dynamic perspective in keeping with the architects' poetic text about the place, where the fundamental idea was precisely a forest with a clearing. The forest motif was an important part of the project right from the outset, and Muusfeldt's simultaneously aesthetic and horticultural perspective on the forest – an eye cultivated by her special expertise as a trained horticulturalist and landscape architect – enables this vision to become a reality.[478]

Agnete Muusfeldt took her starting point in the existing planting and protected it. For example, in 1968, shortly before the swimming pool opened, she – together with the company SITAS (Scandinavian Instant Trees), which specialises in supplying and moving mature trees – has thirty-two ash trees moved, all of them more than twenty years old. Since construction began at the site, the trees have stood a little distance away in a small grove, but as construction comes to a close they are moved closer to the indoor swimming pool so that 'the new building […] truly stands in the middle of nature'.[479] In this way, the planting could facilitate a rich diversity of species, variation in the ground cover in the bright, open deciduous forest, and variation in terms of space and colour throughout the year – all of which form part of an overall aesthetic interaction with the building. The different rooms include the small grove or forest as well as the clearing, the edge of the forest and the Sun Lawn at Kildeskovshallen. In addition, evergreen shrubs and hedges are used to create and define spaces.

Muusfeldt describes how, as soon as the municipal council approved the project in 1963, she quickly began thinning out the trees in order to acclimatise them, letting them grow used to the stronger winds they would later face when part of the forest would be felled.* The building permit was issued in 1965, and when

* In the spring of 1964, the thinning of the trees at the site prompted protests from nearby residents. The outrage was caused less by the overall plans than by the fact that several wooden structures and trees in the adjacent private gardens were destroyed in the process because roots from the trees in Kildeskoven had spread over the years. One of the residents was further angered by the 'council's woman advisor' criticising their gardens, which had been 'extremely well-tended' prior to the thinning.[480]

construction began later that same year, Muusfeldt had secured the trees by setting up iron grids and building protective structures at the trunks to prevent damage when the heavy machinery began their work on the site.[481] This was in the midst of what she describes as her busy and hectic years: the time when the post-war building boom peaked, when construction grew more and more industrialised, and when many architects, planners, engineers and landscape architects like Muusfeldt herself were given many and large commissions.[482] During this period, we also see several examples of projects where the soil was so compacted and destroyed by the large machines that the existing planting was destroyed and the planting of new trees made difficult.[483] In many ways, these were new experiences for architects and landscape architects alike – at any rate on the scale we are dealing with here. This of course says something about the welfare state's orientation towards primarily creating welfare and prosperity for human beings – an anthropocentrism that Muusfeldt essentially shares. Yet she also breaks away from it by devoting space and care to plants and trees. This suggests that opposing ethics and ontologies were at play in the project and in the collaboration, a clash which proved defining for the creation of Kildeskovshallen as an iconic fusion of architecture, construction and landscape. These are ethics that only come to light if we follow a wider field of protagonists than just the central designers – the architects behind the building – and which at the same time make it possible to form a more accurate picture of the ideas behind this design and of its creation.

Agnete Muusfeldt's fondness for trees is reflected in many of her endeavours. Her design for Kildeskoven seems connected to the experiments with a small deciduous forest and different types of ground cover that she carries out in her own garden at Åbrinken 131, a house in a terraced development in Virum north of Copenhagen. While no written evidence of this connection exists, we will try here to demonstrate an overlap in approach and aesthetic expression between Muusfeldt's private garden and her work with the publicly accessible landscape around Kildeskovshallen. We see this overlap partly in photographs, drawings and written descriptions of the garden and of the landscape around Kildeskovshallen, and partly in Muusfeldt's articulations of what she sees as the overall task of the landscape architect.

A key concern for Muusfeldt is the question of how to give trees and plants good growing conditions, combined with a desire to create access to green spaces and to a way of life where we can observe and be in close contact with plants and trees. In her own garden at

Agnete Muusfeldt took a great many photographs, including documentation of her own work. Top l. to r.: stones under old trees; relocated ash trees. Below them is a curved path through a planting with trees of various sizes and the Sun Lawn with a wall. At the bottom left is the new wooded area, next to which is another new forest area to the north-east of the Kildeskovshallen site.

Åbrinken these efforts were about herself, her family or the children in the neighbourhood, and at Kildeskoven she worked with an eye to a wider public, aiming to give them the opportunities for close interaction with deciduous trees, bushes, grass and plants. To better understand what underpins behind this design philosophy, we will now delve deeper into Muusfeldt's private garden in Virum. Our observations will be based on a series of articles she has written – and interviews she has given – over the course of a number of years, expressing her view of the relationship between people and gardens. Muusfeldt's work is, with the exception of a few texts in Danish literature on landscape architecture, relatively unknown, and she rarely appears in a wider architectural historical context. To remedy this, we have chosen to devote extra space to her reflections here.[484]

Agnete Muusfeldt's garden experiments

Agnete Muusfeldt was a highly prolific and successful landscape architect. She has overseen a large number of projects, especially public gardens and parks in the suburbs around Copenhagen and on Zealand. Examples include the large park at the conference facility for adult education LO-skolen in Helsingør[485] and several public parks in Rødovre. She contributed many articles to *Weekendavisen*, the gardening magazines *Haven* and *Havekunst* and the later *Landskap/Landskab*, where she also took on editorial duties.[486] She taught at the landscape architecture programme at the Royal Danish Veterinary and Agricultural College from 1970 to 1973, and was an external examiner there throughout the 1980s.[487] Her large collection of photographs of gardens and landscapes points to a particularly keen interest in using photos as a tool for research, teaching and communication.[488] She was active in the Association of Danish Landscape Architects (DL), where she sat on the board from 1961 to 1963, and she received several awards and accolades for her work, reflecting the great respect she enjoyed in professional circles.[489]

Muusfeldt lived most of her adult life in the house in Åbrinken, where she moved in with her two young children and her then-husband and business partner Erik Mygind immediately upon the area being built in 1954. At that time, she had taken her husband's surname, Mygind. Erik Mygind had helped to develop the landscape architectural framework and communal outdoor spaces for the district, which were designed by the prefab house company Johan Christensen & Søn. The couple separated in 1961, Erik Mygind moved out of the house, and another landscape architect, Jørn Palle Schmidt (1923–2010), moved in. Due to the divorce, Agnete Muusfeldt reverted to her birth name again. She and Jørn Palle Schmidt lived and worked side by side in the house until their cohabitation ended in 1980.*

Long before that, the terraced house in Åbrinken initially formed the setting for Agnete and Erik Mygind's joint design studio, which they founded in 1945. They had met when Erik Mygind taught the horticulture course at the Agricultural Collage and, as Agnete Muusfeldt describes it, he was attentive to the 'daunted and flattered' student.[491] Muusfeldt describes their collaboration in the joint design studio as a form of apprenticeship where she could develop her own professional skills in an ongoing conversation with and under the tutelage of Erik Mygind. Like other architects described in this book, Muusfeldt's career evolved in an ongoing interaction with her partners – but also under her own name in her own design studio.

After the divorce and the dissolution of their joint design studio in 1961, Agnete Muusfeldt founded her own. Her desk and Jørn Palle Schmidt's now stood side by side on the ground floor in Åbrinken. The two did not run a studio together, but Muusfeldt described their working partnership as fluid and informal, as an intellectual space they shared and where ideas and thoughts flowed back and forth as they worked on various tasks at their drawing studios and as teachers of landscape architecture. Muusfeldt wrote:

'I received a great deal of support from my office roommate, colleague and life partner. Throughout these rich and varied years, I have benefited from his wealth of ideas and inexhaustible knowledge of plants, his insight into the well-being and health problems of trees, and his innate sense of lush abundance. Our countless conversations on professional matters have, like a sliding bond of mutual interaction, prompted an ever-deeper immersion in the substance of our profession.'[492]

Although Muusfeldt formally worked alone during the most productive years of her career, she refers to men, women and places as important sources of inspiration and as conversation partners she maintained throughout her life.* Similarly, she describes her garden in Åbrinken, which she can see from her desk, as a source of inspiration and as a fundamental and meaningful reference point in her life and work:

* Agnete Muusfeldt also indulged her professional interests in a garden at a disused homestead on which she worked with Jørn Palle Schmidt over many years.[490]

Inger Ravn (1943–2022) obtained her degree in horticulture from the Royal Danish Veterinary and Agricultural College in 1969. Upon graduating she worked at landscape architect Agnete Muusfeldt's design studio, where she was later made partner. Their projects included a major plan for the outdoor areas around the County Hospital in Frederikssund, a town on West Zealand, which included small, intimate gardens as well as the wider landscape that was to surround the newly built hospital. Ravn taught landscape architecture at the Royal Danish Veterinary and Agricultural College for many years.

* From 1976, Agnete Muusfeldt worked closely with her goddaughter, landscape architect Inger Ravn (1943–2022), who was made partner in the firm in 1978. Ravn left the company in 1987 to become self-employed.[493]

The front garden of Åbrinken 131 as it looks today, with traces still visible of Agnete Muusfeldt's green design.

'I must have trees around me, and I happily give up roses, herbaceous borders and lawns to be allowed to kneel down and weed at their feet. To me, weeding is the most relaxing and thoughtful of all gardening chores.'[494]

The garden in Virum was a place where Muusfeldt could live and work in immediate, physical proximity to plants and trees and with direct access to a green setting. But it was also a place where she could experiment with different types of planting and garden design. These would change as the circumstances of her life altered and her professional interests and tasks evolved. Muusfeldt describes the garden as a place that offers the opportunity to live and work in beautiful, green

The garden in Åbrinken was open to the local children, who often came in to play with Agnete Muusfeldt's offspring. This led to a steady stream of movement in and out of the garden.

surroundings,[495] the very quality she passes on to other people in her work. At the same time, it gave her the opportunity to carry out more non-committal professional experiments that were not dependent on a client, making it an important locus for developing her skills and design philosophy, whether alone or with her professional and life partners.[496]

Muusfeldt's garden in Åbrinken was not alone in playing a major role in her development as a landscape architect. In several texts she describes her childhood garden, not just as a particular place where she became acquainted with the world of plants at an early age, but also as an almost mythical and symbolic reference.[497] Born into a wealthy family, Agnete Muusfeldt grew up in a large house in the affluent suburb of Charlottenlund north of Copenhagen with a romantically landscaped garden, which, among other things, included a large – for a Danish private garden – lake with its own jetty and rowing boat.[498] On several occasions Muusfeldt describes the garden as a place which bestowed upon her a range of formative experiences that proved essential for her life and for her professional work.* She describes these experiences with plants and trees as an essential part of life, highlighting the importance of outdoor life in green surroundings.[500] Thus, her private and professional trajectories in life come together in the gardens, in her private outdoor life and in her professional practice. The combination comes clearly across in a text Muusfeldt wrote together with Jørn Palle Schmidt:

'Was our green design governed by childhood experiences of gardens full of the heft of large trees, green carpets of lawns, bodies of water sent twinkling in the sun by gentle breezes, almost impenetrable secret thickets and an abundance of flowers, their colours full of gaudy fun and delicate grace? Or was it rather directed by a universal, inherent sense of earth's paradises?

Perhaps it was both. For so deeply rooted has the awareness of the luxuriance of growth, the necessity of growth, been for us, that throughout life it has been a constant endeavour for us to prepare everything for people's experiences of the paradisiacal green luxuriance, where plants look as if they were happy in their existence and pass their well-being on to the people who move among them.

The large number of plants, the speed of their growth, their suitability for the climate and soil – these have been the tools we have used. Rich, lush growth is in itself one of the prerequisites for the construction of rooms, walls, vaults, backdrops and colonnades where light and shadow alternate and colours spring to life.'[501]

* As a teenager, Agnete Muusfeldt was unsure of which profession she should pursue. But when she read an interview with landscape architect Anka Rasmussen, she found inspiration that made her confident in her choice. Rasmussen, who was a generation older than Muusfeldt, worked in manor gardens, with fruit growing and at a nursery. Muusfeldt had acquired in-depth knowledge of plants from her horticulture training, meaning that she met the requirement of five years of practical training in order to be admitted.[499]

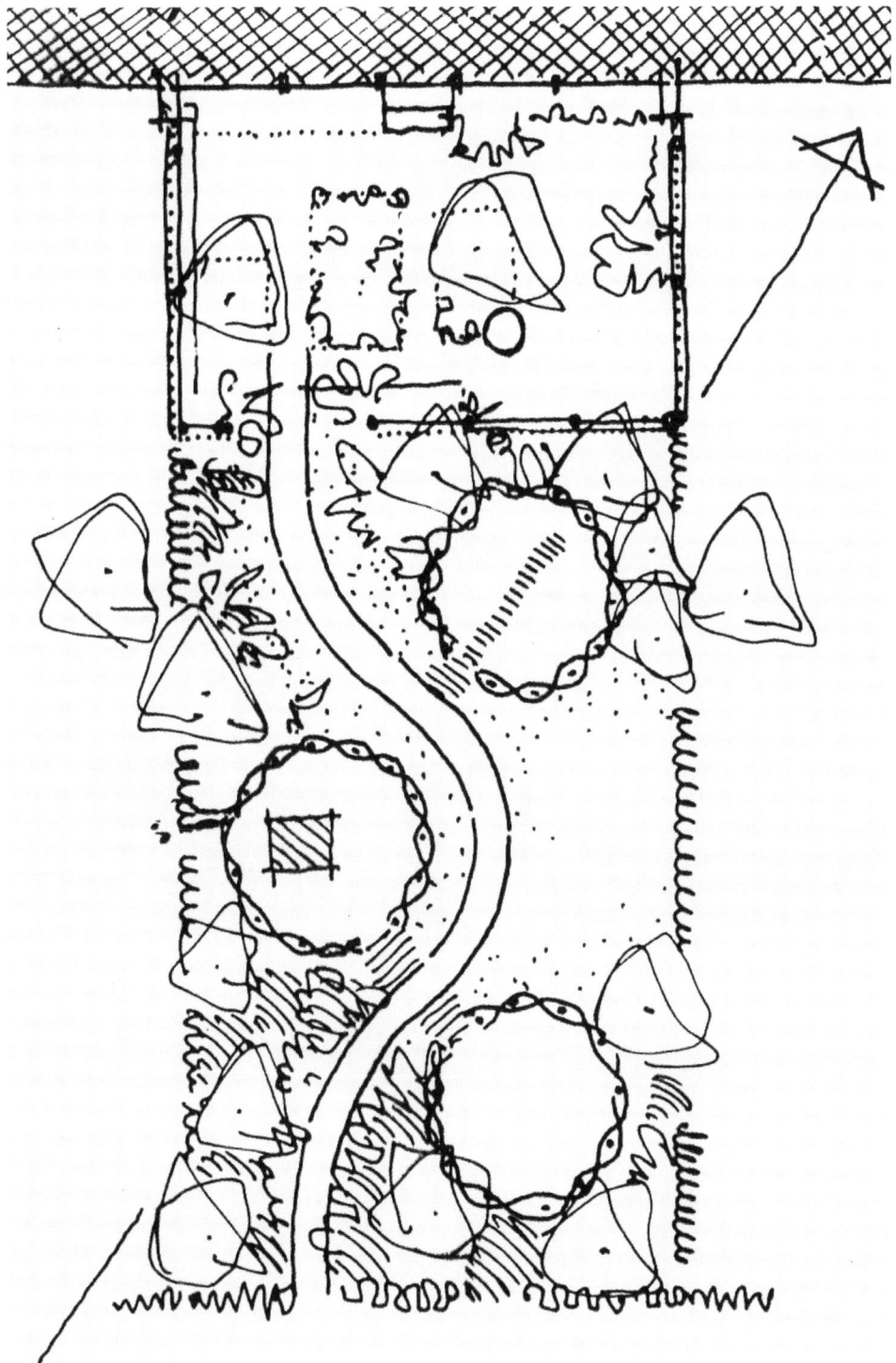

Agnete Muusfeldt's design for her own garden at Åbrinken from 1954. The garden was divided into zones, giving each generation their own section. The children's part of the garden was to the south, while the parents had a terrace closest to the house, to the north.

Agnete Muusfeldt in her childhood garden, which according to her had a major impact on her development as a landscape architect. Born into an affluent family, she was brought up in a large house in Charlottenlund with a garden in the Romantic landscape style, including a lake with its own jetty and rowing boat. For Muusfeldt, outdoor living in green surroundings was the breath of life.

The quote articulates the significance of the formative experiences Muusfeldt had in the kind of 'natural' setting provided by the gardens of suburban Copenhagen. But it also shows a more symbolic layer in the landscapes she produced in her practice, which are characterised by radiating lushness and luxuriance through a great variety of species and colour compositions that change with the seasons. On the one hand, Muusfeldt's work points to some of the important discussions we have about biodiversity, ecology and sustainability today, as well as to the growing interest in pastoral, lush and nature-like design in landscape architecture during the 1960s.[502] On the other hand, her work is poised between the situated experience of lushness at a given place and time and the Garden of Eden as a cultural, metaphysical reference point. As we know it from several religions, Paradise is an eternally blooming and luxuriant garden raised above humanity's progressive, dramatic time and the earth's cyclical time.[503] In this way, Muusfeldt's practice follows in the wake of centuries of using the art of gardening as a medium which conveys an understanding of concepts – in this case eternal life – that cannot be experienced directly by humans. As a design philosophy, Muusfeldt thus posits her work in a field poised between four poles:

> (1) The garden as a place where people have, right from their childhood, the opportunity to gain first-hand knowledge of the world of plants, a practice which allows them to feel a connection with other living beings.

> (2) The garden as a symbolic medium that provides access to something beyond the world of human experience through its lushness and wide-ranging diversity of species.

> (3) The landscape architect's professional knowledge of plants, trees, soil conditions, water, climate, etc., which enables plants and trees to grow in a given place.

> (4) Plants and trees as elements that the landscape architect can use to create inviting sequences of outdoor rooms and spaces, making them places where people want to stay.

Agnete Muusfeldt used, wrote about, developed and reshaped her own private gardens throughout her life, and she saw the garden as a source of a better quality of life, as a space that provides the opportunity for reflection – the *vita contemplativa* in the classical tradition – and as a vehicle for facilitating people's understanding and concern for plants and trees as well as their concrete, physical proximity to them.

Making the lives of plants and people intersect

In the 1960s and 1970s – the period of her life that Agnete Muusfeldt refers to as 'the busy years' – the garden at Åbrinken was rearranged and transitioned into a new phase. In an article from 1987, she describes the garden as a grove, a small open forest with different trees placed at enough of a distance between each other to allow a varied ground cover to grow and bushes to be planted around the garden.[504]

In her writing, Muusfeldt acknowledges that such a forest-like feel is not what one would typically associate with a terraced house plot. As can be seen from the designs for the first garden laid out at the site when the building was new, the couple planted thirteen small false acacias intended to screen off the row of houses behind. Gradually, grass and lawns more or less disappear from the garden, which is instead covered not only by trees, but also by shrubs and various forms of ground cover. As she writes looking back at the period in the 1960s when she had a lot of work on:

'Now the busy years were in full swing, so the garden often had to fend for itself. Looking out from our desk, the trunks and leaves unfurled their patterns towards the sky, and the fence between the terrace and the grove was replaced by a "plug" of boxwood, which is pleasant to look at all year round, and which immediately prevented eye contact with those weeds who are content to languish in the shadows.'[505]

From the perspective of gender history, it is interesting to note that Agnete Muusfeldt carried out so many large and acclaimed projects during this period while appearing only sparingly in the specialist literature on the era. Although women were in many ways under-represented in the architectural professions and to an even greater extent in the histories later written about the architecture and planning of the period, Muusfeldt states that during this period of overall growth it was never difficult for her to find work – quite the contrary.[506] However, the hectic, busy years in the construction industry came to an end due to the energy crisis in the mid-1970s, and this also had an effect on her working life. A time with fewer major commissions followed, and instead she busied herself with teaching. The change of pace in her life was also reflected in the garden. As she writes:

The view from Agnete Muusfeldt's workplace in the family's terraced house in Åbrinken, which changed many times during her time there. The garden acted as a place of experimentation for Muusfeldt, undergoing several redesigns and new phases as changes occurred in her family and work life. She referred to the 1960s as her busy years, while the 1970s brought greater opportunities to potter around the garden and spend more time looking out the window and enjoying the view.

'But in the early '70s, the hectic growth suddenly came to an end. Living conditions also changed for the garden, because now there was time to look out of the window, to potter around a little outside, and to wish for something else. [...] What I wanted now was a grove of light-leaved small trees that would create an open leafy roof over the garden, one where the trees had to be replaced with new ones as soon as they got too big so that new young could be planted.

Underneath those trees I could satisfy my immense curiosity to learn about new plants, because the wandering shadows provide ideal growing conditions for a myriad of plants.'[507]

In the 1980s, after she and Jørn Palle Schmidt separated, Muusfeldt's relationship with her garden seemed to change. We may speculate whether this change, arriving at a point when she lived alone in the house, also marks the time when her commitment to the garden takes a new turn. What is certain is that it is increasingly being described as a place for experimentation with the interaction between trees and ground cover: a modus operandi we also know from several of Muusfeldt's projects, such as the Kildeskovshallen. The garden is now a place that enables her to quench her thirst for knowledge about plants and trees and their growing conditions. It constitutes a private laboratory for plants and trees right outside her windows – and also involves ceaseless negotiation with the neighbours, who often complain about the tall trees casting shadows over their plots. The grove is a well-known type in Danish twentieth-century landscape architecture, and here Muusfeldt works with the theme in a planting design that creates flexibility and vitality. Trees that grow too large can be felled and replaced with smaller ones, and all the while the garden remains lush as it evolves in a process of ceaseless movement and intense dialogue and negotiation with its inhabitants. The garden at the house at Åbrinken 131 has found a new equilibrium in a form of continuous cooperation between people, trees and plants.

We can see that, through her practice and design philosophy, Muusfeldt also adds special value to the new, flat, extended, green welfare city: values about how we humans live with and in the green. Muusfeldt gave trees and plants the opportunity to grow in places where there had often simply been fields or bare land before, or, as we see with Kildeskoven, where a neglected forest planting required great empathy and firm protection on the part of the landscape architect to prevent it from perishing when brutal excavators and cranes began the construction process. Of particular relevance to the present context is the fact that in Muusfeldt's private garden we find aesthetic motifs and a form of practice similar to the one familiar from her work with

Agnete Muusfeldt's own photographs of her garden at Åbrinken in Virum.

Kildeskovshallen, letting us perceive its planting design as a way for the landscape architect to allow human and plant life to reach each other. Aesthetically speaking, the garden reminds us – with the way in which the planting allows room for a wealth of species, for variation in the ground cover in the bright, open deciduous forest as well as for variety in the rooms created and colours found there over the course of during the year, to which we may add the motif of the small grove and the clearing and the practice of using evergreen bushes to define rooms – of the approaches seen at Kildeskovshallen, where we see a similar interaction between elements such as the edge of the forest and the Sun Lawn, the use of shrubs, etc. Claiming that her own garden is a miniature Kildeskovshallen may be overstating matters, but there is something beautiful and generous in seeing elements from the private garden – elements which we know that Muusfeldt saw as an enriching, almost fundamental necessity of life for people, and with which she sought to establish an equilibrium in her own little garden – unfold with such accuracy in a public facility intended for the benefit of many people and as a way of using trees, plants and grasses to add value to civic life. It points to a fundamental anthropocentism in Agnete Muusfeldt's work, but also to a anthropocentism which is mediated by and forms part of a precisely choreographed and physical interaction with the plants, trees and grasses we find in the green spaces around the buildings.

The busy years – when Kildeskovshallen was created

Kildeskovshallen was created as a collaborative project that cut across genders and professions. We have focused on landscape architects and engineers collaborating with architects, but of course many others were also part of the project. We have briefly touched on groups such as politicians, craftsmen, planners and local citizens, and the work with Kildeskovshallen took place in a specific context where we can see the importance of contributions from more than just people: things, materials, plants and the place itself also worked for (and against) the project in terms of helping to create all the new, gigantic, architectural and green structures which the rapidly growing welfare state needed.

Although the project took many years to realise and was based on input from many different people, the process involved one common trait: an outstretched hand inviting interdisciplinary collaboration and attention to issues of compassion, conversation and care. The common basis is the place itself and its qualities as a communal asset, an issue to which the engineer, the architects and the landscape architect are all highly attentive, devoting much energy and intellectual care to the project – although they do so in different ways. In Agnete Muusfeldt's case, the task required several years of working on the building site before the actual building process began. She worked with the trees already found at the site, making them partners in the project and ensuring that they could survive the construction process. In the case of Karen and Ebbe Clemmensen, their community-building efforts included writing a text poem and using Karen Clemmensen's watercolours to reach out to fellow collaborators and create common ground for the project. And for the engineer, the task involved – towards the end of the project – calling for self-reflection, dialogue and productive conflict in future projects, thereby articulating an ethics for what a transformative and responsible co-creator in such enormous societal transformation processes should be like. Kildeskovshallen as a project is an example of different people contributing to just that.

It is also a project created on an obvious basis of collaboration across genders and professions – with all the tribulations, conflicts and tensions this can entail. The project came about in the middle of a period of booming growth and prosperity when there was plenty of work to be had for the parties involved (see Chapter Three), but it was still based on an ethics of cooperation where the issue of welfare, of compassion and care for others is envisioned beyond a narrow framework of understanding which insists that human beings take centre stage. At the same time, it is a project in which the four central protagonists, who entered into an ongoing dialogue on a collaboration that ran over a period of more than ten years, are people where two identify as men and two as women – a representative equality rarely seen at the time at this level of such projects. Agnete, Karen and Ebbe, and Knud. Or Agnete, Karen, Ebbe and Knud. The connections between these four people can be outlined in several different ways when describing the nature of the collaboration. There is much to indicate that their collaboration was strong, yet also fragile – like a tightrope walker carefully putting one foot in front of the other far above Kildeskovshallen's swimming pools. In itself, this reminds us that architecture is about much more than the imagination of a single individual. The process points to a fundamental tension between beauty, creation, ethics and the worn-out relationships that may remain after many long and intense negotiations, and which require a far more nuanced and complicated narrative form than the narrative of the genius coming up with a brilliant idea or beautiful design in a single, swooping gesture. Because this is a building that seeks to

Agnete Muusfeldt's own garden changed many times. Shown here is a photograph of the part she called 'the grove', a recurring motif in Danish landscape architecture. The theme can also be found at Kildeskovshallen, testifying to how Muusfeldt used her garden to experiment.

The use of evergreen ground cover to create visual distance in a small grove is a trait also seen in Muusfeldt's own garden at Åbrinken.

provide an answer to how people should build and be together in the new, expanding welfare state. We know that Agnete Muusfeldt calls this period her 'busy years', a time when she did not even have time to weed her small garden just outside her office window, and we know that the Clemmensen couple are described as workhorses who laboured day and night.

At the same time, we also know that the project's engineer urged all these busy people (himself included) to take more time to talk to each other. Furthermore, we know that these very thoughtful, careful and hard-working people accepted the task they were given, actively responding to each other, to the place, to the materials, to the people who would swim and do sports there, as well as to the trees and plants that grew and still grow around the building complex. If this project reminds us of our obligation to make time for dialogue and productive conflict, we must also hope that the future management, operation, care and development of the facility will take on board more voices – and not just those of human beings. A future where the unified impression produced by the interaction between architecture, construction and landscape architecture can be preserved even as new stories about the place can emerge. And where it can also be adapted to new needs of human beings and other living creatures and provide opportunities for creating a future that makes room for further narratives.

Kildeskovshallen was a collaborative project involving four key professionals entering into an alliance that would last for more than a decade. Many others also contributed to the realisation of the complex sports venue. Kildeskovshallen is a testament to how architecture calls for more nuanced and complicated narratives than simply the notion of a singular genius creating a magnificent, monumental building all on their own.

Postscript

Feminist Architects Who Wanted to Change the World

How can we create more inclusive, sustainable and equitable cities in the future if our knowledge of twentieth-century architecture too often emphasises a handful of 'great' architects and their contribution to architectural design? Our aim with this book has been to tell a different, more nuanced and accurate story. We have brought to light untold stories about women's contribution to the architectural professions in Denmark in the years from 1930 to 1980, thereby expanding the shared fount of architectural historical knowledge of a period when the Danish welfare state was growing and the great post-war building boom was well underway. The book illuminates some of the contributions made by women from various branches of the architectural professions during this period. Their achievements are rarely featured as prominently as those of men in the available literature, even though several of the architects appearing in this book were well-regarded and significant in their day, and even though they all left significant marks on the world. One of our key objectives has been to treat the work of several women in a single, unified narrative so that we may see connections between them. We also wanted to create a basis for a conversation about structural connections between gender and architecture.

Another crucial concern for us was to collect research on several different women in a single publication, because the overemphasis on the work of single individuals – so familiar from the many existing monographs on celebrated architects – paints a distorted picture of how architecture is created. We need to look at broader structural and historical contexts, historiographical traditions and the importance of collaborations and collective efforts, which often end up overlooked in publications that focus on individuals. Instead, we want to highlight the fact that buildings, urban spaces and landscapes are never created by the creative efforts of individuals alone. This book shows how our built environment is shaped by collaborations that cut across genders, professions, scales and many different forms of knowledge and skills.

Our book ends here, but the narrative of women's contribution to architecture as well as landscape and urban planning continues to evolve. The period merits further study than has been possible in this book, and there is still a great deal of work to be done in systematically reviewing the role and contribution of women to the architectural professions after 1980. Furthermore, potential tasks for scholars in the field includes examining the contributions of other protagonists who have often been relegated to the margins of existing architectural research, such as squatters, DIY builders and residents as well as construction workers, gardeners, municipally employed architects, planners, engineers and many others, all of whom have had important roles to play in determining why our built environment looks the way it does today. In several branches of historical research, both within and outside the architectural professions, we now see an interest in expanding the scope of events and persons who are allowed places in historical publications. The hitherto untold stories of women constitute just one potential angle out of many.

In the introduction, we mentioned Agnete Frederikke Laub Hansen, who in 1908, when the School of Architecture at the Royal Danish Academy of Fine Arts opened to women, was the first woman admitted to the programme. Others followed, but women remained outnumbered at the school and in the profession for many decades in the twentieth century. The gender balance in several of the architectural professions has changed significantly over time, and in recent years we have also seen a number of gender-political discussions arising in the light of movements such as #metoo and leaving their mark in the form of various activist initiatives in the world of architecture, such as the list of 'The Shitty Architecture Men'.[508] This has prompted discussion of, for example, the often-precarious working conditions in the industry and of the patriarchal principles that can still be found in architectural education. The discussions have also brought with them a focus on women's conditions, even if existing structural inequalities or various forms of transgressive behaviour cannot be attributed to all men or have personally affected all women – or only women – in the profession. And the critical feminist movements have led to polarising clashes as well as broader discussions of the need for structural changes within the field of architecture. Feminist agendas of today make our historical study of the intersection between architecture and gender particularly topical. We want to contribute historical knowledge to the discussions and to better understand, nuance and correct some of the patriarchal preconceptions that form blind spots in the existing architectural history writing and guiding narratives. Dominating narratives emphasise men's work in the profession and individual artistic achievements, and these narratives have been allowed to dominate the image of how a twentieth-century architect looks, works and best contributes to society. These narratives continue to influence our collective image of how architecture is created and of the importance of the architectural profession in society. In working on this book, we have used the gender and diversity debates of recent years as a catalyst for expanding our historical knowledge and creating a more accurate and nuanced understanding of Danish architectural history.

Feminist initiatives around 1980

Around the time that this book's historical narrative ends, a number of feminist initiatives arose. In Denmark, these are spearheaded partly by trained architects and partly by other protagonists, all of whom had a gender-political mission.[509] The years around 1980 see an increasing number of women enrolling at the Danish schools of architecture, and several groups of architects raise gender-political and feminist agendas which are often in line with various initiatives on the political left. Specifically, the first self-proclaimed women's design studio Thyra is formed at this time, named after Queen Thyra – Denmark's first known woman to commission an architectural project.[510] Furthermore, from the end of the 1970s on, women in the architectural professions begin to organise themselves in new ways: examples include the formation of the organisations Kvinder i Byggesektoren (Women in the Construction Sector) and Kvindelige Arkitekter Jylland K.A.J. (Women Architects in Jutland), both in 1977, and two years later – after a major Nordic conference in Kungälv near Gothenburg featuring numerous participants from Denmark – Nordiske Kvinders Bygge- og Planforum (Nordic Women's Building and Planning Forum, 1979).[511] Here we see a series of initiatives where women take a feminist starting point for focusing not just on gender and structural inequality, but also on the importance of organising to actively oppose unjust structural conditions.

From the mid-1970s on, we also see a number of exhibitions which specifically strive to call attention to and change women's conditions. The art exhibition *Kvindeudstillingen XX* (The Women's Exhibition XX) at Charlottenborg was staged in 1975 (see Chapter Four), as was the travelling exhibition *La femme danoise* (The Danish Woman), curated by architect Karen Zahle. With support from the Ministry of Culture, the latter exhibition was shown in France, Belgium and Switzerland, using several art and architecture projects to ask fundamental questions about women's double burden.[512] Five years later, in 1980, Copenhagen hosted an important event: the mid-term conference of the UN Decade for Women. Due to unrest in Iran, where the international conference was originally scheduled to take place, the Danish capital became the place where politicians, officials and NGOs met to discuss issues of gender and global inequality. On that occasion, a number of Danish architects and artists showed their work in the exhibition *på vej* (On the Way) – a large joint exhibition at Copenhagen City Hall and Aarhus City Hall.[513] Organised by the architects Kirsten Birch, Bodil Damgaard, Anne Fogh, Kirsten Hanson, Bodil Kjær, Karen Kratina and Marianne Nielsen, the exhibition focused on central themes such as the role of women in urban spaces, communal living and the everyday lives of women and families.

Adopting a gender-political perspective, it is important for us as authors to emphasise that our work here relates to themes that have previously been addressed within the architectural professions in Denmark. While this has been done in different contexts and in other ways, those other efforts share a fundamental belief with this book; namely that issues of gender, architecture and justice must be examined in their wider context, and that change does not happen by itself: it requires collective effort and hopeful, unifying narratives about the future.

In the 1980s, the Danish architecture industry was beset by recession and a decline in construction, not least in the capital region. At the same time, many architects – both women and men – applied their specialist knowledge while working in public-sector positions in municipalities, agencies and similar positions: a contribution to the architectural profession that is still often overlooked in specialist literature. During this period, several architects worked on the basis of approaches that would later be named postmodernism, and which often unfolded in abstract experiments and paper architecture, for example in the journal *Scala* and in teaching.[514] But as we have seen with the examples of Ussing + Hoff and Anne Marie Rubin (see Chapter Four) – as well as with the new women's organisations and the exhibition *på vej* – it is important to remember that the architectural professions were not as apolitical as they might seem when reading about the postmodern architects' speculative works.[515] The feminist positions found in the profession in Denmark in the 1980s were not only concerned with women's conditions but also with human-made ecological crises, resource scarcity, pollution and overconsumption. Examples of such thinking can be found in the work of architect Anne Ørum-Nielsen, who was part of the team behind the well-known low-rise social housing development Galgebakken (1972–74) in Albertslund.[516] Ørum-Nielsen grew increasingly keen to put questions of ecology on the agenda within the architectural professions. In connection with the exhibition *på vej*, she stated:

'[…] our activities have turned out to be so extensive and our technology so destructive that the natural balancing of our interventions can no longer keep up – when, for example, the sum of the disruptions we impose on the living conditions of microorganisms impacts the oxygen and carbon cycle to an extent that will affect the Earth's climate.'[517]

Here Anne Ørum-Nielsen clearly anticipates some of our current discussions on the limitations of economic models and the high consumption of resources – debates prompted by our growing awareness of climate and biodiversity crises. In a book published in connection with the *på vej* exhibition, she points out that we humans must 'see ourselves as a co-existing, living part of nature – and choose to use our technology in such a way that it is subordinated to the principle of all things living, which is cyclical'.[518] Whether deliberately or not, she thus inscribes herself within the arguments of ecofeminism as presented by, among others, the American philosopher and historian Carolyn Merchant in the book *The Death of Nature*, also published in 1980.

Several of the architects we have met in this book came from educated backgrounds and, by virtue of their own education and large earning potential during the construction boom, held relatively high positions in society. Hence the question of class is as important as the question of gender. For example, this becomes clear when we see how several of the feminist architects of the 1970s and 1980s were themselves entangled in complex situations where their rebellion was made possible by their privileged upbringing and education and by publicly-funded actions, exhibitions and commissions. In this way, the women's biographies become part of a more nuanced narrative about how change, development and innovation happen in complex collaborations rich in conflicts and dilemmas: collaborations that are just as full of blind spots, coincidences and power struggles as any other. Several of the women whose work we have written about in this book have addressed connections between inequality, women's conditions and opportunities, solidarity and personal identity markers – in this case gender – and so too have the feminist architects from the 1970s onwards, only at a more structural level. Standing on the shoulders of previous feminist architects and thinkers, we have been able to read these women's work and thoughts in the light of feminist theory and of concepts such as equality, equal opportunities, justice, humanity, care, love and the right to integrity as well as a good life regardless of gender, body or background.

Public dialogue as a tool in research

This book focuses on Denmark but speaks into a wider international research context, where these years are seeing worldwide work being done to bring untold stories about women's contributions to the architectural professions to light. The current situation gives rise to hope: academics around the world are helping to expand our common horizons, calling for collaboration and consolidation across national borders, research groups and professional fields. These efforts also prompt a need to forge links between the various research efforts and archives, libraries, museums, educational institutions and the wider public. In addition, in recent years a number of established art and architecture institutions have shown exhibitions about women's contribution to architecture.[519] As authors of this book, we have contributed by curating the historical part of the exhibition *Women in Architecture* (*Kvinder skaber rum*) in collaboration with the Danish Architecture Center, on display from May to October 2022.[520] Concurrently with the exhibition, we released a podcast series *De Glemte Arkitekter* (The Forgotten Architects) and the guidebook *byWomen* and participated in a number of interviews and reports in the Danish and international press.[521] These public dissemination initiatives were developed early in the research process, meaning that they did not only constitute a sharing of knowledge: they were also a way of creating new knowledge. The dialogue with curators, exhibition architects, journalists, exhibition visitors, professional organisations and a wider interested public has contributed to the research on which this book is based. On several occasions we have been contacted by descendants, witnesses and other collaborators who – having heard about the exhibition or read about the project – wanted to share their stories, photographs, documents and drawings. This way of working with the public on research has been fruitful and meaningful, and we have endeavoured to adhere to all applicable principles of good research ethics, respecting the personal commitment shown by our collaborators and the often personal and sensitive nature of the material.[522] While we have not been able to pass on all the stories provided by our collaborators, we hope that the dialogue and collection of testimonies can continue.

Hope for the future

The women whose work we have examined have rarely been directly connected with each other, let alone shared values or goals. Nevertheless, the chapters have revealed connections between the professional histories of many women and the different practices with which they worked. Women with architectural training have erected significant and impactful monuments, but they have also made many other contributions to architecture – such as designing kitchens and town plans, designing and planting gardens, writing articles and reports that have changed the profession's self-understanding, curating exhibitions and managing planning and building legislation.[523] This book offers an opportunity to adjust our image of who and what has value, both in terms of the shared history of how our built environment is created and shaped and in terms of our notions about which – and whose – stories are worth telling. Herein lies an important steppingstone for expanding the scope of the potential roles and positions architects can take up in the future. The book shows how architectural work – regardless of the architect's gender identity – can directly affect people's everyday lives, contribute to good housing for all, create public and inclusive common spaces, produce beautiful things, provide spaces for imagining alternative futures and for incorporating issues of ecology and justice in the work of architects. Conversely, the architectural profession can also contribute to creating disciplining structures, unequal power relations and constricting financial ties and lead to the exploitation of resources, other people and ecosystems, as well as causing deep disappointments for individuals, arising as a result of collaborations that are often subject to conflicts, serendipity and insoluble dilemmas. We hope that by raising awareness of the importance of gender identity in architecture during the period addressed in this book and by understanding the importance of diversity for collaborations and innovative thinking, we can become better equipped to push the field of architecture in a direction that is more diverse and equitable in the future – across genders, bodies and classes, as well as for other living beings and ecosystems with which we share our world.

på vej

ARBEJDER AF KVINDELIGE ARKITEKTER · PLANLÆGGERE · KUNSTNERE
UDSTILLING   KØBENHAVNS RÅDHUS 18.-27. JULI   mandag-fredag 10-18
                                              lørdag-søndag 10-16
1980   ÅRHUS RÅDHUS 6.-14. SEPTEMBER   daglig 10-17

True to the aesthetic of the period, this poster advertising the 1980 exhibition *på vej* (On the Way) is a feminist image, representing the woman's body as a place from which new life can spring. However, the scene can be read in several different ways: the woman's body is depicted as intertwined with nature, with the animal world and with a nostalgic notion of life in the countryside – as is evident from the small, thatched cottages perched on the branches that grow on her dress, or for which the dress forms a canvas. The rural scene points to a typical perception of the woman as being close to nature, inviting the naïvely drawn, barefoot and voluptuous female body to be read in that light, too. Where are we headed if we follow this woman? The poster points ambivalently to romantic notions about life in the countryside, presenting the woman as connected to nature.

Notes

Preface
On Writing a New History of Architecture

1. Anne Tietjen (ed.): *Forstadens bygningskultur 1945-1989. På sporet af velfærdsforstadens bevaringsværdier*, Copenhagen, Dansk Bygningsarv, 2010; Jannie Rosenberg Bendsen, Birgitte Kleis and Mogens A. Morgen: *Bellahøj. Fortællinger om en bebyggelse*, Copenhagen, Strandberg Publishing, 2015; Jannie Rosenberg Bendsen and Dorthe Bendtsen: *Drømmen om eget hus. Statslånshuse 1933–1959*, Copenhagen, Strandberg Publishing, 2021.

2. See for example Ellen Braae and Henriette Steiner: 'The Sustainable Nordic City of the Future is the City We Already Have', in *NORDIC WORKING PAPERS: Opportunities and challenges for future regional development – notes from an open seminar*, 12 September 2019, ed. Kjell Nilsson, Copenhagen, Nordic Council of Ministers, 2019, pp. 31–39, https://doi.org/10.6027/NA2019-910; Ellen Braae and Svava Riesto: 'As Found: A New Design Paradigm', in *Nordic Journal of Architecture*, vol 1, no. 1, 2011, pp. 8–9.

3. See for example Kate Eichhorn: *The Archival Turn in Feminism: Outrage in Order*, Philadelphia, PA, Temple University Press, 2013; Antoinette M. Burton (ed.): *Archive Stories: Facts, Fictions, and the Writing of History*, Durham, NC, London, Duke University Press, 2005.

4. For example, Vibeke Dalgas's and Agnete Laub Hansen's materials are now at The Royal Danish Library, The Danish National Art Library. Some material from Ragna Grubb's family has been handed over to the Women's Building archive. Also, material pertaining to Inger Ravn is now at the Royal Danish Library in the collection of garden and landscape architecture drawings. See also archivist Tina Lund's article: 'Agnete Muusfeldt – skjult i samlingen', in *Revy*, vol. 44, no. 1, 2022, pp. 3–7.

5. Linda Nochlin: *Why Have There Been No Great Women Artists*, 1971, www.writing.upenn.edu/library/Nochlin-Linda_Why-Have-There-Been-No-Great-Women-Artists.pdf, p. 7.

6. See for example Svava Riesto: *Biography of an Industrial Landscape. Carlsberg's Urban Spaces Retold*, Amsterdam, Amsterdam University Press, 2018.

7. See for example Henriette Steiner and Kristin Veel: *Touch in the Time of Corona*, Berlin, De Gruyter, 2020.

8. For a broader survey of women's work with architecture and design in and around Copenhagen than space permits in this book, see Rahbek, Liv Løvetand, Svava Riesto and Henriette Steiner: *By women. En guidebog til hverdagsarkitektur i København og omegn*, Aarhus, Ikaros Press, 2022.

9. Katve-Kaisa Kontturi: *Ways of Following. Art, Materiality, Collaboration*, London, Open Humanities Press, 2018, p. 17.

10. Karen Burns and Lori Brown: 'Telling Transnational Histories of Women in Architecture, 1960–2015', in *Architectural Histories*, vol. 8, no. 1, 2020, p. 15, DOI: http://doi.org/10.5334/ah.403

11. See for example Hélène Frichot, Catharina Gabrielsson and Helen Runting (eds.): *Architecture and Feminisms: Ecologies, Economies, Technologies*, London, New York, Routledge, 2018.

Introduction
Where Are the Women in Danish Architectural History?

12. Wanda M. Corn with contributions by Charlene G. Garfinkle and Annelise K. Madsen: *Women Building History. Public Art at the 1893 Columbian Exposition*, Berkeley, University of California Press, 2010; Jeanne Madeline Weimann: *The Fair Women. The Story of the Women's Building at the World's Columbian Exposition, Chicago 1893*, Chicago, Academy Chicago Publishers, 1981, pp. 26–31.

13. Grethe Holmen: 'Historien bag bygningen' in Tove Koed and Edith Kjærsgaard (eds.): *Historien om Kvindernes Bygning*, Copenhagen, Kvindernes Bygning, 1986, p. 9.

14. Annemarie Balle (ed.): *Fra vision til virkelighed. Kvindernes Bygning 125 år*, Aars, Forlaget Himmerland, Kvindernes Bygning, 2020, pp. 8–11.

15. Sonja Meyer was born Carstensen and appears by this name in the article. Pernille: 'Arkitekterne Carstensen og Westergaard', in *Dagens Nyheder – Nationaltidende*, 11.3.1927, p. 2.

16. Annemarie Lund: 'Anka Rasmussen. Første danske kvindelige havearkitekt', in *Landskab*, vol. 94, no. 4, 2013, pp. 126–135, www.kvinfo.dk/side/597/bio/622/origin/170/

17. The winning project was partially realised in block 7 of Kantorparken in Copenhagen, built between 1939–1941, and the villa is located at Storchsvej 6 and dates from 1936. Ole Buhl: *Socialt Boligbyggeri*, København, Foreningen Socialt Boligbyggeri, 1941, pp. 57–64; Rahbek, Liv Løvetand, Svava Riesto and Henriette Steiner: *By women. En guidebog til hverdagsarkitektur i København og omegn*, Aarhus, Ikaros Press, 2022.

18. See Jannie Rosenberg Bendsen, Svava Riesto and Henriette Steiner: 'Hvor er kvinderne i dansk arkitekturhistorie?', in *Arkitekten*, no. 5, 2020, p. 24.

19. See for example Esbjørn Hiort: *Finn Juhl*, København, Arkitektens Forlag, 1990; Lulu Salto Stephensen: *Tradition og fornyelse i dansk havekunst. G.N. Brandt og de første årtier af 1900 tallet*, Copenhagen, Frangipani, 1993; Carsten Thau and Kjeld Vindum: *Arne Jacobsen*, Copenhagen, Arkitektens Forlag, 1998; Christoffer Harlang, Keld Helmer-Petersen and Krestine Kjærholm (eds.): *Poul Kjærholm*, Copenhagen, Arkitektens Forlag, 1998; Sven-Ingvar Andersson and Steen Høyer: *C.Th. Sørensen – en havekunstner*, 2nd edition, Copenhagen, Arkitektens Forlag, 2001; Martin Keiding and Kim Dirckinck-Holmfeld (eds.): *Utzon og den nye tradition*, Copenhagen, Arkitektens Forlag, 2005; Thomas Bo Jensen: *P.V. Jensen-Klint*, Copenhagen, Kunstakademiets Arkitektskoles Forlag, 2006; Annemarie Lund: *Grøn form – grønt modspil. En bog om landskabsarkitekten Jørn Palle Schmidt*, Copenhagen, Arkitektens Forlag, 2007; Olaf Lind: *Arkitekten Steen Eiler Rasmussen*, Copenhagen, Gyldendal, 2008; Kenn Schoop and Peter Thule Kristensen: *Svenn Eske Kristensen – velfærdsarkitekten*, Copenhagen, Aristo, 2018; Martin Søberg: *Kay Fisker. Works and Ideas in Danish Modern Architecture*, London, Bloomsbury Visual Arts, 2021. See also Michael Sheridan: *Mesterværker. Enfamiliehuset i dansk arkitekturs guldalder*, Copenhagen, Strandberg Publishing, 2011. A few women from the period are addressed in monographs, albeit usually because they set up architecture firms with their husbands; see for example Johannes Hedal Hansen: *Eva & Nils Koppel*, Copenhagen, Strandberg Publishing, 2017 and Thomas Bo Jensen: *Inger og Johannes Exner*, Aarhus, Ikaros Press, 2012. A few exceptions exist, such as Birgitte Thorsen Vilslev and Carsten Hoff (eds.): *Susanne Ussing – mellem arkitektur og kunst*, Copenhagen, Strandberg Publishing, 2017; Peter Beck: *Det essentielle – arkitekt Bodil Kjær om sine internationale arbejder 1950–2000*, Aarhus, Turbine, 2022.

20. www.akademikerbladet.dk/aktuelt/2020/august/se-koensfordelingen-paa-alle-landets-uddannelser

21 In Denmark, examples include two major research projects funded by The Independent Research Fund Denmark: 'Spaces of Danish Welfare' and 'Reconfiguring Welfare Landscapes', to which Svava Riesto and Henriette Steiner have contributed. Also see Mark Swenarton, Tom Avermaete and Dirk van den Heuvel: *Architecture and the Welfare State*, London, New York, Routledge, 2014; Helena Mattsson and Sven-Olov Wallenstein: *Swedish Modernism. Architecture, Consumption, and the Welfare State*, London, Black Dog Publishing, 2010; Katrine Lotz et al.: *Form til velfærd*, Copenhagen, Arkitektens Forlag, 2017; Kirsten Marie Raahauge et al. (eds.): *Architectures of Dismantling and Restructuring. Spaces of Danish Welfare 1970–Present*, Zurich, Lars Müller Publishers, 2022; Ellen Braae and Henriette Steiner: 'Expanding Danish Welfare Landscapes – Steen Eiler Rasmussen and Tingbjerg Housing Estate', in Jeanne Haffner (ed.): *Landscapes of Housing. Design and Planning in the History of Environmental Thinking*, London, New York, Routledge, 2021, pp. 145–167; Henriette Steiner: 'Gigantic Welfare Landscapes and the Ground Beneath Høje Gladsaxe', in *Landscape Research*, vol. 46, no. 4, 2021, pp. 527–541; Ellen Marie Braae et al.: 'Welfare Landscapes: Open Spaces of Danish Social Housing Estates Reconfigured', in Svava Riesto and Miles Glendinning (eds.): *Mass Housing of the Scandinavian Welfare States: Exploring Histories and Design Strategies*, Edinburgh, University of Edinburgh/Docomomo, 2020, pp. 13–23; Lærke Sophie Keil, Svava Riesto and Tom Avermaete: 'Welfare Landscapes Between Individuality and Communality. Social Housing in Albertslund Syd', in *Landscape Research*, vol. 46, no. 4, 2021, pp. 456–473.

22 This is described in Olaf Forchhammer: *Københavnsegnens Grønne Omraader. Forslag til et System af Omraader for Friluftsliv*, Copenhagen, Nyt Nordisk Forlag,1936; C.Th. Sørensen *Parkpolitik i Sogn og Købstad*, Copenhagen, Gyldendal 1931 and in Egnsplankontoret: *Skitseforslag til Egnsplan for Storkøbenhavn*, 1947 (also known as *Fingerplanen/the Finger Plan*), Copenhagen, Dansk Byplanlaboratorium; Ellen Marie Braae et al.: 'Welfare Landscapes: Open Spaces of Danish Social Housing Estates Reconfigured', in Svava Riesto and Miles Glendinning (eds.): *Mass Housing of the Scandinavian Welfare States: Exploring Histories and Design Strategies*, Edinburgh, University of Edinburgh/ Docomomo, 2020, pp. 13–23.

23 See for example Scott E. Page: *The Diversity Bonus*, Princeton, N.J., Princeton University Press, 2019.

24 We base this assumption on surveys counting the amount of women's work referenced in specialist literature seen in relation to counts we have also made of the number of students in and graduates from the schools of architecture. Of course, this tells us nothing about the quality of their work, but it does tell us that they were present. Det Kongelige Danske Kunstakademi: *Sager over kvindelige Elever 1888–1923; Kartotek over Elever (Mænd og Kvinder) 1923–1933*; The Royal Danish Academy of Fine Arts: Inventory of Graduates 1915–1968; *Fortegnelse over Danske Havebrugskandidater 1865–1955*. Supplement for vol. 5, 1947, Copenhagen, Foreningen af Danske Havebrugskandidater, 1955.

25 Despina Stratigakos: *Where are the Women Architects?*, Princeton, N.J., Princeton University Press, 2016.

26 See for example the themed issue on women's architecture, 'Kvindearkitektur', in *Blød By*, no. 24, 1983.

27 See for example Landsforeningen Dansk Arbejde by Johan Nielsen (ed.): 'En Nuance', in *Dansk Arbejde*, vol. 27, 1 February, 1936, p. 2

28 Ragna Grubb: 'Kvindernes Bygning', in *Arkitekten* Ugehæfte, vol. 38, 1936, pp. 13–14.

29 Olga Eggers (ed.): *Kendte danske Kvinder*, Copenhagen, Arthur-Jensens Forlag, 1934, p. 44.

30 For example, the building is not mentioned in either Tobias Faber: *Dansk arkitektur*, 2nd edition., Copenhagen, Arkitektens Forlag, 1977, in Martin Keiding, Marianne Amundsen and Kim Dirckinck-Holmfeld (eds.): *Dansk arkitektur siden 1754*, 2nd edition, Copenhagen, Arkitektens Forlag, 2007 or in Jørgen Hegner Christiansen: *Dansk betonarkitektur*, Copenhagen, Forlaget Vandkunsten, 2018. It is mentioned in brief entries in *Weilbachs Kunstnerleksikon*, *Dansk Kvindebiografisk Leksikon* and *Wikipedia*.

31 Det Kongelige Danske Kunstakademi: *Sager over kvindelige Elever 1888–1923; Kartotek over Elever (Mænd og Kvinder) 1923–1933*.

32 Gösta Esping-Andersen: *The Three Worlds of Welfare Capitalism*, Princeton, N.J., Princeton University Press, 1990.

33 Ibid.

34 www.danmarkshistorien.dk/vis/materiale/kanslergadeforliget-1933 and Jannie Rosenberg Bendsen and Dorthe Bendtsen: *Drømmen om eget hus. Statslånshuse 1933–1959*, Copenhagen, Strandberg Publishing, 2021.

35 See for example Lasse Horne Kjældgaard: *Meningen med velfærdsstaten. Da litteraturen tog ordet – og politikerne lyttede*, København, Gyldendal, 2018.

36 Ibid.

37 Anette Borchorst: 'Feminist Thinking about the Welfare State', in Myra Marx Ferree, Judith Lorber and Beth B. Hess: *Revisioning Gender*, New York, Oxford, Altamira Press, 1999, p. 100.

38 Tanja Jordan and Rikke Lequick Larsen (eds): *Female forces of architecture. Women's centennial anniversary at the Royal Danish Academy of Fine Arts, School of Architecture, Copenhagen*, Copenhagen, Kunstakademiets Arkitektskole, 2010; Pernille Ipsen: *Et åbent øjeblik. Da mine mødre gjorde noget nyt*, Copenhagen, Gyldendal, 2020.

39 Prior to being accepted at the Royal Danish Academy of Fine Arts, she had attended classes at Vilhelm Klein's drawing school. Det Kongelige Danske Kunstakademi, *Sager over kvindelige Elever 1888–1923* and Emma Salling and Claus Smidt, 'Fundamentet', in Anneli Fuchs and Emma Salling, *Kunstakademiet 1754–2004*, vol. I, Copenhagen: Det Kongelige Akademi for de Skønne Kunstner & Arkitektens Forlag, 2004, p. 374.

40 See the Danish National Art Library, part of the Royal Danish Library, where her small archive is located. Agnete Frederikke Laub Hansen was subsequently a part-time assistant in the design studio operated by her husband, the architect Henning Hansen (1880–1945). Claus Smidt, 'Fra tempel til boligblok. Arkitektur i første halvdel af 1900-tallet', in Anneli Fuchs and Emma Salling, *Kunstakademiet 1754–2004*, vol. I, Copenhagen: Det Kongelige Akademi for de Skønne Kunster & Arkitektens Forlag 2004, p. 374.

41 Tip: 'Den første kvindelige Arkitekt', *Nationaltidende*, 2 May 1915, p. 3.

42 The Royal Danish Academy of Fine Arts: *Sager over kvindelige Elever 1888–1923; Kartotek over Elever (Mænd og Kvinder) 1923–1933*.

43 Olaf Lind: *Arkitekten Steen Eiler Rasmussen*, Copenhagen, Gyldendal, 2008.

44 Claus M. Smidt: 'Fra tempel til boligblok. Arkitektur i første halvdel af 1900-tallet', in Anneli Fuchs and Emma Salling (eds.): *Kunstakademiet 1754–2004*, vol. 1, Copenhagen, Det Kongelige Akademi for de Skønne Kunster & Arkitektens Forlag, 2004, pp. 325–330.

45 Tanja Jordan and Rikke Lequick Larsen (eds.): *Female forces of architecture. Women's centennial anniversary at the Royal*

Danish Academy of Fine Arts, School of Architecture, Copenhagen, Copenhagen, Kunstakademiets Arkitektskole, 2010, p. 44.

46 *Fortegnelse over Danske Havebrugskandidater 1865–1955.* Supplement to the 5th edition 1947, Copenhagen, Foreningen af Danske Havebrugskandidater, 1955.

47 *Undervisnings- og Eksamensplan for Den Kongelige Veterinær og Landbohøjskole*, 6th edition., Copenhagen, 1910.

48 *Fortegnelse over Danske Havebrugskandidater 1865-1955.* Supplement to the 5th edition 1947, Copenhagen, Foreningen af Danske Havebrugskandidater, 1955.

49 Vilhelmine Busck also graduated from Vilvorde in 1891 and from the Rødkilde Havebrugsskole (Horticultural School) in 1892, *Fortegnelse over Danske Havebrugskandidater 1865-1955.* Supplement to the 5th edition 1947, Copenhagen, Foreningen af Danske Havebrugskandidater, 1955, p. 13.

50 www.skbl.se/en/article/EsterClaesson; Catharina Nolin: 'International Training and National Ambitions. Female Landscape Architects in Sweden, 1900–1950', in Sonja Dümpelmann and John Beardsley (eds.): *Women, Modernity, and Landscape Architecture*, New York, Routledge, 2015, pp. 38–59.

51 Ester Claesson: 'Några minnen från min skoltid på Vilvorde', in *Havebrugshøjskolen Vilvorde. Skolen gennem 50 Aar. 1875-1925*, Charlottenlund, 1925, p. 78.

52 Annemarie Lund: 'Anka Rasmussen. Første danske kvindelige havearkitekt', in *Landskab*, vol. 94, no. 4, 2013, p. 129.

53 www.kvinfo.dk/side/597/bio/1346/origin/170/; see also Annemarie Lund: *Danmarks havekunst*, vol. 3: *1945–2002*, Copenhagen, Arkitektens Forlag, 2002.

54 Annemarie Lund: 'Anka Rasmussen. Første danske kvindelige havearkitekt', in *Landskab*, vol. 94, no. 4, 2013, p. 126.

55 Foreningen for Socialt Boligbyggeri: *Foreningen for Socialt Boligbyggeri 1945–1985*, vol. 2, Foreningen for Socialt Boligbyggeri, 1986; Anja Boserup: 'Havearkitekten Agnete Petersen', in *Landskab*, vol 112, no. 1, 2021, pp. 24–27; Svava Riesto and Henriette Steiner: *By women. En guidebog til hverdagsarkitektur i København og omegn*, Aarhus, Ikaros Press, 2022.

56 Anna Weber: *Kvinden som Gartner og Havebruger*, Copenhagen, Nyt Nordisk Forlag Arnold Busck, 1933.

57 Anna Weber: 'Kan kvinder blive gartnere?', excerpt from Anna Weber's lecture at Vilvorde in 1928, www.rts.dk/images/temaer/historie/pdf/Vilvorde_125_aar.pdf

58 Sonja Dümpelmann and John Beardsley: 'Introduction', in Sonja Dümpelmann and John Beardsley (eds.): *Women, Modernity, and Landscape Architecture*, New York, Routledge, 2015, p. 7.

59 Ibid.

60 Malene Lytken: 'The Danish School of Interior Architecture. A Visionary Functionalist, a Visionary Aesthete, and Their Women Students', in *Journal of Interior Design*, vol. 38, no. 3, 2013, pp. 1–19.

61 *Havebrugshøjskolen Vilvorde. Skolen gennem 50 Aar. 1875–1925*, Charlottenlund, 1925.

62 Ibid., p. 39–42. The same could be said of many male architects who worked on developing the modern-day kitchen, such as Edvard Heiberg, Svenn Eske Kristensen and Bent Salicath.

63 Anna Weber: *Kvinden som Gartner og Havebruger*, Copenhagen, Nyt Nordisk Forlag Arnold Busck, 1933, p. 22.

64 Ibid., p. 44.

65 Ibid., p. 15.

66 Ibid., pp. 38–39.

67 Anna Weber: *Kvinden som Gartner og Havebruger*, Copenhagen, Nyt Nordisk Forlag Arnold Busck, 1933, p. 38.

68 See www.leksikon.org/art.php?n=1504?

69 Ibid., p. 103.

70 Pernille: 'Arkitekterne Carstensen og Westergaard', in *Dagens Nyheder – Nationaltidende*, 11.3.1927, p. 2.

71 Selverhvervende Kvinder: 'De kvindelige Arkitekter af K. F. U. K.s nye Bygning', in *Berlingske Tidende*, 24.12.1916, p. 6.

72 Gamin: 'En Konkurrence i Mandsværk', in *B.T.*, 16.11.1921, p. 9. See also Mary-Ann: 'Kvindelige Arkitekter. Hvad vi trænger til', in *Klokken 5*, 20.8.1930, p. 4.

73 Tanja Jordan and Rikke Lequick Larsen (eds.): *Female forces of architecture. Women's centennial anniversary at the Royal*

Danish Academy of Fine Arts, School of Architecture, Copenhagen, Copenhagen, Kunstakademiets Arkitektskole, 2010, p. 44.

74 Sestoft, Kirsten, Karen Clemmensen and Vibeke Fischer Thomsen: '3 Kvinder i arkitektfaget', in *Blød By*, no. 11, 1981, p. 18.

75 Interview with Svava Riesto, 5 May 2021.

76 Karen Zahle: *Udelukket og indelukket. Arkitekten Karen Zahle*, Nykøbing Sj., Bogværket, 2021.

77 In Vibeke Dalgas: 'Byplanhistorie – og kvindehistorie', in *Byplanhistoriske noter*, no. 37, 1997, p. 30.

78 Sestoft, Kirsten, Karen Clemmensen and Vibeke Fischer Thomsen: '3 Kvinder i arkitektfaget', in *Blød By*, no. 11, 1981, p. 21.

79 Founded in 1965.

80 *Blød By*, no. 11, 1981.

Chapter 1
Visions – A Revolution in the Kitchen

81 SPF: 'Vi skal bo helt anderledes', in *Aftenbladet*, 1.4.1937, p. 5.

82 Steph: 'Uhyggelige Tal fra de overbefolkede Lejligheder. København har Boliger med kun 4½ Kubikmeter Luft til hver Beboer. En Familie med Mand, Kone og 5 Børn bor i et enkelt Værelse', in *Politiken*, 11.11.1937, p. 14.

83 Kay Fisker: 'Socialt Boligbyggeri's konkurrence om boligtyper i etagehuse', in *Arkitekten* Ugehæfte, vol. 39, no. 14, 1937, pp. 65–76. Also see Jannie Rosenberg Bendsen and Dorthe Bendtsen: *Drømmen om eget hus. Statslånshuse 1933–1959*, Copenhagen, Strandberg Publishing, 2021, pp. 26–31.

84 Anon.: 'Hvert Familiemedlem sit Kammer!', in *Hejmdal*, 5.4.1937, p. 2.

85 FM: 'En ny Lejlighedstype', in *Bygge og bo*, vol. 4, no. 1, 1937, p. 27.

86 Anon.: 'Hjem & Bohave i Tivoli 17–26 sept', in *Politiken*, 18.9.1937, p. 16.

87 Jørn Guldberg: 'Stockholm i Danmark. Den danske reception af Stockholmsudstillingen 1930', in *Architectura*, vol. 33, 2011, pp. 103–150.

88 Lisbet Balslev Jørgensen: *Den sidste guldalder. Danmark i 1950'erne*, Copenhagen, Arkitektens Forlag, 2004.

89 Several books have been written about the kitchen from a design perspective in a Danish context, but these have not concerned

89 themselves with the role of women in the development of the kitchen. See for example Lars Dybdahl and Ida Engholm (eds.): *Design – køkkenet*, København, Gyldendal, 2008 or, adopting an ethnological perspective, Birgit Vorre: *Boligen i det 20. århundrede. Indretning og brug*, Copenhagen, Nyt Nordisk Forlag Arnold Busck, 2008.

90 Sara Bonnemaison and Christine Macy: 'The Dwelling-Garden Dyad in Twentieth-Century Affordable Housing', in Charissa N. Terranova and Meredith Tromble (eds.): *The Routledge Companion to Biology in Art and Architecture*, New York, London, Routledge, 2019, pp. 105–107.

91 See for example Barbara Penner: 'Designed-in Safety: Ergonomics in the Bathroom', in Kenny Cupers (ed.): *Use Matters. An Alternative History of Architecture*, London, New York, Routledge, 2013.

92 www.bolius.dk/danskerne-skifter-koekkenet-efter-11-aar-mange-aar-foer-det-er-udtjent-97149

93 Vibeke Gulmann: 'Et spørgsmål om at gide', in *Weekendavisen Berlingske Aften*, 28.10.1977, p. 18; Lili Ochsner: 'Frygtløs og nysgerrig', in *Morgenavisen Jyllands-Posten*, 22.5.1983, p. 53.

94 Gytte Rue and Rut Speyer: Til bestyrelsen for Overretssagfører Zeuthens Mindelegat, Copenhagen, 30 September 1944.

95 See for example Lars Dybdahl: 'Scientific management i hjemmets fabrik', in Lars Dybdahl and Ida Engholm (eds.): *Design – køkkenet*, Copenhagen, Gyldendal, 2008, pp. 25–46; William J.R. Curtis: *Modern Architecture Since 1900*, 3rd edition, London, New York, Phaidon, 1996, pp. 183–216; Sigfried Giedion: *Space, Time, and Architecture. The Growth of a New Tradition*, 5th edition, Cambridge, Mass., London, Harvard University Press, 2008, pp. 429–706.

96 www.denstoredanske.lex.dk/husmoder and Helle Juhl: *Husmødre. Historier fra landets største arbejdsplads*, Copenhagen, Gyldendal, 2012, pp. 19–50.

97 Dolores Hayden: *The Grand Domestic Revolution*, Cambridge, Mass., London, MIT Press, 1982; June Freeman: *The Making of the Modern Kitchen. A Cultural History*, Oxford, New York, Berg, 2004; Lars Dybdahl: 'Scientific management i hjemmets fabrik', in Lars Dybdahl and Ida Engholm (eds.): *Design – køkkenet*, Copenhagen, Gyldendal, 2008, pp. 25–46.

98 June Freeman: *The Making of the Modern Kitchen. A Cultural History*, Oxford, New York, Berg, 2004, pp. 29–32; Lars Dybdahl: 'Scientific management i hjemmets fabrik', in Lars Dybdahl and Ida Engholm (eds.): *Design – køkkenet*, Copenhagen, Gyldendal, 2008, p. 29.

99 Carmen Espegel: *Women Architects in the Modern Movement*, New York, London, Routledge, 2018, p. 183; Susan R. Henderson: 'A revolution in the woman's sphere. Grete Lihotzky and the Frankfurt Kitchen', in Barbara Miller Lane (ed.): *Housing and Dwelling. Perspectives on Modern Domestic Architecture*, New York, London, Routledge, 2007, pp. 248–258; Marcel Bois and Bernadette Reinhold (eds.): *Margrete Schütte-Lihotzky. Architektur, Politik, Geschlecht. Neue Perspektiven auf Leben und Werk*, Basel, Birkhäuser, 2019.

100 Carmen Espegel: *Women Architects in the Modern Movement*, New York, London, Routledge, 2018, p. 178.

101 Ulla Tafdrup: 'Køkkenundersøgelsen', in *Kvinden og samfundet*, vol. 65, no. 4, 1949, p. 52.

102 Karen Braae: 'Moderne Køkkener', in *Architekten*, vol. 25, 1923, pp. 16–18, 82–86.

103 Ingrid Møller Dyggve sat on the board of De Danske Husmoderforeninger (The Danish Housewives' Associations) from 1922 to 1925 and on the board of the Women's Building in Copenhagen from 1926 to 1928. Olga Eggers (ed.): *Kendte danske Kvinder*, Copenhagen, Arthur-Jensens Forlag, 1934, p. 36; Ingrid Møller Dyggve: 'Køkkenet', in *Architekten*, vol. 28, no. 9/10, 1926, pp. 104–108; www.kvinfo.dk/side/597/bio/622/

104 www.kvinfo.dk/side/597/bio/622/

105 Lars Dybdahl: 'Scientific management i hjemmets fabrik', in Lars Dybdahl and Ida Engholm (eds.): *Design – køkkenet*, Copenhagen, Gyldendal, 2008, p. 41; Leif Leer Sørensen: *Edvard Heiberg og dansk funktionalisme. En arkitekt og hans samtid*, Copenhagen, Arkitektens Forlag, 2000, pp. 64–68.

106 www.biografiskleksikon.lex.dk/Viggo_Sten_Møller

107 Viggo Sten Møller: 'Boligforhold', in *Nyt Tidsskrift for Kunstindustri*, 1943, p. 133.

108 Statens Husholdningsråd participated from 1945 onwards.

109 S. Haunsø, Viggo Sten Møller and Bent Salicath (eds.): *Køkkenundersøgelse*, København, Fællesudvalget for Boligundersøgelser, 1949, p. 5 and *Boligen*, no. 2, 1945, p. 28.

110 Viggo Sten Møller: 'Boligforhold', in *Nyt Tidsskrift for Kunstindustri*, 1943, p. 133. For an international angle on the subject, see Kenny Cupers (ed.): *Use Matters. An Alternative History of Architecture*, London, New York, Routledge, 2013.

111 S. Haunsø, Viggo Sten Møller and Bent Salicath: *Køkkenundersøgelse*, Copenhagen, Fællesudvalget for Boligundersøgelser, 1949, pp. 7–8.

112 Ibid., p. 5.

113 Also Bodil Foss, Birgit Karberg, Lea Stein, Inger Lythans and Else Margrethe Nielsen. The overview of employees appears in the book, but we do not know whether all employees are mentioned. For example, Rut Speyer is not mentioned, and as is apparent from an interview in the newspaper *B.T.* in March 1945, she contributed alongside Gytte Rue in late 1944 and the beginning of 1945. Unfortunately, not much material from the study itself has been preserved; only a single box is kept in the National Archives. S. Haunsø, Viggo Sten Møller and Bent Salicath: *Køkkenundersøgelse*, Copenhagen, Fællesudvalget for Boligundersøgelser, 1949, p. 6; Blondie: 'De københavnske Køkkener fulde af Mangler', in *B.T.*, 9.3.1945, p. 5.

114 Letter to Miss Rut Speyer from Aarhus Tekniske Skole, 4 May 1937; letter from S. Klostergaard-Sørensen on 19 January 1935 (both from a private collection).

115 Gytte Rue and Rut Speyer: Til bestyrelsen for Overretssagfører Zeuthens Mindelegat, Copenhagen, 30 September 1944.

116 Ibid.

117 Ibid.

118 Carsten Nielsen: 'Frivillig Husundersøgelse', in *Berlingske Tidende*, 13.9.1944, p. 6.

119 Blondie: 'De københavnske Køkkener fulde af Mangler', in *B.T.*, 9.3.1945, p. 5.

120 Ibid.

121 Ibid.

122 Ibid.

123 S. Haunsø, Viggo Sten Møller and Bent Salicath: *Køkkenundersøgelse*, Copenhagen, Fællesudvalget for Boligundersøgelser, 1949, p. 5; Blondie: 'De københavnske Køkkener fulde af Mangler', in *B.T.*, 9.3.1945, p. 5.

124 S. Haunsø, Viggo Sten Møller and Bent Salicath: *Køkkenundersøgelse*, Copenhagen, Fællesudvalget for Boligundersøgelser, 1949, p. 9.

125 During the war, from 1943 until 1 December 1944, Edvard Heiberg worked at Svenska

Riksbyggen, which gave him in-depth knowledge of Swedish housing construction and construction theory. Leif Leer Sørensen: *Edvard Heiberg og dansk funktionalisme. En arkitekt og hans samtid*, Copenhagen Arkitektens Forlag, 2000, p. 247.

126 Edvard Heiberg: 'Om køkkener', in *Arkitekten Ugehæfte*, vol. 50, 1948, pp. 37–40.

127 Bent Salicath: 'Køkkenforholdene i Boligbyggeriet', in *Boligen*, no. 3, 1948, p. 80; S. Haunsø, Viggo Sten Møller and Bent Salicath: *Køkkenundersøgelse,* Copenhagen, Fællesudvalget for Boligundersøgelser, 1949, p. 7; Viggo Sten Møller: 'Hemmens Forskningsinstitut', in *Nyt Tidsskrift for Kunstindustri*, vol. 18, 1945, pp. 65–66; Per H. Hansen: *Da danske møbler blev moderne. Historien om dansk møbeldesigns storhedstid*, Copenhagen, Aschehoug and Syddansk Universitetsforlag, 2006, p. 272.

128 Ragna Grubb: 'Boligundersøgelser', in *Arkitekten Ugehæfte*, vol. 48, no. 17, 1946, p. 99; Blondie: 'De københavnske Køkkener fulde af Mangler', in *B.T.*, 9.3.1945, p. 5.

129 S. Haunsø, Viggo Sten Møller and Bent Salicath: *Køkkenundersøgelse*, Copenhagen, Fællesudvalget for Boligundersøgelser, 1949.

130 Ibid., p. 31.

131 Blondie: 'De københavnske Køkkener fulde af Mangler', in *B.T.*, 9.3.1945, p. 5.

132 The Ministry of Housing's committee on collective facilities: *Fællesanlæg til lettelse af hjemmets arbejde*, vol. 1, *Betænkning*, no. 57, Copenhagen, Statens Trykningskontor, 1954, pp. 3–5.

133 Esbjørn Hiort and Birte Ludovica Rasmussen (eds.): *Håndbog for Kvinde og Hjem. Danske kvinders udstilling for rationel husførelse, Forum 1.-17. september 1950*, Copenhagen, 1950, p. 11.

134 The Ministry of Housing's committee on collective facilities: *Fællesanlæg til lettelse af hjemmets arbejde*, vol. 1, *Betænkning*, no. 57, Copenhagen, Statens Trykningskontor, 1954, p. 7; the Ministry of Housing's committee on collective facilities: *Fællesanlæg til lettelse af hjemmets arbejde*, vol. 2: *Bilag*, *Betænkning*, no. 57, Copenhagen, Statens Trykningskontor, 1954, pp. 202–204.

135 Eva: 'Samfundet kræver meget af Kvinderne, og vi kræver alt af os selv ...', in *Berlingske Tidende*, 16.1.1949, p. 6.

136 Lili Ochsner: 'Frygtløs og nysgerrig', in *Morgenavisen Jyllands-Posten*, 22.5.1983, p. 53.

137 Ellen Bisgaard: '"EN FINSTUE" blev til køkken – og hele familien har glæde og nytte af forandringen', in *ALT for damerne*, 6.1.1953, p. 19.

138 Ibid.

139 Vibeke Gulmann: 'Et spørgsmål om at gide', in *Weekendavisen Berlingske Aften*, 28.10.1977, p. 18.

140 Ibid.

141 Mazelle: 'Det er køkkenet, det drejer sig om', in *ALT for damerne*, 10.8.1954, p. 3.

142 Anon.: 'Mærkedage', in *Aftenbladet*, 6.9.1940; Anon.: 'Navne og Nyheder', in *Morgenbladet*, 12.10.1930.

143 Vibeke Gulmann: 'Et spørgsmål om at gide', in *Weekendavisen Berlingske Aften*, 28.10.1977, p. 18; editors: 'Familie-Nyt', in *Nationaltidende*, 24.8.1940, p. 2; Lili Ochsner: 'Frygtløs og nysgerrig', in *Morgenavisen Jyllands-Posten*, 22.5.1983, p. 53.

144 Ibid.

145 Ibid.

146 Ulla Tafdrup: 'Det rigtige køkken', in *Bygmesteren*, vol. 41, 1948, p. 129.

147 Johan Pedersen (ed.): *Vore køkkener. En forsøgsrapport*, Copenhagen, Dansk Almennyttigt Boligselskab, 1951.

148 Ibid., pp. 9–10.

149 Ibid., p. 46.

150 Ulla Tafdrup: 'Kærnen i boligen – køkkenet', in *Kvinder og samfundet*, vol. 64, no. 9, 1948, p. 136.

151 N: 'Gode og dårlige køkkener og vaskekældre i Amerika og Danmark', in *Ingeniøren*, no. 14, 1950, pp. 302–303.

152 Anon.: 'Husmoderens arbejde i nationaløkonomisk perspektiv', in Esbjørn Hiort and Birte Ludovica Rasmussen (eds.): *Håndbog for Kvinde og Hjem. Danske kvinders udstilling for rationel husførelse, Forum 1.-17. september 1950*, Copenhagen, 1950, pp. 14–15.

153 Esbjørn Hiort and Birte Ludovica Rasmussen (eds.): *Håndbog for Kvinde og Hjem. Danske kvinders udstilling for rationel husførelse, Forum 1.-17. september 1950*, Copenhagen, 1950, pp. 6–7.

154 Perikon: 'Det ideale Køkken – næsten!', in *Nationaltidende*, 28.2.1947, p. 8; Steen Sørensen (eds.): *Søndergård Park – verdens navle i 60 år. Historien om en bebyggelse og beboerdemokrati i Gladsaxe almennyttige Boligselskab*, Gladsaxe, Søndergård Park, Afdelingsbestyrelsen, 2012, p. 11; Ulla Tafdrup: 'Det rigtige køkken', in *Bygmesteren*, vol. 41, 1948, p. 133.

155 Perikon: 'Det ideale Køkken – næsten!', in *Nationaltidende*, 28.2.1947, p. 8.

156 Eva: 'Samfundet kræver meget af Kvinderne, og vi kræver alt af os selv ...', in *Berlingske Tidende*, 16.1.1949, p. 6.

157 Perikon: 'Det ideale Køkken – næsten!', in *Nationaltidende*, 28.2.1947, p. 8

158 The Ministry of Housing's committee on collective facilities: *Fællesanlæg til lettelse af hjemmets arbejde*, vol. 1, *Betænkning*, nr. 57, Copenhagen, Statens Trykningskontor, 1954, pp. 43–50; Lars Dybdahl: 'Scientific management i hjemmets fabrik', in Lars Dybdahl and Ida Engholm (eds.): *Design – køkkenet*, Copenhagen, Gyldendal, 2008, p. 44.

159 The development consists of terraced houses built in 1952–53 designed by Mogens Jacobsen, Alex Poulsen, Magnus Stephensen and Knud Thorball together with Ulla Tafdrup. A communal house was added in 1958–59. Aksel Andersen and Jørn Palle Schmidt were landscape architects. Arne Jacobsen contributed to the design of the development plan. Elisabeth Hermann: *50'er boligen. En eksempelsamling*, Copenhagen, Byggeriets Studiearkiv, 2000, pp. 75–86.

160 Annette Vasström: 'Kollektivbyen Carlsro – en by i byen', in Sigurd Rambusch (ed.): *Rødovre 1901–1976*, Rødovre, Rødovre Kommune, 1978, p. 225.

161 Anon.: 'Gaarden Carlsro forvandles til By med 4500 Indbyggere', in *Billed-Bladet*, no. 30, 1952, pp. 16–17. Inge and Christian Hansen's kitchen is shown under the headline 'Stue og køkken går i et' ('Combining the living room and kitchen), in *ALT for damerne*, 19.5.1953, p. 19.

162 Anon.: 'Gaarden Carlsro forvandles til By med 4500 Indbyggere', in *Billed-Bladet*, no. 30, 1952, p. 17.

163 Annette Vasström: 'Kollektivbyen Carlsro – en by i byen', in Sigurd Rambusch (eds.): *Rødovre 1901–1976*, Rødovre, Rødovre Kommune, 1978, p. 225.

164 Eva: 'Samfundet kræver meget af Kvinderne, og vi kræver alt af os selv ...', in *Berlingske Tidende*, 16.1.1949, p. 6.

165 Annette Vasström: 'Kollektivbyen Carlsro – en by i byen', in Sigurd Rambusch (ed.): *Rødovre 1901–1976*, Rødovre, Rødovre Kommune, 1978, p. 225.

166 Ibid.

167 Ulla Tafdrup: 'Det rigtige køkken', in *Bygmesteren*, vol. 41, 1948, p. 130; Birte: 'En køkkenvask skal være stor', in *Aftenbladet*, 29.7.1948, p. 2.

168 Erna: 'Køkkenarkitekten paa opdagelsestogt i USA', in *Ekstra Bladet*, 18.1.1950 (from the archives of Statens Byggeforskningsinstitut [now BUILD]); Barbara Penner: 'The Cornell Kitchen. Housing and Design Research in Postwar America', in *Technology and Culture*, vol. 59, no. 1, 2018, p. 52.

169 Barbara Penner: 'The Cornell Kitchen. Housing and Design Research in Postwar America', in *Technology and Culture*, vol. 59, no. 1, 2018, pp. 48–94.

170 Erna: 'Køkkenarkitekten paa opdagelsestogt i USA', in *Ekstra Bladet*, 18.1.1950 (from the archives of Statens Byggeforskningsinstitut [now BUILD]); Pan: 'Hvor et moderne dansk Køkken er gammeldags', in *Berlingske Aftenavis*, 4.3.1950 (from the archives of Statens Byggeforskningsinstitut [now BUILD]). See also Iben Vyff: 'Kold krig i en dansk køkkenkultur, 1945–1965', in *Arbejderhistorie*, no. 2, 2012, pp. 40–56.

171 Stated by Ulla Tafdrup and Ib Martin Jensen's son, Michael Martin Jensen, in an email, May 2022.

172 Pan: 'Hvor et moderne dansk Køkken er gammeldags', in *Berlingske Aftenavis*, 4.3.1950 (from the archives of Statens Byggeforskningsinstitut [now BUILD]).

173 Perikon: 'Jeg mødte ikke en eneste overbelastet Husmoder i USA', in *Nationaltidende*, 28.11.1949, p. 5.

174 Pan: 'Hvor et moderne dansk Køkken er gammeldags', in *Berlingske Aftenavis*, 4.3.1950 (from the archives of Statens Byggeforskningsinstitut [now BUILD]).

175 Ibid.

176 Perikon: 'Jeg mødte ikke en eneste overbelastet Husmoder i USA', in *Nationaltidende*, 28.11.1949, p. 5.

177 N: 'Gode og dårlige køkkener og vaskekældre i Amerika og Danmark', in *Ingeniøren*, no. 14, 1950, pp. 302–303.

Chapter 2
Love – Three Houses Built for Women's Work, Family and Love Lives

178 Lundwall Nilsen: 'Et penalhus med mange rum', in *ALT for damerne*. The house was featured in the magazine in the mid-1960s; the exact date is unknown.

179 'Arkitekterne Inger og Johannes Exner', www.ingerogjohannesexner.dk/

180 Thomas Bo Jensen: *Inger og Johannes Exner*, Aarhus, Ikaros Press, 2012, pp. 30–33; 'Arkitekterne Inger og Johannes Exner', www.ingerogjohannesexner.dk/

181 See Whitney Chadwick and Isabelle de Courtivron: *Significant Others. Creativity and Intimate Partnership*, London, Thames & Hudson, 1998 (1993).

182 See Thomas Bo Jensen: *Inger og Johannes Exner*, Aarhus, Ikaros Press, 2012, pp. 8–33, for more comprehensive biographical information.

183 Ibid.

184 Gorm Harkær: *Kaare Klint*, vols. 1–2, Copenhagen, Klintiana, 2010.

185 Eva Illouz: *Why Love Hurts. A Sociological Explanation*, Cambridge, Mass., Polity Press, 2012.

186 Joshua S. Goldstein: *War and Gender*, Cambridge, Cambridge University Press, 2003.

187 For a more in-depth treatment of this discussion, see: Henriette Steiner: 'Between Passion and Possession. Women Architects and the Houses They Built for Family, Love and Work', approved for publication in *Journal of Architecture*. To be published in 2023.

188 'Arkitekterne Inger og Johannes Exner', www.ingerogjohannesexner.dk/

189 Thomas Bo Jensen: *Inger og Johannes Exner*, Aarhus, Ikaros Press, 2012, pp. 8–33; 'Arkitekterne Inger og Johannes Exner', www.ingerogjohannesexner.dk/

190 'Arkitekterne Inger og Johannes Exner', www.ingerogjohannesexner.dk/

191 'Arkitekterne Inger og Johannes Exner', www.ingerogjohannesexner.dk/

192 See *Søllerødbogen*, vol. 1988, for a discussion of the topography and possible origins of the hill, including the uncertainties attached to the issue.

193 Ibid.

194 Jens-Peter Thomsen and Stefan Bastholm Andrade: 'Vi gifter os med dem, der ligner os', Copenhagen, VIVE, 2 December 2018, www.vive.dk/da/udgivelser/vi-gifter-os-med-dem-der-ligner-os-11750/

195 Hadley Keller: 'The Power Couples of Architecture and Design', in *AD*, 31.1.2015, www.architecturaldigest.com/gallery/power-couples-of-architecture-and-design-slideshow

196 Jens Clemmensen: 'Ghettoer i det nordlige København?', in Niels Helberg and Hans Kristensen (eds.): *På fri fod. Gamle byplanlæggere ser tilbage på barndomslivet*, Byplanhistorisk Skriftserie, no. 75, 2015, pp. 62–63.

197 Sestoft, Kirsten, Karen Clemmensen and Vibeke Fischer Thomsen: '3 Kvinder i arkitektfaget', in *Blød By*, no. 11, 1981, p. 20.

198 Ibid.

199 Dag Lénard: 'Huset er ladet med sol, lys og lykke', in *ALT for damerne*, 19.10.1954.

200 Sestoft, Kirsten, Karen Clemmensen and Vibeke Fischer Thomsen: '3 Kvinder i arkitektfaget', in *Blød By*, no. 11, 1981, p. 20.

201 Dag Lénard: 'Huset er ladet med sol, lys og lykke', in *ALT for damerne*, 19.10.1954; Sestoft, Kirsten, Karen Clemmensen and Vibeke Fischer Thomsen: '3 Kvinder i arkitektfaget', in *Blød By*, no. 11, 1981, p. 20.

202 Dag Lénard: 'Huset er ladet med sol, lys og lykke', in *ALT for damerne*, 19.10.1954.

203 Ibid.

204 Ibid.

205 See Jannie Rosenberg Bendsen and Dorthe Bendtsen: *Drømmen om eget hus. Statslånshuse 1933–1959*, Copenhagen, Strandberg Publishing, 2021, pp. 46–53.

206 Dag Lénard: 'Huset er ladet med sol, lys og lykke', in *ALT for damerne*, 19.10.1954.

207 Diary entries found in Karen and Ebbe Clemmensen's business archives in the Royal Danish Library, the Danish National Art Library.

208 Eva Illouz: *Why Love Hurts. A Sociological Explanation*, Cambridge, Mass., Polity Press, 2012.

209 www.kulturarv.dk/kid/VisWeilbach.do?kunstnerId=10634&wsektion=alle

210 Frank: 'De unge Arkitekter slog de store Kanoner ud', in *B.T.*, 28.11.1944, p. 2.

211 Ibid.

212 Lise Skjøt-Pedersen: 'Lyngby-Taarbæk i 1950'erne', in *Lyngby-bogen*, 2015, pp. 5–128.

213 Lyngby-Taarbæk Kommune: *Lyngby Taarbæk Dispositionsplan*, 1949; *Hovedstadsmetropolen efter 1945*, Henning Bro et al. (eds), Copenhagen, Hovedstadsområdets Kulturhistoriske Arkiver, 2011; *Den grønne metropol. Natur- og rekreative områder i hovedstadsmetropolen efter 1900*, Caspar Christiansen et al. (eds.), Copenhagen, Frydenlund Academic, 2016.

214 Johannes Hedal Hansen: *Eva & Nils Koppel*, Copenhagen, Strandberg Publishing, 2017.

215 According to the agreement document as supplied by Erik Frank Jeppesen, dated 4 April 1950.

216 Erik Frank Jeppesen: 'Min opvækst i Hjortekær', in *Lyngby-bogen*, 2005, pp. 5–54; *Weilbachs Kunstnerleksikon*: 'Rut Speyer', www.kulturarv.dk/kid/VisWeilbachRefresh.do?kunstnerId=10634&wsektion=alle

217 Jannie Rosenberg Bendsen's and Henriette Steiner's interview with Rut Speyer's daughters, Elsebet and Karen Speyer, 12 January 2022.

218 Ibid.

219 Ibid.

220 Henriette Steiner in conversation with one of Rut Speyer's neighbours at Hjortekærbakken, Annelise Holstebroe, 1 September 2021.

221 Letter provided by Rut Speyer's daughters.

222 Jannie Rosenberg Bendsen's and Henriette Steiner's interview with Rut Speyer's daughters, Elsebet and Karen Speyer, 12 January 2022.

223 *Hovedstadsmetropolen efter 1945*, ed. Jenning Bro et al, Copenhagen, Hovedstadsområdets Kulturhistoriske Arkiver, 2011.

224 Rut Speyer: 'Politik er det umuliges kunst', in *Morgenavisen Jyllands-posten*, 18.10.1989, p. 9; Henriette Steiner: 'Constructing Copenhagen in a Time of Economic Downturn', in *Architecture and Culture*, vol. 10, no. 1, 2022, pp. 76–95.

225 Rose Etherington: 'Denise Scott Brown Petition for Pritzker Recognition Rejected', in *Dezeen*, 14.6.2013, www.dezeen.com/2013/06/14/pritzker-jury-rejects-denise-scott-brown-petition/

226 MoMA: 'New Furniture Designs and Techniques Have Initial Showing at Museum of Modern Art', press release, 1946, www.assets.moma.org/documents/moma_press-release_325508.pdf

227 Eva Illouz: *Why Love Hurts. A Sociological Explanation*, Cambridge, Mass., Polity Press, 2012.

228 Joshua S. Goldstein: *War and Gender*, Cambridge, Cambridge University Press, 2003.

229 See Gösta Esping-Andersen: *The Three Worlds of Capitalism*, Princeton, N.J., Princeton University Press, 1990. Also see Steiner's article on the politics and architecture of the Danish welfare state: Henriette Steiner: 'Gigantic Welfare Landscapes and the Ground Beneath Høje Gladsaxe', in *Landscape Research*, vol. 46, no. 4, 2021, pp. 527–541, www.doi.org/10.1080/01426397.2020.1808953

230 Ana Alacovska: 'From Passion to Compassion. A Caring Inquiry into Creative Work as Socially Engaged Art', in *Sociology*, vol. 54, no. 4, 2020, pp. 727–744, www.doi.org/10.1177/0038038520904716

Chapter 3
Growth – Stories of a More Caring Approach to Urban Planning

231 RB: 'Ulykkelige følger af sommerhusbyggeriet', in *Aalborg Amtstidende*, 20.6.1967, p. 3. The Hindsgavl course is also referenced in the article 'Dårlig planlægning af sommerhus-byggeri', in *Folkebladet*, 20.6.1969, p. 7.

232 Line Vestergaard Knudsen: *De første sommerhuse – 1886*, Aarhus, Aarhus Universitetsforlag, 2022, p. 74.

233 Anne Marie Rubin in Ejvind Bjørnkjær: 'Moderne gårdhus-bebyggelse midt i vestkystens klitter', in *Ny tid*, 17.3.1968, p. 7.

234 www.danmarkshistorien.dk/vis/materiale/danmarks-befolkningsudvikling

235 Niels Albertsen and Bülent Diken: 'Welfare and the City', in *Nordisk Arkitekturforskning*, vol. 17, no. 2, 2004, pp. 7–22.

236 Anne Tietjen (ed.): *Forstadens bygningskultur 1945–1989. På sporet af velfærdsforstadens bevaringsværdier*, Copenhagen, Dansk Bygningsarv, 2010.

237 Ole Nørgård: 'Albertslund Syd', in *Landskab*, vol. 50, no. 2, 1969–1970, p. 21.

238 See Asbjørn Jessen and Anne Tietjen: 'Assembling Welfare Landscapes of Social Housing: Lessons from Denmark', in *Landscape Research*, vol. 46, no. 4, 2021, pp. 474–494.

239 Henrik Vejre: *Fingerbyens grønne handske. Planlægning og virkeliggørelse af Københavnsegnens grønne områder 1950-2020*, Aalborg, BUILD, Aalborg University, 2021, pp. 206–209.

240 Arne Gaardmand: *Dansk byplanlægning. Plan over land 1938-1992*, 2nd edition, Nykøbing Sj., Bogværket, 2016.

241 Jannie Rosenberg Bendsen and Mogens A. Morgen: *Fredet. Bygningsfredning i Danmark 1918–2018*, Copenhagen, Strandberg Publishing, 2018, pp. 173, 182–184; 'Heritage as sector, factor and vector: conceptualizing the shifting relationship between heritage management and spatial planning', by Joks Janssen et al., in *European Planning Studies*, vol. 25, no. 9, 2017, pp. 1654–1672; Svava Riesto and Anne Tietjen: 'Planning with Heritage. A Critical Debate Across Landscape Architecture Practice and Heritage Theory', in Ellen Braae and Henriette Steiner (eds.): *Routledge Reseach Companion to Landscape Architecture*, London, New York, Routledge, 2019.

242 Ellen Braae and Svava Riesto: 'As Found: A New Design Paradigm', in *Nordic Journal of Architecture*, vol. 1, no. 1, 2011, pp. 8–9; 'Plans for Uncertain Futures: Heritage and Climate Imaginaries in Coastal Climate Adaptation', by Svava Riesto et al., in *International Journal of Heritage Studies*, vol. 28, no. 3, 2022, pp. 358–375.

243 Joan C. Tronto: 'Caring Architecture', in Angelika Fitz and Elke Krasny (eds.): *Critical Care: Architecture and Urbanism for a Broken Planet*, Wien, Architekturzentrum, 2019, p. 28.

244 Joan C. Tronto and Berenice Fisher describes the world as consisting of 'our bodies, our selves, and our environment, all of which we seek to interweave in a complex, life-sustaining web', Joan C. Tronto and Berenice Fisher: 'Toward a Feminist Theory of Caring', in Emily K. Abel and Margaret K. Nelsen (eds.): *Circles of Care*, Albany, New York, State University of New York Press, 1990, 35–62.

245 Svava Riesto in interview with Sussa Rubin, Anne Marie Rubin's sister, 13 July 2021.

246 Finn Monies and Karen Zahle (eds.), *Tiden i Stockholm*, Copenhagen, Arkitektens Forlag, 1999. Rubin is referenced in, for example, Erik Christian Sørensen's article 'Arkitekt næsten og næsten svensk'.

247 www.kvinfo.dk/side/597/bio/1634/origin/170/

248 Arne Gaardmand: *Dansk byplanlægning. Plan over land 1938–1992*, 2nd edition, Nykøbing, Sj., Bogværket, 2016, pp. 25–32; *Byplankonsulenttegnestuerne i 1960'erne og 70'erne. En interviewundersøgelse*, ed. Vibeke Dalgas et al., in *Byplanhistoriske noter*, no. 65, 2011.

249 Erik Kaufmann: *27 slags planer. Oversigt over og kritisk analyse af den offentlige fysiske planlægning i Danmark*, Copenhagen, Statens Byggeforskningsinstitut, 1966, pp. 38–46.

250 Arne Gaardmand: *Dansk byplanlægning. Plan over land 1938–1992*, 2nd edition, Nykøbing, Sj., Bogværket, 2016, pp. 25–32.

251 Anon.: 'Nye Arkitekter. Akademiets Afgangsprøve for Arkitekter er blevet bestaaet af Poul Hessellund Andersen, Mogens Leth, Anne Marie Rubin og Jørgen Thomsen', i *Nationaltidende*, 19.11.1946, p. 6.

252 George: 'Kvinden bag sommerlandets "byplan"', in *Politiken*, 24.9.1959, p. 13.

253 www.kvinfo.dk/side/597/bio/1634/origin/170/. Regarding the role and history of 'den kommitteredes', see Arne Gaardmand: *Dansk byplanlægning. Plan over land 1938–1992*, 2nd edition, Nykøbing, Sj., Bogværket, 2016, pp. 24–34.

254 Arne Gaardmand: *Dansk byplanlægning. Plan over land 1938–1992*, 2nd edition, Nykøbing, Sj., Bogværket, 2016, p. 30.

255 Anne Marie Rubin and architect K. Bosmann Pedersen carried out this work from 1952 to 1954, undoubtedly in their leisure time. Sven Illeris: 'Anne Marie Rubins tegnestue', in *Byplankonsulenttegnestuerne i 1960'erne og 70'erne. En interviewundersøgelse*, ed. Vibeke Dalgas et al., in *Byplanhistoriske noter*, no. 65, 2011, p. 164.

256 Sven Illeris: 'Anne Marie Rubins tegnestue', in *Byplankonsulenttegnestuerne i 1960'erne og 70'erne. En interviewundersøgelse*, ed. Vibeke Dalgas et al., in *Byplanhistoriske noter*, no. 65, 2011, p. 164

257 See for example Jack: 'Hun skal hjælpe Korsør', in *Politiken,* 26.9.1963, p. 29.

258 Sven Illeris: 'Anne Marie Rubins tegnestue', in *Byplankonsulenttegnestuerne i 1960'erne og 70'erne. En interviewundersøgelse*, ed. Vibeke Dalgas et al., in *Byplanhistoriske noter*, no. 65, 2011, p. 164.

259 Ibid.

260 She initially accepted the commission with Claus Bremer, but Anne Marie Rubin was the one who attended the meetings, and of the two it was she who had special professional insight in planning. Sven Illeris: 'Anne Marie Rubins tegnestue', in *Byplankonsulenttegnestuerne i 1960'erne og 70'erne. En interviewundersøgelse*, ed. Vibeke Dalgas et al., in *Byplanhistoriske noter*, no. 64, 2010, p. 164. See also Arne Gaardmand: *Dansk byplanlægning. Plan over land 1938–1992*, 2nd edition, Nykøbing, Sj., Bogværket, 2016, p. 89.

261 See also Vibeke Dalgas: 'Kampen om bykernerne', in *Byplanhistoriske noter*, no. 66, 2011, pp. 47–67; Kristian Buhl Thomsen: *Da de danske byer blev revet ned. Praksis og ideologi i dansk sanerings- og byfornyelsespolitik 1939–1983*, PhD diss., Aarhus, Aarhus University, 2015.

262 Sven Illeris: 'Anne Marie Rubins tegnestue', in *Byplankonsulenttegnestuerne i 1960'erne og 70'erne. En interviewundersøgelse*, Vibeke Dalgas et al. (eds.), in *Byplanhistoriske noter*, no. 65, 2011, p. 164.

263 Arne Gaardmand: *Dansk byplanlægning. Plan over land 1938–1992*, 2nd edition, Nykøbing, Sj., Bogværket, 2016, p. 89.

264 Jn: 'Professor – uden titel', in *Politiken*, 9.10.1968, p. 18.

265 www.kvinfo.dk/side/597/bio/1634/origin/170/

266 www.kvinfo.dk/side/597/bio/1634/origin/170/; jn: "Professor – uden titel", i *Politiken*, 9.10.1968, p. 18.

267 Ferieloven af 1938 (the Danish Holiday Act of 1938).

268 Nan Dahlkild (ed.): *Sommerlandets arkitektur. Drømmen om det gode liv*, Copenhagen, Museum Tusculanums Forlag, 2018.

269 Vibeke Fischer Thomsen: 'Byafgrænsning – byudvikling', in *Vort åbne land. Danmarks Naturfredningsforenings årsskrift*, 1968, p. 60.

270 Michael Varming: 'Vestkystens fremtid', in *Fonden for Bygnings- og Landskabskultur. 10 års-beretning 1964–1974*, Copenhagen, Fonden for Bygnings- og Landskabskultur, 1974, p. 25.

271 Ejvind Bjørnkjær: 'Moderne gårdhus-bebyggelse midt i vestkystens klitter', in *Ny tid*, 17.3.1968, p. 7.

272 For example, at her lecture on urban planning at the Øresundskonferencen in 1965. Her lecture is published in the journals *Havekunst*, *Arkitekten* and *Louisiana Revy*.

273 Cited from the Øresundskonferencen, published in *Havekunst* and in *Arkitekten*. Anne Marie Rubin, Knud W. Jensen and J.-F. Gravier: 'Byplanlægningen i fritidens epoke', in *Louisiana Revy*, vol. 6, no. 4, 1965/66, pp. 25–31.

274 Kaj Gottlob: 'Vestkysten ødelægges af feriehuse', in *Arkitekten*, vol. 72, no. 7, 1970, pp. 153–159.

275 Henrik Knuth-Winterfeldt: *Naturfredning i Danmark*, Copenhagen, Danmarks Naturfredningsforenings Forlag, 1981, p. 11.

276 Ibid., p. 6.

277 Cf. her lecture at Øresundskonferencen, published in *Havekunst* and in *Arkitekten*. Anne Marie Rubin, Knud W. Jensen and J.-F. Gravier: 'Byplanlægningen i fritidens epoke', in *Louisiana Revy*, vol. 6, no. 4, 1965/66, pp. 25–31.

278 George: 'Kvinden bag sommerlandets "byplan"', in *Politiken*, 24.11.1959, p. 13.

279 Henrik Knuth-Winterfeldt: *Naturfredning i Danmark*, Copenhagen, Danmarks Naturfredningsforenings Forlag, 1981, p. 62.

280 Anne Marie Rubin's plan from 1964 for the coast of South Lolland, 'The Rubin Plan', at the local history archive in Rudbjerg.

281 Dan Raahauge: *Rudbjerg kommune: Det 45. danske byplanmøde d. 13. oktober 1995. Tur til Rudbjerg om landskab og mennesker*. Unpublished document in the local history archive in Rudbjerg.

282 Anne Marie Rubin's plan from 1964 for the coast of South Lolland, 'The Rubin Plan', at the local history archive in Rudbjerg includes a chart enumerating the holiday homes in the area, whether legal or illegal.

283 Anon.: 'Lollands sommerland', in *Fyns Aktuelt*, 16.7.1965, p. 2.

284 Anon.: 'Sommerhus- og vandplan for Sydlolland', in *Politiken*, 14.7.1964, p. 2.

285 Anon.: 'Lollands sommerland', in *Fyns Aktuelt*, 16.7.1965, p. 2.

286 Anne Marie Rubin's plan from 1964 for the coast of South Lolland, 'The Rubin Plan', at the local history archive in Rudbjerg.

287 *Nær Salten Østerstrand*, television broadcast on Danmarks Radio, 15 July 1965. Cinematographer: Poul H. Hansen. Producers: Anne Marie Rubin and Bent Børge Larsen.

288 Ibid.

289 Anne Marie Rubin's plan from 1964 for the coast of South Lolland, 'The Rubin Plan', at the local history archive in Rudbjerg.

290 Ibid.

291 Ibid., ad article 3.

292 *Nær Salten Østerstrand*, television broadcast on Danmarks Radio, 15 July 1965. Camera:

Poul H. Hansen. Producers: Anne Marie Rubin and Bent Børge Larsen.

293 Anne Marie Rubin's plan from 1964 for the coast of South Lolland, 'The Rubin Plan', at the local history archive in Rudbjerg. They state no reason for this.

294 www.kvinfo.dk/side/597/bio/1634/origin/170/

295 Anne Marie Rubin's plan from 1964 for the coast of South Lolland, 'The Rubin Plan', at the local history archive in Rudbjerg.

296 Newspaper cutting in the local history archives at Rudbjerg: 'Gloslunde-Græshave uenig med punkt på Rubinplanen' from 15 November 1966, but there is no information indicating which newspaper it was taken from.

297 The same held true for the plans regarding water supply. Anon.: 'Sommerhus- og vandplan for Sydlolland', in *Politiken*, 14.7.1964, p. 2. The plan was originally intended to also prompt a major renewal of the local water systems. State geologist (Head of Department) Ole Bertelsen wanted to see the drinking water supplies in Lolland-Falster rationalised based on the idea that it was best to have a few, but large, waterworks, reminiscent of the approach to electricity supply. This would ensure the best and cheapest drinking water. Efforts were made to make this happen, but it was not carried out in the plan.

298 *Lolland-Falsters Folketidende*, 11.9.1975, p. 7.

299 See for example Lolland Kommune: *Strategisk udviklingsplan for Lollands sydkyst*, a strategic development plan for the south coast of Lolland adopted by the town council on 25 May 2022.

300 Henrik Vejre: *Et århundrede med planlægning for grønne områder i Storkøbenhavn*, Copenhagen, Kraks Fond, 2017.

301 Vibeke Dalgas: 'Byplanhistorie – og kvindehistorie', in *Byplanhistoriske noter*, no. 37, 1997, p. 30.

302 Ibid.; Vibeke Dalgas: 'Byplanlægning – en kvindehistorie', in Katrine Dirckinck-Holmfeld and Honey Biba Beckerlee (eds.): *Jubil96um. At forhandle kønnet. At introducere kvindelige erfaringsverdener. At kæmpe for ligeberettigelse. Kunstakademiets rolle i fremtiden*, Copenhagen, Kunstakademiet, 2004, unpaged.

303 Egnsplankontoret: *Skitseforslag til Egnsplan for Storkøbenhavn*, Copenhagen, 1947.

304 Vibeke Dalgas: 'Byplanhistorie – og kvindehistorie', *Byplanhistoriske noter*, no. 37, 1997, p. 31.

305 Vibeke Dalgas: 'Byplanlægning – en kvindehistorie', in Katrine Dirckinck-Holmfeld and Honey Biba Beckerlee (eds.): *Jubil96um. At forhandle kønnet. At introducere kvindelige erfaringsverdener. At kæmpe for ligeberettigelse. Kunstakademiets rolle i fremtiden*, Copenhagen, Kunstakademiet, 2004, unpaged.

306 Kunstakademiets Arkitektskole: 'Fortegnelser over indskrevne elever 1948-1949 til 1961–1962', year 1952/53.

307 Vibeke Dalgas: 'Byplanlægning – en kvindehistorie', in Katrine Dirckinck-Holmfeld and Honey Biba Beckerlee (eds.): *Jubil96um. At forhandle kønnet. At introducere kvindelige erfaringsverdener. At kæmpe for ligeberettigelse. Kunstakademiets rolle i fremtiden*, Copenhagen, Kunstakademiet, 2004, unpaged.

308 Vibeke Dalgas: 'Kvindehistorie i en foranderlig tid', in Vibeke Dalgas and Jens Kristian Krarup (eds.): *Stenhusstudent 1952 – og hvad så?* Published by the students celebrating their fiftieth anniversary (1952–2002) on the occasion of the school's hundredth anniversary, 4 September 2006, p. 19.

309 She does not, however, state exactly how this aspect was incorporated in the assignment. Vibeke Dalgas: 'Byplanhistorie – og kvindehistorie', *Byplanhistoriske noter*, no. 37, 1997, p. 31.

310 Sven Illeris: 'Vibeke Fischer Thomsens (Dalgas) tegnestue', in *Byplanhistoriske noter*, no. 65, 2011, p. 67.

311 Ibid., p. 70.

312 Vibeke Dalgas: 'Byplanlægning – en kvindehistorie', in Katrine Dirckinck-Holmfeld and Honey Biba Beckerlee (eds.): *Jubil96um. At forhandle kønnet. At introducere kvindelige erfaringsverdener. At kæmpe for ligeberettigelse. Kunstakademiets rolle i fremtiden*, Copenhagen, Kunstakademiet, 2004, unpaged.

313 Sestoft, Kirsten, Karen Clemmensen and Vibeke Fischer Thomsen: '3 Kvinder i arkitektfaget', in *Blød By*, no. 11, 1981, p. 21; Sven Illeris: 'Vibeke Fischer Thomsens (Dalgas) tegnestue', in *Byplanhistoriske noter*, no. 65, 2011, pp. 67–77.

314 Vibeke Dalgas: 'Byplanlægning – en kvindehistorie', in Katrine Dirckinck-Holmfeld and Honey Biba Beckerlee (eds.): *Jubil96um. At forhandle kønnet. At introducere kvindelige erfaringsverdener. At kæmpe for ligeberettigelse. Kunstakademiets rolle i fremtiden*, Copenhagen, Kunstakademiet, 2004, unpaged.

315 Fredningsplanudvalget for Sorø og Præstø Amter. Vibeke Fischer Thomsen: *Øen Nyord*, Copenhagen, Fonden for Bygnings- og Landskabskultur, 1968, p. 3.

316 Vibeke Fischer Thomsen: *Øen Nyord*, Copenhagen, Fonden for Bygnings- og Landskabskultur, 1968, p. 3.

317 Anon.: 'Ingen fredning på lille ø', in *Berlingske Tidende*, 9.9.1966, p. 18.

318 Vibeke Fischer Thomsen: *Øen Nyord*, Copenhagen, Fonden for Bygnings- og Landskabskultur, 1968, p. 3.

319 Jannie Rosenberg Bendsen and Mogens A. Morgen: *Fredet. Bygningsfredning i Danmark 1918-2018*, Copenhagen, Strandberg Publishing, 2018, p. 173, pp. 182–184; 'Heritage as sector, factor and vector: conceptualizing the shifting relationship between heritage management and spatial planning', by Joks Janssen et al., in *European Planning Studies*, vol. 25, no. 9, 2017, p. 1654–1672.

320 The foundation was founded by the architect and professor Palle Suenson with funding from the New Carlsberg Foundation. Jannie Rosenberg Bendsen and Mogens A. Morgen: *Fredet. Bygningsfredning i Danmark 1918–2018*, Copenhagen, Strandberg Publishing, 2018, p. 187; Fonden for Bygnings- og Landskabskultur, Selskabet for Bygnings- og Landskabskultur and Sammenslutningen for Bygnings- og Landskabskultur, *Beretning for årene 1964–1974 i anledning af 10-året for oprettelsen af Fonden for Bygnings- og Landskabskultur*, Copenhagen, Fonden for Bygnings- og Landskabskultur, 1974, pp. 1–11.

321 Joks Janssen et al.: 'Heritage as sector, factor and vector: conceptualizing the shifting relationship between heritage management and spatial planning', in *European Planning Studies*, vol. 25, no. 9, 2017, pp. 1654–1672; Svava Riesto and Anne Tietjen: 'Planning with Heritage. A Critical Debate Across Landscape Architecture Practice and Heritage Theory', in Ellen Braae and Henriette Steiner (eds.): *Routledge Research Companion to Landscape Architecture*, London, Routledge, 2019.

322 Mo: 'Æstetiske miljøer og gamle bygninger', in *Aktuelt*, 30.3.1965 (cutting found in Kaj Gottlob's business archive).

323 Anon.: 'Lodsejerudvalg på Nyord', in *Næstved Tidende*, 19.12.1966, p. 3.

324 Ibid.

325 Fonden for Bygnings- og Landskabskultur: *Beretning for året 1969*, Copenhagen, Fonden for Bygnings- og Landskabskultur, 1969, p. 2.

326 The committee consisted of the Academy of Technical Sciences, the Ministry of Housing's commissioner for urban planning matters (architect Kirsten Andersen), the

Conservation Committee for the Sorø and Præstø Counties, representatives from the sailing community, the Ministry of Culture, the Royal Danish Academy of Fine Arts (three departments), the Cooperative Danish Farmers' Associations, the National Museum of Denmark, the Danish Society for Nature Conservation, Stege County Parish Council's Nyord Committee, the Greater Municipality's Nyord Committee and finally the Nyord residents' island committee. Vibeke Fischer Thomsen: *Øen Nyord*, Copenhagen, Fonden for Bygnings- og Landskabskultur, 1968, p. 2. Architect Kirsten Andersen was the Housing Ministry's commissioner for urban planning matters, and in an interview in April 2022, Vibeke Dalgas emphasised the excellent cooperation with 'the commissioner' – not only in the Nyord survey, but in general.

327 Vibeke Fischer Thomsen: *Øen Nyord*, Copenhagen, Fonden for Bygnings- og Landskabskultur, 1968, p. 3.

328 Vibeke Dalgas: 'Byplanhistorie – og kvindehistorie', *Byplanhistoriske noter*, no. 37, 1997, p. 30.

329 Vibeke Dalgas's business archive, box 33: *Redegørelser, Møn, Christiansfeld 1957*.

330 Ibid.

331 Ibid.

332 Vibeke Fischer Thomsen: *Øen Nyord, København*, Fonden for Bygnings- og Landskabskultur, 1968, p. 29.

333 Ibid., pp. 4–27.

334 This applied to the buildings Nordgade 7, Nordgade 9, Nordgade 11, Østergade 7 and Østergade 9, which were added to the list of protected buildings in the early 1970s, www.kulturarv.dk/fbb/

335 Vibeke Fischer Thomsen: *Øen Nyord, København*, Fonden for Bygnings- og Landskabskultur, 1968, p. 31.

336 The Overfredningsnævnet: printout of the Overfredningsnævnet's decision protocol, 10 September 1975. In 1975, the Danish protection authorities issued a decision, protecting the high-lying farmland from developments.

337 The purpose is not expressed particularly clearly in § 1, subsection 3 of the Town Planning Act itself, but is elaborated in the Ministry of the Interior's circular of 21 October 1939. Erik Kaufmann: *27 slags planer. Oversigt over og kritisk analyse af den offentlige fysiske planlægning i Danmark*, Copenhagen, Statens Byggeforskningsinstitut, 1966, p. 29.

338 Gaardmand: *Dansk Byplanlægning. Plan over land 1938–1992*, 2nd edition., Nykøbing, Sj., Bogværket, 2016, pp. 96–101; Erik Kaufmann: *27 slags planer. Oversigt over og kritisk analyse af den offentlige fysiske planlægning i Danmark*, Copenhagen, Statens Byggeforskningsinstitut, 1966, pp. 29–37.

339 Møns Kommune: Nyord By. Partial town planning statute, 1973, § 6, subsection 1.

340 Fonden for Bygnings- og Landskabskultur: Report for 1968, Copenhagen, Fonden for Bygnings- og Landskabskultur, 1968, p. 2.

341 Ibid.

342 Jannie Rosenberg Bendsen and Mogens A. Morgen: *Fredet. Bygningsfredning i Danmark 1918–2018*, Copenhagen, Strandberg Publishing, 2018, p. 110.

343 Sven Illeris: 'Vibeke Fischer Thomsens (Dalgas) tegnestue', in *Byplanhistoriske noter*, no. 65, 2011, pp. 69–70.

344 Jannie Rosenberg Bendsen's interview with Vibeke Dalgas, April 2022.

345 Ibid.

346 Vibeke Dalgas: 'Byplanlægning – en kvindehistorie', in Katrine Dirckinck-Holmfeld and Honey Biba Beckerlee (eds.): *Jubil96um. At forhandle kønnet. At introducere kvin– delige erfaringsverdener. At kæmpe for ligeberettigelse. Kunstakademiets rolle i fremtiden*, Copenhagen, The Royal Danish Academy of Fine Arts, 2004, unpaged.

347 Sven Illeris: 'Vibeke Fischer Thomsens (Dalgas) tegnestue', in *Byplanhistoriske noter*, no. 65, 2011, p. 70.

348 Interview with Vibeke Dalgas, April 2022; Sven Illeris: 'Vibeke Fischer Thomsens (Dalgas) tegnestue', in *Byplanhistoriske noter*, no. 65, 2011, p. 74.

349 Vibeke Dalgas: 'Byplanlægning – en kvindehistorie', in Katrine Dirckinck-Holmfeld and Honey Biba Beckerlee (eds.): *Jubil96um. At forhandle kønnet. At introducere kvin– delige erfaringsverdener. At kæmpe for ligeberettigelse. Kunstakademiets rolle i fremtiden*, Copenhagen, The Royal Danish Academy of Fine Arts, 2004, unpaged; Anne Marie Rubin: 'Vores situation, tid og omverden', in *Byplan*, vol. 18, no. 3, 1966, pp. 90–94.

350 Vibeke Dalgas: 'Byplanlægning – en kvindehistorie', in Katrine Dirckinck-Holmfeld and Honey Biba Beckerlee (eds.): *Jubil96um. At forhandle kønnet. At introducere kvin– delige erfaringsverdener. At kæmpe for ligeberettigelse. Kunstakademiets rolle i fremtiden*, Copenhagen, The Royal Danish Academy of Fine Arts, 2004, unpaged.

351 Sven Illeris: 'Vibeke Fischer Thomsens (Dalgas) tegnestue', in *Byplanhistoriske noter*, no. 65, 2011, p. 72.

352 Vibeke Fischer Thomsen: *Bevaringsplanlægning*, in Kommuneplanorientering, no. 1, 1979, p. 2.

353 Vibeke Fischer Thomsen: *Bevaringsplanlægning*, in Kommuneplanorientering, no. 1, 1979.

354 www.kvinfo.dk/side/597/bio/1634/origin/170/

355 Jannie Rosenberg Bendsen's interview with Vibeke Dalgas in 2022 and Dalgas's application for a professorship at Lund University (private material, provided by Vibeke Dalgas), 1986.

356 Among other things, Vibeke Dalgas writes about how she believes that it is good to have both men and women employed at the same workplace.

357 A key figure in the development of the SAVE system was the architect Gregers Algreen-Ussing (b. 1938), see Gregers Algreen-Ussing, Grethe Silding and Allan de Waal: *Byens træk. Om by- og bygningsbevaringssystemet SAVE*, Copenhagen, Planstyrelsen, 1992; Jannie Rosenberg Bendsen and Mogens A. Morgen: *Fredet. Bygningsfredning i Danmark 1918–2018*, Copenhagen, Strandberg Publishing 2018, p. 217.

358 Jorge Otero–Pailos: 'On self–effacement: The aesthetics of preservation', in Thordis Arrhenius et al. (eds.), *Place and Displacement: Exhibiting Architecture*, Zurich, Lars Müller Publishers, 2014, pp. 231–243.

359 See for example Jin Xue and Wojciech Kębłowski: 'Spatialising degrowth, degrowing urban planning', in *Local Environment*, vol. 27, no. 4, 2022, pp. 397–403.

360 Joan C. Tronto: 'Caring Architecture', in Angelika Fitz and Elke Krasny (eds.): *Critical Care: Architecture and Urbanism for a Broken Planet*, Vienna, Architekturzentrum, 2019, pp. 26–31.

361 The history of twentieth-century architecture and planning has often happened at the same time as events were taking place – or shortly after – which has greatly influenced the narratives. See for example Jannie Rosenberg Bendsen: *Enkelhed, mådehold og funktionalitet – en analyse af fremtrædende danske arkitekters udlægninger af dansk arkitektur*,

PhD dissertation, Copenhagen, University of Copenhagen, 2009; Anthony Vidler: *Histories of the Immediate Present: Inventing Architectural Modernism*, Cambridge, Mass., MIT Press, 2008. Panayotis Tournikiotis: *The Historiography of Modern Architecture*, Cambridge, Mass., MIT Press, 1999.

362 Jorge Otero-Pailos: 'On self-effacement: The aesthetics of preservation', in Thordis Arrhenius et al. (eds.), *Place and Displacement: Exhibiting Architecture*, Zurich, Lars Müller Publishers, 2014, pp. 231–243.

363 See for example Svava Riesto: *Biography of an Industrial Landscape. Carlsberg's Urban Spaces Retold*, Amsterdam, Amsterdam University Press, 2018; Svava Riesto and Anne Tietjen: 'Doing Heritage Together: New Heritage Frontiers in Collaborative Planning', in Torgrim Sneve Guttormsen and Grete Swensen (eds.): *Heritage, Democracy and the Public. Nordic Approaches*, London, New York, Routledge, 2017, pp. 159–175.

364 See for example Egil Fischer's plan for the old town in Dragør 1949, Arne Gaardmand: *Dansk byplanlægning. Plan over land 1938–1992*, 2nd edition, Nykøbing, Sj., Bogværket, 2016, p. 27.

365 Danish literature on the history of architecture has placed little focus on conservation history except for some studies on the history of protection and listing measures, see Jannie Rosenberg Bendsen and Mogens A. Morgen: *Fredet. Bygningsfredning i Danmark 1918–2018*, Copenhagen, Strandberg Publishing, 2018.

366 See for example Kenneth R. Olwig: 'Introduction: The Nature of Cultural Heritage, and the Culture of Natural Heritage – Northern Perspectives on a Contested Patrimony', in *International Journal of Heritage Studies*, vol. 11, no. 1, 2005, pp. 3–7.

367 See for example 'Plans for Uncertain Futures: Heritage and Climate Imaginaries in Coastal Climate Adaptation', by Svava Riesto et al., in *International Journal of Heritage Studies*, vol. 28, no. 3, 2022, pp. 358–375.

Chapter 4
Alternatives – A New Architecture for a New Society

368 Martin Hartung: 'Skal vi bo sådan?', in *Berlingske Tidende*, 25.6.1977, p. 1.

369 *Louisiana Revy*, special edition, *Alternativ Arkitektur*, vol. 17, no. 3, 1977.

370 Knud W. Jensen: 'Introduktion', in *Louisiana Revy*, special edition, *Alternativ Arkitektur*, vol. 17, no. 3, 1977, p. 3.

371 The exhibition *Women in American Architecture: A Historic and Contemporary Perspective* was shown at Brooklyn Museum from February–April 1977. Susana Torre (ed.): *Women in American Architecture. A Historic and Contemporary Perspective*, New York, Watson–Guptill Publishers, 1977.

372 Jan Gehl: *Livet mellem husene. Udeaktiviteter og udemiljøer*, 5th edition, Copenhagen, Arkitektens Forlag, 2003. First edition published in 1971; Ingrid Gehl: *Bo-miljø*, SBI–rapport, no. 71, 1971.

373 Helena Mattsson: 'Revisiting Swedish Postmodernism. Gendered Architecture and Other Stories', in *Konsthistorisk Tidskrift*, vol. 85, no. 1, 2016, pp. 109–125. In Denmark, postmodernism has recently been addressed in a series of contributions about men with an interest in form and symbol in a double special issue of *Arkitekten*, see for example Kasper Lægring: 'Gensyn med postmodernismen', in *Arkitekten*, vol. 123, no. 2, 2021, pp. 52–55.

374 Birgitte Thorsen Vilslev and Carsten Hoff (eds.): *Susanne Ussing – mellem kunst og arkitektur*, Copenhagen, Strandberg Publishing, 2017.

375 Monika Kaiser: *Neubesetzungen des Kunst-Raumes. Feministische Kunstausstellungen und ihre Räume, 1972–1987*, Bielefeld, Transcript Verlag, 2013.

376 Information provided in an email exchange between Carsten Hoff and Svava Riesto, 16 May 2022.

377 See also Hans-Christian Jensen and Anders V. Munch: 'Environment and Emancipation through Design. Avant-garde Intervention and Experiments with Social Design in Denmark around 1970', in *AIS/Design: Storia e Ricerche*, vol. 7, nos. 12–13, 2019–20, pp. 88–109; Susanne Ussing and Carsten Hoff: 'Alternative Rum/Spatial Alternative/Alternative räume/Alternatives', in *Mobilia*, no. 180, 1970, unpaged.

378 See for example Jane Bennett: *Vibrant Matter. A Political Ecology of Things*, Durham, NC, Duke University Press, 2010; Katve-Kaisa Kontturi: *Ways of Following. Art, Materiality, Collaboration*, London, Open Humanities Press, 2018. See also Birgitte Thorsen Vilslev and Carsten Hoff (eds.): *Susanne Ussing – mellem arkitektur og kunst*, Copenhagen, Strandberg Publishing, 2017, p. 16–54.

379 Sara Staunsager and Emilie Victoria Raundahl (eds.): *Verner Panton – Farver en ny verden*, Kolding, Trapholt, 2022.

380 Flemming Flyvholm: 'Vi forsøger at vise virkeligheden – ikke som den er, men så den opdages', in *Socialistisk Dagblad*, 9.2.1979, p. 9.

381 Susanne Ussing in an interview with Flemming Flyvholm: 'Når det bliver kunst – så skip det', in *Socialistisk Dagblad*, 23–24.1.1982, p. 17.

382 Ibid.

383 Else Bülow: 'Indledning', in Susanne Ussing: *Susanne Ussing – arbejder mellem 1957–1987. Beskrivelse af en proces*, Aalborg, Nordjyllands Kunstmuseum, 1987, p. 5.

384 It is reproduced in Wolfgang Pohl and Ueli Schnelzer (eds.): *Architektur des Unfertigen. Die Arbeiten von Susanne Ussing und Carsten Hoff*, Düsseldorf, Archipol-Verlag, 1982.

385 Hilde Heynen: 'A Feminist in Disguise? Sibyl Moholy-Nagy's Histories of Architecture and Its Environment', in Hélène Frichot, Catharina Gabrielsson and Helen Runting (eds.): *Architecture and Feminisms: Ecologies, Economies, Technologies*, London, New York, Routledge, 2018, p. 47.

386 R. W. Connell and James W. Messerschmidt: 'Hegemonic Masculinity: Rethinking the Concept', in *Gender & Society*, vol. 19, no. 6, 2005, p. 829–859.

387 See for example Christian Norberg-Schulz: *Genius Loci. Towards a Phenomenology of Architecture*, New York, Rizzoli, 1980. (First published in Italian as *Genius loci – paesaggio, ambiente, architettura* in 1979); Gordon Cullen: *The Concise Townscape*, London, New York, Routledge, Taylor & Francis, 1961.

388 Gitte Just: 'Ærens slagmark', in *Det Fri Aktuelt*, 20.5.1989, section 2, p. 8.

389 Susanne Ussing and Carsten Hoff: 'Eksperimentbyggeri i Thy', in *Arkitekten*, vol. 72, no. 26, 1970, p. 638.

390 The cardboard was sponsored by Neopak in Randers, while Ussing + Hoff rented the scaffolding, pipes, wooden boards, etc. in Aalborg. Information provided in email from Carsten Hoff to Svava Riesto, 23.05.2022.

391 Kenny Cupers (ed.): *Use Matters. An Alternative History of Architecture*, New York, Routledge, 2013; 'User' and 'Flexibility' in Adrian Forty: *Words and Buildings. A Vocabulary of Modern Architecture*, London, Thames & Hudson, 2019. See also Carsten Thau: 'Ussing og Hoff – arkitekturen frisat', in Birgitte Thorsen Vilslev and Carsten Hoff (eds.): Susanne *Ussing – mellem arkitektur og kunst*, Copenhagen, Strandberg

Publishing, 2017, pp.81–82. See also Birgitte Thorsen Vilslev and Carsten Hoff (eds.): *Susanne Ussing – mellem arkitektur og kunst*, Copenhagen, Strandberg Publishing, 2017.

392 Tom Avermaete and Janina Gosseye: *Urban Design in the 20th Century – a History*, Zurich, gta Verlag, 2021, pp. 302–305.

393 Interview with Carsten Hoff, 14.4.2021.

394 *Ussing/Hoff Bygge eksperiment Thy Lejren. Sommeren 1970 (varighed tre måneder).* Camera: Susanne Ussing and Carsten Hoff (Super 8 film). Editing: Cecilie Gravesen. The Carsten Hoff and Susanne Ussing Archive.

395 Nils Ufer: 'Kampen om Thylejren', in *Information*, 12.5.1971, p. 5.

396 Susanne Ussing and Carsten Hoff: 'Eksperimentbyggeri i Thy', in *Arkitekten*, vol. 72, no. 26, 1970, p. 638.

397 See for example Mari Hvattum: 'Nordic Nonumentality', in *Nordic Journal of Architecture*, vol. 2, no. 1, 2012, pp. 8–10.

398 Birgitte Thorsen Vilslev and Carsten Hoff (eds.): *Susanne Ussing – mellem kunst og arkitektur*, Copenhagen, Strandberg Publishing, 2017; Susanne Ussing: 'Byggeeksperiment på Vejlø', in *Land og By*, vol. 2, no. 1, 1975.

399 Susanne Ussing and Carsten Hoff: 'Eksperimentbyggeri i Thy', in *Arkitekten*, vol. 72, no. 26, 1970, p. 641.

400 The proposal was signed by Ussing + Hoff in collaboration with Kjeld Ussing Arkitektfirma, architect Svend Møller and engineer Malmstrøm. The Royal Danish Library, the Danish National Art Library.

401 'DAL's konkurrence om etageboligformer: Program for konkurrencens 2. etape', in *Danske Arkitekters Landsforbund*, February 1973, p. 2.

402 Ibid.

403 Ibid.

404 Interview with Susanne Ussing and Carsten Hoff by Flemming Madsen in the news broadcast TV-Aktuelt, 12 August 1977.

405 Gitte Just: 'Ærens slagmark', in *Det Fri Aktuelt*, 20.5.1989, section 2, p. 8.

406 Susanne Ussing: 'MEDIET mellem KUNST og ARKITEKTUR', in Kirsten Birch et al. (eds.), *Kvinder ytrer sig om omgivelserne. Kommentarer til udstillingen pa vej som viser arbejder af kvindelige arkitekter, planlæggere og kunstnere*, Aarhus, Modtryk, 1980, pp. 63–65.

407 Annelise Bistrup: 'Jeg har kæmpet for at ødelægge min gode smag', in *Berlingske Tidende*, 3.3.1974, p. 9.

408 Ibid., p. 8.

409 TV-Aktuelt. First broadcast 12 August 1977. *Byggeri for mennesker*. Producer: Flemming Madsen. Camera: Gergely Szabo, 8.44–11.48.

410 Annelise Bistrup: 'Jeg har kæmpet for at ødelægge min gode smag', in *Berlingske Tidende*, 3.3.1974, p. 8.

411 Ibid., p. 9.

412 Interview with Carsten Hoff, 14 April 2021. Susanne Ussing cited in Annelise Bistrup: 'Jeg har kæmpet for at ødelægge min gode smag', in *Berlingske Tidende*, 3.3.1974, p. 9.

413 Interview with Kjeld Kjeldsen, curator, Louisiana, 13 December 2021.

414 Carsten Hoff in conversation with Svava Riesto and Niels Bjørn in the podcast *De glemte arkitekter*, www.realdania.dk/tema/de–glemte–arkitekter

415 SMK (2015), Den Frie (2014), The Nordic Biennial of Contemporary Art (2017), KØS Museum for kunst i det offentlige rum (2016–2017).

416 See The Royal Danish Library, the Danish National Art Library.

417 www.susanneussing.dk/

418 See for example Chapter Two.

419 Carmen Espegel: *Women Architects in the Modern Movement*, New York, London, Routledge, 2018.

420 Examples include the exhibition *How We Live Now. Reimagining Spaces with Matrix Feminist Design Co-operative* at the Barbican in London, 17 May 2021–30 January 2022 and this chapter on the architect's collective BIG: Helena Mattsson and Meike Schalk: 'Action Archive. Oral History as Performance', in Janina Gosseye, Naomi Stead and Deborah van der Plaat (eds.): *Speaking of Buildings. Oral History in Architectural Research*, New York, N.Y., Princeton Architectural Press, 2019, pp. 94–113.

421 Birgit Pontoppidan: *Det skete på Kvindeudstillingen Charlottenborg 1975*, Holte, Birgit Pontoppidan Forlag, 2017, p. 28.

422 Ibid.

423 Else Bülow: 'Indledning', in Susanne Ussing: *Susanne Ussing – arbejder mellem 1957–1987. Beskrivelse af en proces*, Aalborg, Nordjyllands Kunstmuseum, 1987, p. 6.

424 Niels Michael Jacobsen: 'Børn er et folk – og Louisiana et helt andet land', in *Landsavisen Aktuelt*, no. 23, August 1978, pp. 24–25.

425 Interview with Kjeld Kjeldsen, 13 December 2021.

426 Anne Tietjen, Svava Riesto and Pernille Skov (eds.): *Forankring i forandring. Christiania og bevaring som ressource i byomdannelsen*, Aarhus, Arkitektskolens Forlag, 2007.

427 *Christianias Børn: Skyggesiden af eventyret*, Danmarks Radio, August 2015.

428 Information from Harvey Davies, who was employed at Christopher Alexander's design studio in the 1970s, and from Anne Marie Rubin's sister, Sussa Rubin, on 13 July 2021.

429 Anne Marie Rubin: *Billeder fra Christiania*, Aalborg, Aalborg Universitetscenter, 1977, p. 11.

430 Steen Eiler Rasmussen: *Omkring Christiania – med en fyldig dokumentation*, Copenhagen, Gyldendal, 1976.

431 Anne Marie Rubin: *Billeder fra Christiania*, Aalborg, Aalborg Universitetscenter, 1977, p. 11.

432 Excerpts from Robert Venturi and Denise Scott Brown's study of Levitton, which they conducted with Yale students in 1970, were featured in the exhibition *Signs of Life: Symbols in the American City* at Renwick Gallery in Washington, 1976. Philippe Boudon: *Pessac de Le Corbusier: 1927–1967: Étude socio-architecturale: Pessac II, Le Corbusier: 1969–1985*, Paris, Dunod, 1985.

433 Anne Marie Rubin: *Billeder fra Christiania*, Aalborg, Aalborg Universitetscenter, 1977, p. 11.

434 Ibid.

435 Ibid.

436 Anne Marie Rubin: 'Vores situation, tid og omverden', in *Byplan*, vol. 18, no. 3, 1966, p. 92.

437 Dolores Hayden: 'What Would a Non-Sexist City Be Like? Speculations on Housing, Urban Design, and Human Work', in *Women and the American City*, vol. 5, no. 3, 1980, supplement, pp. 170–187 (originally presented in a longer version as a lecture in 1979).

438 Anne Marie Rubin: 'Om behovet for en byplanforskning', in Ulla Koch (ed.): *Køn og videnskab*, Aalborg, Aalborg Universitetsforlag, 1989, p. 220.

439 Matthew Pratt Guterl: *Josephine Baker and the Rainbow Tribe*, Cambridge, Mass., London, The Belknap Press of Harvard University Press, 2014, p. 87.

440 Matthew Pratt Guterl: *Josephine Baker and the Rainbow Tribe*, Cambridge, Mass., London, The Belknap Press of Harvard University Press, 2014.

441 Ibid., p. 110.

442 Anon.: 'Les Milandes – et nutidigt kulturcenter', in *Arkitekten*, vol. 69, no. 23, 1967, pp. 509–517.

443 Matthew Pratt Guterl: *Josephine Baker and the Rainbow Tribe*, Cambridge, Mass., London, The Belknap Press of Harvard University Press, 2014, p. 93.

444 Anon., cited in Karen Burns: 'Feminist Theory and Praxis, 1991–2003. Questions from the Archive', in Hélène Frichot, Catharina Gabrielsson and Helen Runting (eds.): *Architecture and Feminisms: Ecologies, Economies, Technologies*, London, New York, Routledge, 2018, p. 15.

Chapter 5
Collaboration – A Story About how Architecture Comes Into Being

445 See for example Martin Keiding, Marianne Amundsen and Kim Dirckinck-Holmfeld (eds.): *Dansk arkitektur siden 1754*, 2nd edition., Copenhagen, Arkitektens Forlag, 2007, pp. 294–297; Vibeke Andersson Møller: *Dansk arkitektur i 1960'erne*, Copenhagen, Forlaget Rhodos in collaboration with Nationalmuseet and Syddansk Universitetsforlag, 2019, pp. 88–90; Tobias Faber: *Dansk arkitektur*, 2nd edition, Copenhagen, Arkitektens Forlag, 1977, pp. 302–303; Anne Tietjen (ed.): *Forstadens bygningskultur 1945–1989. På sporet af velfærdsforstadens bevaringsværdier*, Copenhagen, Dansk Bygningsarv, 2010, p. 118.

446 www.kulturarv.dk/fbb/sagvis.pub?sag=3757721

447 For examples of how conservation practices focus on buildings, and how this ties in with concepts of canon, see for example Svava Riesto: *Biography of an Industrial Landscape. Carlsberg's Urban Spaces Retold*, Amsterdam, Amsterdam University Press, 2017; Svava Riesto and Rikke Stenbro: 'Mesterværkerne, eliten og dem, der var flest af. Værdiopfattelser og blinde vinkler i fredningen af velfærdssamfundets boliger', in *Fabrik og Bolig*, no. 1, 2019, pp. 32–48.

448 www.kulturarv.dk/fbb/sagvis.pub?sag=3757721

449 www.slks.dk/fileadmin/user_upload/SLKS/Omraader/Kulturarv/Bygningsfredning/Fredninger/Dokumenter/WEB_Afgoerelse_Adolphsvej_25_Gentofte.pdf

450 www.sn.dk/gentofte-kommune/ny-svoemmehal-i-kildeskovshallen-kan-staa-klar-i-2022-men-fredning-kan-forhindre-planerne/

451 Karen and Ebbe Clemmensen had several employees in their design studio, but the surviving archive material has not made it possible to determine exactly who took part in in the work on Kildeskovshallen. The scope of our project did not permit us to delve into a closer examination of these possible collaborations.

452 What is more, the Ministry of Housing also played a major role, partly in terms of approving the location of Kildeskovshallen, and partly in terms of greenlighting the construction process.

453 Draft cooperation agreement 7 October 1966. Karen and Ebbe Clemmensen's business archive. The Royal Library, the Danish National Art Library.

454 Agnete Muusfeldt: 'Idrætshaller i Kildeskoven', in *Landskab*, vol. 52, no. 8, 1971, p. 160.

455 See also our other publications on the period's welfare architecture and landscape planning, for example Ellen Marie Braae et al.: 'Welfare Landscapes: Open Spaces of Danish Social Housing Estates Reconfigured', in Svava Riesto and Miles Glendinning (eds.): *Mass Housing of the Scandinavian Welfare States: Exploring Histories and Design Strategies*, Edinburgh, University of Edinburgh/Docomomo, 2020, pp. 13–23; Lærke Sophie Keil, Svava Riesto and Tom Avermaete: 'Welfare Landscapes Between Individuality and Communality. Social Housing in Albertslund Syd', in *Landscape Research*, vol. 46, no. 4, 2021, pp. 456–473.

456 https://sportspark.gentofte.dk/da/Om-os/Historie

457 Chr. Ostenfeld and W. Jønsson and Karen and Ebbe Clemmensen: *Svømmehal ved Gentofte Stadion. Skitseprojekt april 1961*. The publication is in the Kildeskovshallen archive.

458 *Gentofte Kommunalbestyrelses offentlige forhandlinger – i året 1. april 1962–31. marts 1963*, Hellerup, 1963, p. 37.

459 In addition, the architects are asked to propose a project that can be realised in two stages – the swimming pool first and a sports venue later. Gentofte Kommunalbestyrelse: *Gentofte Kommunalbestyrelses offentlige forhandlinger – i året 1. april 1962–31. marts 1963*, Hellerup, 1963, p. 37.

460 O: 'Kommunen må ikke fælde træerne uden at få kompensation', in *Villabyerne*, 25.1.1962, page unknown (cutting found in Karen and Ebbe Clemmensen's business archive, The Royal Danish Library, the Danish National Art Library).

461 Karen and Ebbe Clemmensen: *Svømmehaller i Kildeskoven*, year unknown. Karen and Ebbe Clemmensen's business archive, The Royal Danish Library, the Danish National Art Library.

462 Ibid.

463 The watercolours are not signed, but it is likely that Karen Clemmensen painted them. In the early 1950s, she designed the annual Danish Christmas stamps twice, and in 1953 she received the Knud V. Engelhardt's Mindelegat, a grand awarded to artists, architects or designers who have excelled in graphic design and the like. Karen and Ebbe Clemmensen's business archive, The Royal Danish Library, the Danish National Art Library.

464 Svend E. Petersen: 'Arkitektur og/eller ingeniørkunst', in *Ingeniørens Ugeblad*, vol. 14, no. 30, 1970, pp. 3–4.

465 The business archive of the Clemmensen couple contains a letter from Bergholt in which he sends them the manuscript accompanied by some slides he borrowed for the occasion, enclosing a note saying that it was a pity the architects could not be present. Knud Bergholt: letter to the architects Karen and Ebbe Clemmensen on 12 March 1970, Karen and Ebbe Clemmensen's business archive, The Royal Danish Library, the Danish National Art Library.

466 Svend E. Petersen: 'Arkitektur og/eller ingeniørkunst', in *Ingeniørens Ugeblad*, vol. 14, no. 30, 1970, p. 3.

467 Knud Bergholt: Lecture (BSS), 10.3.1970, found in Karen and Ebbe Clemmensen's business archive, The Royal Danish Library, the Danish National Art Library.

468 Ibid.

469 Ibid.

470 Ibid.

471 Svend E. Petersen: 'Arkitektur og/eller ingeniørkunst', in *Ingeniørens Ugeblad*, vol. 14, no. 30, 1970, p. 4.

472 Knud Bergholt: Lecture (BSS), 10.3.1970, found in Karen and Ebbe Clemmensen's

473 Ibid.

474 It is not clear from the archive material when Agnete Muusfeldt was attached to the project, but the most likely date is 1962. At the end of 1961 and in early 1962, inspections of the new construction site, Kildeskoven, are carried out by the Geotechnical Institute to find out whether it is even possible to build on the plot. In April 1962, the municipal council considered the case again at a meeting. Muusfeldt is not mentioned by name at this meeting, but a decision is made to go ahead with the new location and the new adapted drawings. Surviving drawings by Muusfeldt from 1962 are linked to the location in Kildeskoven. In the spring of 1963, the municipal council was presented with the final project in the publication *Idrætshaller i Kildeskoven*, where Muusfeldt is credited. Gentofte Kommunalbestyrelse: *Gentofte Kommunalbestyrelses offentlige forhandlinger – i året 1. april 1962–31. marts 1963*, Hellerup, 1963, pp. 33–39, and Karen and Ebbe Clemmensen, Chr. Ostenfeld and W. Jønsson and Agnete Muusfeldt: *Idrætshaller i Kildeskoven*, Gentofte Kommune, September 1963.

475 Agnete Muusfeldt: 'Idrætshaller i Kildeskoven', in *Landskab*, vol. 52, no. 8, 1971, p. 160.

476 O: 'Kommunen må ikke fælde træerne uden at få kompensation', in *Villabyerne*, 25.1.1962, page unknown (cutting found in Karen and Ebbe Clemmensen's business archive, The Royal Danish Library, the Danish National Art Library).

477 In March 1964, the Gentofte Municipal Council allocates an extra DKK 220,000 to the project, which is to be used for improvement works before construction begins. Gentofte Kommunalbestyrelse: *Gentofte Kommunalbestyrelses offentlige forhandlinger – i året 1. april 1963–31. marts 1964*, Hellerup, 1964, pp. 209–211.

478 Agnete Muusfeldt: 'Idrætshaller i Kildeskoven', in *Landskab*, vol. 52, no. 8, 1971, p. 161.

479 Anon.: 'Køber haverne fuldt færdige', in *Villabyerne*, 30.10.1968 (cutting found in Karen and Ebbe Clemmensen's business archive, The Royal Danish Library, the Danish National Art Library).

480 Unknown: 'Skarp protest mod uheldig træfældning i Kildeskoven', in *Villabyerne*, 8.4.1964 (cutting found in Karen and Ebbe Clemmensen's business archive, The Royal Danish Library, the Danish National Art Library).

481 Agnete Muusfeldt: 'Idrætshaller i Kildeskoven', in *Landskab*, vol. 52, no. 8, 1971, p. 162.

business archive, The Royal Danish Library, the Danish National Art Library.

482 Agnete Muusfeldt: 'En have som en lund', in *Haven*, vol. 87, no. 7/8, 1987, p. 373.

483 See for example statements by landscape architect Ole Nørgaard cited in Lærke Sophie Keil: *Microhistories of Landscape Elements in Albertslund Syd: Plant Beds, a Canal and Garden Fences of Welfare*, PhD dissertation, Copenhagen, University of Copenhagen, Department of Geosciences and Natural Resource Management, 2021.

484 Mathilde Lundt Larsen: 'Empati for det levende – om Agnete Muusfeldts liv og virke', in *Landskab*, vol. 103, no. 3, 2022, pp. 20–25; Annemarie Lund: *Guide til dansk havekunst år 1000–2000*, Copenhagen, Arkitektens Forlag, 2000; Annemarie Lund: *Danmarks havekunst, bd. 3: 1945–2002*, Copenhagen, Arkitektens Forlag, 2002.

485 www.kulturarv.dk/fbb/sagvis.pub?sag=75518752

486 She was an editor from 1958 to 1961 and sat on the editor's committee from 1964 to 1968, www.kvinfo.dk/side/597/bio/1167/origin/170/query/muusfeldt/

487 Now the University of Copenhagen.

488 See the collection of garden and landscape architecture drawings at the Copenhagen University Library Frederiksberg, The Royal Danish Library.

489 Agnete Muusfeldt became an honorary member of Foreningen af Danske Landskabsarkitekter in 1982 and received the Substralprisen award in 1983. See Andreas Bruun: 'En festtale. I anledning af 50 året for stiftelsen af "Dansk Havearkitektforening" – idag kaldet "Foreningen af Danske Landskabsarkitekter"', in *Landskab*, vol. 63, no. 7/8, 1982, pp. 145–146; Annemarie Lund: 'Agnete Muusfeldt', www.kvinfo.dk/side/597/bio/1167/origin/170/

490 See Agnete Muusfeldt and Line Mygind: 'Rundt i haven', in *Haven*, vol. 90, no. 2, 1990, pp. 52–56; Agnete Muusfeldt: 'En have på landet', in *Haven*, vol. 78, no. 4, 1978, pp. 168–171.

491 Agnete Muusfeldt: 'Tilbageblik', in *Landskab*, vol. 63, no. 7/8, 1982, p. 149.

492 Ibid.

493 www.kvinfo.dk/side/597/bio/1167/origin/170/

494 Agnete Muusfeldt: 'En have som en lund', in *Haven*, vol. 87, no. 7/8, 1987, p. 373.

495 Ibid.

496 Rather like when architects design their own house, see for example Chapter Two.

497 Agnete Muusfeldt: 'En idyllisk have', in *Fra kvangaard til humlekule*, no. 13, 1983, pp. 37–46.

498 Ibid.

499 www.kvinfo.dk/side/597/bio/1167/origin/170/: Annemarie Lund: 'Anka Rasmussen. Første danske kvindelige havearkitekt', in *Landskab*, vol. 94, no. 4, 2013, p. 129; Jette Abel and Per Stahlschmidt: 'Landskabsarkitektuddannelsen på KVL har 25-års jubilæum', in *Ugeskrift for jordbrug*, vol. 130, no. 35, 1985, pp. 943–951.

500 Agnete Muusfeld: 'Tilbageblik', in *Landskab*, vol. 63, nos. 7/8, 1982, p. 147.

501 Agnete Muusfeldt and Jørn Palle Schmidt: 'Løvværk', in *Landskab*, vol. 71, no. 8, 1990, p. 133.

502 Malene Hauxner: *Fra naturlig natur til supernatur. Europæisk landskabsarkitektur 1967–2007 set fra Danmark*, Aarhus, Ikaros Press, 2010.

503 John Dixon Hunt: *Greater Perfections. The Practice of Garden Theory*, Philadelphia, PA, University of Pennsylvania Press, 2000.

504 Agnete Muusfeldt: 'En have som en lund', in *Haven*, vol. 87, nos. 7/8, 1987, pp. 372–376.

505 Ibid., p. 373.

506 'Nej, det har aldrig været noget problem [at skaffe arbejde som kvindelig landskabsarkitekt], hvilket helt klart fremgår af tegnestuens årlige sagsregister.' Karen Permin: 'Samtale med landskabsarkitekt Agnete Muusfeldt', in *Landskab*, vol. 69, no. 8, 1988, p. 188.

507 Agnete Muusfeldt: 'En have som en lund', in *Haven*, vol. 87, nos. 7/8, 1987, p. 373.

Postscript
Feminist Architects Who Wanted to Change the World

508 Suzanne LaBarre: interview with anonymous spokesperson for the initiative, in FastCompany: 'Exclusive: Why I Started A "Shitty Architecture Men" List' (fastcompany.com).

509 See for example Pernille Ipsen: *Et åbent øjeblik. Da mine mødre gjorde noget nyt*, Copenhagen, Gyldendal, 2020 and Kirsten Birch et al. (eds.): *Kvinder ytrer sig om omgivelserne. Kommentarer til udstillingen på vej som viser arbejder af kvindelige arkitekter, planlæggere og kunstnere*, Aarhus, Modtryk, 1980.

510 Eva Würtz: 'Et tilbageblik over "Kvinder i Byggesektoren" & Tegnestuen Thyras historie', in Tanja Jordan og Rikke Lequick Larsen (eds.): *Female forces of architecture. Women's centennial anniversary at the Royal Danish Academy of Fine Arts, School of Architecture, Copenhagen*, Copenhagen, Kunstakademiets Arkitektskole, 2010, pp. 90–91.

511 Kirsten Hanson and Sigrun Kaul (eds.): 'Bygge og bo på kvinners vilkår. Rapport fra en konferanse Kungälv 4.–6. maj 1979. Nordiske Kvinners Bygge- og Planforum', in Kirsten Birch et al. (eds.): *Kvinder ytrer sig om omgivelserne. Kommentarer til udstillingen på vej som viser arbejder af kvindelige arkitekter, planlæggere og kunstnere*, Aarhus, Modtryk, 1980, pp. 125–131.

512 Karen Zahle: 'Fællesskaber og boligbyggeri i 1970'erne', in Tanja Jordan and Rikke Lequick Larsen (eds.): *Female forces of Architecture. Women's centennial anniversary at the Royal Danish Academy of Fine Arts, School of Architecture, Copenhagen*, Copenhagen, Kunstakademiets Arkitektskole, 2010, pp. 86–87.

513 Kirsten Birch et al. (eds.): *Kvinder ytrer sig om omgivelserne. Kommentarer til udstillingen på vej som viser arbejder af kvindelige arkitekter, planlæggere og kunstnere*, Aarhus, Modtryk, 1980.

514 Kasper Lægring: 'Gensyn med postmodernismen', in *Arkitekten*, vol. 123, no. 2, 2021, pp. 51–97; Henriette Steiner: 'Constructing Copenhagen in a Time of Economic Downturn', in *Architecture and Culture*, vol. 10, no. 1, 2022, pp. 74–95.

515 Helena Mattsson: 'Revisiting Swedish Postmodernism. Gendered Architecture and Other Stories', in *Konsthistorisk Tidskrift*, vol. 85, no. 1, 2016, pp. 109–125.

516 The Galgebakken development was designed by architects J.P. Storgaard, Hanne Marcussen, Anne and Jørn Ørum-Nielsen and landscape architect Jørgen Vesterholt.

517 Anne Ørum-Nielsen: 'Planlegging og økologi', in *Byggekunst*, vol. 62, no. 8, 1980, p. 368.

518 Ibid.

519 Examples include the German travelling exhibition *Frau Architekt* at the Deutsches Architekturmuseum in 2017, later shown at other venues over the course of several years; *Women in Architecture*, shown at MAXXI in Rome, 2021–22; *Here We Are! Frauen im Design 1900–heute*, Vitra Design Museum, 2021–22; *How We Live Now: Reimagining Spaces with Matrix Feminist Design Co-operative*, Barbican, London, 2021–22; *A Room of One's Own. Feminist's Questions to Architecture*, Estonian Museum of Architecture, Tallinn, 2019.

520 www.dac.dk/udstillinger/kvinder–skaber–rum/. Exhibition created in collaboration with the Danish Architecture Center: Tanya Lindkvist, Sara Hatla Krogsgaard, Lykke Ley and Maya Lahmy.

521 www.realdania.dk/tema/de–glemte–arkitekter. The exhibition has received coverage in 100+ media, including many major features in media such as *Dezeen, Byggeri, Arkitektur, Børsen Pleasure, Berlingske Tidende, Politiken, Metropolis* Magazine, *ArchDaily, Topos Magazine, El País, Corriere della Sera, AD Magazine, Stylepark, Sydsvenska Dagbladet, Bauwelt, STIRworld* and *SPACE Magazine*. Stated by the Danish Architecture Center on 9 November 2022.

522 For example, we have checked all direct quotes (in the original Danish version) from our interviews by running them past the interviewees. We have let descendants read the factual descriptions of the lives and projects of the women of which they have special knowledge. And we have been careful to store data securely. In our close dialogue with contemporaries, descendants and others who have helped us with information, we have endeavoured to be generous and open to the wishes and needs of each individual.

523 In all these roles we also find men with a background in architecture.

Bibliography

UNPUBLISHED SOURCES

The Danish National Archives

— Ministry of Housing, 5th office, housing matters
— Ministry of Housing, the commissioner for urban planning matters
— Archives of the Danish Association for Arts and Crafts (Foreningen for Kunsthåndværk)
— Archives of the Danish Association of Architects (Danske Arkitekters Landsforbund, DAL)
— Archives of the Royal Danish Academy of Fine Arts' School of Architecture
— Archives of the Statens Byggeforskningsinstitut [now BUILD]
— Business archives of the design studio of Vibeke Fischer Thomsen (Vibeke Dalgas)
— Overretssagfører Zeuthens Mindelegat
— Women's History Collection (Kvindehistorisk Samling)

The Royal Danish Library
The Danish National Art Library

— Archives of Ib Martin Jensen and Hans Erling Langkilde
— Business archives of Claus Bremer
— Business archives of Kaj Gottlob
— Business archives of Karen and Ebbe Clemmensen
— Susanne Ussing and Carsten Hoff

The Royal Danish Library, the collection of garden and landscape architecture drawings

— Archives of Anka Rasmussen
— Archives of Erik Mygind
— Archives of Jørn Palle Smidt
— Curricula and study material from the College of Agriculture (Landbohøjskolen)
— Slide collection of Agnete Muusfeldt

Other archives

— ALT for damerne's archive
— Arkiv.dk
— DAB's archive
— fsb's archive
— Gentofte Lokalarkiv
— Grethe Meyer's archive, Designmuseum Danmark
— Kildeskovshallen's archive
— Louisiana Museum of Modern Art photo archive
— Lyngby-Taarbæk Stadsarkiv
— Royal Danish Academy – Architecture, Design, Conservation, the School of Architecture archive
— Rudbjerg Lokalhistoriske Arkiv
— Rødovre Lokalarkiv
— Women's Building archive

Private archives

— Frank Erik Jeppesen
— Gerda Tosti Nielsen's photographic collection
— Ragna Grubb
— Rut Speyer
— Susanne Ussing / Carsten Hoff's archive
— Vibeke Dalgas

PUBLISHED SOURCES

The following journals have been systematically reviewed and used as base material:

— *Arkitekten* (1900–1985), *Arkitektur DK* (1958–1975), *Boligen* (1941–1980), *Byplan* (1950–1985), *Haven* (1969–1990), *Havekunst/Landskab* (1920–1980).

Searches have also been conducted on all the women mentioned in this book in the Royal Danish Library's media collections Mediestream and in the newspaper *Politiken*.

Articles

— Abel, Jette and Per Stahlschmidt: 'Landskabsarkitektuddannelsen på KVL har 25 års jubilæum', in *Ugeskrift for jordbrug*, vol. 130, no. 35, 1985, pp. 943–951.
— Alacovska, Ana: 'From Passion to Compassion. A Caring Inquiry into Creative Work as Socially Engaged Art', in *Sociology*, vol. 54, no. 4, 2020, pp. 727–744, www.doi.org/10.1177/0038038520904716
— Albertsen, Niels and Bülent Diken: 'Welfare and the City', in *Nordisk Arkitekturforskning*, vol. 17, no. 2, 2004, pp. 7–22.
— Anon.: 'Navne og Nyheder', in *Morgenbladet*, 12.10.1930, p. 8.
— Anon.: 'Hjem & Bohave i Tivoli 17–26 sept', in *Politiken*, 18.9.1937, p. 16.
— Anon.: 'Mærkedage', in *Aftenbladet*, 6.9.1940, p. 5.
— Anon.: 'Nye Arkitekter. Akademiets Afgangsprøve for Arkitekter er blevet bestaaet af Poul Hessellund Andersen, Mogens Leth, Anne Marie Rubin og Jørgen Thomsen', in *Nationaltidende*, 19.11.1946, p. 6.
— Anon.: 'Husmoderens arbejde i nationaløkonomisk perspektiv', in Esbjørn Hiort and Birte Ludovica Rasmussen (eds.): Håndbog for Kvinde og Hjem. Danske kvinders udstilling for rationel husførelse, Forum 1.–*17. september 1950*, Copenhagen, 1950, pp. 14–15.
— Anon.: 'Gaarden Carlsro forvandles til By med 4500 Indbyggere', in *Billed-Bladet*, no. 30, 1952, pp. 16–17.
— Anon.: 'Skarp protest mod uheldig træfældning i Kildeskoven', in *Villabyerne*, 8.4.1964 (cutting found in the business archive of Karen and Ebbe Clemmensen).
— Anon.: 'Sommerhus- og vandplan for Sydlolland', in *Politiken*, 14.7.1964, p. 2.
— Anon.: 'Lollands sommerland', in *Fyns Aktuelt*, 16.7.1965, p. 2.
— Anon.: 'Ingen fredning på lille ø', in *Berlingske Tidende*, 9.9.1966, p. 18.
— Anon.: 'Lodsejerudvalg på Nyord', in *Næstved Tidende*, 19.12.1966, p. 3.
— Anon.: 'Les Milandes – et nutidigt kulturcenter', in *Arkitekten*, vol. 69, no. 23, 1967, pp. 509–517.
— Anon.: 'Køber haverne fuldt færdige', in *Villabyerne*, 30.10.1968 (cutting found in the business archive of Karen and Ebbe Clemmensen).
— Anon.: 'Dårlig planlægning af sommerhus-byggeri', in *Folkebladet*, 20.6.1969, p. 7.
— Balle, Annemarie (ed.): *Fra vision til virkelighed. Kvindernes Bygning 125 år,*

Aars, Forlaget Himmerland, Kvindernes Bygning, 2020, pp. 8–11.
— Bendsen, Jannie Rosenberg, Svava Riesto and Henriette Steiner: 'Hvor er kvinderne i dansk arkitekturhistorie?', in *Arkitekten*, no. 5, 2020, pp. 24–29.
— Birte: 'En køkkenvask skal være stor', in *Aftenbladet*, 29.7.1948, p. 2.
— Bisgaard, Ellen: '"EN FINSTUE" blev til køkken – og hele familien har glæde og nytte af forandringen', in *ALT for damerne*, 6.1.1953, p. 19.
— Bisgaard, Ellen: 'Stue og køkken går i et', in *ALT for damerne*, 19.5.1953, pp. 19.
— Bistrup, Annelise: 'Jeg har kæmpet for at ødelægge min gode smag', in *Berlingske Tidende*, 3.3.1974, p. 9.
— Bjørnkjær, Ejvind: 'Moderne gårdhus-bebyggelse midt in vestkystens klitter', in *Ny tid*, 17.3.1968, p. 7.
— Blondie: 'De københavnske Køkkener fulde af Mangler', in *B.T.*, 9.3.1945, p. 5.
— Bonnemaison, Sara and Christine Macy: 'The Dwelling-Garden Dyad in Twentieth-Century Affordable Housing', in Charissa N. Terranova and Meredith Tromble (eds.): *The Routledge Companion to Biology in Art and Architecture*, New York, London, Routledge, 2019, pp. 105–107.
— Borchorst, Anette: 'Feminist Thinking about the Welfare State', in Myra Marx Ferree, Judith Lorber and Beth B. Hess: *Revisioning Gender*, New York, Oxford, Altamira Press, 1999, pp. 100.
— Boserup, Anja: 'Havearkitekten Agnete Petersen', in *Landskab*, vol. 112, no. 1, 2021, pp. 24–27.
— Bruun, Andreas: 'En festtale i anledning af 50 året for stiftelsen af "Dansk Havearkitektforening" – idag kaldet "Foreningen af Danske Landskabsarkitekter"', in *Landskab*, vol. 63, no. 7/8, 1982, pp. 145–146.
— Braae, Ellen and Svava Riesto: 'As Found: A New Design Paradigm', in *Nordic Journal of Architecture*, vol. 1, no. 1, 2011, pp. 8–9.
— Braae, Ellen and Henriette Steiner: 'The Sustainable Nordic City of the Future is the City We Already Have', in *NORDIC WORKING PAPERS: Opportunities and challenges for future regional development – notes from an open seminar*, 12.9.2019, Kjell Nilsson (ed.), Copenhagen, Nordic Council of Ministers, 2019, pp. 31–39, https://doi.org/10.6027/NA2019-910
— Braae, Ellen and Henriette Steiner: 'Expanding Danish Welfare Landscapes – Steen Eiler Rasmussen and Tingbjerg Housing Estate', in Jeanne Haffner (ed.): *Landscapes of Housing. Design and Planning in the History of Environmental Thinking*, London, New York, Routledge, 2021, pp. 145–167.
— Braae, Karen: 'Moderne Køkkener', in *Architekten*, vol. 25, 1923, pp. 16–18, 82–86.
— Burns, Karen: 'Feminist Theory and Praxis, 1991–2003. Questions from the Archive', in Hélène Frichot, Catharina Gabrielsson and Helen Runting (eds.): *Architecture and Feminisms: Ecologies, Economies, Technologies*, London, New York, Routledge, 2018, pp. 11–24.
— Burns, Karen and Lori Brown: 'Telling Transnational Histories of Women in Architecture, 1960–2015', in *Architectural Histories*, vol. 8, no. 1, 2020, DOI: http://doi.org/10.5334/ah.403
— Bülow, Else: 'Indledning', in Susanne Ussing: *Susanne Ussing – arbejder mellem 1957–1987. Beskrivelse af en proces*, Aalborg, Nordjyllands Kunstmuseum, 1987, pp. 7–11.
— Claesson, Ester: 'Några minnen från min skoltid på Vilvorde', in *Havebrugshøjskolen Vilvorde. Skolen gennem 50 Aar. 1875–1925*, Charlottenlund, 1925, pp. 78.
— Clemmensen, Jens: 'Ghettoer in det nordlige København?', in Niels Helberg and Hans Kristensen (eds.): *På fri fod. Gamle byplanlæggere ser tilbage på barndomslivet*, Byplanhistorisk Skriftserie, no. 75, 2015, pp. 57–67.
— Connell, R.W. and James W. Messerschmidt: 'Hegemonic Masculinity: Rethinking the Concept', in *Gender & Society*, vol. 19, no. 6, 2005, pp. 829–859.
— Dalgas, Vibeke: 'Byplanhistorie – og kvindehistorie', in *Byplanhistoriske noter*, no. 37, 1997, pp. 29–33.
— Dalgas, Vibeke: 'Byplanlægning – en kvindehistorie', in Katrine Dirckinck-Holmfeld and Honey Biba Beckerlee (eds.): *Jubil96um. At forhandle kønnet. At introducere kvindelige erfaringsverdener. At kæmpe for ligeberettigelse. Kunstakademiets rolle i fremtiden*, Copenhagen, Kunstakademiet, 2004, unpaged.
— Dalgas, Vibeke: 'Kvindehistorie i en foranderlig tid', in Vibeke Dalgas and Jens Kristian Krarup (eds.): *Stenhusstudent 1952 – og hvad så? Udgivet af 50-års studenterjubilarerne 1952–2002 i anledning af skolens 100-års jubilæum*, 4 September 2006, pp. 15–26.
— Dalgas, Vibeke: 'Kampen om bykernerne', in *Byplanhistoriske noter*, no. 66, 2011, pp. 47–67.
— Dybdahl, Lars: 'Scientific management i hjemmets fabrik', in Lars Dybdahl and Ida Engholm (eds.): *Design – køkkenet*, Copenhagen, Gyldendal, 2008, pp. 25–46.
— Dyggve, Ingrid Møller: 'Køkkenet', in *Architekten*, vol. 28, no. 9/10, 1926, pp. 104–108.
— Erna: 'Køkkenarkitekten paa opdagelsestogt i USA', in *Ekstra Bladet*, 18.1.1950 (from the archives of Statens Byggeforskningsinstitut [now BUILD].
— Etherington, Rose: 'Denise Scott Brown Petition for Pritzker Recognition Rejected', in *Dezeen*, 14.6.2013, www.dezeen.com/2013/06/14/pritzker-jury-rejects-denise-scott-brown-petition/
— Eva: 'Samfundet kræver meget af Kvinderne, og vi kræver alt af os selv ...', in *Berlingske Tidende*, 16.1.1949, p. 6.
— Fisker, Kay: 'Socialt Boligbyggeri's konkurrence om boligtyper i etagehuse', in *Arkitekten* Ugehæfte, vol. 39, no. 14, 1937, pp. 65–76.
— Flyvholm, Flemming: 'Vi forsøger at vise virkeligheden – ikke som den er, men så den opdages', in *Socialistisk Dagblad*, 9.2.1979, p. 9.
— Flyvholm, Flemming: 'Når det bliver kunst – så skip det', in *Socialistisk Dagblad*, 23.–24.1.1982, p. 17.
— FM: 'En ny Lejlighedstype', in *Bygge og bo*, vol. 4, no. 1, 1937, p. 27.
— Frank: 'De unge Arkitekter slog de store Kanoner ud', in *B.T.*, 28.11.1944, p. 2.
— Gamin: 'En Konkurrence i Mandsværk', in *B.T.*, 16.11.1921, p. 9.
— George: 'Kvinden bag sommerlandes "byplan"', in *Politiken*, 24.11.1959, p. 13.
— Gottlob, Kaj: 'Vestkysten ødelægges af feriehuse', in *Arkitekten*, vol. 72, no. 7, 1970, pp. 153–159.
— Grubb, Ragna: 'Kvindernes Bygning', in *Arkitekten* Ugehæfte, vol. 38, 1936, pp. 13–14.
— Grubb, Ragna: 'Boligundersøgelser', in *Arkitekten* Ugehæfte, vol. 48, no. 17, 1946, p. 99.
— Guldberg, Jørn: 'Stockholm i Danmark. Den danske reception af

— Stockholmsudstillingen 1930', in *Architectura*, vol. 33, 2011, pp. 103–150.
— Gulmann, Vibeke: 'Et spørgsmål om at gide', in *Weekendavisen Berlingske Aften*, 28.10.1977, p. 18.
— Hartung, Martin: 'Skal vi bo sådan?', in *Berlingske Tidende*, 25.6.1977, p. 1.
— Hayden, Dolores: 'What Would a Non-Sexist City Be Like? Speculations on Housing, Urban Design, and Human Work', in *Women and the American City*, vol. 5, no. 3, 1980, supplement, pp. 170–187.
— Heiberg, Edvard: 'Om køkkener', i *Arkitekten* Ugehæfte, vol. 50, 1948, pp. 37–40.
— Henderson, Susan R.: 'A revolution in the woman's sphere. Grete Lihotzky and the Frankfurt Kitchen', in Barbara Miller Lane (ed.): *Housing and Dwelling. Perspectives on Modern Domestic Architecture*, New York, London, Routledge, 2007, pp. 248–258.
— 'Heritage as sector, factor and vector: conceptualizing the shifting relationship between heritage management and spatial planning', by Joks Janssen et al., in *European Planning Studies*, vol. 25, no. 9, 2017, pp. 1654–1672.
— Heynen, Hilde: 'A Feminist in Disguise? Sibyl Moholy-Nagy's Histories of Architecture and Its Environment', in Hélène Frichot, Catharina Gabrielsson and Helen Runting (eds.): *Architecture and Feminisms: Ecologies, Economies, Technologies*, London, New York, Routledge, 2018, pp. 39–48.
— Holmen, Grethe: 'Historien bag bygningen', in Tove Koed and Edith Kjærsgaard (eds.): *Historien om Kvindernes Bygning*, Copenhagen, Kvindernes Bygning, 1986, pp. 9–36.
— Hvattum, Mari: 'Nordic Nonumentality', in *Nordic Journal of Architecture*, vol. 2, no. 1, 2012, pp. 8–10.
— Illeris, Sven: 'Anne Marie Rubins tegnestue', in *Byplankonsulenttegnestuerne in 1960'erne og 70'erne. En interviewundersøgelse*, in Vibeke Dalgas et al. (eds.), *Byplanhistoriske noter*, no. 65, 2011, pp. 163–171.
— Illeris, Sven: 'Vibeke Fischer Thomsens (Dalgas) tegnestue', in *Byplanhistoriske noter*, no. 65, 2011, pp. 67–77.
— Jack: 'Hun skal hjælpe Korsør', in *Politiken*, 26.9.1963, p. 29.
— Jacobsen, Niels Michael: 'Børn er et folk – og Louisiana et helt andet land', in *Landsavisen Aktuelt*, no. 23, August 1978, pp. 24–25.
— Jensen, Hans-Christian and Anders V. Munch: 'Environment and Emancipation through Design. Avant-garde Intervention and Experiments with Social Design in Denmark around 1970', in *AIS/Design: Storia e Ricerche*, vol. 7, nos. 12–13, 2019–2020, pp. 88–109.
— Jensen, Knud W.: 'Introduktion', *Louisiana Revy*, vol. 17, no. 3, 1977, p. 3.
— Jeppesen, Erik Frank: 'Min opvækst i Hjortekær', in *Lyngby-bogen*, 2005, pp. 5–54.
— Jessen, Asbjørn and Anne Tietjen: 'Assembling Welfare Landscapes of Social Housing: Lessons from Denmark', in *Landscape Research*, vol. 46, no. 4, 2021, pp. 474–494.
— Jn: 'Professor – uden titel', in *Politiken*, 9.10.1968, p. 18.
— Just, Gitte: 'Ærens slagmark', in *Det Fri Aktuelt*, 20.5.1989, section 2, p. 8.
— Keil, Lærke Sophie, Svava Riesto and Tom Avermaete: 'Welfare Landscapes Between Individuality and Communality. Social Housing in Albertslund Syd', in *Landscape Research*, vol. 46, no. 4, 2021, pp. 456–473.
— Keller, Hadley: 'The Power Couples of Architecture and Design', in *AD*, 31.1.2015, www.architecturaldigest.com/gallery/power-couples-of-architecture-and-design-slideshow
— Kristensen, Frederik Buhl: 'KHR Architecture kæmper mod konkurs', in *Byrummonitor*, 2.3.2022, www.byrummonitor.dk/Nyheder/art8646725/KHR-Architecture-kæmper-mod-konkurs
— 'Kvindearkitektur', *Blød By*, no. 24, 1983.
— Larsen, Mathilde Lundt: 'Empati for det levende – om Agnete Muusfeldts liv og virke', in *Landskab*, vol. 103, no. 3, 2022, pp. 20–25.
— Lénard, Dag: 'Huset er ladet med sol, lys og lykke', in *ALT for damerne*, 19.10.1954, pp. 12–13, 26.
— Lund, Annemarie: 'Anka Rasmussen. Første danske kvindelige havearkitekt', in *Landskab*, vol. 94, no. 4, 2013, pp. 126–135.
— Lund, Tina: 'Agnete Muusfeldt – skjult i samlingen', in *Revy*, vol. 44, no. 1, 2022, pp. 3–7.
— Lytken, Malene: 'The Danish School of Interior Architecture. A Visionary Functionalist, a Visionary Aesthete, and Their Women Students', in *Journal of Interior Design*, vol. 38, no. 3, 2013, pp. 1–19.
— Lægring, Kasper: 'Gensyn med postmodernismen', in *Arkitekten*, vol. 123, no. 2, 2021, pp. 52–55.
— Mary-Ann: 'Kvindelige Arkitekter. Hvad vi trænger til', in *Klokken 5*, 20.8.1930, p. 4.
— Mattsson, Helena: 'Revisiting Swedish Postmodernism. Gendered Architecture and Other Stories', in *Konsthistorisk Tidskrift*, vol. 85, no. 1, 2016, pp. 109–125.
— Mattsson, Helena and Meike Schalk: 'Action Archive. Oral History as Performance', in Janina Gosseye, Naomi Stead, Deborah van der Plaat (eds.): *Speaking of Buildings. Oral History in Architectural Research*, New York, N.Y., Princeton Architectural Press, 2019, pp. 94–113.
— Mazelle: 'Det er køkkenet, det drejer sig om', in *ALT for damerne*, 10.8.1954, p. 3.
— Mo: Æstetiske miljøer og gamle bygninger', in *Aktuelt*, 30.3.1965 (cutting found in the business archives of Kaj Gottlob).
— Muusfeldt, Agnete: 'Idrætshaller in Kildeskoven', in *Landskab*, vol. 52, no. 8, 1971, pp. 160–164.
— Muusfeldt, Agnete: 'En have på landet', in *Haven*, vol. 78, no. 4, 1978, pp. 168–171.
— Muusfeldt, Agnete: 'Tilbageblik', in *Landskab*, vol. 63, no. 7/8, 1982, pp. 147–152.
— Muusfeldt, Agnete: 'En idyllisk have', in *Fra kvangaard til humlekule*, no. 13, 1983, pp. 37–46.
— Muusfeldt, Agnete: 'En have som en lund', in *Haven*, vol. 87, no. 7/8, 1987, pp. 372–376.
— Muusfeldt, Agnete and Jørn Palle Schmidt: 'Løvværk', in *Landskab*, vol. 71, no. 8, 1990, pp. 133–141.
— Muusfeldt, Agnete and Line Mygind: 'Rundt i haven', in *Haven*, vol. 90, no. 2, 1990, pp. 52–56.
— Møller, Viggo Sten: 'Boligforhold', in *Nyt Tidsskrift for Kunstindustri*, vol. 16, 1943, p. 133.
— Møller, Viggo Sten: 'Hemmens Forskningsinstitut', in *Nyt Tidsskrift for Kunstindustri*, vol. 18, 1945, pp. 65–66.
— N: 'Gode og dårlige køkkener og vaskekældre in Amerika og Danmark', in *Ingeniøren*, no. 14, 1950, pp. 302–303.
— Nielsen, Carsten: 'Frivillig Husundersøgelse', in *Berlingske Tidende*, 13.9.1944, p. 6.

— Nielsen, Johan (eds.): 'En Nuance', i *Dansk Arbejde*, vol. 27, 1 February, 1936, p. 2.
— Nilsen, Lundwall: 'Et penalhus med mange rum', in *ALT for damerne*. The house was featured in the magazine in the mid-1960s; the exact year is unknown.
— Nochlin, Linda: *Why Have There Been No Great Women Artists*, 1971, p. 7, www.writing.upenn.edu/library/Nochlin-Linda_Why-Have-There-Been-No-Great-Women-Artists.pdf
— Nolin, Catharina: 'International Training and National Ambitions. Female Landscape Architects in Sweden, 1900–1950', in Sonja Dümpelmann and John Beardsley (eds.): *Women, Modernity, and Landscape Architecture*, New York, Routledge, 2015, pp. 38–59.
— Nørgård, Ole: 'Albertslund Syd', in *Landskab*, vol. 50, no. 2, 1969–1970, p. 21.
— O: 'Kommunen må ikke fælde træerne uden at få kompensation', in *Villabyerne*, 25.1.1962, page no. unknown (cutting found in the business archives of Karen and Ebbe Clemmensen).
— Ochsner, Lili: 'Frygtløs og nysgerrig', in *Morgenavisen Jyllands-Posten*, 22.5.1983, p. 53.
— Olwig, Kenneth R.: 'Introduction: The Nature of Cultural Heritage, and the Culture of Natural Heritage – Northern Perspectives on a Contested Patrimony', in *International Journal of Heritage Studies*, vol. 11, no. 1, 2005, pp. 3–7.
— Otero-Pailos, Jorge: 'On self-effacement: The aesthetics of preservation', in *Place and Displacement: Exhibiting Architecture*, Thordis Arrhenius et al. (eds.), Zürich, Lars Müller Publishers, 2014, pp. 231–243.
— Ostenfeld, Chr. and W. Jønsson and Karen and Ebbe Clemmensen: *Svømmehal ved Gentofte Stadion. Skitseprojekt april 1961* (found in the Kildeskovshallen's archive).
— Pan: 'Hvor et moderne dansk Køkken er gammeldags', in *Berlingske Aftenavis*, 4.3.1950 (from the archives of Statens Byggeforskningsinstitut [now BUILD].
— Penner, Barbara: 'Designed-in Safety: Ergonomics in the Bathroom', in Kenny Cupers (ed.): *Use Matters. An Alternative History of Architecture*, London, New York, Routledge, 2013, pp. 153–168.
— Penner, Barbara: 'The Cornell Kitchen. Housing and Design Research in Postwar America', in *Technology and Culture*, vol. 59, no. 1, 2018, pp. 48–94.
— Perikon: 'Det ideale Køkken – næsten!', in *Nationaltidende*, 28.2.1947, pp. 8.
— Perikon: 'Jeg mødte ikke en eneste overbelastet Husmoder in USA', in *Nationaltidende*, 28.11.1949, p. 5.
— Permin, Karen: 'Samtale med landskabsarkitekt Agnete Muusfeldt', in *Landskab*, vol. 69, no. 8, 1988, pp. 185–190.
— Pernille: 'Arkitekterne Carstensen og Westergaard', *Dagens Nyheder – Nationaltidende*, 11.3.1927, p. 2.
— Petersen, Svend E.: 'Arkitektur og/eller ingeniørkunst', in *Ingeniørens Ugeblad*, vol. 14, no. 30, 1970, pp. 3–4.
— 'Plans for Uncertain Futures: Heritage and Climate Imaginaries in Coastal Climate Adaptation', by Svava Riesto et al., in *International Journal of Heritage Studies*, vol. 28, no. 3, 2022, pp. 358–375.
— RB: 'Ulykkelige følger af sommerhusbyggeriet', in *Aalborg Amtstidende*, 20.6.1967, p. 3.
— Redaktionen: 'Familie-Nyt', in *Nationaltidende*, 24.8.1940, p. 2.
— Riesto, Svava and Anne Tietjen: 'Doing Heritage Together: New Heritage Frontiers in Collaborative Planning', in Torgrim Sneve Guttormsen and Grete Swensen (eds.): *Heritage, Democracy and the Public. Nordic Approaches*, London, New York, Routledge, 2017, pp. 159–175.
— Riesto, Svava and Anne Tietjen: 'Planning with Heritage. A Critical Debate Across Landscape Architecture Practice and Heritage Theory', in Ellen Braae and Henriette Steiner (eds.): *Routledge Reseach Companion to Landscape Architecture*, London, New York, Routledge, 2019, pp. 240–253.
— Riesto, Svava and Rikke Stenbro: 'Mesterværkerne, eliten og dem, der var flest af. Værdiopfattelser og blinde vinkler i fredningen af velfærdssamfundets boliger', in *Fabrik og Bolig*, no. 1, 2019, pp. 32–48.
— Rubin, Anne Marie: 'Vores situation, tid og omverden', in *Byplan*, vol. 18, no. 3, 1966, p. 92.
— Rubin, Anne Marie. 'Om behovet for en byplan-forskning', in Ulla Koch (ed.): *Køn og videnskab*, Aalborg, Aalborg Universitetsforlag, 1989, pp. 219–229.
— Rubin, Anne Marie, Knud W. Jensen and J.-F. Gravier: 'Byplanlægningen i fritidens epoke', in *Louisiana Revy*, vol. 6, no. 4, 1965/66, pp. 25–31.
— Salicath, Bent: 'Køkkenforholdene i Boligbyggeriet', in *Boligen*, no. 3, 1948, p. 80.
— Selverhvervende Kvinder: 'De kvindelige Arkitekter og K. F. U. K.s nye Bygning', in *Berlingske Tidende*, 24.12.1916, p. 6.
— Sestoft, Kirsten, Karen Clemmensen and Vibeke Fischer Thomsen: '3 kvinder in arkitektfaget', in *Blød By*, no. 11, 1981, pp. 18–22.
— Smidt, Claus M.: 'Fra tempel til boligblok. Arkitektur in første halvdel af 1900-tallet', in Anneli Fuchs and Emma Salling (eds.): *Kunstakademiet 1754–2004*, vol. 1, Copenhagen, Det Kongelige Akademi for de Skønne Kunster & Arkitektens Forlag, 2004, pp. 321–382.
— Speyer, Rut: 'Politik er det umuliges kunst', in *Morgenavisen Jyllands-Posten*, 18.10.1989, p. 9.
— SPF: 'Vi skal bo helt anderledes', in *Aftenbladet*, 1.4.1937, p. 5.
— Steiner, Henriette: 'Gigantic Welfare Landscapes and the Ground Beneath Høje Gladsaxe', in *Landscape Research*, vol. 46, no. 4, 2021, pp. 527–541.
— Steiner, Henriette: 'Constructing Copenhagen in a Time of Economic Downturn', in *Architecture and Culture*, vol. 10, no. 1, 2022, pp. 76–95.
— Steiner, Henriette: 'Between Passion and Possession. Women Architects and the Houses They Built for Family, Love and Work', to be published in *Journal of Architecture* in 2023.
— Steph: 'Uhyggelige Tal fra de overbefolkede Lejligheder. København har Boliger med kun 4½ Kubikmeter Luft til hver Beboer. En Familie med Mand, Kone og 5 Børn bor i et enkelt Værelse', in *Politiken*, 11.11.1937, p. 14.
— Tafdrup, Ulla: 'Det rigtige køkken', in *Bygmesteren*, vol. 41, 1948, p. 129.
— Tafdrup, Ulla: 'Kærnen i boligen – køkkenet', in *Kvinder og samfundet*, vol. 64, no. 9, 1948, p. 136.
— Tafdrup, Ulla: 'Køkkenundersøgelsen', in *Kvinden og samfundet*, vol. 65, no. 4, 1949, p. 52.
— Thau, Carsten: 'Ussing og Hoff – arkitekturen frisat', in Birgitte Thorsen Vilslev and Carsten Hoff (eds.): *Susanne Ussing – mellem arkitektur og kunst*, Copenhagen, Strandberg Publishing, 2017, pp. 81–82.

— Thomsen, Jens-Peter and Stefan Bastholm Andrade: 'Vi gifter os med dem, der ligner os', Copenhagen, VIVE, 2. december 2018, www.vive.dk/da/udgivelser/vi-gifter-os-med-dem-der-ligner-os-11750/
— Thomsen, Vibeke Fischer: 'Byafgrænsning – byudvikling', in *Vort åbne land. Danmarks Naturfredningsforenings årsskrift*, 1968, pp. 56–61.
— Tip: 'Den første kvindelige Arkitekt', in *Nationaltidende*, 2.5.1915, p. 3.
— Tronto, Joan C. and Berenice Fisher: 'Toward a Feminist Theory of Caring', in Emily K. Abel and Margaret K. Nelsen (eds.): *Circles of Care*, Albany, New York, State University of New York Press, 1990, pp. 35–62.
— Tronto, Joan C.: 'Caring Architecture', in Angelika Fitz and Elke Krasny (eds.): *Critical Care: Architecture and Urbanism for a Broken Planet*, Wien, Architekturzentrum, 2019, pp. 26–31.
— Ufer, Nils: 'Kampen om Thylejren', in *Information*, 12.5.1971, p. 5.
— Ussing, Susanne: 'Byggeeksperiment på vejlø', in *Land og By*, vol. 2, no. 1, 1975.
— Ussing, Susanne: 'MEDIET mellem KUNST og ARKITEKTUR', in *Kvinder ytrer sig om omgivelserne. Kommentarer til udstillingen på vej som viser arbejder af kvindelige arkitekter, planlæggere og kunstnere*, Kirsten Birch et al. (eds.), Aarhus, Modtryk, 1980, p. 65.
— Ussing, Susanne and Carsten Hoff: 'Alternative Rum/Spatial Alternative/Alternative räume/Alternatives', in *Mobilia*, no. 180, 1970, unpaged.
— Ussing, Susanne and Carsten Hoff: 'Eksperimentbyggeri in Thy', in *Arkitekten*, vol. 72, no. 26, 1970, pp. 638–641.
— Varming, Michael: 'Vestkystens fremtid', in *Fonden for Bygnings- og Landskabskultur. 10 års-beretning 1964–1974*, Copenhagen, Fonden for Bygnings- og Landskabskultur, 1974, p. 25.
— Vasström, Annette: 'Kollektivbyen Carlsro – en by i byen', in Sigurd Rambusch (ed.): *Rødovre 1901–1976*, Rødovre, Rødovre Kommune, 1978, pp. 219–238.
— Vyff, Iben: 'Kold krig i en dansk køkkenkultur, 1945–1965', in *Arbejderhistorie*, no. 2, 2012, pp. 40–56.
— 'Welfare Landscapes: Open Spaces of Danish Social Housing Estates Reconfigured', by Ellen Marie Braae et al., in Svava Riesto and Miles Glendinning (eds.): *Mass Housing of the Scandinavian Welfare States: Exploring Histories and Design Strategies*, Edinburgh, University of Edinburgh/Docomomo, 2020, pp. 13–23.
— Würtz, Eva: 'Et lille tilbageblik over 'Kvinder in Byggesektoren' & Tegnestuen Thyras historie', in Tanja Jordan and Rikke Lequick Larsen (eds.): *Female forces of architecture. Women's centennial anniversary at the Royal Danish Academy of Fine Arts, School of Architecture, Copenhagen*, Copenhagen, Kunstakademiets Arkitektskole, 2010, pp. 90–93.
— Xue, Jin and Wojciech Kębłowski: 'Spatialising degrowth, degrowing urban planning', in *Local Environment*, vol. 27, no. 4, 2022, pp. 397–403.
— Zahle, Karen: 'Fællesskaber og boligbyggeri i 1970'erne', in Tanja Jordan and Rikke Lequick Larsen (eds.): *Female forces of architecture. Women's centennial anniversary at the Royal Danish Academy of Fine Arts, School of Architecture, Copenhagen*, Copenhagen, Kunstakademiets Arkitektskole, 2010, pp. 86–89.
— Ørum-Nielsen, Anne: 'Planlegging og Økologi', in *Byggekunst*, no. 8, 1980, pp. 365–368.

Books

— Algreen-Ussing, Gregers, Grethe Silding and Allan de Waal: *Byens træk. Om by- og bygningsbevaringssystemet SAVE*, Copenhagen Planstyrelsen, 1992.
— Andersson, Sven-Ingvar and Steen Høyer: *C. Th. Sørensen – en havekunstner*, 2nd edition, Copenhagen, Arkitektens Forlag, 2001.
— *Architectures of Dismantling and Restructuring. Spaces of Danish Welfare 1970–Present*, Kirsten Marie Raahauge et al. (eds.), Zurich, Lars Müller Publishers, 2022.
— Avermaete, Tom and Janina Gosseye: *Urban Design in the 20th Century – a History*, Zürich, gta Verlag, 2021.
— Bay, Helle et al. (eds.): *Women in Danish Architecture*, Copenhagen, Arkitektens Forlag, 1991.
— Beck, Peter: *Det essentielle – arkitekt Bodil Kjær om sine internationale arbejder 1950–2000*, Aarhus, Turbine, 2022.
— Bendsen, Jannie Rosenberg: *Enkelhed, mådehold og funktionalitet – en analyse af fremtrædende danske arkitekters udlægninger af dansk arkitektur*, PhD dissertation, Copenhagen, Københavns Universitet, 2009.
— Bendsen, Jannie Rosenberg, Birgitte Kleis and Mogens A. Morgen: *Bellahøj. Fortællinger om en bebyggelse*, Copenhagen, Strandberg Publishing, 2015.
— Bendsen, Jannie Rosenberg and Mogens A. Morgen: *Fredet. Bygningsfredning in Danmark 1918–2018*, Copenhagen, Strandberg Publishing, 2018.
— Bendsen, Jannie Rosenberg and Dorthe Bendtsen: *Drømmen om eget hus. Statslånshuse 1933–1959*, Copenhagen, Strandberg Publishing, 2021.
— Bennett, Jane: *Vibrant Matter. A Political Ecology of Things*, Durham, NC, Duke University Press, 2010.
— Bisgaard, Ellen: *Køkken-ideer*, Copenhagen, J.Fr. Clausens Forlag, 1955.
— Bois, Marcel and Bernadette Reinhold (eds.): *Margrete Schütte-Lihotzky. Architektur, Politik, Geschlect. Neue Perspektiven auf Leben und Werk*, Basel, Birkhäuser, 2019.
— Boligministeriets udvalg vedrørende kollektive anlæg: *Fællesanlæg til lettelse af hjemmets arbejde*, vol. 1, *Betænkning*, no. 57, Copenhagen, Statens Trykningskontor, 1954.
— Boligministeriets udvalg vedrørende kollektive anlæg: *Fællesanlæg til lettelse af hjemmets arbejde*, vol. 2: *Bilag, Betænkning*, no. 57, Copenhagen, Statens Trykningskontor, 1954.
— Boudon, Philippe: *Pessac de Le Corbusier: 1927–1967: Étude socio-architecturale: Pessac II, Le Corbusier: 1969–1985*, Paris, Dunod, 1985.
— Buhl, Ole: *Socialt Boligbyggeri*, Copenhagen, Foreningen Socialt Boligbyggeri, 1941.
— Burton, Antoinette M. (ed.): *Archive Stories: Facts, Fictions, and the Writing of History*, Durham, NC, London, Duke University Press, 2005.
— Chadwick, Whitney and Isabelle de Courtivron: *Significant Others. Creativity and Intimate Partnership*, London, Thames & Hudson, 1998 (1993).
— Christiansen, Caspar et al. (eds.): *Den grønne metropol. Natur- og rekreative områder i hovedstadsmetropolen efter 1900*, Copenhagen, Frydenlund Academic, 2016.

— Christiansen, Jørgen Hegner: *Dansk betonarkitektur*, Copenhagen, Forlaget Vandkunsten, 2018.
— Clemmensen, Karen, Ebbe Clemmesen, Chr. Ostenfeld, W. Jønsson and Agnete Muusfeldt: *Idrætshaller in Kildeskoven, Gentofte Kommune september 1963*.
— Corn, Wanda M., Charlene G. Garfinkle and Annelise K. Madsen: *Women Building History. Public Art at the 1893 Columbian Exposition*, Berkeley, University of California Press, 2010.
— Cullen, Gordon: *The Concise Townscape*, London, New York, Routledge, Taylor & Francis, 1961.
— Cupers, Kenny (eds.): *Use Matters. An Alternative History of Architecture*, London, New York, Routledge, 2013.
— Curtis, William J.R.: *Modern architecture since 1900*, 3rd edition, London, New York, Phaidon, 1996.
— Dahlkild, Nan (ed.): *Sommerlandets arkitektur. Drømmen om det gode liv*, Copenhagen, Museum Tusculanums Forlag, 2018.
— Dahlsgård, Inga, M.K. Michaelsen and Viggo Sten Møller (eds.): *Bosætningsbogen. En grundbog for studiekredse*, Copenhagen, Schultz, 1953.
— *DAL's konkurrence om etageboligformer. Program for konkurrencens 2. etape*, Copenhagen, Danske Arkitekters Landsforbund, 1973.
— Dalgas, Vibeke et al. (eds.): 'Byplankonsulenttegnestuerne i 1960'erne og 70'erne. En interviewundersøgelse', in *Byplanhistoriske noter*, no. 65, 2011.
— Dybdahl, Lars and Ida Engholm (eds.): *Design – køkkenet*, Copenhagen, Gyldendal, 2008.
— Dümpelmann, Sonja and John Beardsley (eds.): *Women, Modernity, and Landscape Architecture*, New York, Routledge, 2015.
— Eggers, Olga (ed.): *Kendte danske Kvinder*, Copenhagen, Arthur-Jensens Forlag, 1934.
— Egnsplankontoret: *Skitseforslag til Egnsplan for Storkøbenhavn*, Copenhagen, 1947.
— Eichhorn, Kate: *The Archival Turn in Feminism: Outrage in Order*, Philadelphia, PA, Temple University Press, 2013.
— Espegel, Carmen: *Women Architects in the Modern Movement*, New York, London, Routledge, 2018.

— Esping-Andersen, Gösta: *The Three Worlds of Capitalism*, Princeton, N.J., Princeton University Press, 1990.
— Faber, Tobias: *Dansk arkitektur*, 2nd edition., Copenhagen, Arkitektens Forlag, 1977.
— Fonden for Bygnings- og Landskabskultur: *Beretning for året 1968*, Copenhagen, Fonden for Bygnings- og Landskabskultur, 1968.
— Fonden for Bygnings- og Landskabskultur: *Beretning for året 1969*, Copenhagen, Fonden for Bygnings- og Landskabskultur, 1969.
— Fonden for Bygnings- og Landskabskultur, Selskabet for Bygnings- og Landskabskultur og Sammenslutningen for Bygnings- og Landskabskultur: *Beretning for årene 1964-1974 i anledning af 10-året for oprettelsen af Fonden for Bygnings- og Landskabskultur*, Copenhagen, Fonden for Bygnings- og Landskabskultur, 1974.
— Forchhammer, Olaf: *Københavnsegnens grønne Omraader. Forslag til et System af Omraader for Friluftsliv*, Copenhagen Nyt Nordisk Forlag, 1936.
— Foreningen for Socialt Boligbyggeri: *Foreningen for Socialt Boligbyggeri 1945-1985*, vol. 2, Foreningen for Socialt Boligbyggeri, 1986.
— *Form til velfærd*, Katrine Lotz et al., Copenhagen, Arkitektens Forlag, 2017.
— *Fortegnelse over Danske Havebrugskandidater 1865-1955*. Supplement to the 5th edition, 1947, Copenhagen, Foreningen af Danske Havebrugskandidater, 1955.
— Forty, Adrian: *Words and Buildings. A Vocabulary of Modern Architecture*, London, Thames & Hudson, 2019.
— Freeman, June: *The making of the modern kitchen. A cultural history*, Oxford, New York, Berg, 2004.
— Frichot, Hélène, Catharina Gabrielsson and Helen Runting (eds.): *Architecture and Feminisms: Ecologies, Economies, Technologies*, London, New York, Routledge, 2018.
— Gehl, Ingrid: *Bo-miljø. SBI-Rapport*, no. 71, 1971.
— Gehl, Jan: *Livet mellem husene. Udeaktiviteter og udemiljøer*, 5th edition, Copenhagen, Arkitektens Forlag, 2003.
— Gentofte Kommunalbestyrelse: *Gentofte Kommunalbestyrelses offentlige forhandlinger – i året 1. april 1962-31. marts 1963*, Hellerup, 1963.
— Gentofte Kommunalbestyrelse: *Gentofte Kommunalbestyrelses offentlige forhandlinger – i året 1. april 1963-31. marts 1964*, Hellerup, 1964.
— Giedion, Sigfried: *Space, Time, and Architecture. The Growth of a New Tradition*, 5th edition., Cambridge, Mass., London, Harvard University Press, 2008.
— Goldstein, Joshua S.: *War and Gender*, Cambridge, Cambridge University Press, 2003.
— Guterl, Matthew Pratt: *Josephine Baker and the Rainbow Tribe*, Cambridge, Mass., London, The Belknap Press of Harvard University Press, 2014.
— Gaardmand, Arne: *Dansk byplanlægning. Plan over land 1938–1992*, 2nd edition, Nykøbing Sj., Bogværket, 2016.
— Hansen, Johannes Hedal: *Eva & Nils Koppel*, Copenhagen, Strandberg Publishing, 2017.
— Hansen, Per H.: *Da danske møbler blev moderne. Historien om dansk møbeldesigns storhedstid*, Copenhagen, Ascheoug and Syddansk Universitetsforlag, 2006.
— Harkær, Gorm: *Kaare Klint*, vols. 1–2, Copenhagen, Klintiana, 2010.
— Harlang, Christoffer, Keld Helmer-Petersen and Krestine Kjærholm (eds.): *Poul Kjærholm*, Copenhagen, Arkitektens Forlag, 1998.
— Haunsø, S., Viggo Sten Møller and Bent Salicath (eds.): *Køkkenundersøgelse*, Copenhagen, Fællesudvalget for Boligundersøgelser, 1949.
— Hauxner, Malene: *Fra naturlig natur til supernatur. Europæisk landskabsarkitektur 1967–2007 set fra Danmark*, Aarhus, Ikaros Press, 2010.
— *Havebrugshøjskolen Vilvorde. Skolen gennem 50 Aar. 1875-1925*, Charlottenlund, 1925.
— Hayden, Dolores: *The Grand Domestic Revolution*, Cambridge, Mass., London, MIT Press, 1982.
— Hermann, Elisabeth: *50'er boligen. En eksempelsamling*, Copenhagen, Byggeriets Studiearkiv, 2000.
— Hiort, Esbjørn and Birte Ludovica Rasmussen (eds.): *Håndbog for Kvinde og Hjem. Danske kvinders udstilling for rationel husførelse, Forum 1.-17. september 1950*, Copenhagen, 1950.
— Hiort, Esbjørn: *Finn Juhl*, København, Arkitektens Forlag, 1990.
— *Hovedstadsmetropolen efter 1945*, Henning Bro et al. (eds.), Copenhagen, Hovedstadens Kulturhistoriske Arkiver, 2011.

- Hunt, John Dixon: *Greater Perfections. The Practice of Garden Theory*, Philadelphia, PA, University of Pennsylvania Press, 2000.
- Illouz, Eva: *Why Love Hurts. A Sociological Explanation*, Cambridge, Mass., Polity Press, 2012.
- Indenrigsministeriet: *Betænkning afgivet af det af Indenrigsministeriet den 11. September nedsatte Udvalg vedrørende Statens Forhold til Byggeriet. Udviklingen af det spredte Byggeri m. m.*, Copenhagen, Schultz, 1943.
- Ipsen, Pernille: *Et åbent øjeblik. Da mine mødre gjorde noget nyt*, Copenhagen, Gyldendal, 2020.
- Jensen, Thomas Bo: *P.V. Jensen-Klint*, Copenhagen, Kunstakademiets Arkitektskoles Forlag, 2006.
- Jensen, Thomas Bo: *Inger og Johannes Exner*, Aarhus, Ikaros Press, 2012.
- Jordan, Tanja and Rikke Lequick Larsen (eds.): *Female forces of architecture. Women's centennial anniversary at the Royal Danish Academy of Fine Arts, School of Architecture, Copenhagen*, Copenhagen, Kunstakademiets Arkitektskole, 2010.
- Juhl, Helle: *Husmødre. Historier fra landets største arbejdsplads*, Copenhagen, Gyldendal, 2012.
- Jørgensen, Lisbet Balslev: *Den sidste guldalder. Danmark i 1950'erne*, Copenhagen, Arkitektens Forlag, 2004.
- Kaiser, Monika: *Neubesetzungen des Kunst-Raumes. Feministische Kunstausstellungen und ihre Räume, 1972–1987*, Bielefeld, Transcript Verlag, 2013.
- Kaufmann, Erik: *27 slags planer. Oversigt over og kritisk analyse af den offentlige fysiske planlægning in Danmark*, Copenhagen, Statens Byggeforskningsinstitut, 1966.
- Keiding, Martin and Kim Dirckinck-Holmfeld (eds.): *Utzon og den nye tradition*, Copenhagen, Arkitektens Forlag, 2005.
- Keiding, Martin, Marianne Amundsen and Kim Dirckinck-Holmfeld (eds.): *Dansk arkitektur siden 1754*, 2nd edition, Copenhagen, Arkitektens Forlag, 2007.
- Keil, Lærke Sophie: *Microhistories of Landscape Elements in Albertslund Syd: Plant Beds, a Canal and Garden Fences of Welfare*, PhD dissertation, Copenhagen, University of Copenhagen, Department of Geosciences and Natural Resource Management, 2021.
- Kjældgaard, Lasse Horne: *Meningen med velfærdsstaten. Da litteraturen tog ordet – og politikerne lyttede*, Copenhagen, Gyldendal, 2018.
- Knudsen, Line Vestergaard: *De første sommerhuse – 1886*, Aarhus, Aarhus Universitetsforlag, 2022.
- Knuth-Winterfeldt, Henrik: *Naturfredning in Danmark*, Copenhagen, Danmarks Naturfredningsforenings Forlag, 1981.
- Koed, Tove and Edith Kjærsgaard (eds.): *Historien om Kvindernes Bygning*, Copenhagen, Kvindernes Bygning, 1986.
- Kontturi, Katve-Kaisa: *Ways of Following. Art, Materiality, Collaboration*, London, Open Humanities Press, 2018, pp. 17.
- *Kvinder ytrer sig om omgivelserne. Kommentarer til udstillingen på vej som viser arbejder af kvindelige arkitekter, planlæggere og kunstnere*, Kirsten Birch et al. (eds.), Aarhus, Modtryk, 1980.
- Lind, Olaf: *Arkitekten Steen Eiler Rasmussen*, Copenhagen, Gyldendal, 2008.
- *Louisiana Revy*, special edition, 'Alternativ Arkitektur', vol. 17, no. 3, 1977.
- Lund, Annemarie: *Guide til dansk havekunst år 1000–2000*, Copenhagen, Arkitektens Forlag, 2000.
- Lund, Annemarie: *Danmarks havekunst*, vol. 3: *1945–2002*, Copenhagen, Arkitektens Forlag, 2002.
- Lund, Annemarie: *Grøn form – grønt modspil. En bog om landskabsarkitekten Jørn Palle Schmidt*, Copenhagen, Arkitektens Forlag, 2007.
- Lund, Hakon and Anne Lise Thygesen: *C.F. Hansen*, vols. 1–2, Copenhagen, Arkitektens Forlag, 1995.
- Lyngby-Taarbæk Kommune: *Lyngby Taarbæk Dispositionsplan*, 1949.
- Mattsson, Helena and Sven-Olov Wallenstein: *Swedish Modernism. Architecture, Consumption, and the Welfare State*, London, Black Dog Publishing, 2010.
- Meadows, Donatella H. et al.: *The Limits to Growth. A Report for The Club of Rome's Project on the Predicament of Mankind*, Washington, Potomac Associates, 1972.
- Ministeriet for Landbrug og Fiskeri: *Undervisnings- og Eksamensplan for Den Kongelige Veterinær- og Landbohøjskole. Approberet af Ministeriet for Landbrug og Fiskeri ved Skrivelse af 6. Marts og 24. Juni 1939 til at træde i Kraft for de Studerende, som begynder deres Studium ved Højskolen 1. September 1940 eller senere*, Copenhagen, 1939.
- Monies, Finn and Karen Zahle (eds.): *Tiden i Stockholm*, Copenhagen, Arkitektens Forlag, 1999.
- Møller, Vibeke Andersson: *Dansk arkitektur in 1960'erne*, Forlaget Rhodos in collaboration with Nationalmuseet and Syddansk Universitetsforlag, 2019.
- Møns Kommune: *Nyord By. Partiel byplanvedtægt*, 1973.
- Norberg-Schulz, Christian: *Genius Loci. Towards a Phenomenology of Architecture*, New York, Rizzoli, 1980.
- Page, Scott E.: *The Diversity Bonus*, Princeton, N.J., Princeton University Press, 2019.
- Pedersen, Johan (ed.): *Vore køkkener. En forsøgsrapport*, Copenhagen, Dansk Almennyttigt Boligselskab, 1951.
- Pohl, Wolfgang and Ueli Schnelzer (eds.): *Architektur des Unfertigen. Die Arbeiten von Susanne Ussing u. Carsten Hoff*, Düsseldorf, Archipol-Verlag, 1982.
- Pontoppidan, Birgit: *Det skete på Kvindeudstillingen Charlottenborg 1975*, Holte, Birgit Pontoppidan Forlag, 2017.
- Rahbek, Liv Løvetand, Svava Riesto and Henriette Steiner: *byWomen. En guidebog til hverdagsarkitektur in København og omegn*, Aarhus, Ikaros Press, 2022.
- Rasmussen, Steen Eiler: *Omkring Christiania – med en fyldig dokumentation*, Copenhagen, Gyldendal, 1976.
- Riesto, Svava: *Biography of an Industrial Landscape. Carlsberg's Urban Spaces Retold*, Amsterdam, Amsterdam University Press, 2017.
- Riesto, Svava and Miles Glendinning (eds.): *Mass Housing of the Scandinavian Welfare States: Exploring Histories and Design Strategies*, Edinburgh, University of Edinburgh/Docomomo, 2020.
- Rubin, Anne Marie: *Billeder fra Christiania*, Aalborg, Aalborg Universitetscenter, 1977.
- Schoop, Kenn and Peter Thule Kristensen: *Svenn Eske Kristensen – velfærdsarkitekten*, Copenhagen, Aristo, 2018.
- Sheridan, Michael: *Mesterværker. Enfamiliehuset in dansk arkitekturs guldalder*, Copenhagen, Strandberg Publishing, 2011.

— Staunsager, Sara and Emilie Victoria Raundahl (eds.): *Verner Panton – Farver en ny verden*, Kolding, Trapholt, 2022.
— Steiner, Henriette and Kristin Veel: *Touch in the Time of Corona*, Berlin, De Gruyter, 2020.
— Stephensen, Lulu Salto: *Tradition og fornyelse in dansk havekunst. G.N. Brandt og de første årtier af 1900 tallet*, Copenhagen, Frangipani, 1993.
— Stratigakos, Despina: *Where are the Women Architects?*, Princeton, N.J., Princeton University Press, 2016.
— Swenarton, Mark, Tom Avermaete and Dirk van den Heuvel: *Architecture and the Welfare State*, London, New York, Routledge, 2014.
— Søberg, Martin: *Kay Fisker. Works and Ideas in Danish Modern Architecture*, London, Bloomsbury Visual Arts, 2021.
— *Søllerødbogen*, vol. 1988.
— Sørensen, C.Th.: *Parkpolitik in Sogn og Købstad*, Copenhagen, Gyldendal, 1931.
— Sørensen, Leif Leer: *Edvard Heiberg og dansk funktionalisme. En arkitekt og hans samtid*, Copenhagen, Arkitektens Forlag, 2000.
— Sørensen, Steen (eds.): *Søndergård Park – verdens navle in 60 år. Historien om en bebyggelse og beboerdemokrati in Gladsaxe almennyttige Boligselskab*, Gladsaxe, Søndergård Park, Afdelingsbestyrelsen, 2012.
— Thau, Carsten and Kjeld Vindum: *Arne Jacobsen*, Copenhagen, Arkitektens Forlag, 1998.
— Thomsen, Kristian Buhl: *Da de danske byer blev revet ned. Praksis og ideologi i dansk sanerings- og byfornyelsespolitik 1939-1983*, PhD dissertation, Aarhus, Aarhus Universitet, 2015.
— Thomsen, Vibeke Fischer: *Øen Nyord*, Copenhagen, Fonden for Bygnings- og Landskabskultur, 1968.
— Thomsen, Vibeke Fischer: *Bevaringsplanlægning*, in *Kommuneplanorientering*, no. 1, 1979.
— Tietjen, Anne, Svava Riesto and Pernille Skov (ed.): *Forankring in forandring. Christiania og bevaring som ressource in byomdannelsen*, Aarhus, Arkitektskolens Forlag, 2007.
— Tietjen, Anna (ed.): *Forstadens bygningskultur 1945-1989. På sporet af velfærdsforstadens bevaringsværdier*, Copenhagen Dansk Bygningsarv, 2010.

— Torre, Susana (eds.): *Women in American Architecture. A Historic and Contemporary Perspective*, New York, Watson-Guptill Publishers, 1977.
— Tournikiotis, Panayotis: *The historiography of modern architecture*, Cambridge, Mass., MIT Press, 1999.
— *Undervisnings- og Eksamensplan for Den Kongelige Veterinær- og Landbohøjskole*, 6th edition., Copenhagen, 1910.
— Vejre, Henrik: *Et århundrede med planlægning for grønne områder in Storkøbenhavn*, Copenhagen, Kraks Fond, 2017.
— Vidler, Anthony: *Histories of the immediate present: inventing architectural modernism*, Cambridge, Mass., MIT Press, 2008.
— Vilslev, Birgitte Thorsen and Carsten Hoff (eds.): *Susanne Ussing – mellem arkitektur og kunst*, Copenhagen, Strandberg Publishing, 2017.
— Vorre, Birgit: *Boligen in det 20. århundrede. Indretning og brug*, Copenhagen, Nyt Nordisk Forlag Arnold Busck, 2008.
— Weber, Anna: *Kvinden som Gartner og Havebruger*, Copenhagen, Nyt Nordisk Forlag Arnold Busck, 1933.
— Weimann, Jeanne Madeline: *The Fair Women. The Story of the Women's Building at the World's Columbian Exposition, Chicago 1893*, Chicago, Academy Chicago Publishers, 1981.
— Winding, Ole, Lisbeth Wolters and Elith Juul Møller (eds.): *Arkitektskolernes byplanuddannelse 1930–1997. 13. seminar 30. maj 1997, Charlottenborg*, in *Byplanhistoriske noter*, no. 37, 1997.
— Zahle, Karen: *Udelukket og indelukket. Arkitekten Karen Zahle*, Nykøbing Sj., Bogværket, 2021.

Online

The following websites have been searched for references to women in Danish architecture: www.kvindebiografiskleksikon.lex.dk and www.kulturarv.dk/kid/Forside.do

— Akademikerbladet: 'Universiteterne er delt op i mænd og kvinder: Se kønsfordelingen på alle landets uddannelser'. Last amended 7 August 2020, www.akademikerbladet.dk/aktuelt/2020/august/se-koensfordelingen-paa-alle-landets-uddannelser

— 'Arkitekterne Inger og Johannes Exner'. Accessed 13 November 2022, www.ingerogjohannesexner.dk/
— Bay, Helle: 'Anne Marie Rubin'. Accessed 20 October 2022, www.kvinfo.dk/side/597/bio/1634/origin/170/
— Bolius: 'Danskerne skifter køkkenet efter 11 år – mange år, før det er udtjent'. Last amended 17 May 2021, www.bolius.dk/danskerne-skifter-koekkenet-efter-11-aar-mange-aar-foer-det-er-udtjent-97149
— Faber, Tobias: 'Rut Speyer'. Accessed 20 October 2022, www.kulturarv.dk/kid/VisWeilbach.do?kunstnerId=10634&wsektion=alle
— Gentofte Kommune: 'Historie. Gentofte Stadion, nu Gentofte Sportspark'. Accessed 13 November 2022, https://sportspark.gentofte.dk/da/Om-os/Historie
— Harding, Marie and Esbjørn Hiort: 'Viggo Sten Møller'. Accessed 2 February 2022, https://biografiskleksikon.lex.dk/Viggo_Sten_M%C3%B8ller
— Kold, Lone Flugt: 'Kanslergadeforliget'. Accessed 13 November 2022 https://danmarkshistorien.dk/vis/materiale/kanslergadeforliget-1933
— *Kvinder in dansk arkitektur*: 'Podcast: *De glemte arkitekter*'. Producers: Niels Bjørn and Ane Skak. Podcast on the research project *Women in Danish Architecture* featuring Jannie Rosenberg Bendsen, Henriette Steiner, Svava Riesto and guests. Accessed 13 November 2022, www.realdania.dk/tema/de-glemte-arkitekter
— Suzanne Labarre: Interview with anonymous spokesperson for the initiative FastCompany, Exclusive: Why in Started a 'Shitty Architecture Men' List (fastcompany.com). Accessed 28 November 2022.
— Leksikon.org: 'Kvindearbejde'. Accessed 13 November 2022, www.leksikon.org/art.php?n=1504?
— Lund, Annemarie: 'Agnete Muusfeldt'. Accessed 20 October 2022, www.kvinfo.dk/side/597/bio/1167/origin/170/query/muusfeldt/
— Lund, Annemarie: 'Erna Sonne Friis'. Accessed 20 October 2022, www.kvinfo.dk/side/597/bio/1346/origin/170/
— Marcussen, Ole, Hans Melgaard and Jacob Christiansen: 'Vilvorde 125 år',

- 2001, www.rts.dk/images/temaer/historie/pdf/Vilvorde_125_aar.pdf
- Miljø- og Energiministeriet and Skov- og Naturstyrelsen: 'Vejledning om 300 m strandbeskyttelses- og klitfredningszone'. Accessed 13 November 2022, www.naturstyrelsen.dk/media/nst/attachments/81194/vejledningom300mstrandbeskyttelsesogklitfredningsz.pdf
- MoMA: 'New Furniture Designs and Techniques Have Initial Showing at Museum of Modern Art', press release, 1946, www.assets.moma.org/documents/moma_press-release_325508.pdf
- Nolin, Catharina: 'Ester Laura Matilda Claesson'. Accessed 20 October 2022, www.skbl.se/en/article/EsterClaesson
- Pedersen, Lykke: 'Ingrid Møller Dyggve'. Accessed 20 October 2022, https://kvindebiografiskleksikon.lex.dk/Ingrid_M%c3%b8ller_Dyggve
- Schriver, Astrid Ølgaard Christensen: 'Danmarks befolkningsudvikling'. Accessed 13 November 2022, www.danmarkshistorien.dk/vis/materiale/danmarks-befolkningsudvikling
- Slots- og Kulturstyrelsen: 'Fredede og bevaringsværdige bygninger'. Accessed 13 November 2022, www.kulturarv.dk/fbb/
- Slots- og Kulturstyrelsen: 'Sag: Kildeskovshallen'. Accessed 13 November 2022, www.kulturarv.dk/fbb/sagvis.pub?sag=3757721
- Slots- og Kulturstyrelsen: 'Udvidelse af fredningen af Kildeskovshallen', 18 September 2019, www.slks.dk/fileadmin/user_upload/SLKS/Omraader/Kulturarv/Bygningsfredning/Fredninger/Dokumenter/WEB_Afgoerelse_Adolphsvej_25_Gentofte.pdf
- 'Susanne Ussing'. Accessed 13 November 2022, http://www.susanneussing.dk/
- Vorre, Birgit: 'Husmoder'. Last amended 30 January 2009, www.denstoredanske.lex.dk/husmoder

Television and film

- Madsen, Flemming: Interview with Susanne Ussing and Carsten Hoff. *TV-Aktuelt*, 12 August 1977.
- *Nær Salten Østerstrand*. Television broadcast, Danmarks Radio, 15 July 1965. Camera: Poul H. Hansen. Producers: Anne Marie Rubin and Bent Børge Larsen.
- *Ussing/Hoff Bygge eksperiment Thy Lejren. Sommeren 1970 (varighed tre måneder)*. Camera: Susanne Ussing and Carsten Hoff (Super 8 film). Editing: Cecilie Gravesen. Archives of Carsten Hoff and Susanne Ussing.

Miscellaneous

- Lolland Kommune: *Strategisk udviklingsplan for Lollands sydkyst*, adopted by the council 25 May 2022.

Earlier versions of the chapters 'Love' and 'Alternatives' have been published in *Journal of Architecture*, no. 3, 2023 under the titles 'Creating Alternatives: Stories About Participation, Collaboration and Gender in Architecture, the 1960s and 70s' (by Svava Riesto) and 'Between Passion and Possession: Women Architects and the Houses They Built for Family, Love and Work' (by Henriette Steiner).

Index

Abel, Jette (b. 1937) – 41
Acropolis, Athens – 243, 245
Adelgade, Copenhagen – 161
Agency for Culture and Palaces – 251
Akademiraadet – 152
Akademisk Arkitektforening / Danish Association of Architects – 61–62
Albertslund – 154–155, 301
Albuen – 166
Alexander, Christopher (1936–2022) – 237
Alternativ Arkitektur / Alternative Architecture, Louisiana 1977 – 203–208, 210, 227–228, 234–235, 237–238, 246
Andersen, Aksel (1903–1952) – 86
Andersen, J.P. (1877–1942) – 30
Andersen, Lisbeth (1916–1996) – 128
Andersen, Rigmor (1903–1995) – 17, 26
Anne Marie Rubin's studio – 162, 166, 174, 192–193, 240
Arbejdernes Andels-Boligforening (AAB) – 76
Athens, Greece – 243

Backberger, Barbro (1932–1999) – 239
Bådsmandsstrædes Kaserne, Copenhagen – 234, 237
Baker, Josephine (1906–1975) – 240–243, 245
Begtrup, Bodil M. (1902–1987) – 76
Behrndt, Anne (1942–2018) – 210
Bellahøj, Copenhagen – 137
Bentzon, Eva Weis (1944–2018) – 210
Bergholt, Knud (1921–2006) – 252, 264–267, 269
Bernadotte, Sigvard (1907–2002) – 98
Bernstorffsvej, Gentofte – 258
BIG – 232
Birch, Kirsten (b. 1940) – 300
Bjørn, Acton (1910–1992) – 98
Blågård Seminarium, Copenhagen – 114
Bo, Jørgen (1919–1999) – 38, 114
Borchorst, Anette (b. 1951) – 29
Borgergade, Copenhagen – 161
Børneengen, Christiania – 227
Børneudstillingen / The Children's Exhibition, Louisiana 1978 – 206
Boston, USA – 85
Boudon, Philippe (b. 1941) – 238
Boye, Georg (1906–1972) – 41
Braae, Karen (1882–1962) – 61
Bredsdorff, Peter (1913–1981) – 177, 191
Bremer, Claus (1919–1983) – 167, 174
Brown, Denise Scott (b. 1931) – 111, 145, 232, 238
Brown, Lori (b. 1969) – 14
Brummer, Carl (1864–1953) – 27
Buckminster Fuller, Richard (1895–1983) – 203
Burns, Karen (b. 1962) – 14
Busck, Vilhelmine (1869–1954) – 36, 40
Byker, Newcastle – 228
Byplanhistorisk Udvalg / Committee on Town Planning History – 179

C.Th. Sørensen's design studio – 57
Carlsro, Rødovre – 72, 78, 82–85, 91, 95
Caroline Mathilde, Queen of Denmark and Norway (1751–1775) – 110–111

Centralforeningen af Møbelhandlere i Danmark / Central Association of Furniture Dealers in Denmark – 62–63
Château des Milandes, Dordogne – 240–243, 245
Chr. Ostenfeld & W. Jønsson – 252, 255, 258
Christensen, Dan (life dates unknown) – 240
Christian VII (1749–1808) – 110
Christiania, Copenhagen – 206, 208, 227, 234–240, 243
City of Copenhagen – 63, 177
Claesson, Ester (1884–1931) – 33, 37, 40, 42
Clemmensen, Ebbe (1917–2003) – 24, 31, 111–112, 114–117, 120–127, 132–133, 135, 250–252, 255, 258, 264, 267–268, 291, 294
Clemmensen, Karen (1917–2001) – 24, 31, 111–112, 115–117, 120–128, 130–133, 135, 250–252, 255, 258–259, 264, 267–268, 291, 294
Copenhagen City Hall – 300
Copenhagen Technical School – 18, 27, 29
Cornell University, Ithaca, New York – 85
Council of Practising Architects – 48
County Hospital, Frederikssund – 278

Dalgas, Vibeke (b. 1933) – 31, 48, 152, 157, 176–182, 184–186, 188–198, 200
Danish Planning Agency – 192–194
Danish Women's Society's housing committee – 22
Danish Wood Award – 112
Danmarks Naturfredningsforening / Danish Society for Nature – 180, 184
Danmarks Radio (DR) – 58
Danmarks Tekniske Universitet / Technical University of Denmark (then the Polytechnic Institute / Polytekniske Læreanstalt) – 25, 138
Dansk Almennyttigt Boligselskab (DAB) – 75–76, 78–79, 81, 82
Dansk Arkitektforening / Danish Architects' Association – 62
Dansk Arkitektur Center / Danish Architecture Center, Copenhagen – 302
Dansk Bygge- og Boligudstilling, Forum 1926 – 61
Dansk Byplanlaboratorium / Danish Town Planning Institute, Copenhagen – 179
Dansk Folkeferie – 171, 174
Dansk Havearkitektforening (later the Association of Danish Landscape Architects) – 30, 254, 277
Dansk Kvindesamfund / Danish Women's Society – 18, 22
Dansk Selskab for Byggestatik / Danish Society for Structural Engineering – 264, 266
Danske Kvinders Nationalråd / National Council of Danish Women (now the Women's Council Denmark) – 72
De Danske Husmoderforeninger / The Danish Housewives' Associations – 18, 61
De Danske Møbelfabrikkers Handelsforening / The Danish Furniture Manufacturers' Trade Association – 62
de Neergaard, Hans Rottbøll (1897–1964) – 76

De Samvirkende Danske Landboforeninger / The Cooperative Danish Farmers' Associations – 180
Dehlholm, Kirsten (b. 1945) – 210
Det Internationale Forbund af Arkitekter / UIA, International Union of Architects – 85
Det Ny Samfund – 218
Detroit, USA – 85
Dyggve, Ejnar (1887–1961) – 27
Dyggve, Ingrid Møller (1890–1969) – 17, 21, 27, 61

Eames, Charles (1907–1978) – 111, 145
Eames, Ray (1912–1988) – 111, 145
École de l'Urbanisme, Paris – 47
École des Beaux-Arts, Paris – 47
Elsebet and Kjeld Ussing's studio – 226, 228, 230
Enghavegård School, Søborg – 115
Ermelundsvej 100, Gentofte – 116
Ernst May's studio – 60
Erskine, Ralph (1914–2005) – 228
Exner, Anna Mette (b. 1962) – 107
Exner, Inger (b. 1926) – 31, 97–99, 101, 103–107, 110–111
Exner, Johan (1897–1981) – 98, 101
Exner, Johannes (1926–2015) – 31, 97–99, 102–107, 111
Exner, Karen (b. 1957) – 98, 107

Fællesorganisationen for Almennyttige Danske Boligselskaber / Association of Non-Profit Danish Social Housing Organisations (now BL – Danmarks Almene Boliger) – 62, 69
Fællesudvalget for Boligundersøgelser / Joint Committee for Housing Studies – 58, 62, 64–65, 69, 93
Fællesudvalgets Køkkenundersøgelse / The Joint Committee's Kitchen Survey – 58, 62–64, 65–66, 69, 71, 73, 78, 93
Finger Plan – 153, 166, 175, 177
Foreningen af Danske Landskabsarkitekter / Association of Danish Landscape Architects – 30, 254, 277
foreningen socialt boligbyggeri (fsb) – 23, 29, 39, 40, 52, 55, 71
Frederick, Christine (1883–1970) – 60
Frederiksberg Hospital – 18
Frederiksberg Municipality – 18
Frederiksborg County – 184
Friis, Erna Sonne (1902–1990) – 31, 40

Gaardmand, Arne (1926–2008) – 154
Galgebakken, Albertslund – 301
Gehl, Ingrid (b. 1940) – 206
Gehl, Jan (b. 1936) – 206
Gentofte Municipality – 22, 31, 76, 111, 113, 115–116, 250–252, 254–255, 258
Gentofte Stadium, Gentofte – 255, 258
Gerstrøm, Ole (1934–2009) – 166–167, 169, 170–171, 173–174, 188, 197, 199, 200, 240
Gottlob, Kaj (1887–1976) – 164
Grantoften, Ballerup – 116
Grubb, Ragna (1903–1961) – 17–19, 21–23, 26–29, 33, 52–53, 55, 57–58, 184

330

Grupp 8 – 239
Grut, Flemming (1911–1987) – 18
Guterl, Matthew Pratt (b. 1970) – 241

H.C. Ørsted Institute, Copenhagen – 111
Hans Erling Langkilde and Ib Martin Jensen's studio – 72
Hansen, Agnete Frederikke Laub (1886–1970) – 32–33, 36, 298
Hansen, Henning (1880–1945) – 32–33, 52
Hansen, Per H. (b. 1957) – 93
Hansen, Sven (1910–1989) – 254
Hansen, Urban (1908–1986) – 153
Harvard University, Cambridge, Massachusetts – 145
Haunsø, Svend (life dates unknown) – 63, 71
Hayden, Dolores (b. 1945) – 239
Heger, Jarl (1929–1998) – 114
Heiberg, Edvard (1897–1958) – 62, 70, 93–94,
Hemmens Forskningsinstitut / Swedish Home Research Institute, Stockholm – 69
Henning Hansen's studio – 32
Henningsen, Poul (1894–1967) – 26
Herløw, Erik (1913–1991) – 226
Herning Municipality – 162
Hillerød Municipality – 178, 180
Hirschholm Palace, Hørsholm – 110
Hjortekær – 138, 140, 145
Hjortekærbakken, Jægersborg Dyrehave – 60, 139–140, 142–146, 148
Hoff, Carsten (b. 1934) – 205–206, 210, 212–213, 217–222, 226, 228–230, 232–233, 238, 246
Hoff, Povl Ernst (1903–1992) – 86
Holstebro Kunstmuseum, Holstebro – 46
Holte Gymnasium, Holte – 152
Hotel Cecil, Copenhagen – 18
Hundesømosen, Gentofte – 111, 113, 115, 117, 124–125, 127, 130, 134
Husby Strand, Ejby – 166
Hvistendahl, Karen (1903–2003) – 21–23, 29, 52–53, 55, 57–58
Hyllekrog, Rødby – 166

I.H. Mundts Vej 16, Virum – 62
Illouz, Eva (b. 1961) – 103, 147
Ingeniørforeningen / Danish Society of Engineers – 79
Inger and Johannes Exner's studio – 98–99, 101, 106
Ingrid, Queen of Denmark (1910–2000) – 66
Ingwersen, Ingwer (1911–1969) – 31
Irming, Mogens (1915–1993) – 137
Ithaca, New York, USA – 85

Jacobsen, Arne (1902–1971) – 255
Jægersborg Dyrehave, Kongens Lyngby – 138–140
Jægersborg Hegn, Nærum – 101
Jensen, Fanny (1890–1969) – 72
Jensen, Ib Martin (1906–1979) – 72, 75
Jensen, Knud W. (1916–2000) – 38, 204
Jensen, Thomas Bo (b. 1964) – 98, 105
Johan Christensen & Søn – 278
Jolie, Angelina (b. 1975) – 241
Jordemoderforeningen / Danish Association of Midwives – 18

Kantorparken, Copenhagen – 29, 55, 57
Karen and Ebbe Clemmensen's studio – 111, 115, 122, 125, 127–128, 130
Kastrup Glasværk, Kastrup – 63
Keynes, John Maynard (1883–1946) – 152
KFUK – 47
Kildeskoven, Gentofte – 254, 258–259, 260, 268–271, 274–275, 277, 288
Kildeskovshallen, Gentofte – 31, 114, 122, 250–255, 257–261, 263–265, 268–269, 273–275, 277, 288, 290–292, 295
King, Jr., Martin Luther (1929–1968) – 240
Kjældgaard, Lasse Horne (b. 1974) – 29
Kjær, Bodil (b. 1932) – 300
Kjærgaard, Poul (1912–1999) – 176
Kjærholm, Hanne (1930–2009) – 36, 46–47
Kjærholm, Poul (1929–1980) – 46
Klint, Kaare (1888–1954) – 26, 102
Klint, Morten (1918–1978) – 40
Kluge, Helen Lait (1947–2017) – 210
Københavns Almindelige Boligselskab (KAB) – 227, 229
Københavns Lærerforening – 18
Koldinghus, Kolding – 98
Kollektivhuset Høje Søborg, Søborg – 72, 86, 89
Kontturi, Katve-Kaisa (life dates unknown) – 14
Koppel, Eva (1916–2006) – 25, 111, 113
Koppel, Nils (1914–2009) – 25, 111, 113
Korngården, Ballerup – 113, 116
Kramnitze, Lolland – 166, 171, 174–175
Kristensen, Svenn Eske (1905–2000) – 70, 93–94
Krohn & Hartvig Rasmussen (KHR) – 137
Krohn, Bodil Merete (1915–1979) – 60, 136–138
Krohn, Gunnar (1914–2005) – 136–38, 144–145
Kruse, Jytte (life dates unknown) – 76
Kungliga Tekniska Högskolan / Royal Institute of Technology, Stockholm – 152, 158
Kunsthal Charlottenborg, Copenhagen – 210
Kunsthåndværkerskolen / The School of Decorative Art, Copenhagen – 206
Kvinde og Hjem. Danske kvinders udstilling for rationel husførelse, Forum 1950 – 76, 81
Kvindelig Læseforening / Women Readers' Association – 33
Kvindelige Arkitekter i Jylland / Women Architects in Jutland – 32, 300
Kvinder for fred / Women for Peace – 58
Kvinder i Byggesektoren / Women in the Construction Sector – 31, 300
Kvinder skaber rum / Women in Architecture, Danish Architecture Center 2022 – 302
Kvinderegensen, Copenhagen – 26
Kvindernes Udstilling fra Fortid til Nutid / The Women's Exhibition from Past to Present, 1895 – 18
Kvindeudstillingen XX / The Women's Exhibition XX, Kunsthal Charlottenborg 1975 – 206, 209–210, 232–233, 300

La Femme Danoise, Maison du Danemark / Danish Cultural Institute in Paris 1975 – 300
Laboratory for Housing Construction, Copenhagen – 47
Landsforeningen Dansk Kunsthaandværk og Kunstindustri / National Association of Danish Crafts and Applied Art – 62

Langeliniepavillonen, Copenhagen – 111
Langkilde, Hans Erling (1906–1997) – 72, 75–76
Lauritzen, Vilhelm (1894–1984) – 55
Laursen, Christian (1902–1973) – 22
Le Corbusier (1887–1965) – 56, 59, 232
Le Unité d'Habitation, Marseille – 56
LO-skolen, Helsingør – 114, 277
Löfquist, Helfrid (1895–1972) – 254
Lolland – 161, 163, 166–167, 169–171, 173, 175–176, 189, 197–200
Louisiana Museum of Modern Art, Humlebæk – 38, 40, 203, 205–206, 208, 218, 227–228, 230, 234–235, 238, 246
Lund University, Lund – 179–180
Lundevænget, Copenhagen – 55
Lundtoftesletten, Lundtofte – 138
Lundtoftevej, Kongens Lyngby – 138, 141–142
Lütken, Tutti (1914–2012) – 57, 63
Lyngby-Taarbæk Municipality – 136, 138, 140–142

Madonna (b. 1958) – 241
Malmstrøm, Povl Egon (1917–1985) – 226
Maribo County – 167
Mathildenhöhe Artists' Colony, Darmstadt – 33
May, Ernst (1886–1970) – 60
Merchant, Carolyn (b. 1936) – 301
#Metoo – 299
Meyer, Grethe (1918–2008) – 44, 62–63, 66, 71, 94
Meyer, Sonja Emmy (1898–1981) – 17–18, 20–21, 45
Mies van der Rohe, Ludwig (1886–1969) – 232
Mindelunden, Hellerup – 117
Ministry of Culture – 180, 300
Ministry of Housing – 47, 72, 81, 152, 160–161, 188
Ministry of Housing's committee on collective facilities – 72
Ministry of Social Affairs – 72
Ministry of the Interior – 159–160
Møller, Svend (1890–1981) – 226
Møller, Viggo Sten (1897–1990) – 60, 62–63, 69
MoMA, New York – 145
Møn Municipality – 185
Mørch, Ibi Trier (1910–1980) – 63, 71
Mozartgård, Copenhagen – 76
Municipal council, Gentofte Municipality – 258
Muusfeldt and Mygind's studio – 254, 278
Muusfeldt, Agnete (1918–1991) – 40, 114, 250–252, 254, 257–258, 264, 270–271, 273–275, 277–279, 281–294
Muusfeldt's studio – 254, 278
Mygind, Erik (1916–1978) – 254, 277–278

N. Zahles Skole, Copenhagen – 18, 31
Nakskov – 160–162, 179, 189
Napoléon Bonaparte (1769–1821) – 241
Nationalmuseet / National Museum of Denmark, Copenhagen – 180
New Furniture Designed by Charles Eames, MoMA 1946 – 145
Niels Hemmingsens Gade, Copenhagen – 18–19, 27
Nielsen, Andrea Maria Norn (1888–date unknown) – 30
Nielsen, Gerda Tosti (1928–2020) – 206, 234–239
Nielsen, Tage (1914–1991) – 137

Nochlin, Linda (1931–2017) – 13, 194
Nordiska institutet för samhällsplanering, Stockholm – 162
Nordiske Kvinders Bygge– og Planforum / Nordic Women's Building and Planning Forum – 32, 300
Nørgaard, Edith (1919–1989) – 25
Nørgaard, Ole (1925–1978) – 25, 153–155
Nyboe-Pedersen, Paul (1904–1991) – 22
Nyeland, Stephan (1845–1922) – 44
Nyord – 152, 176–182, 184–186, 188–191, 193, 195–197, 200
Nyrop, Martin (1849–1929) – 47
Nyvig, Anders (1914–1986) – 161, 178

Olbrich, Joseph Maria (1867–1908) – 33
Olsen, Emilie (life dates unknown) – 76
Ordrupgaard, Charlottenlund – 231
Otero-Pallos, Jorge (b. 1971) – 194, 197
Ott, Stefan (1928–1997) – 177

på vej, Copenhagen City Hall /Aarhus City Hall 1980 – 206, 300–301, 304–305
Panton, Verner (1926–1998) – 214
Panum Institute, Copenhagen – 111
Pedersen, Johan (1902–1970) – 76
Perriand, Charlotte (1903–1999) – 56, 232
Petersen, Agnete (1916–2000) 38–40
Petersen, Lene Adler (b. 1944) – 209–210
Petersen, Torben Miland (1909–1994) – 136–137
Pio, Louis (1841–1894) – 44
Pontoppidan, Birgit (b. 1942) – 210, 233
Præstø – 179–180
Pritzker Prize – 145, 232
Privatbanken, Copenhagen – 23, 29, 52, 55, 71
Psyak, Copenhagen – 227

Randers Statsgymnasium – 99, 106
Rasmussen, Anka (1893–1977) – 21, 30, 38, 40, 282
Rasmussen, Eigil Hartvig (1905–1980) – 31, 60, 68, 135–139, 141–142, 144–146, 148
Rasmussen, Steen Eiler (1898–1990) – 36, 235, 238
Ravn, Inger (1943–2022) – 278
Reich, Lilly (1885–1947) – 232
Risom, Sven (1880–1971) – 30
Rødby Fjord, Lolland – 166, 171
Rødhus Klit, Pandrup – 174
Rødovre Almennyttige Boligselskab (RAB) – 82
Rømer, Hilda (1906–1964) – 17, 22
Rosenborg, Copenhagen – 31
Rosenkjær, Nina (b. 1939) – 152, 182, 184, 186, 188, 190–191, 195, 197
Roskilde Technical School – 55
Royal Danish Academy of Fine Arts' Model School, Copenhagen – 32
Royal Danish Academy of Fine Arts' School of Architecture, Copenhagen – 17–19, 22, 26–27, 29–30, 32–33, 36–37, 40, 45–48, 52, 55, 58, 60, 62–63, 65, 72, 76, 98–99, 111, 114, 116, 136, 152, 158–159, 162, 177, 180, 182, 184, 192, 226, 229, 298
Royal Danish Academy of Fine Arts' School of Furniture, Copenhagen – 26, 55
Royal Danish Horticultural Society's Garden, Frederiksberg – 31

Rubin Plan – 166, 175–176
Rubin, Anne Marie (1919–1993) – 29, 31, 47, 151–153, 157–167, 169–171, 173–177, 188, 192–194, 197–199, 206, 234–235, 237–241, 243–246, 301
Rubin, Edgar (1886–1951) – 158
Rudbjerg Municipality – 175
Rue, Gytte Berner (1918–1993) – 31, 44, 52, 58, 63–65, 68, 71, 94, 120, 137
Rut Speyer and Eigil Hartvig Rasmussen's studio – 31, 60, 136–139, 142–143, 145

Sabroe, Karen (life dates unknown) – 86
Salicath, Bent (1915–1973) – 63, 69–71, 93–94
Sankt Clemens Church, Randers – 98
Schäffer, Gerda (1884–1960) – 17, 21, 29
Schmidt, Ingeborg Lange (1905–1986) – 21–23, 29, 52–53, 55, 57–58
Schmidt, Jørn Palle (1923–2010) – 278, 282, 288
Schultze–Naumburg, Paul (1869–1949) – 33
Schütte-Lihotzky, Margrete (1897–2000) – 60
Schweizerdalsparken, Rødovre – 254
Seagull Colony – 174
Sensory Spaces, Den frie Udstillingsbygning 1970 – 212–214
Sestoft, Kirsten (1936–1990) – 47–48
Skive Teachers' College (now a high school), Skive – 24, 114
Snedkerlaugets Møbelsnedkerafdeling / Carpenters' Guild's Furniture Joinery Department – 63
Soleri, Paolo (1919–2013) – 203
Solgården, Copenhagen – 52
Sølvhøj, Hans (1919–1989) – 153
Sønderborg Statsskole, Sønderborg – 114
Søndergård Park, Bagsværd – 72, 78
Sonnengarten, Zurich – 85
Sørensen, C. Th. (1893–1979) – 39, 57
Speyer, Rut (1914–2003) – 31, 44, 52, 58, 60, 63–65, 68–69, 71–72, 94, 120, 135–139, 141–142, 144–148
Statens Byggeforskningsinstitut / Danish Building Research Institute, Copenhagen – 62, 226
Statens Bygningsdirektorat / National Building Directorate – 62
Statens Husholdningsråd / Danish Home Economics Council – 63, 81
Stauning, Thorvald (1873–1942) – 44, 164
Stege Landsogn – 180
Stockholmsutställningen, Stockholm 1930 – 52
Store Vejleå, Albertslund – 154
Stratigakos, Despina (b. 1963) – 26
Struensee, Johann Friedrich (1737–1772) – 110
Strynø – 189–190
Suenson, Palle (1904–1987) – 47, 65, 181, 192
Swanley Horticultural College, Berkeley, University of California – 36

Tafdrup, Ulla (1906–1996) – 29, 31, 36, 44, 52, 58, 72–76, 79, 81–86, 88–92, 94–95, 126
Taylor, Frederick W. (1856–1915) – 60
Technological Institute, Copenhagen – 81
Tegne- og Kunstindustriskolen for Kvinder (School of Drawing and Applied Art for Women) – 32, 46
The Royal Veterinary and Agricultural University, Frederiksberg – 31, 36, 40–41, 277–278

The Shitty Architecture Men – 299
The Woman's Building, Chicago – 18
Thiesen, Hedevig Elisabeth Marie (1891–1965) – 158
Thorball, Knud (1904–1980) – 76
Thylejren, Frøstrup – 218–219, 222, 226
Thyra Danebod, Queen of Denmark (c. 880 CE–c. 959 CE) – 299
Thyra, studio – 32, 299
Tibirke Bakker, Tisvildeleje – 27, 29
Tinggården – 228
Tivoli, Copenhagen – 52–53
Tronto, Joan C. (b. 1952) – 157, 197

Ussing + Hoff, studio – 205–206, 218–222, 226–230, 232, 234, 238–240, 244, 301
Ussing, Elsebet (1915–1978) – 111, 113–114, 116, 217, 226, 230
Ussing, Kjeld Juul (1913–1977) – 111, 113–114, 116, 217, 226, 230
Ussing, Susanne (1940–1998) – 31, 205–206, 209–210, 212–222, 226, 229–234, 238–239, 243–244, 246, 301

Vældegårdsvej 22, Gentofte – 22
Vældegårdsvej 59, Gentofte – 22
Vattenbyggnadsbyrån studio – 152, 159
Vejby Strand – 166–167
Vejlø – 221–222, 226
Venturi, Robert (1925–2018) – 111, 145, 232, 238
Vestersøhus, Copenhagen – 55
Vibeke Fischer Thomsen's studio (later Vibeke Dalgas's studio) – 178–179, 180, 182, 184–185, 189, 193–194, 196
Vilvorde Havebrugsskole / Vilvorde School of Horticulture, Charlottenlund – 33, 36, 40, 42, 44

Weber, Anna (1893–1993) – 40, 42–45
Westergaard, Kirsten (1901–1994) – 17–18, 20–21
Windinge, Bennet (1905–1986) – 86
Women in American Architecture, Brooklyn Museum 1977 – 204, 246
Women's Building, Copenhagen – 18–19, 26–30, 40, 45

Zahle, Karen (b. 1931) – 47, 300

Ærø – 189, 196, 200
Ærøskøbing – 189–190, 196, 200

Ørnsholt, Laust (1924–1974) – 175
Ørum-Nielsen, Anne (b. 1937) – 301
Øster Voldgade 8, Fredericia – 29
Østerbrogården, Copenhagen – 116
Østerled 17, Copenhagen – 18

Åbrinken 131, Virum – 275, 277–279, 282–283, 286–289, 293
Aakirkeby – 190
Aalborg University – 152, 162, 234, 237
Aarhus City Hall – 300
Aarhus School of Architecture, Aarhus – 49, 98, 102, 105
Aarhus Technical School – 60, 63, 137
Aarre, Mette (b. 1943) – 210

Acknowledgements

This book could not have been written without the help and assistance of numerous people. First of all, we would like to mention the research team behind project *Women in Danish Architecture 1925–1975* which has worked tirelessly and made invaluable contributions throughout the project period: Mathilde Lundt Larsen, Mathilde Elisabeth Merolli, Liv Løvetand Rahbek and Frida Irving Søltoft. In particular, we would like to highlight Liv Løvetand Rahbek's beautiful photographs which also can be seen in the book *byWomen*. Other colleagues at the University of Copenhagen, in Denmark and internationally have also provided important input and assistance at various stages of the research process. We owe a special thank you to the many architects, descendants, witnesses, collaborators and others who have generously and trustingly shared their knowledge, perspectives and images with us.

We would like to extend our warmest thanks to: Jette Abel, Annette Ussing Bah, Annemarie Balle, Niels Bjørn, Ellen Braae, Isabel Bernadette Brammer, Per Boje, Ning de Coninck-Smith, Luca Csepely-Knorr, Vibeke Dalgas and Hans Andersson, Torben Dam, Howard Davis, Anna Mette Exner, Karen Exner, Line Grubb, Marianne Gyldendal, Carsten Hoff, Annelise Holstebroe, Kjeld Kjeldsen, Bodil Kjær, Uwe Jahn, Birgit Jensen, Bent Jensen, Frank Erik Jeppesen, Tanja Jordan, Gregers Kirkegaard, Rikke Lequick Larsen, Annemarie Lund, Ane Skak Nielsen, Pia Nielsen, Catharina Nolin, Christian Olesen, Birgit Pontoppidan, Lene Rasmussen, Rune Rosenberg Rasmussen, Inger Ravn, Lars Refn, Nina Rosenkjær, Sussa Rubin, Carsten Sestoft, Peter Sestoft, Lise Skjøt-Pedersen, Jens Rønholt Schmidt, Claus M. Smidt, Elsebet Speyer, Karen Speyer, Heidi Svenningsen Kajita, Martin Søberg, Maiken Thorsen, Mikael Tosti, Mette Ussing, Henrik Vejre, Christine Waage, Karen Zahle, Marie Drost Aakjær and many more.

Archives and libraries have been invaluable resources, and the skilled professionals working there have helped us find material and solve some of the many puzzles inherent in archival research. A very special thank you goes to information specialist Tina Lund at the Royal Danish Library, research librarian Rikke Lyngsø Christensen at the Royal Danish Library – Danish National Art Library and Martin Toft Burchardi Bendtsen at the Royal Danish Academy – Library.

Special thanks also go to our international advisory board: Barbara Penner from University College London, Meike Schalk from KTH Stockholm and Despina Stratigakos from the University at Buffalo.

During the project, our collaboration with the Danish Architecture Center gave us the opportunity to further develop certain ideas and to pursue valuable interactions with a wider public. We would like to thank the Danish Architecture Center for excellent and inspiring contributions, especially: Luise J. Holm-Rathje, Sara Hatla Krogsgaard, Maya Lahmy, Lykke Ley, Tanya Lindkvist, Pia Rost Rasmussen and Johanne Troelsgaard Toft. We also would like to express our gratitude to Niels Bjørn and Ane Skak for their work on the podcast and, last but not least, Strandberg Publishing and our wonderful editor Marianne Krogh.

Finally, we are grateful to the University of Copenhagen and to the many foundations that have made the research project and the book possible: the Augustinus Foundation, the Beckett Foundation, the Bergia Foundation, the Karin and Georg Boye Foundation, the Independent Research Fund Denmark, Dreyers Fond, Queen Margrethe's and Prince Henrik's Foundation, the National Building Fund, the New Carlsberg Foundation, Realdania, Politiken-Fonden and the Danish Arts Foundation.

We owe special thanks to Stine Jacobi, Vera Noldus and Simon Harboe from Realdania, who believed in the project right from the outset.

About the authors

JANNIE ROSENBERG BENDSEN is an architectural historian and holds a PhD from the University of Copenhagen; her thesis was on Danish architectural historiography. She has previously held positions at the Danish Agency for Culture and Palaces and at the Aarhus School of Architecture. Rosenberg Bendsen's research and dissemination activities include a number of books and articles on Danish architectural history with a particular focus on architecture and preservation from the twentieth century, including *Bakkehusene* (with Birgitte Kleis, Strandberg Publishing, 2022), *Drømmen om eget hus. Statslånshuse 1933–1959* (with Dorthe Bendtsen, Strandberg Publishing, 2021), *Fredet – Bygningsfredning i Danmark 1918–2018* (with Mogens A. Morgen, Strandberg Publishing, 2018) and *Bellahøj. Fortællinger om en bebyggelse* (with Birgitte Kleis and Mogens A. Morgen, Strandberg Publishing, 2015).

SVAVA RIESTO is an associate professor and research group leader at the University of Copenhagen. She has studied art history in Tromsø, Berlin and Copenhagen and holds a PhD in landscape architecture. Riesto works with the history of designed landscapes and built environments of twentieth-century welfare states seen in the light of the current urban issues of ecology, climate and social justice. Her books include *Biography of an Industrial Landscape. Carlsberg's Urban Spaces Retold* (Amsterdam University Press, 2017), *Vademecum. 77 Minor Concepts for Writing Urban Places* (with Klaske Havik, Kris Pint and Henriette Steiner, NAi Publishers, 2021) and *byWomen. A Guidebook to Everyday Architecture in Greater Copenhagen* (with Henriette Steiner and Liv Løvetand Rahbek, Ikaros Press, 2022).

HENRIETTE STEINER is an associate professor and Head of Section at the University of Copenhagen. She holds a PhD in the history and philosophy of architecture from the University of Cambridge. Steiner works with issues of diversity and justice in architecture and urban history often through feminist writing collectives; publications include *Tower to Tower. Gigantism in Architecture and Digital Culture* (with Kristin Veel, MIT Press, 2020) and *Touch in the Time of Corona. Reflections on Love, Care, and Vulnerability in the Pandemic* (with Kristin Veel, De Gruyter, 2021, Danish translation published in 2023) and most recently *byWomen. A Guidebook to Everyday Architecture in Greater Copenhagen* (with Svava Riesto and Liv Løvetand Rahbek, Ikaros Press, 2022).

Photo credits

Aftenbladet – 23, 30, 52, 55
Agnete Muusfeldt – 276, 279, 280–281, 283, 287, 289, 292
Aktuelt – 165, 235, 241
ALT for damerne – 74, 100, 118–119, 132
Anne Marie Rubin's studio – 160, 163, 172–173, 174, 245
Annikke Tirkkala – 304
Berlingske Tidende – 112
Byplanhistoriske Noter – 152
Carsten Hoff – 206, 213, 216, 231
Danmark set fra luften – 155, 156
DR Archives – 168, 169
Emil Christensen/Ritzau Scanpix – 211
Esbjerg Byhistorie Arkiv – 20
FDB Archives – 53
Photo: Aage Strüwing © Jørgen Strüwing – 75, 78, 80, 82, 87, 91, 92, 250, 253b, 265, 268, 272–273, 295
Gentofte Lokalarkiv – 37, 284
Gerda Tosti Nielsen – 236, 237
Gladsaxe Byarkiv – 86, 89
Goodwin – 33t
Grethe Meyers Arkiv – 62, 66, 67
Hans Søndergaard – 19t, 22, 27b, 28, 29b, 33b
Holstebro Kunstmuseum – 46r
Jonals Co. – 121, 258
Jørgen Sperling/Ritzau Scanpix – 212
Liv Løvetand Rahbek – 25, 38b, 57, 104, 113t, 115t, 134, 143, 146, 167, 170, 181, 195, 199, 256–257, 262–263, 293, 334

Louisiana Museum of Modern Art – 208
Louisiana Museum of Modern Art. Photo: Marianne Grøndahl – 205, 207
Lyngby-Taarbæk Stadsarkiv – 136t
Margrete Schütte-Lihotzky – 61
Maurice Zalewski / adoc-photos – 242
Mogens Falk-Sørensen, Stadsarkivets fotografiske Atelier – 54
Nationaltidende – 18b
Ole Meyer – 102
Private photo – 32b, 34–35, 47, 48, 60, 98, 106, 107, 114r, 116, 123, 136b, 148, 180, 184, 278
Royal Danish Library – Danish National Art Library – 19n, 24, 26, 31, 32t, 72, 99, 108–109, 111, 113n, 114l, 122, 124, 127, 128–129, 131, 217, 222, 223, 224–225, 228, 253t, 260, 261, 267
Royal Danish Academy – DOCS – 46l
Rut Speyer and Eigil Hartvig Rasmussen – 141, 142
Rødovre Lokalarkiv – 83
Scan from Blød By (vol. 24, May 1983) – 49
Scan from Boligen (1951) – 59, 66t
Scan from Fortegnelse over Danske Havebrugskandidater 1945–1955 (1955) – 40, 254
Scan from Havekunst (1966) – 153
Scan from Kendte danske kvinder 1934 (1934) – 18t, 22b, 27t, 29t
Scan from Kvinden som Gartner og Havebruger (1933) – 42, 43
Scan from Køkkenundersøgelse (1949) – 64

Scan from Moderne Haver (1929) – 38t
Scan from Planlægning af køkkener i etagehuse (1950) – 70
Scan from Vore køkkener (1951) – 77
Skovlund Sognearkiv – 159
Sonja Iskov – 233
Sorø Amts Tidende (6 August 1955) – 39
Susanne Mertz/BAM/Ritzau Scanpix – 209
Sylvest Jensen Luftfoto – 140, 270
Ugeskrift for Jordbrug (no. 35, 1985) – 41
Ulla Tafdrup – 85
Ussing/Hoff experiment, Thylejren festival/encampment, summer 1970 – 219
Vibeke Dalgas – 178, 183, 186, 187, 190, 191, 193, 196
Wikimedia Commons – 63

Every effort has been made to trace and credit all known copyright or reproduction right holders for materials printed in this book. If any rights holders should find any errors or omissions in the credits, the publishers would welcome this being brought to their attention. Said rights holders will be remunerated as if an agreement had been entered into in advance of publication.

UNTOLD STORIES
on Women, Gender and Architecture in Denmark

© Strandberg Publishing and the authors

Editor: Marianne Krogh
Translation: René Lauritsen
Copyeditor: Sarah Quigley
Photo editors: the authors
Photo co-ordinator: Claudia Rebecca Juul Kassentoft
Illustrations: see p. 335
Front Cover: Ragna Grubb, Anne Marie Rubin, Kildeskovshallen
Back Cover: Ulla Tafdrup and Inge Hansen
Design and cover: Alexis Mark and Orin Bristow
Fonts: Adobe Caslon Pro, AM Kosmos and AM Partitur (by Alexis Mark and Beate Bloch)
Paper: 130 g Munken Lynx
Image processing: Narayana Press, Denmark
Printing and binding: Jelgavas Tipogrāfija, Latvia
1st edition, 1st printing
ISBN: 978-87-94102-67-4
Printed in Latvia 2023

In keeping with Danish ministerial requirements, the contributions to this book have been peer reviewed, meaning that a peer at PhD level has carried out a review and a written assessment confirming the academic validity of this book.

Copying of this book may only take place at institutions that have entered into an agreement with Copydan and only within the terms and conditions set down in said agreement.

Strandberg Publishing A/S
Gammel Mønt 14
DK-1117 København K
www.strandbergpublishing.dk

Published with the generous support of:
Beckett-Fonden
Bergiafonden
Karin og Georg Boyes Fond
Danmarks Frie Forskningsfond
Dronning Margrethes og Prins Henriks Fond
Landsbyggefonden